a gift from my
friend Herbert Engstrom
Oakland May '68

Juarez

AND HIS MEXICO

VOLUME I

Other Books by Ralph Roeder

SAVONAROLA

THE MAN OF THE RENAISSANCE

CATHERINE DE' MEDICI AND THE LOST REVOLUTION

JUAREZ AS PRESIDENT

Juarez
AND HIS MEXICO

A BIOGRAPHICAL HISTORY BY
Ralph Roeder

I

NEW YORK · THE VIKING PRESS
1947

SET IN GRANJON AND GARAMONT TYPES
AND PRINTED IN U.S.A. BY THE COLONIAL PRESS INC.

To My Wife

Grateful acknowledgment is made to Señor Pedro Hurtado, Lic. Pablo Prida Santacilia, and Arq. Carlos Obregon Santacilia for access to the personal archives of Benito Juarez in their possession and for generous assistance in the preparation of this book.

Contents

List of Illustrations

PART ONE

Education

I

THE road rises steeply, and we nose our way slowly around the shoulder of the mountain, hugging the treacherous curves, and halting wherever a brook breaks through the underbrush to water the white-hot engine and to rest the human machine. The engine wears out in four months, and though the Indian who drives the truck has been trained from time immemorial not to tire, habit has not made the haul easy, and the passengers help the ascent by their silence: every word is a weight, and not one is spoken until we reach the crest. Then they look back and bid us take our leave of Oaxaca. Below, infinitely far below, lies the floor of the valley with its fertile farm lands and the distant domes of the city, where the presence of man has made some impression upon nature; before us, and no less far below, opens a vast basin of valleys and mountains multiplying, in labyrinthine confusion, in every direction—the land of the man whose fame has risen from the wilderness in which he was born and whose origin we have come to seek—the Sierra Juarez.

The road runs along a ridge that divides two worlds, and here, level with the eagle, the one ahead seems to be completely uninhabited, but our destination is already in sight, and our companions lean forward and point to something, visible to them at least, halfway up one of those far slopes, we are not sure which, which is San Pablo Guelatao. Why we are going there is a mystery to them, but, being sensible people, they suppose that we are going to look at the lake. The lake is enchanted and one of the natural wonders of the region. Man is not, and the memory of the one who was born there, or of any man, means so little that when we mention it they relapse into silence. So we slip into the other world. One by one our companions, who have been our fellows for an hour or two, drop away and set off afoot for some solitude of their own in the mountains. The road winds on and on, dipping, rising, disappearing, skirting an occasional settlement indistinguishable from the mud of which it is made and the green into which it grows, and fading immediately into the vacant immensity that dwarfs it. Once we pass through a village deserted by day and pause to drop provisions for a woman, who stands by the wayside taking leave of a man; as he swings away, she retreats into her doorway and stands there weeping,

3

and indifferent to the food laid at her feet. The Sierra is poorer by one more man, and she clings to her memories while they last.

After six hours on the road the truck drops us in another vacant village and winds its way on up the mountain to the mines at the end of the run. There is no one in sight, and we are free to wander at will; and we discover with surprise that the place is conscious of the man. A statue of him stands in a diminutive garden; a plinth marks the site of the hut in which he was born; an official portrait hangs in the municipal office. But by-and-by the people appear, and we discover that the cult has been imported and imposed on a community that has only a remote and casual connection with it. Three of his kin come in from the fields, and we make their acquaintance. They are willing to talk of their famous ancestor, but bewildered to know what we want and pained to find nothing to say. "We were not in the world then," they plead in apology of their ignorance, and we stand rebuked for disturbing it. They are of the sixth generation, and after so long a lapse of time, in a people without memory, immersed in an everlasting and unvarying present, there is not even a thread of family tradition by which to recover the trace of that distant kinsman who left his people one hundred and twenty-nine years ago, and who has returned to them in the form of a statue on a pedestal in the village green. The continuity lies in their ignorance, and curiosity breaks the connection. Time has long since severed the tie, and so has the statue standing there, a stranger like us, scanning the horizon like a solitary bronze tourist.

So they send us to school. The school is a better memorial than the statue, for it honors by a living return the memory of the boy who fled the wilderness in search of knowledge: here some eighty young men have come from all parts of the Sierra to gain some consciousness and control of life; but by its very progress the school marks the passage of time no less irrevocably than the statue. What the students know of Juarez is what we know ourselves—the conventional knowledge drawn from books—and that we should have come so far to borrow or to better it by some intimate truth out of the mouths of his own people seems to them a strange foreign notion, as it is; but they humor it. After nightfall, when the work of the day is done, masters and pupils troop with us to the municipal office, where the whole community assembles to satisfy our curiosity and to wonder at it. The mayor lights a lamp and opens a ledger and waits patiently while we read the few lines in which one of his predecessors transcribed, in 1902, the little that could then be gleaned from local tradition; for our notion is neither new nor original; others before us have burrowed in the placid oblivion of San Pablo Guelatao for some hint of his forgotten humanity, and left their meager findings to satisfy and silence all future intruders. We close the book, convinced that our curiosity is cloud-mining, and willing to admit that we have come to look at the lake.

The meeting breaks up, and on our way to bed we are shown a little cattle pool which we had noticed before without suspecting that we were looking upon wonders.

No. To know is to be, and here where his being began all that remains of the man is the statue that he has become, the metallic cast from which the living substance has long since fled. The road to San Pablo Guelatao leads nowhere; and not until we turn back and follow it, as he did, in the reverse direction does the journey make sense and the road remember the traveler.

2

BIOGRAPHY being a composite of what a man thinks of himself and what others think of him, we should begin with a blank but for an autobiographical fragment left by Juarez himself. Late in life he began a memoir for his children, which is valuable less for the information it contains than for that self-revelation which in the case of any man, and above all of one so bitterly disputed, will always be the most veracious of truths. The *Notes for My Children,* however, were written by one who had long since lost all connection with his origin, and who recalled his childhood with the detachment of maturity: it is a bare record of facts, and its self-revelation lies in his reticent and matter-of-fact recital of them.

Two dates lingered in his memory. The first was borrowed from the parish register. His birth on March 21, 1806, would have passed as unnoticed as the birth of an animal, had he awakened to it with no other witness than the spring equinox; but on the following day his father, his godmother, and his grandparents carried him up the mountain to Santo Tomas Ixtlan, where the vicar baptized him and entered the name of Pablo Benito Juarez in the book of life. The material facts that followed the end of his prenatal sleep were equally remote from his ken. "I had the misfortune," we are told, "not to have known my parents, Marcelino Juarez and Brigida Garcia, Indians of the primitive race of the country, for I was hardly three years old when they died, leaving me and my sisters, Maria Josefa and Rosa, to the care of our paternal grandparents, Pedro Juarez and Justa Lopez, Indians also of the Zapotec nation." He knew his nation, and that was enough. A few years later his grandparents died, his sisters married, and he was left

to the care of an uncle. Here were the common facts of Indian life—
birth and death, baptism and burial, dispersal and adoption, where the
burden of fertility was borne by everyone in turn—but within the immemorial pattern the will to escape it was also born, and with the
awakening of that urge his own memories begin.

"As my parents had left me no patrimony and my uncle lived by his
own toil, as soon as I could reason I applied myself, so far as my tender
years would permit, to the work in the fields. In some idle moments
my uncle taught me to read and impressed on me how useful and help-
ful it was to learn the Spanish tongue, and as it was extremely difficult
then for poor people, and especially for the native class, to pursue any
learned profession other than the ecclesiastic, he wished me to study for
ordination. These promptings and the examples of some of my countrymen who knew how to read and write and speak the Spanish
tongue, and who exercised the sacred ministry, awoke in me a vehement desire to learn, so much so indeed that when my uncle called me
to take my lesson, I myself brought him the whip to punish me if I
did not know it; but his occupations and my application to the daily
toil thwarted my desires, and I made little or no progress in my studies.
Moreover, in a little village like mine, where there were hardly twenty
families, and at a time when little or no attention was paid to the education of youth, there was no school; the Spanish tongue was not even
spoken, so that fathers who could afford the schooling of their children
took them to the City of Oaxaca for that purpose, and those who
could not pay the fees put them into service in private homes on condition that they be taught to read and write. This was the only method
of education generally in use, not only in my village, but in the whole
district of Ixtlan, so that it was a remarkable fact in that period that
most of the servants in the houses in the City were young people of
both sexes from that district. Because of these facts which I felt, rather
than by any mature reflection, of which I was yet incapable, I came to
the conclusion that only by going to the City could I learn, and indeed
I often begged my uncle to take me to the capital; but whether because
of the affection he felt for me or for some other reason, he came to no
decision and merely gave me hope that he would take me there some
day."

The accuracy of his memories is fully confirmed—save for one small
detail—by the recollections of his oldest living kin collected in 1902 in
the municipal ledger. Centenarians or near-centenarians, they remembered that even at that remote period their *pueblo* boasted a school,
run by a native, and that the boy attended it every morning before leaving for the fields. If there was some disagreement as to the school, there
was none as to the scholar. He was very much devoted to study and
showed application and profit in his letters. "His character was obedient; he was reserved in his thoughts and usually shy; he had friends,

but few, and to them he showed formality and good sense." He practiced his chosen vocation even in the fields while he was minding his flocks, and it was not uncommon to see him "mount a tree and harangue his sheep in his native Zapotec tongue."

The day when he would exercise his vocation in Oaxaca, however, was indefinitely deferred, his uncle being a man of small means "whose interests were limited to a small flock of sheep and a parcel of ground by the lake." With little to do but to count sheep or convert them, the most unsleeping ambition may well have nodded, and the boy was obedient. The years wore away uneventfully, their even tenor unbroken save by a single adventure, and that inadvertent. One day, or once upon a time, he fell asleep on the shore of the enchanted lake and woke to find himself adrift in the dark, on a clump of bushes, under a driving downpour of rain, wind, thunder, and lightning. It was the most terrifying experience in his life. He spent the night on the treacherous waters, where long ago another shepherd had fallen asleep and been drowned, and his body never found, unless by the water-witch down below; but whether she was asleep, or dead, or did not want him, he drifted safely ashore in the morning, and her legendary haunts became once more what they had been the day before, a standing lure no larger than a cattle pool in his back yard.

In his twelfth year he was no nearer Oaxaca. His uncle was loath to part with him, and the lad with his uncle. Had it been left to them, the decision might never have been made. But a sheep made up their minds for both of them.

The second date that lingered in his memory was indelibly imprinted on it—the year, the month, the day of the week, and even the hour of the day. "It was Wednesday, December 16, 1818. I was in a field, as usual, with my flock, when some muleteers chanced to pass, at eleven in the morning, leading their mules on the road to the Sierra. I asked them if they came from Oaxaca. They replied that they did, and at my request they described some of the things they had seen there and went on their way." Fatal curiosity! for when he went back to counting his sheep he found that one of them was missing and, worse yet, "another boy, who was much older than I and whose name was Apolonio Conde, approached and told me, on learning the cause of my grief, that he had seen one of the muleteers make away with the sheep." Weighing what his uncle would or would not do, he anticipated the worst, and "that fear and my natural desire to amount to something decided me to walk to Oaxaca."

Then and there the boy discovered himself. Of that mishap no mention is made, however, in the memoir: what the man chose to remember was the compunction it cost him to part with his uncle. "For my part," he wrote in the notes for his children, "I was loath to leave his side and to forsake the house that had harbored me as a child and an orphan, and to abandon the tender companions of infancy with whom one always forms profound ties and affections that suffer by absence, which withers the heart. Cruel was the conflict between these feelings and my desire to go to another society, new and unknown to me, to secure my education. Nevertheless, the desire was stronger than the sentiment, and on the 17th day of December of 1818, and at twelve years of age, I fled from my home and walked to the city of Oaxaca, where I arrived the same night."

The brevity of the account of his childhood sufficiently testifies to its truth. His birthplace was the background of his being, and his first twelve years of life merely a prelude to the day when he obeyed the lure of the road and followed it out of the cramping immensity of the mountains, through the echoless solitude of the valleys, across the crest that divides the two worlds, and down to the City, where a society new and unknown to him quickened his self-consciousness, and he became aware at last of us. San Pablo Guelatao was the point of departure; the starting-point was Oaxaca.

3

ARRIVING in Oaxaca on the night of the fatal day that followed the theft of the sheep, he found shelter in the house of Don Antonio Mazza, where one of his sisters, who had tired of marriage, was working as a cook. Here he earned his keep by watching the grain, which could not run away anyway, while he looked about for a place. Three weeks later he found one—thanks to the time-honored system by which young people from the Sierra secured an education in return for domestic service, and the charitable householders of Oaxaca an abundant supply of cheap labor—in the home of Don Antonio Salanueva. His employer was a bookbinder by trade, and by vocation a lay brother of the Third Order of Saint Francis. "Although very much addicted to devotion and religious practices, he was fairly unprejudiced and a friend to the education of youth," and was familiar with the books which he bound. His favorite reading was the Epistles of St. Paul and the collected works of Feijoo—who? no matter, he, too, promised to teach the heathen to read and write. A pious and honorable man, Dr. Salanueva fully lived up to his side of the bargain. He adopted the boy, body and soul, became his godfather, and gave him the benefit of all the educational facilities available in Oaxaca in 1818.

Before long the lad discovered their limitations. In the primary schools of New Spain, Spanish grammar was not taught at that period, reading, writing, and reciting the catechism of Padre Ripalda being hard enough to learn by heart; and as Juarez spoke what was still a foreign tongue to him, "without rules and with all the faults of the vulgar," he himself soon became dissatisfied with his progress, which was slow and imperfect. He applied, accordingly, for admission to a higher institution. Here the headmaster set him a task and he formed a page, which was faulty of course, "since I was a pupil and not a professor"— but the master, not knowing the pupil, lost his temper and, "instead of showing me my mistakes and how to correct them, merely said that it would not do and ordered me to be punished." Now, this would not do, not at all, not with Pablo Benito Juarez. "This injustice offended me profoundly, and so did the inequality with which instruction was dispensed in that institution, which was called 'The Royal School'; for while the master taught a certain number of so-called respectable pupils correctly in a separate apartment, I and the other poor boys like myself were relegated to another room, under the direction of a man who called himself the Assistant, and who was as little fitted to teach, and of a character as harsh, as the master himself." Class consciousness was all that he learned in the Royal School, and as his native handicaps were aggravated by those of being a charity pupil, he took his education in hand himself. "I was disgusted with this wretched method of instruction, and, since there was no other establishment in the City to which I could go, I decided definitely to leave school and to practice the little I had learned by myself, so as to be able to express my ideas in writing, although the form might be poor, as it still is today."

His ideas developed rapidly. The mechanics of schooling he mastered by slow and solitary application, working late into the night by the light of a stump of resin which a woman in the next courtyard lent him. Though the lad had exhausted the elementary facilities of Oaxaca so quickly, he was ill fitted to teach himself; but within less than three years he was ready for the next step. He had noticed many young men of his age going in and out of the Seminary every day, "which reminded me of the counsels of my uncle, who wished me to be an ecclesiastic" —counsels that might have been forgotten but for another fact which spurred him at fifteen. "Moreover, it was an opinion generally accepted then, not only among the vulgar but in the upper classes of society, that clerics, and even those who were merely students without being ecclesiastics, knew a great deal, and I noticed that they were respected and considered for the knowledge attributed to them. This circumstance rather than any thought of becoming a cleric, for which I felt an instinctive dislike, decided me to beg my godfather to let me study in the Seminary, offering to do everything to make the fulfillment of my obligations in his service compatible with my devotion to the study to which I was going to consecrate myself."

Dr. Salanueva not only agreed but encouraged him to adopt a calling in which he could turn his deficiencies to excellent account, explaining that, as he possessed his native Zapotec tongue, he could be ordained by right of it, under the ecclesiastical law of America, without having to possess some patrimony as well, as was required of other boys while they were waiting for a benefice. This consideration carried some weight with Salanueva and increased the satisfaction with which he welcomed the choice of a sacred career by his charge. As the motives that led the boy to embrace it were religious only in the candor with which he confessed them to himself, a mutual understanding was reached. On October 21, 1821, he donned a mantle larger than his little body and, carrying a copy of his birth certificate, joined the other young men flocking into the Seminary.

The memoir, up to this point, gives us a picture of solitary youth exclusively devoted to study; but though it is true to the dominant motive of his development, it is incomplete. In Oaxaca, as in Guelatao, his habits were noticed by the neighbors, and what is wanting is supplied by other witnesses. The nearest was the woman next door who contributed a stub of resin to his progress; the farthest, an old lady living down the block, who spent a long life there and who could still remember in her nonage that the houseboy of Dr. Salanueva was "very humble, very much devoted to study, and always to be seen with a book in his hand." These habits, she supposed, were part of his housework, since she had never seen him going to school or anywhere else for that matter, except down the street on days of religious processions. Dr. Salanueva kept in his house a figure of Christ carrying the Cross, and every day, when it went out, out came the houseboy clad in spotless linen, book in hand, reciting the *Via Crucis*. What the women saw, as they sat in their windows, was limited, however, by their powers of observation: the boys on the block saw something more, and in the reminiscences of one of them we catch a glimpse of other habits. "Although Juarez was very timid," we are told, "he was also very lively. He would buy apples and distribute them, not to eat but to pelt people buying and selling in the shops that we passed. On nights of religious exercises, and in moments of discipline, he would do the same thing when the churches were darkened, and we would throw apples until we were discovered by Salanueva and punished; but we played the same prank the next time, only more carefully." This habit was as incorrigible as his inability to distinguish between a shop and a church. Exercise of some sort was a necessity, and while Dr. Salanueva was nodding over St. Paul or Feijoo, or both at once, Juarez would slip out and join his friends around the corner. Their favorite sports were running and jumping, and he excelled in them to his cost: one day he dared the crowd to run down the Street of the Bells leaping the gutter, and with a single bound he fell in and had to be hauled out, "and though he was not soiled, since there was no filth, he made himself thoroughly wet and for that he won his whipping."

Among these larks some were more memorable than others. Most memorable of all were the outings which they made beyond the bounds of the City, across the River Atoyac, to the Lake of Montoyac. This lake was not enchanted, and here he built a springboard of his own invention, with barrels, turf, and timber borrowed from some work-men near by. Like his copybooks in school, the experiment "produced the picture we expected, not quite perfect, but nearly so." Before test-ing it the boys studied one another, "for a bold spirit was needed to make the jump." Anyone would follow the leader, and "finally Juarez made up his mind with all the courage of a good seaman, but as he came to the center of the plank or the end, both tipped and went over-board; fortunately the plank fell short and the body fell far, and he was not crushed by it." Undrowned, he was undaunted. On their next holiday he led them back to the swimming hole and repaired the con-traption with the help of a clever friend who knew the mechanics of springboards. This time it worked perfectly. The spirit of enterprise developing, he charged the boys who collected around them three or four pennies a jump, and with the profits he fed his own crowd fruit candy. Then came philanthropic cravings. "Juarez had an aversion for the strong and always favored the weak, and often he would say to us, 'When I have money I shall give it to that poor man—and some day I shall have it.'" But at fifteen, fruit candy came first.

Rambles were rare, however, and at the end of the day the road led back to the beaten path. "On the nights when we went to chapel early, Salanueva would read to us from the book that explained the mysteries of religion, the mystery of the Trinity, and the preservation of the Church and the destruction of Jerusalem, and I forget what else. When Salanueva wearied of reading, Juarez would take up the lesson, and he explained it to us fairly clearly. Then came the Rosary, or whatever office fell on that day, until eight or a quarter past eight at night." By then everyone was nodding, and curfew concluded the accustomed routine. So the memorable but dateless days of his boyhood ended, for "all this happened in our last years, about the year '20. Juarez changed his clothes and I left the chapel of Salanueva never to return, since it had been decided that I should enter the Seminary."

The reminiscences of his boyhood friend were written on the margin of the main theme: in the memoir the dominant motive develops with-out digression. His formal education was slow. When he entered the Seminary he was as ignorant of Spanish grammar as when he left the

Royal School, but this was not a serious drawback since the other students were equally deficient. In the Seminary, however, he mastered
Latin grammar; four years were spent on this study, and in August
1825 he passed or, as he said, suffered, the statutory examinations with
the rating of "Excellent." He was now qualified for the higher learning; but a serious difficulty arose with his godfather. The course in
Philosophy, which followed the mastery of grammar, was not to be
given that year, and Salanueva decided that Juarez might very well dispense with it, take up the study of Moral Theology at once, and be ordained the following summer. "This suggestion was very painful to
me, both because of the repugnance which I felt for an ecclesiastical
career, and because of the bad opinion which people held of priests
who studied nothing but Latin grammar and Moral Theology, and
who were ridiculed for that reason and called 'Mass-and-Meal Priests'
or *Larragos*. The former nickname was given them because in their
ignorance they sang Mass merely as a means of subsistence and were
not permitted to preach or to exercise any other function requiring
learning and ability; and the latter because they studied Moral Theology only in the manual of Padre Larragos." Having embraced an uncongenial calling for the sake of social advancement, Juarez meant to
make the best of a bad bargain and had no mind to be cheated of four
years of domestic servitude for the sake of a small curacy and the life
of an ecclesiastical menial somewhere in the mountains.

In his haste to hatch his charge, Salanueva made a serious mistake.
As an employer of native labor, he might have known that a discon-
tented domestic, however docile, devoted, and obedient, always ends by
having his way, and that he would have done better not to begin what
he could not finish; for Juarez had a will of his own and was not to be
hurried into holy orders. As best he could, he defended his claim to a
complete education, explaining to his godfather that he was too young
yet for the Presbytery and that nothing would be lost by taking a
course in Arts. As they were both reasonable beings, who had lived
under the same roof for seven years, the difficulty was overcome by
mutual agreement. Arts it was.

Thereafter the youth advanced at his own pace. He managed to prolong the reprieve for two years more and to stretch the persuasive appeal of immaturity well beyond the age at which it lost all legal validity. His years of schooling in Oaxaca wore away slowly, like the years
of his ignorance in Guelatao, and the plodding pace of the narrative
eloquently testifies to their dreary aridity. The calendar is dated by the
curriculum, the milestones are the opening and closing of courses, and
the record is as narrow and confined as the corridors of the convent
and the dwindling vista of doors opening and closing on his adolescence. The outer world never intrudes, no companions appear. The
memoir is a monologue, and the self-portrait is painted in mono-

chrome. Dr. Salanueva is not even mentioned; his guardian had been tamed, and the greatest difficulty under which he labored was himself, for despite his distaste for his chosen profession he displayed a marked aptitude for his studies and could not deny his abilities or defer the dreaded day indefinitely. In 1827 he suffered and passed the statutory examinations in scholastic Philosophy, sustaining two theses in public with the rating of *Excelente nemine discrepante,* and winning the unanimous commendation of his synodics. He was twenty-one, it was impossible to stall any longer, he was a man, and the next term he began the study of Moral Theology.

It was the beginning of the end, and his dilemma now became acute. He knew that he was not fitted for the Church, and he knew that there was no escape from it. The secular professions were inaccessible, since they could be pursued only in the capital or in foreign parts, and "for poor people like myself there was no hope." The monopoly of education exercised by the Church left him no choice. He was trapped by his own essential needs and the limited opportunities for satisfying them, which had driven him from Guelatao nine years before; his plight was repeated on a larger scale in Oaxaca and aggravated by the knowledge he had picked up since then of a society no longer new and unknown to him. He had found a place, and a privileged one, in Oaxaca, adopted by a sympathetic patron and given all the advantages that the philanthropic facilities of the provincial capital provided for his people. There was no further to go, and he could not go back to Guelatao. He had enjoyed all the benefits and exhausted all the resources of the City, from the Royal School with its class distinctions to the Seminary, which offered the refuge of religious equality to those who renounced the world for it; and he found himself in an impasse, advancing consciously toward a dead end. The dilemma was cruel, but it was of his own choosing, and he could not complain. The Church it was.

So his last years in the Seminary slipped away. He was bored, he was listless, he found the principles of Moral Theology incomprehensible, but he completed his contract. Nothing less than a direct intervention of Divine Providence, or a change in the whole social order, could break it, and he knew too little of Moral Theology to believe in miracles. Before the year was out, however, something happened in Oaxaca that completely altered his destiny. Here the narrative breaks off in a digression that is an integral part of the chronicle and necessary to explain how it was that in the course of time he was able to write those notes for his children.

4

"IN THAT period great events had already occurred in the Nation." The words with which the digression begins read like the belated acknowledgment of a debt; and so they were. The Nation is a new word in the narrative, and a new fact in his consciousness, and it is introduced at the precise moment when it begins to have a meaning for him. Born in 1806, he grew up in the period during which a Crown colony of Spain was gradually transformed into an independent people. His childhood coincided with the birth throes, and his adolescence with the growth, of the movement for national emancipation, but between that development and his own there was no connection until he reached manhood and reaped its benefits in 1827. The debt was acknowledged when he was ripe to appreciate it; but the great events of that period were too familiar to require more than a passing mention in the memoir, and the brief allusion which he makes to them there deserves some enlargement because of the far-reaching effect which they exercised on his destiny, recasting it and foreshadowing the forces that determined his future.

The separation of the colony from the mother country had long been foreseen by the Spanish themselves as a natural phenomenon foreordained by its very constitution and born in the bowels of the world. Predestined by political geography, the distance of one continent from the other, the remote control of the colony by the mother country, and the detachment of the offspring from the parent—nature and human nature combined to make it inevitable. Geopolitical generalities are less important, however, than the specific factors—the time, the place, and the human agents—that produced the foregone conclusion. The *why* was foreseen, but not the *how* and the *when*. Like other fatalities, though the rupture could not be prevented, it could at least be postponed by the normal precautions of human prudence; and no safeguard was neglected to defer it. The colony was isolated and preserved in hermetic seclusion from the outer world, and for two centuries after the founding of New Spain the policy was applied with success, breeding a race of political minors and a dependent mentality in the colonials, which provided the best means of perpetuating their bondage; but eventually the parental hand slipped.

The process of emancipation was common to the whole continent and contagious, and for New Spain it began with the rebellion of the British colonies in North America. When the peace treaty was signed in Paris in 1783, France and Spain were parties to it, as they had been to the revolt, which they abetted to cripple a rival empire. The Conde de Aranda, who signed the treaty in the name of Spain, improved the occasion to read his royal master a lesson. "The independence of the English colonies has been recognized, and this fact is for me an occasion of sorrow and fear," he wrote. "France has few possessions in America, but she should have considered that Spain, her closest ally, has many, and that henceforth they will be exposed to dreadful convulsions. From the first France has worked against her own interests in favoring and stimulating this independence. I have said as much more than once to the ministers of that nation. I shall not dwell on the difficulty of preserving our domination in America. Never have possessions so extensive and lying at so great a distance from the metropolis been successfully preserved for any length of time. Without entering into such considerations, I shall confine myself to what concerns us now, the fear of finding ourselves exposed to the perils that threaten us from the new Power that we just recognized in a land where no other State exists to check its advance. This Federal Republic was born a pygmy, so to speak, and needed the support of two Powers as mighty as Spain and France to achieve its independence. A day will come when it will become a giant, a colossus to be dreaded in those parts. It will then forget the benefits it received from both Powers and will think only of its own aggrandizement. The first step of this new Power, when once it begins to grow, will be to gain possession of the Floridas to dominate the Gulf of Mexico. After thus hampering our commerce with New Spain, it will aspire to the conquest of that vast empire, which we shall be unable to defend against a formidable Power established on the same continent and adjoining it as well."

The prophet of doom, however, was also a statesman determined to outwit it, and he crowned his complaint with a remarkable recommendation. Since the loss of the colonies was inevitable, and the proximity of the new nation certain to speed it, either by example or conquest, it was obviously the part of wisdom to yield to necessity and to forestall it gracefully. Startling as his advice seemed, what the Conde de Aranda had in mind was no wanton flight of reason, but a completely hardheaded scheme: he proposed to abandon all the overseas possessions of Spain with the exception of Cuba and Puerto Rico and some islands to the south to serve as a route and a storehouse for colonial trade, and to convert the dominions into a commonwealth of autonomous American monarchies bound to the mother country by an issue of Bourbons who would sit, one on the throne of Peru, another on that of New Spain, and a third on the coast of Costa Firma.

Nor was the shadow of sovereignty to be the sole compensation for abandoning its substance. The condition of this great cession was that the transatlantic kings should recognize the King of Spain as the head of the family and pay tribute to him in kind—gold from Peru, silver from New Spain, and colonial commodities from Costa Rica; trade would be conducted on a basis of complete reciprocity, binding the four thrones together in a close defensive and offensive alliance for their mutual protection and prosperity. Since the factories of Spain could not meet the demand in America for manufactured articles, France would be invited as an ally to supply the shortage, to the absolute exclusion of England, and the boycott against the British would be embodied in formal trade treaties. The contributions of the three kings would be more valuable than all the silver currently drawn from America, Aranda believed; the population would increase, emigration from Spain would be checked, and the power bloc would be strong enough to prevent the aggrandizement of the Anglo-American colonies or of any other competitor in that part of the world. "In short," he concluded, "we shall enjoy all the advantages of the possession of America without suffering any of its drawbacks."

The admonitions of the Conde de Aranda have often been cited for the accuracy of his forecasts; they are no less notable as the statement by a contemporary of the causes which were already apparent in 1783 for the imminent dissolution of the Spanish empire. Spain at the close of the eighteenth century was no longer the nation that had colonized a hemisphere in the sixteenth, but a weakening world Power barely able to maintain its position on the old continent, and incapable of retaining its possessions overseas without adapting its colonial system to the changing times. The consciousness of that fact pervades the recommendations of Aranda, and the best advice he could offer under the circumstances was necessarily senile. The proposal to transform the colonies into a protectorate and to lend a new lease of life to the decrepit Spanish empire by an act of fraudulent political bankruptcy was one of those schemes, dear to the minds of lawyers and chancellors alike, which had the merit of professional shrewdness but which could not cheat the facts; it was an accommodation to change which merely encouraged the delusion of past grandeur. The proposal to form an economic bloc between France and Spain against Great Britain was inspired, on the other hand, by a clear grasp of the forces which were to determine the future and, speeded by the industrial revolution, to tip the balance of power.

With his long view of history and his limited means of controlling it, the Conde de Aranda was a typical *fin-de-siècle* statesman, looking backward and forward in impotent perception of a dilemma which could be met only by makeshifts. His whole scheme might be described as the daydream of a senile realist, had it not influenced the course of independence and caught the fancy of later and no less level-headed statesmen who tested it in the nineteenth century. At the time, it was taken seriously by no one but its author. His warning was addressed to an enlightened monarch; but not even a liberal Bourbon could transcend his regal limitations and the settled inertia of two centuries of colonial empire. Institutions, and not men, govern such situations, and Carlos III, a liberal, a Bourbon, but not an anomaly, found no better means of postponing the loss of his dominions in America than to tighten his grip on them, increasing the garrisons and adopting all the traditional precautions best calculated to produce the traditional results of repression. The real interest of the recommendations of his minister lies in the forlorn attempt, one of the first and not the last of its kind, to foresee historic processes, to anticipate inevitable defeats, and to avert unnecessary conflicts. As such, it fully demonstrated the futility of sparing humanity and the impossibility of writing history painlessly.

Of the two partners to the mutiny in North America, France was the first to suffer the consequences of her reckless philanthropy. The Rights of Man, discovered in America and the first colonial commodity to be exported abroad, were proclaimed in Paris in the thick of a revolution and weakened the control of the metropolis over the Crown colonies in the Caribbean. As the conflagration progressed, the sparks crossed the ocean. In Haiti, the French portion of Santo Domingo, where the accumulation of class, caste, and race conflicts lay packed and inflammable, a series of social explosions followed, of such intensity that slaveholders all over the world, and above all in the New World, saw in the column of smoke rising from the tropical island a warning to redouble their vigilance and tighten the rigor of repression, so plainly warranted by the reprisals to which they were exposed if they weakened. The upheaval in Haiti brought the danger measurably nearer to New Spain; but the Spaniards were not disturbed by the troubles of their neighbors, and their indifference was the more remarkable in that the proximity of Santo Domingo to New Spain, as close politically as it was geographically, heightened the hazards of contagion.

Both provinces were ruled by the Colonial Compact; by the terms, that is, of a code to which that misnomer added the final touch of absurdity, since it involved no reciprocity and was designed to secure the complete exploitation of the colony by the mother country. The Colonial Compact embodied the mania of monopoly in its most senseless forms and developed it to the highest degree to which human ingenuity could carry it: monoply of trade to the exclusion not only of foreign nations, but of intercolonial commerce; monopoly of industry, to the suppression of any local commodity that might compete with the exports of the home market; monopoly of office by Europeans, to the exclusion not only of the natives, but of their own offspring born in the colony, who, thus disqualified, formed a class apart, the anomalous Creoles, Europeans by blood and natives by law, belonging neither to one world nor to the other; monopoly of privilege, with the consequent division of families into classes and classes into castes, according to color and origin, each jealous of the other and all destined to support the ruling caste by their divisions; and lastly, monopoly of education, entrusted to the Church and enforced by censorship—though the last was not a serious privation, perhaps, in tropical countries where the climate provided the best censorship, all the labor essential to life was performed by illiterates, and the need for mental exertion was unknown to their betters. On those broad principles all the possessions of France and Spain were run and the structure of colonial society was built. They had the rational merit, at least, of reducing to their simplest terms and revealing in their crudest forms the natural relations governing all empires and all colonies, without attenuating compensations to make them tolerable to the colonials themselves, and were admirably adapted, therefore, to provoke them to revolt. Although the rules had been relaxed in some respects by contraband trade and administrative laxity by the end of the eighteenth century, these involuntary concessions to necessity had merely served to adulterate the system with the contagious dram of delivery.

While the regime was identical in Santo Domingo and New Spain, some social differences there were which explained the indifference of the Spaniards to the upheaval in Haiti. There the bottom class, which supported the structure of colonial society, was composed of black slaves, and slavery was an institution repugnant to the Spaniards in the raw form of human bondage. Without it, they obtained the same labor from their serfs, bound to the land by feudal service and aboriginal habit, and the submissive Indian of the mainland was not the same breed of primitive as the jungle-bred black of the islands, nor liable to the same ferocity that marked the insurrection in Santo Domingo. What happened there showed very clearly, nevertheless, that the initial danger lay not in the lowest, but in the upper, strata of the community. The insurrection began at the top between Europeans and Creoles, in the friction of fathers and sons who were foreigners to each other under the terms of the Colonial Compact. It spread with the natural virulence of a family quarrel to the subordinate castes and half-castes, degenerated rapidly into the aboriginal rages of race war, and brought the whole structure crashing to the ground in a complete demonstration of human brotherhood. The servile class was not the first danger but the last; and the saving difference between the Negro and the Indian was a feeble safeguard against a duplication of the Haitian experience in New Spain, in a Crown colony bound by the same practices, the same monopolies, the same discriminations, and the same servitudes to the parent Power.

Nevertheless, the Spaniards preserved their immunity. They trusted in God: a special Providence protected the land that they had covered with convents and churches, and in New as in Old Spain the Church had performed its social mission and subdued a heterogeneous population by divine precept to the security of the State. They trusted in man: the docility of the native and his hermetic seclusion had preserved him in a state of political innocence so incorruptible that in two and a half centuries only five small flares of revolt betrayed his original depravity. And the confidence of the Spaniards was warranted. After five years of conflagration the insurrection in Santo Domingo flickered out without affecting the Spanish dominions either on the island or on the mainland. The French Revolution, from which it caught the spark, also burned itself out, and the years of crisis abroad passed without disturbing the settled peace of the colony. It was not until France turned against Spain that the ties with the mother country became actually strained.

Out of the embers came the phoenix. It was Napoleon who, by diverting the energies of the French Revolution to the conquest of Europe, finally relayed, indirectly and inadvertently, the impulse of colonial emancipation to Spanish America. By 1808 his armies had overrun Spain; the Bourbons were his captives; his brother sat on their throne; the defense of the peninsula was carried on by popular insurrection and patriotic committees; and the dismemberment of the old country created a dilemma for the Viceroy of New Spain. To whom or to what was his allegiance due? To the dynasty represented by a captive monarch? Or to the nation represented by the self-constituted regional bodies? Each horn of the dilemma was worse than the other, but he hit upon a solution that evaded them both. He decided to hold the colony in trust, under temporary self-government and in a state of suspended animation, until the return of normal times. While professing absolute loyalty to the sovereign, he met the emergency by adopting the example of the patriotic committees, which also swore allegiance to Ferdinand VII, and summoned an assembly of the local administrative bodies—the Audiencia, the Archbishopric, the Municipality of Mexico, the Delegates of the Tribunals, the secular and ecclesiastical bodies of the Nobility, the leading citizens, and the military commanders— which ratified his decision, declared for the sovereignty of New Spain, and invested him with supreme authority. To protect the colony against the possibility of foreign attack, either by the English who were tampering with the integrity of the empire in South America, or by the French or the Dutch who were based on the islands of the Caribbean, the Viceroy mobilized the military forces on an unprecedented scale and put them through imposing maneuvers between the capital and the coast.

Sensible and loyal as the solution was, it alarmed the conservatives of the colony, always more orthodox than those of the old country, and now deprived of their protection. To the party of Old Spaniards, as they called themselves, self-government, even as a provisional measure, spelled a dangerous precedent. Suspecting the Viceroy of ulterior aims and personal ambitions, they formed a conspiracy to nip them in the bud. He was deposed, deported, and replaced by one of their own choosing. The coup was approved by the provincial authorities in Spain, who claimed jurisdiction over the colony, and who profited by it, collecting fourteen million pesos from the coffers of New Spain for the defense of the peninsula, and appointing their own regents in Mexico. These changes, and the confusion and uncertainty of the situation, inevitably produced an unsettling effect on the colony, and the party of Old Spaniards kept a close watch over the lower orders, lest they improve on the precedent. The masses did not move; they had not moved for centuries. It was in the higher classes that the danger lay, and there the damage was done. The name of self-government had been pronounced, and by a Viceroy, sanctioned by legitimate authority and fostered by his forcible overthrow; the idea had been sown, the precedent set; and the seed settled among the Creoles. Fretting to free themselves from the inferiority to which they were condemned by the accident of colonial birth, they were not slow to perceive the favorable opportunity which the flux of the times offered them, but they were themselves confused by it. The inferiority was fictitious, class barriers had become blurred, they were favored with wealth and position, the driving motive was feeble, and if the Creoles, as a class, were restless, they were not rebellious, being by nature and training both indolent and mercurial, and the vigilance of the Old Spaniards held them in check. The colony remained quiet—for a year—for two years—and vigilance had already relaxed when the outbreak came.

Belated as it was historically, the long-awaited revolt was nonetheless premature. In September 1810 the military commander of Queretaro was informed of a seditious conspiracy by one of its members, who, alarmed by its consequences, denounced himself. In an access of conscience he betrayed one of its leaders, a captain of Dragoons stationed in the neighboring town of San Miguel el Grande and well known as a scion of the Creole aristocracy of the region, by the name of Ignacio Allende. Warned by his confederates in Queretaro, where he was spending the day, Allende made his escape, carried the alarm to his friends in San Miguel, and galloped on to the village of Dolores to take counsel with the parish priest, who was the head of the movement. Arriving after nightfall, Allende lost a precious hour in locating him in the home of a local Spaniard, where a dance was in progress, and in inducing him, after some dallying, to withdraw to his own house and hear him out. There Father Hidalgo insisted on sitting down to a cup of chocolate while he sent for their confederates in Dolores.

About nine, when they were assembled, came another cavalryman, Captain Aldama, from San Miguel, with a message from the Colonel of the Regiment for Allende and his friends to escape. The offer was warmly welcomed and hotly debated until Father Hidalgo forbade them to discuss it, reminding them that it would be an unpardonable crime to desert the cause and their comrades who were compromised and defenseless. "Forget it," he said, "for such an idea is neither honorable nor, far less, great." But what else could they do? someone protested. Die, he replied; when men had sworn as highly as they to redeem their country. . . . The company was not convinced. The classic cry of the patriot seemed to be aimed at posterity, not at them. It was then that the priest displayed his peculiar generalship. "An idea occurs to me, gentlemen, and it will be our real salvation," he said. "Come on, Valleza. Now, and without losing time, you are going to arrest the *gachupin* priests. You, Mariano"—turning to his brother—"the *gachupin* traders. You too, Aldama, and Don Santos Villa. To prison with all of them, without touching their interests."

The company stood aghast, protesting that they were unprepared and would be the sole victims of their temerity. "That is how children talk," he replied, "who never measure the circumstances of a situation nor calculate that the most insignificant details, if one has the skill to combine them, will form a strong and terrible whole. With the cry against the *gachupines,* tomorrow we shall have all and more than we need. Pocket your fears and to work, without losing a moment." Every man to his trade—soldiers were trained to be commanded and men of action to be occupied—and without leaving them time to think, Hidalgo sent them out to round up the local Spaniards. "This bold feat, carried out by eleven men," says the account of one who witnessed it, "will appear fabulous, and some may consider it such, but it is entirely true." A silent patrol made the rounds of the *pueblo,* collecting the sleeping *gachupines* one by one. By five in the morning the last one had been bagged and put behind bars. The intervening hours were spent by Hidalgo and Allende in mapping their next move—a one-sided conference, for the problem so precipitately created could be met only by the qualities of inspiration peculiar to the priest, and he had yet to conceive his next step when he took the first.

So, in the small hours of September 16, 1810, a new nation was forced into being in the brains of a country curate and a few fugitives who followed his lead unquestioningly, hypnotized by his self-possession and obeying it blindly. The idea was not new—Hidalgo had nursed it for years and matured it patiently with a little group of initiates; but the original plan called for a concerted uprising by selected troops in December, and its premature disclosure compelled him to modify it in a manner which profoundly altered its character. Captain Allende had sought converts in his regiment and in those with which he had come into contact in the capital during the maneuvers ordered by the Viceroy two years before, and had declared himself ready to draw the sword as soon as he could find five hundred. But he found his countrymen deaf to the idea of independence, and to go off at half-cock before so vast a movement could be organized was so obviously foolhardy that he would have abandoned it, no doubt, but for his partner. The adventure so recklessly begun, without adequate preparation and against great odds, could survive only by consistently attempting the impossible. Hidalgo guided it accordingly, step by step, himself always well ahead of his lieutenants.

The next day was a Sunday. By five in the morning the *pueblo* was swarming with the usual crowd of Indians from the surrounding countryside, gathering for early Mass, market, and gossip. When word spread that there might be no Mass that morning, and no market, as Señor Hidalgo had spent the night locking up the *gachupines,* they assembled before his house to learn what remained of their only occupations in life. Their numbers increased with their uncertainty, and "seeing them swell," says the chronicle, "that estimable priest thought that the time had come to address a few words to the crowd and to explain his reasons for so novel and unknown a movement." The words were few but effective. He informed them that there was no longer a king, nor tribute to be levied, that the shameful tax, which was the badge of their slavery and which they had paid for two hundred years, was abolished, that the day of deliverance was at hand, and that the cause was holy and God would protect it. Raising a shout for America and the Virgin of Guadalupe, he bade them march. Accustomed to unquestioning obedience and the responses of the liturgy, the crowd caught up the cry and carried the day by acclamation. By ten o'clock, when Hidalgo reappeared on horseback, he was surrounded by thousands of men, armed with knives, cudgels, poles, slings and stones.

The hold which Hidalgo had over his flock was not due to his cloth alone, nor even to his war cry; for he was one of those rare priests in New Spain who brought his religion out of doors and applied it to the relief of the native. Fostering his crafts, extending his industries, and cultivating the prohibited vine of the Colonial Compact, he introduced into his district potteries and tanneries, beehives and silkworms, vineyards and distilleries. He could always be found, after Mass, at the silk works or the pottery, supervising the output or sitting in a corner, on call. He had advanced ideas. "He wanted every industry to be protected by societies," says the chronicle, "which would supply it with sufficient funds, every member holding one or more shares; the officials and workers would co-operate with the value of their labor, being given an advance to allow them to subsist until the utility was divided in which they were all to have a proportionate part. He was opposed, in short, to the tyranny of capital. He said also that every stranger who established himself in the country would have to belong to a society of industry, either as a shareholder or by means of his knowledge and labor, otherwise he could not live in the country. In sum, he wanted everyone to be useful to all. Theories these were which would have had some modification in practice; but at bottom there was an abundance of good intentions which aimed at the general good, since even our men of means in the whole Mexican country would have had to belong to the commercial or industrial societies, for he was opposed to the softness of our powerful men. Sometimes he would be heard to cite the aphorism of Hippocrates, 'To know the evil is half the cure.'" It was. If not the technique, Hidalgo created the habit of co-operation and the spirit of self-help in his community, and he reaped the fruits in the multitude that mustered to his call on the morning of September 16.

Long before he preached his subversive sermon, he had endeared himself profoundly to his charges; and when he took leave of his potters to whom he recommended the care of the silkworms and the beehives, "which formed a great resource for the poor, and the flax-seed of which he had high hopes, even of deriving something substantial from it," he gathered an abundant harvest and resowed it. Those whom he left behind were not the least in his sight. "Uniting them all, he embraced them and begged them to attend to their tasks. There were some tears, and he consoled them, saying that he would return soon," for they were the root. Thus, out of the root and the fruit of his pastoral labors, the curate of Dolores conjured up a movement revolutionary in its promise, its mass character, its contagious scope. The individual roles were still indistinct: leadership belonged by right to the man who provided the inspiration and the manpower, and the professional soldier fell inevitably into the background.

The crowd poured forth from Dolores, and the flock became a herd on the highroad, heading for San Miguel el Grande, gathering recruits on the way and growing prodigiously with the parade of the captives, for the *gachupines* under guard of Allende brought up the rear, and it was they, according to all accounts, "who provided the impulse for so colossal a revolution." Halfway to San Miguel, which was reported to be arming in haste, a halt was called while Allende with a hundred horsemen galloped ahead to reconnoiter the town. In the public square he found two companies, in fact, under arms, and was accosted by a subordinate who upbraided him and clutched his bridle, but he rode him down, and the troops broke ranks and joined him. An enthusiastic crowd followed them to the doors of the *Casas Reales,* where the Spaniards had taken refuge after appealing in vain to the military authorities for protection. Colonel Narciso Maria Loreto de la Canal bore a name that was synonymous with San Miguel, his family having en-them. Here the first battle was fought. The building, a solid block-house built on a steep slope, was an impregnable position that defied the very idea of storming it.

The siege which the insurgents set to it with volleys of slingstones would have lasted indefinitely, or until the arrival of relieving forces, but for the feat of an individual who detached himself from the mass and whose exploit remained famous. On the slope above the citadel, Hidalgo commanded a clear view of it and nothing else, when he was informed that a miner had volunteered to burn the gate with the loss of no more than one life. He sent for him. A sickly little man, consumed by a chronic disease in the mines, appeared, explained his plan, and was permitted to try it. All that he needed was a big flagstone to cover his back, a rope, and a fuse, and off he went, downhill, slowly but steadily, like an invalid Atlas, under a hail of missiles that missed him, straight to the gate and fired it. As the door crumbled, the Intendant was seen behind it, repairing the damage; a slingstone killed him. Amid the crying confusion within, the besiegers swarmed in and massacred the garrison before Hidalgo and Allende could climb through the breach and proclaim the laws of civilized warfare.

The citadel was conquered, but the townspeople had still to be won. In Guanajuato Hidalgo had many friends. They came to call on him in the barracks where he set up his bed. The room was small, the affluence was great, and as there were only two chairs they sat on the cot or the floor, while one spoke for all. "Well, sir," said Hidalgo, after the preliminary compliments had been exchanged, "what do you think of my visit?"—"It is not like the others that you deigned to make me," was the reply.—"What is the difference?"—"The difference is that you come accompanied by much blood and destruction, and followed by much mourning and by no less fear, which we still feel." The speaker was his most intimate friend.—"You may be right, Señor Licenciado," Hidalgo replied, "but what is remarkable is that you were not alarmed by the terrible destruction which the Lion of Spain made, without pity and in cold blood, of the country, the life, and the welfare of our ancestors, ending with the people and forcing them into a shameful and humiliating situation which still exists, and which the backs of the mexicans have borne without murmuring for the long term of three centuries. By this destruction was formed the foundation of that terrible power, and the cement which our conquerors used to form and raise the structure of their abominable domination which is wet with the blood and tears of our elders, and though it is still very strong and high, all that you have seen, and that surprises and terrifies you, is no more than the first blow; it will not fall by it, because it is solidly built; but the blows to come will make it tremble and destroy it, perhaps. It is very high and it must fall, for its shadow or bulk prevents the rays of liberty from penetrating to fertilize the small grass that surrounds it.

Consult France in her revolution and you will see that we are mere pygmies and cannot compare with those terrible events; but the motives are not unlike ours. Courage, then Señor Licenciado, you shall see more, much more, we are only in the prologue."

The words which he put into the mouth of his friend remained there, however, and seeing him stand tongue-tied and embarrassed, Hidalgo changed the subject and asked him whether he had suffered any harm in his interests. "No, not yet, nothing but a great fear," the lawyer admitted, "and in spite of it I have come out into the street to beg a mercy."—"And of whom do you expect it?"—"Of you, in favor of some europeans who have been arrested, and their interests embargoed." The favor was readily granted, Hidalgo referring them to the offer which he had made to the Intendant and of which his friends were thus informed for the first time. But the terms of capitulation which he offered them would have made no difference, as it made none now, in their attitude: they showed their political instinct by petitioning him for the release of his European prisoners. The response was the same when he called a meeting of the Town Council to explain the aims of the movement and rally their support: the members sat speechless and dumfounded. When it came to organizing a government, he could find no one willing to accept a post of responsibility, not even to maintain law and order. They had seen him distributing silver bars to the men who made them and who neither needed nor waited for his permission to take them. The storming of the Alhondiga and its capture barehanded by a horde of half-armed rebels was a portent of what an aroused people could accomplish; and the fall of the local Bastille confounded, without converting, the bureaucrats. Since no one spoke up, Hidalgo said that he regarded their silence "either as a vague fear that his plans and ideas would not be realized for lack of imitators or as a real and pronounced neutrality, which, as it was so harmful in the present circumstances, he would punish as a declared partiality." They tried to reply but could not; before they could open their mouths he made the appointments, which were proclaimed and cheered by the populace celebrating the fall of the citadel.

Independence was two weeks old. Though word came that many places had declared for it, or would soon do so, in the immediate vicinity, Hidalgo was worried by the silence of his partisans in San Luis Potosi, where the preliminary organization of the conspiracy had been carried furthest and men of high position and powerful influence had pledged themselves to promote the movement. He decided to march there without delay. Guanajuato was not a guarantee but a warning. The respectable classes were not the only ones to be shocked by the license and alarmed by the success with which they were liberated by the lower orders. The reduction of the Alhondiga was a revolutionary feat, or a freak of fortune, too unscientific to satisfy the military mind:

an accident from which nothing could be argued and upon which folly
alone would presume to found further operations; and a strong royalist force was reported to be assembling at San Luis Potosi. Allende took
time out, therefore, to complete the training, interrupted by the triumph, of his nondescript troops. The miners made good shock troops;
two wooden cannon were built and tested without exploding; they
were of small caliber, but they were made to prove, as Hidalgo said,
that "any people can be free that wants to be." But there were still,
there would always be, more Alhondigas to burn.

Time was pressing, and Hidalgo started ahead with six thousand
men. The march was made through the Sierra by night, with thousands of torches dispelling the solitude, if not the gloom, of the mountains. In the morning they passed through Dolores, where he was welcomed with sincere affection by his flock, his friends, his co-operatives.
His return fired their faith in his other promises. But beyond Dolores
it was different. The radius of confidence had not reached San Luis
Potosi. Halfway there, he received a message from his confederates
urging him to turn back and attack the capital first and promising, for
their part, to follow up his success and cover his rear. San Luis Potosi
was also a mining town. He hesitated; he turned back.

Returning to Guanajuato, where his reappearance restored public
confidence for four days, he left it again on the fifth with his whole
army and hurried on to Valladolid. One month after it had begun, the
insurrection was still tentative, a magnified reconnaissance movement,
a rising of the masses, but not yet a popular revolt. Possession of the
capital was indispensable to its success, to catch the imagination and
determine the loyalty of the country at large; and whatever the value
of the advice from a military point of view, politically the partisans in
San Luis Potosi did Hidalgo a service by restoring him to his inspiration and the giant strides of his instincts. Formidable in numbers, for
the original five thousand had multiplied tenfold, the teeming multitude advanced on Valladolid and overran it. Here Hidalgo was on
home ground. In the ancient University he had been student, teacher,
and rector, in turn. In the citadel of books he had dipped into the forbidden volumes of French revolutionary literature and had drawn the
blood of books with which he returned at the head of fifty thousand
barefooted disciples, acclaimed by Indians, Creoles, and ecclesiastics
alike. The reward of abounding in boldness was a triumphant entrance
into the calm academic town—a triumphant entrance, not a triumphant welcome. Furious preparations had been made for defense; the
Bishop had fled, casting excommunications behind him, the priests had
rallied all the villages of that levitic valley; but as the shadow fell
across it and the spell of an army of victorious and veteran vagrants
spread, all resistance was abandoned and the excommunications were
lifted at the point of the sword. There was some irregular looting,

promptly suppressed by Allende, and Hidalgo helped himself to a million pesos from the coffers of the Cathedral; but the best of the booty was the garrison, which went over to the insurgents and supplied them with their first professional leaven. Thus fortified, Hidalgo started for the capital at the end of October; but with the increase in numbers and the difficulty of controlling them, his self-confidence clouded. Challenged by a critic to justify the upheaval, he replied that he knew what it ought to be but not what it was.

His best friends now were the enemy. The enemy knew what it was and what it ought to be from the day it began. His house in Dolores had long been called *la Francia chiquita,* and everyone foresaw what was coming when he left "little France" with his hordes of land-hungry insurgents: the movement for independence was at the same time a social revolution. The one was inseparable from the other and indispensable to its triumph. In Valladolid he issued a decree abolishing slavery, ignoring the legal fiction that there was no such thing in New Spain, and followed up his Emancipation Proclamation with decrees abolishing castes and tributes, reducing taxes and landed estates, and proscribing the accepted servitudes that were its substance.

The authorities anticipated his next step; they thought as he did, and faster. The Bishop of Valladolid had once been a reformer himself. Recognizing "the ignorance and misery of the Indians," which placed them "at an infinite distance from a Spaniard," he had recommended long ago the free distribution of some acreage among the castes and the Indians, the division of the communal lands in each *pueblo,* and an agrarian law, like that of Galicia or the Asturias, allowing the people to settle gradually, over a period of twenty or thirty years, upon the uncultivated lands of the great proprietors. But the reform remained on paper, and when the revolution came rolling to his door, he hurled anathemas at it, protesting that in this part "the plan of the Curate Hidalgo constitutes a private civil war, of anarchy and destruction, efficient also and necessary, between the Indians, Castes, and Spaniards, who compose all the children of this Country." The cry traveled. Another bishop discovered another danger and warned the country that, if the revolt succeeded, they would all be at the mercy of the first maritime Power that appeared off their coasts. Everyone knew that British, French, and American agents were trying to revolutionize the colony —everyone, that is, but Hidalgo. The authorities were better informed.

As the embattled farmers approached the capital, panic prevailed there. The Inquisition exorcised the leader, and the Archbishop of Mexico exhorted his followers. "Hidalgo errs," he warned them, "and his plan of reconquering America for the Indians is not only anti-Catholic but chimerical, extravagant, ridiculous, and supremely prejudicial to the author who proposes it. Even supposing that the plan of casting off the Europeans could be accomplished, would not a cruel war be kindled between the Indians and the Spanish-Americans for the estates, the mines, the riches wrested from the subjects of Spain and those of the Americans? And what would the length and outcome of such a war be? Who would be the gainers by it, and who the losers? Would not the Indians insist, as they are now being told by Hidalgo, that they are lords and masters of the land of which the Spaniards despoiled them by conquest?" Across the narrowing gulf between Indian and Spaniard, Creole called to Creole in supreme appeal, and the Indians were cautioned against the tempter. "Be not deceived, my sons, be not seduced! The Curate Hidalgo is on trial for heresy. He seeks not your fortune but his own, as we already said in our exhortation of the 24th of September. Now he flatters you with the attractive lure that he will give you the land. He will not, he will break faith with you, he will impose tributes and personal services, because otherwise he cannot subsist in the elevation to which he aspires, and he will shed your blood and the blood of your children to preserve and increase it, as Bonaparte has done. You are already free of tributes; enjoy this blessing in peace; shun the man whose doctrines are reproved by Holy Scripture and our blessed Mother Church, and that would put an end to the world, if they were practiced, yourselves being the first victims. Long live Religion!—as it will not with those who oppose the teachings of Holy Mother Church! Long live the Virgin of Guadalupe!—as she will not with him who decries her virginity, or those who subvert and overturn the lands of that Lady! Long live Ferdinand VII!—as he cannot with the independence of his vassals!" Hidalgo and the Archbishop came within shouting distance of the end of the world; and the protests, the appeals, the persuasions of an enemy already reduced to reason were the best proof that he was on the right road.

From Valladolid the unseen congregation of the Archbishop pressed on to Toluca; and on the last lap of the road to the capital, in a winding defile of the descent to the valley of Mexico, they met the troops hastily assembled by the Viceroy. These numbered no more than two thousand, but they were regulars, entrenched on high ground with cannon, commanding the winding road, on which the rebels lost the value of numbers and were raked, hour after hour, with accurate fire. The generalship of Allende rose to the test: hour after hour, he flung an inexhaustible supply of raw human material, or matter, against the guns overhead, while he mounted a single cannon above both, directing flank attacks by his few trained troops and head after head of the huge herd, with which he drew and drained the fire of the enemy. The slaughter lasted from ten in the morning until four in the afternoon. Finally, falling, scattering, and scrambling back for yet another and another rush, by sheer weight of numbers and uncounted sacrifices, the victims dislodged and overwhelmed the regulars and carried the

day. The road lay open, and the victors followed it to within sight of
the promised land. There it was learned that royalist troops were advancing by forced marches from San Luis Potosi. The position was
critical. Caught between fresh troops and the unconquered capital,
Hidalgo called a council of war. The roles were reversed: Allende
recommended an immediate attack on the city, but Hidalgo decided on
a tactical retreat. His inspiration was spent, he had stretched the movement as far as the momentum of improvisation could carry it, and
within sight of the goal he faltered and fell back.

From that day disaster ensued. His star deserted him, his followers
hugged his heels, and the retreat was a series of irresistible reverses.
When they passed the Monte de las Cruces, where they had fought the
battle that marked the crest of their advance two days before, the dispirited thousands broke ranks to bury their dead, and they were still
disheartened when they were overtaken at Aculco by the troops from
San Luis Potosi, whom they were trying to avoid. Neither side dared
to engage the other, but a runaway horse, dragging a headless rider,
stampeded the rebels, who abandoned the field without battle. Allende
managed to bring the bulk of his best troops back to Guanajuato,
where weeks were wasted in drilling men and casting cannon for a
new stand, for when the government troops appeared, he found himself outflanked and abandoned the town, falling back on Guadalajara,
which had declared for the cause and where Hidalgo had gone ahead
to raise a fresh army. And at the gates of Guadalajara a great battle was
lost, unfought, by another accident. Hidalgo had mustered an army of
seventy thousand men. They were drawn up on the plain, awaiting the
attack of the enemy, when the munitions exploded, the stubble caught
fire, and the plain became a sea of flame, blown by a strong north wind
against the rebels, who melted away in confusion and terror.

With a few officers, Hidalgo and Allende made their way northward, gathering recruits, ready, as one of them said, "for a long and
perhaps eternal migration," their destination being their distance from
the enemy. An agent whom they had sent to the United States to secure support and conclude an alliance was caught and shot, but they
themselves eluded pursuit, although the local authorities were on the
alert to prevent any contact with the fatal constellation of seventeen
northern stars. Their worst enemies were the heat and thirst that retarded their progress as they worked their way slowly northward
through the burning wastes of Coahuila. There they were overtaken by
the final disaster, and not by accident. At a waterhole in the desert they
walked into a trap laid by a traitor, and were captured on March 21,
1811. The lesser confederates, after rotting in the torrid jail of Mon-
clova and corrupting their keepers, were farmed out for forced labor
to the great landowners of the region. The ringleaders were sent to

Chihuahua, where they were shot four months later. Hidalgo died hard. Seated in a chair, and blindfolded, he pointed to his heart to guide the firing squad, but they were trembling "like whipped men," as the sergeant said, and their aim was poor. The first volley broke the belly and one arm; the second smashed the guts and one shoulder; the blindfold slipped, and the sight of his tears troubled the marksmen, who fired a third round without finding the heart. Not until the muzzles were placed on it, was he fit to be shown to the public. His head was sent to Guanajuato, with those of his three captains, Allende, Aldama, and Jimenez, and the trophies were suspended in cages from the four corners of the Alhondiga, where they remained for years, while time gave them new bodies.

The uprising had lasted six months. But it was not over. Between the autumn and spring equinoxes Hidalgo sowed the seed of a movement destined both to die and endure. Conservative historians have laid two charges on his tomb: that the enterprise which he initiated was premature and without plan. Premature it undoubtedly was, as he himself admitted, and in the conditions in which it was undertaken it could not have been anything else; and it was premature by more than three months. When he carried his cause to the people, he gave a revolutionary turn to the promotion of independence, which prejudiced it at the start, antagonizing the upper classes and converting the nebulous dream of national liberation into the dread, and the foretaste, of class war. The depredations of the rebels spared neither Creole nor Spaniard: the rich were all *gachupines;* and the resistance which he encountered and could not break compelled Hidalgo to countenance reprisals which he could not control against both. Marauding and massacre loom larger in the books of historians than they do in history; but the inevitable excesses of a servile insurrection were sufficient to determine the loyalty of the propertied classes. They rallied to the government or remained neutral; and to this position they clung for ten years, until independence was won without them. In this respect, the rising would have been premature at any time; but in another, and deeper one, it also suffered from precipitation. The masses were the one element ripe to receive the inspiration with which Hidalgo fired them, but they were incapable of sustaining it against trained troops. Despite the exceptional triumph at the Monte de las Cruces, Hidalgo himself was convinced by that costly success, and bowed to the dictates of common sense in beating his retreat from the capital. But the movement was not born of common sense and could not survive it, and he sacrificed at the same time the imponderable power, the unreckoning onrush, that made it possible. When he left Dolores a woman shouted after him, "Where are you going, Señor Cura?"—

"To free you of the yoke," he replied. —"Worse if you lose even the oxen," she cried. The woman was right. When he failed, the masses relapsed into their age-old submission and the apathy of abject disillusionment.

The second charge is of a piece with the first. The pace of events was too swift for the plan. What the conspirators originally contemplated is uncertain: Hidalgo himself compressed his creed into one word, *Independencia,* and his followers into a hue and cry against *gachupines;* but it was to have been carried out by the army and the educated classes. At first loyalty to the throne figured among the slogans, and the cry of "Long live Ferdinand VII!" among the flags of rebellion, a fluttering rag of Creole conscience, soon abandoned with the development of the movement; for his ideas developed with his motive power. The Emancipation Proclamation he issued in Valladolid, the promise of a Constitution and of the redistribution of the land, were picked up in the capital and re-echoed with enormous resonance in the excommunications of the Inquisition and the exhortations of the Archbishop. A movement which inspired such panic could hardly be said to have suffered from the want of a political plan; but whatever the ultimate aims of the heretic may have been, they were swept away in the whirlwind which he raised and could not ride.

A pioneer, he fulfilled the design of the pathfinder. He was the wind in the wilderness, but he was also the trail-blazer. He performed the function of every forerunner of revolution, advancing it against insuperable odds, by example and sacrifice. Premature, experimental, visionary, invertebrate, the enterprise he launched was doomed from its inception to disaster—but not to extinction. Even in retreat, and with a defeated following, he struck a spirit wherever he made a stand; and six months of mutiny precipitated changes that quickened the pulse of past and present and cheated time of its tenses. In Guanajuato, where the return of the rebels redoubled their ruin, the people fight for the honor of manning the guns and the women drag them to battle with songs "in the manner of the Marseillaise." In Guadalajara, where he raised an army twice as large as the one he had lost, he kindles a spark that is unquenched by the blazing field that scatters his battle. Fleeing northward, he still meets friends on whose faith he rests the burden of defeat and finds them willing and able to bear it. Defeat advances the cause; and knowing that no one else can kill it, the authorities extract a recantation from his corpse and drum it up as his testament. But they cannot undo his work, and the dead heretic himself cannot deed a doubt of his faith. His was merely the first wave of a seminal and unseasonable urge; and between the autumn and spring equinoxes the new seed has been sown. The insurrection is crushed; the resurrection begins.

The second wave also fell short of the goal, but it was deeper, more enduring, and incomparably more efficient than the first. Instead of six months, the next upsurge lasted for four years and was carried forward by a conspiracy of forces as well as of men—the spread of its ideas, the development of its spirit, the formation of its following, and the capacities of a leader fully equal to the test. José-Maria Morelos was also a priest, of the same militant temper as Hidalgo, endowed with the same social vision, and gifted with military talents and organizing ability in which he far surpassed his master. A pupil of Hidalgo at Valladolid, he became his disciple in the first days of the insurrection and was sent south to muster support for it. Cast on his own resources by the collapse of the revolt in the north, he abandoned the old methods of reckless dash after an unsuccessful raid on Acapulco, dug himself into his territory, and built up a body of partisans to repair the defeat of the cause. Starting with scarcely a score, he collected three thousand recruits, with whom at Cuautla, in 1812, he stood off a siege by government troops for two months. Though the besieged were finally reduced by hunger, the besiegers were reduced to offering them an amnesty and the honors of war, which Morelos ignored, beating his way out with flying colors and the garrison intact. Thereafter he took the offensive, and in a series of successful campaigns, which forced the Viceroy to describe him as "the genius of greatest strength, resourcefulness, and cunning" among the rebels, he held the enemy at bay and harassed him in his stronghold, threatening and at times cutting the trade routes to the capital. Swinging around from coast to coast, alternating periods of intensive training with well-timed blows, and adding new names to the patriotic rosary—Acapulco, Tehuacan, Orizaba, Huajuapam, Oaxaca—he dominated the south for two years with a force whose mobility compensated for the small numbers with which he controlled so large a territory.

Brilliant episodes without strategic plan, these sporadic successes have been called; but they followed a plan carefully laid and consistently pursued. What Morelos accomplished was to make good the defects of Hidalgo and to supply the movement, after a false start, with the preparation that should have preceded it. Instead of a mass rising, blind, chaotic, and blundering to destruction, he produced, without the help or hindrance of professional soldiers, an organized insurrection. Early in his progress he was joined by a few influential landowners with their *rancheros,* men of feudal fidelity and fighting traditions developed in the clanlike communities of the great estates; and out of these embattled families he formed the backbone of a compact and flexible force well adapted to the conditions of the struggle and the country. Less than an army, more than a guerrilla band, and transformed at will into the one or the other by the fortunes of war, this tenacious and elastic militia enabled Morelos to retrieve the failure of the first insurgents, to start anew with fresh methods in fresh territory, to gain experience and to secure credit, and to return to the north to recover the ground his forerunner had forfeited. In December 1813 he was ready, and two years after starting his mission he laid siege to Valladolid. There he was attacked in force by the troops of the Viceroy and disastrously defeated. After two years of fugitive efforts to recover, he was captured and shot in December 1815.

As a military leader, the function of Morelos in the development of independence was to redeem and discipline the crude initial impulse. But he was not merely a military leader: in the field of ideas he was also an emancipator, and here he extended the aims of the movement far beyond those of his master. Recognizing that the principal impediment to its progress lay in the latent conflicts of class interests and patriotic loyalty, he exploited social forces not merely as makeshifts imposed by expediency, but consciously and deliberately as revolutionary levers of popular insurrection. "All the rich, the noble, and the civil servants of the first class, *creole* and *gachupin* alike," he wrote in his instructions to his lieutenants in the field, "must be considered enemies of the nation and addicted to the party of tyranny, since they find sanction for their passions and vices in the system and legislation of Europe, the plan of which comes down in substance to severely punishing poverty and stupidity; that is to say, the lack of money or talent, the only crimes recognized by the Magistrates and Justices of our corrupt Courts." His officers were directed to confiscate the property of the bureaucracy, half the proceeds going to the war chest and half to the relief of the poor, to lay the same levies on the wealth of the Church, and to expropriate the great estates wherever the arable lands exceeded two leagues and were uncultivated, breaking them up into small holdings for the benefit of the landless peons. Military expedients were transformed into social strategy, and in the agricultural provinces of the south, where he operated, the land might have supported him, had his triumphs not been too transient to test his policies. The masses, hypnotized by Hidalgo and magnetized by Morelos, remained passive, sobered by the collapse of the master and slow to trust the disciple. His program succeeded merely in neutralizing the propertied classes, already shocked by the casual and unscientific looting that had followed the progress of Hidalgo, and the movement remained equally isolated socially; but he drove a furrow in the wilderness.

Conscious of the mortality of his cause, and unwilling to be indispensable to it, Morelos provided for the future as soon as he was master of his territory. In 1813 he called a Congress in Chilpancingo to draft a Constitution and create an embryo of national life capable of surviving him. Here he showed his full measure. In this prenatal Constitution Morelos developed a democratic conception of independence, which marked the growth of national consciousness since he caught the impulse from Hidalgo, and the advance he had made over the hazy ideals of his model. The claims of Morelos began with the sole eligibility to office of Americans, and the exclusion of foreign immigration, except for skilled artisans likely to be socially useful; but they went far beyond protective restrictions and attacked the alien elements within the nation and the settled institutions incompatible with the existence of a free people. He proclaimed as cardinal principles and indispensable conditions of independence the abolition of slavery in all its forms, not only of bestial bondage and caste distinctions, but of class privileges and legal immunities of every kind, including those of the military and ecclesiastics, the extinction of the Inquisition, the disestablishment of the Church, and the moderation of poverty and opulence by measures providing rates of pay and means of subsistence for the poor to protect them against the vices of their class, "ignorance, rapine, and theft."

As superior to Hidalgo in social insight as he was in military talents, Morelos was even further ahead of his time; but he spoke of times present in terms of times to come, and belonged to the future because he believed in it. The importance which he attached to the preservation of his ideas and the survival of their custodians was such, indeed, that it cost him his life: it was while he was protecting his Congress from capture and shepherding its flight that he fell, a hunted outlaw, into the hands of the enemy.

His trial was conducted by the Inquisition, and that Court, which he had so lightly vowed to extinction, consecrated the occasion and fully manifested its vitality as the guardian of colonial society. For two hundred years the Holy Office had fed on a small diet of relapsed converts, blasphemous slaves, and Jewish recreants without encountering a case worthy of the functions for which it had been founded until Hidalgo and his disciple fell into its lap and supplied it with legitimate fare. The indictments brought against the first and second insurgents were the best measure of how far the subversive movement had progressed by 1815. Hidalgo was arraigned as a religious rather than as a civil schismatic, and was condemned for his heretical views on a variety of canonical questions—Hell, auricular confession, the virtues of the Eucharist, for every reason, in short, but the real one for which he was brought to book and defrocked by the Church before he was handed over to the secular arm. So strenuous was the conspiracy of silence and the determination to stifle his ideas that not only was a recantation wrung from his shroud, but the recantation itself was buried. After his death a campaign of espionage was conducted by a force of monastic police in a systematic attempt to efface every vestige of his memory, and so thoroughly that no authentic portrait of him survived.

The first count brought against Morelos, in fact, was that he had defied the ban against "all persons who approve the sedition of Hidalgo or receive his proclamations, keep his portrait and epistolary correspondence, lend him any manner of aid or comfort, harbor his revolutionary ideas, and in any way promote and propagate them," and that he had used the paper on which it was printed for his cartridges. In the case of Morelos, however, the Inquisitors came directly to the point and condemned him frankly for his secular offense. They attacked his Constitution and denounced the self-determination of peoples, "which is as much as to say that law is an expression of will and not of necessity; whence comes the habit of considering Man independently of God, of His eternal Justice, and of Nature, Reason, and Honor. As human society in the system of this libertine is neither necessary nor natural, he has decided in his abominable constitution that rational beings have no other obligations than those which they assume by reason of the social contract or the expression of the general will deriving from general representation, as the impious authors already cited declare, and as is categorically stated by this infamous man in Article 18 of his perverse and preposterous Constitution. . . ."

An attempt was made to secure a recantation from Morelos as well— and before he died—but the Court was reduced to parading as such an admission which he made in the course of his questioning that his charter was hastily drawn and impractical. Morelos could not recant, not only because of the strength of his convictions and his character, but because the power of the movement could no longer be repudiated. The pressure of time was beginning to tell, and the behavior of the Court demonstrated it: its frankness in facing the issue, its condescension in arguing as well as its fury in denouncing it, and the expostulation of panic and recrimination, betrayed an insecurity that transformed every item of accusation into another of self-defense; for, indeed, the days of the Inquisition were counted, and the Inquisitors knew it. The trials of Hidalgo and Morelos were not only the first but the last cases with which the Holy Office justified its existence in New Spain. In 1815 it was already doomed to extinction by another Constitution, upon which Morelos modeled his own, equally profane and equally implacable, and coming, moreover, from the mother country. An ally had appeared on the horizon; merely by carrying on the movement for four years, Morelos had advanced it immeasurably.

Morelos was shot close to the capital, as he deserved, for his doctrines had penetrated to the heart of the citadel.

The second wave also fell short, but it came within sight of the goal. The third wave reached it. It lasted longer, but it was also weaker; and it crossed the mark muddied, adulterated, diluted, and drained of its original power.

Reporting to the Viceroy, who wished to muffle the death of Morelos, the Inquisitors justified the publicity which the trial had given to his ideas and the fair hearing he had received, "because of the good effect produced on the innumerable disciples whom he had made, since many have ceased to pity him and have even received his death well, and others have been convinced of the bad cause of the rebels, seeing it cemented with such perverse principles and sustained by leaders so wicked." But Inquisitors are notoriously men of limited acquaintance and accustomed by their activities to a conformity of opinion which affects their judgment. Conversely, they convince no one but themselves. The movement continued, beaten, broken, but stubborn, for six long years after the death of Morelos. It was reduced in scale, however, and in scope, scattered and dispersed, localized, isolated, and confined to spasmodic flares of guerrilla warfare by fugitive lieutenants of Morelos, of whom the foremost was Vincente Guerrero. Without the same talent but with no less tenacity, the third champion of insurgency operated in the south, in the territory which Morelos had made his own and by his tested methods, with a small following of impenitent patriots, repeatedly routed and repeatedly re-forming, whose campaigns roused the people in the only way in which the cowed and the inert could be convinced, by slow unrelenting example and seemingly useless sacrifice. By heroic drudgery Guerrero managed to keep the movement alive, but he could do no more; he succeeded in harassing the government, but at no time was he strong enough to challenge it seriously; and there is no doubt that independence would not have been achieved had it been left to the efforts of Guerrero and his fellows alone. Help came, however, and from an unexpected quarter—from the mother country itself.

In 1812, the last free corner of the Spanish peninsula was held, and the last shred of sovereignty claimed, by a Cortes sitting in Cadiz, which wrote a liberal Constitution born of the boldness of extremity and the freedom of disaster. When the French were driven out and the Bourbons returned from exile, the Constitution was imposed on the King, Ferdinand VII, who accepted it provisionally and repudiated it as soon as he was securely restored to the throne. For the next few years absolutism resumed its old unfettered sway in Spain; but in 1820 a military revolt compelled the King to restore the Constitution. The effect of these events on the colony was a series of reflex actions. In 1812 the Constitution of Cadiz, emanating from a proscribed parliament without authority either to promulgate or enforce it, could be safely ignored overseas; countenanced by the King, it was accepted officially but disregarded in fact; but when a copy of it was produced by Morelos, the authorities became alarmed, and the native version was banned by the Church and its author hunted down by the military with the blessing of the absolutists abroad. In 1820, however, when the Constitution of Cadiz became the basic law of the realm, a crisis was precipitated in the colony. The growing power of liberalism in the old country could no longer be ignored, and steps were taken to check the spread of its ravages to America.

The interested parties comprised all the privileged classes in the colony—the great landowners, the official bureaucracy, the military, the magistracy, the ecclesiastics—and they found their natural center in the most comprehensive and powerful of all the privileged bodies, the Church. The Constitution of Cadiz contained most of the charter principles of liberalism obnoxious to the Church—freedom of opinion and of the press, popular elections, national sovereignty invested in the Cortes—and, in addition, it included provisions directly affecting its interests and curtailing its sovereign attributes as a temporal power.

In Spain ecclesiastical reform had long been recognized as a social necessity and had recently been attempted by a Minister of the Crown. He failed, but he made the name of Manuel Godoy memorable merely by grappling with the problem of the most priest-ridden country in Europe, where the revenues of the Church cut into those of the State, and the impoverishment of the people required drastic reforms of the one or the other. "I thought it possible, if not to cure it completely, at least to prevent it from developing gangrene," he wrote in apology for his failure. "This sacred industry was all the more exacting because of the immense competition, for it was not limited to a few: the Order of Saint Francis alone, with its various families and colors, already reduced from its former estate, still counted in Spain (I do not mention the colonies) seven hundred and twenty-five thousand inmates living on charity, with no other industry but religion and no property but the purse of the people. And then there were the other mendicant orders, shod and unshod, which supplement their income with the offerings of the faithful, although most of them possess property. . . . It was a difficult, a very difficult matter to reform them, but not impossible." Not impossible, that is, as long as there were colonies to relieve the congestion of the mother country; but this solution had already been tried with disappointing results. "Look at the statistics of the American regions, and one is amazed by the neglect of the propagation of the Gospel with two or three million pagans at our door, while here, overcrowded and superabundant and pernicious, we have so many home-keeping apostles and sedentary prophets."

To dump the surplus population of parasites on the colonies was a cure worse than the disease, for the colonies suffered from the same complaint in an even more acute form. There the plethora of churches, the competition of convents, the culture of drones, the manipulation of piety and the milking of faith, magnified by the extent of the territory, the ignorance of the people, and the opportunities of the religious market, eclipsed the conditions prevailing in Spain. The quality of emigration that the colony drew was determined by the function for which the colony was founded and the New World providentially created. Fortune-hunting was not confined to the Crown, and in the course of centuries the ecclesiastics had built up a society there thoroughly mercenary and theocratic, with a tax-gatherer in every village collecting the first fruits for the Church, with a confessor in every household molding opinion, and with half the wealth of the country in the hands of the hierarchy. Such a society could be revolutionized, it could not be reformed, as Manuel Godoy discovered. "Laws are nothing when they touch abuses only in the branch and not in the root. Laws are powerless against those numerous bodies that govern conscience and manipulate opinion at their pleasure." He failed. Nevertheless, another attempt to regulate the position of the Church was made by the liberals when they framed the Constitution of Cadiz. The features directly affecting the Church ranged from the suppression of monastic orders, the reduction of convents in proportion to population, and facilities for the secularization of nuns and friars at the expense of the State, to the abolition of ecclesiastical immunities in penal cases under civil jurisdiction, and the extinction of the Inquisition. Though these reforms lopped off the branches, they cut closer to the root. If this was not yet disestablishment, it was not far from it; and the Constitution of Morelos and his proscript Congress proposed the next step.

Accordingly, when the Constitution of Cadiz was restored in 1820 and the interested parties met to consult on its consequences for the colony, it was in the backroom of a fashionable Oratory that they assembled, and under the direction of an ex-Inquisitor. Dr. Monteagudo had been one of the judges who convicted Morelos and one of the abductors of the Viceroy who recommended local autonomy for the colony in 1808—a record which placed his loyalty to Spain beyond question and allowed him to propose solutions which would have cost anyone else his head. The workings of his mind were never more professional than in this predicament. He first proposed to the Viceroy that all knowledge of the Constitution be suppressed in New Spain, or if this was impractical, to ignore it as they had done in 1813, and for the same reasons, the sovereign being a prisoner of the liberals and not his own master. But the Viceroy, though no liberal, was a responsible functionary, and not only published the Constitution, but put some of its provisions into effect, including the expulsion of the Jesuits and the extinction of the Inquisition.

Thereupon Dr. Monteagudo dispensed with the Viceroy and took counsel with his congregation. The time for drastic measures had come; the Church was a power which had overruled more than one Viceroy in the past; and as the emergency called for heroic measures, Dr. Monteagudo ruled that the only way to preserve the colony from contamination was to sever its connection with the metropolis—to proclaim its independence, in short. The idea, advanced by a man who had deposed a Viceroy and convicted an insurgent to prevent that very consummation, won the approval of his confederates. Their qualms were settled by a letter from Ferdinand VII, lamenting his captivity to the liberals and suggesting that he might emigrate to the colony to recover his independence; and with the sovereign as a prospective accomplice, the consultations rapidly developed into a conspiracy.

To engineer the separation only a tool remained to be found. Among those who frequented the Oratory was a young Creole officer of good family, Agustin Iturbide, who had distinguished himself by defeating Morelos at the siege of Valladolid in 1813. Since then he had also distinguished himself by fleecing the traders who supplied the army, and it was in consequence of their complaints that he landed his historic mission. Summoned to the capital to answer their charges, he frequented the right people, attended the Oratory, and cultivated the acquaintance of Dr. Monteagudo. The spiritual director of aristocratic society quashed the charges of embezzlement, initiated him into his scheme, and secured him the command of an army which the Viceroy was raising to crush the lingering mutiny of Guerrero in the south. Iturbide was not equal to this assignment; victory in the field eluded him, but he secured the desired result by diplomacy. Overtures were made to Guerrero to combine with him in the common cause of colonial liberation, and though his advances were rebuffed at first, his emissaries persisted and his adversary, simple-minded, suspicious, but wearied by years of fruitless struggle, and aware of his weakness, agreed to a compromise. It was the meeting of two infirmities, and in the Plan of Iguala they coalesced.

By the terms of this compact, independence was proclaimed on the basis of three principles: union of Europeans and Americans, preservation of the Catholic faith without toleration of any other creed, and the establishment of a moderate monarchy to be known as the Mexican Empire, the throne to be offered to Ferdinand VII or one of his relatives. The army flocked to the banner of the "Three Guarantees," and on September 21, 1821, the combined forces of Guerrero and Iturbide entered the capital in triumph. The Viceroy vanished, relieved of his office and his responsibility by the arrival of his successor, who landed just in time to witness the accomplished fact, to ratify it by treaty, and to return to Spain with the loyal troops.

So ended a decade of struggle. Eleven years after Hidalgo launched the movement, independence was achieved by intrigue. A new nation was born, but under such conditions as to raise the question whether it was a birth or an abortion. Independence had been won by its enemies, and the aims of the original insurgents had been completely defeated by the Three Guarantees: union instead of separation of Europeans and Americans by the first; reversion of the colony to the Crown by the third; and between them, connecting and explaining them, the guaranteed supremacy of the Church. Independence had been won—but of what? The answer to that question was Mexican history. When the successors of Hidalgo and Morelos realized that what had happened on September 21, 1821, was not the culmination, but the contradiction, of what had occurred on September 16, 1810, a new phase of the insurgent movement began. The struggle for political independence ended, the struggle for social liberation began, with the meretricious triumph of the Plan of Iguala, and thenceforth Mexican history was governed by its results. Two congenital conditions determined its course. The false start condemned the country to a revolutionary development, and to follow foreign movements, as the pathfinders had done, with a time lag that further retarded its progress. The realization came slowly, and the new movement was long in forming. The rebels who came to power in 1821 were incapable of correcting the swindle, and the task of redeeming it fell to another generation. Of that generation of social insurgents Juarez was one. A month after Iturbide entered the capital, he entered the Seminary.

5

THE muddled beginnings of national life cleared with the first attempts to reconstitute the colony as an independent country. The antagonistic elements which combined to proclaim the Plan of Iguala were soon winnowed by its application. The Mexican Empire was proclaimed by a provisional Governing Board, in which none of the old insurgents was represented, and a Constituent Congress, elected by professional representation, ratified the assumption of the Crown by Iturbide, who substituted himself for the Bourbons with the backing of a barracks revolt and a popular demonstration. The *parvenu* Emperor rapidly lost popularity and political support, however, by plundering the Spanish plutocracy and dissolving Congress and arresting its recalcitrant members, and in 1823 he was overthrown by a military revolt, banished, and on his return to the country a year later captured and shot. The ephemeral reign of Iturbide abolished the Third Guarantee. Monarchy answered the needs of the classes which had engineered independence and which desired a mere modification of the colonial regime to secure their vested interests, and was readily accepted by the people at large, the popular patriots being so devoid of political experience and self-confidence that even Guerrero and the old guard rallied to it enthusiastically; but after the fall of Iturbide republican sentiment gained strength, and the experiment in domestic monarchy was followed by an experiment in self-government. Another Constituent Congress proclaimed the Republic in October 1824, and the first President and Vice-President, Guadalupe Victoria and Nicolas Bravo, were both old insurgents. A Constitution was drawn on the best available model, borrowed from the United States; but the basic charter of 1824 was also a compromise, like the declaration of independence, between incompatible partners. Modeled on the American Constitution in its administrative structure, it recognized popular sovereignty and some of the corollaries of that principle, but none of the radical features embodied in the prenatal Constitution of Chilpancingo, save for the abolition of slavery, and it reasserted the principle of religious intolerance and ecclesiastical supremacy proclaimed in the Plan of Iguala.

The republicans who came to power in 1824 gradually eliminated the Spaniards and abolished the First Guarantee; but the Second remained inviolable. Though the flag of Spain was furled, the structure of colonial society over which it had ruled for three centuries remained intact; and in the liberating tricolor of the new nation, between the green of Hidalgo and the red of Morelos, it was the white flag of truce that still represented the national colors. Within a few years of the False Independence of 1821, as it came to be called by political coroners, the rulers of the Republic were forced to recognize the miscarriage of the insurgent movement in their relations with the midwife. During the decade of insurgency the Church had shown its colors: though the movement had been led by two priests, and many members of the lower clergy had rallied to it, the Church as an institution had consistently opposed it until the day when it appropriated the cause for its own protection and condoned independence conditionally. The hierarchy resigned itself to the Republic and accepted a situation which offered some appreciable compensations for the status of the Church in the colony, the most valuable of which was the reversion to the Church of the right of ecclesiastical appointment and patronage hitherto exercised by the Spanish Crown; and it was over this right that the first difference arose between the two powers. As an attribute of sovereignty, inherited from the Spanish Crown, this prerogative was claimed by the government, but it met with such resistance that the attempt was abandoned. During the debate in Congress and the press, however, public attention was focused on the relations of Church and State, and the dispute created intense feeling on both sides, aggravated by the appearance, in the midst of the crisis, of a Papal Encyclical reserving recognition of the Republic and urging the late subjects of Ferdinand VII to return to their allegiance. Though the question of patronage was a minor and debatable issue, the spirit which it aroused and the contention which it raised were neither negligible nor negotiable; and the controversy cleared the air. Henceforth it was manifest that, of all the liabilities under which the infant Republic labored, the greatest, because the most organic, was the existence of a huge, hard, impenetrable foreign body embedded in its very constitution, defying its control and defeating its functions at will. To master that impediment was too formidable a task for the government of the day; but the passionate concern of a small group of liberals was enlisted, within and without Congress, who applied themselves to the task in an independent campaign. Few but farsighted, they realized that the contest would be long and unequal and that it would require time, patience, preparation, and a power more compelling than official initiative, unsupported by the pressure of public opinion. The skirmish over the patronage question was followed by a flank attack on the main issue and the start of a long-range political strategy. They bent their efforts to circumventing the monopoly of education held by the Church and emancipating the coming generation by founding lay schools. They undermined the Second Guarantee, and here and there they succeeded.

Thus it was that, after describing so long an arc, far beyond the horizon of Oaxaca, the rainbow of independence finally reached Juarez. The red and green and white of the national colors spanned a world beyond his ken, luminous with the afterglow of sun and storm, and beyond his reach until the long concatenation of events and remote connection of forces, the delayed action of ideas and indirect urge of their agents that combined to create a new nation—the revolt of the British colonies, and the French Revolution, and the Napoleonic Wars, and the weakening of colonial bonds, and a decade of battling to break them, and the belated but foreordained conclusion—resulted in one more school.

In 1827 a Liberal majority in the local legislature created a Civil College in Oaxaca and provided Juarez with the opening for which he had been unconsciously waiting and which the transformation of his country alone could supply. As soon as the Institute of Arts and Science opened its doors, desertions from the Seminary began, and though he did not commit himself immediately, he went so far as to attend the inaugural ceremony. "Whether because of this example, or of curiosity, or of the impression that the speech of Dr. Canseco made on me, or of the boredom which the study of Theology caused me because of its incomprehensible principles, or of my natural desire to pursue some career other than the ecclesiastic," he confessed, "the fact is that I found no pleasure in following the course of Theology." The variety of his motives reflected as yet nothing more than an unsettled state of mind. In deference to his godfather, he completed the course in Theology; and it was not until a year and a half later that, haunted by the rainbow, he entered the Institute. Dr. Salanueva consented, as usual; and with that final concession, his name fades from the record. Henceforth, having completed his contract, Juarez transferred his allegiance to the State; whatever his obligations to his benefactor may have been for the past, he was now bound to the nation of which he was the ward.

Boredom, ambition, curiosity—whatever the motive that drew him to the Institute, conviction was not among them as yet; that was to come as a consequence of the others. For the flight from the Seminary was in itself a political step. The first announcement of a secular school created less opposition than might have been expected in Oaxaca. The somnolent provincial town was becoming accustomed to progress. Thirty years before, paving had been introduced, and the great square before the Cathedral, which every rain turned into a quagmire, consolidated; street-lighting began about the same time; and in 1824 a normal school opened, unnoticed, without anyone being the worse for these costly conveniences. Material improvements were assimilated, and mental advances survived. But Oaxaca was slow, slow in the pace of life, slow in public perceptions, slow to realize the implications of the latest innovation; and it was not until the Institute actually functioned that its significance as the seminary of a new world was recognized. Then the protests arose, and the constancy of the pupils was tested, and Juarez discovered his convictions. "The Director and the instructors of the new establishment were all liberals and took part, naturally, in all the political questions that arose in the State. For this reason, and for a truer one, the clergy, knowing that this new nursery of learning, where no trammels were placed on the mind in the search for truth, was bound to become in time, as it has, the ruin of its power based on error and interest, declared a cruel and systematic war upon it, employing the very powerful influence which it then exercised over families, the civil authority, and the whole of society. They called the Institute 'a house of prostitution,' and the teachers and pupils 'heretics' and 'libertines.' Parents refused to send their sons to it, and the few students who attended classes were ill considered and excommunicated by the immense majority of that ignorant, fanatical, and miserable society. Many of my companions deserted, terrified by the powerful enemy that persecuted us. A few, but a very few, continued to support the house by attending classes daily."

Man and boy, Juarez was no backslider. For a young man born beyond the pale, with no family to blush for him, and with no social standing to maintain but that of a favored domestic, persecution and ostracism were a less trying ordeal, perhaps, than for other libertines; but for one who had worked his way through the Seminary with the sole aim of improving his prospects in life, it was sufficiently severe to test his stamina. He had the advantage, however, of being an orphan—with all due respect to Dr. Salanueva—and he had the most compelling of all reasons to persist, for in the Institute he discovered his latent capacities and grasped the true bent of his mind; and from that satisfaction there was no turning back.

So his re-education began, at the age of twenty-two. It was late to make a fresh start, but he was old enough to appreciate the necessity of beginning anew. The native ignorance which he had brought to the Seminary had been refined and developed there into the dogmatic ignorance indispensable to the sacred calling; and whatever else might be said of the knowledge he acquired there, it was completely divorced from actual life and calculated, as an intellectual discipline, to prepare the adept for a purely contemplative existence and a passive and unproductive part in the activities of the world. That education as a social function was limited by the society which it served was an axiom which he had spent seven of the best and most formative years of his life in learning; but they were not wasted. He had been an apt pupil and had improved his opportunities to the satisfaction of everyone but himself; if the result was unprofitable, the fault clearly lay elsewhere. Where, he discovered in the Institute. What he learned there was not anticlericalism or incredulity, for the Director was a churchman and there were priests on the staff, but the limitations which the Second Guarantee imposed on the growth of his ignorance.

The education provided in the Institute represented only a relative advance over that dispensed in the Seminary. The professors were not far ahead of their pupils, and some of the novices acted as their substitutes, doubling between the bench and the platform, so that the whole enterprise resembled a common adventure, teachers and taught beating out the untrodden paths of knowledge together; but the spirit was progressive. What made the Institute so subversive a departure was the approach to knowledge—the appeal to experience, the untrammeled search for truth, and the range of studies. A ferment of fresh wine was poured into the old bottles: instead of the curriculum laid down by the Council of Trent and confined to four courses in the Seminary—Latin grammar, Philosophy, Elementary Physics, and Theology—the qualifications for contemporary life in the nineteenth century; instead of Latin grammar, living languages and free access to foreign thought; instead of scholastic Philosophy, Political Economy; instead of elementary Physics, taught as a branch of dialectics and as a metaphysical exercise, experimental science itself; instead of a small scale of sterile accomplishments, a broad range of socially useful knowledge, above all in the branch which Juarez elected to pursue. In the study of Jurisprudence the Institute offered, besides Canon Law, courses in Natural, Civil, and Constitutional Law, undermining the concept of dogmatic authority by the comparative study of various systems of law, all deriving from the concept of society as a contract and a partnership, imperfect, experimental, progressive, and all developing the exciting and abstract sense of justice as a science advancing by trial and error. The proficiency which Juarez showed in his studies in the Institute was as marked as in the Seminary; and with the widening of his mental horizon and the confidence of manhood awakening, he felt for the first time the full pulse of a mind that was positive, active, and rational.

His progress was rapid and marked by recognition more conspicuous than the honors bestowed on him in the Seminary. In 1830, a brief year after entering the Institute, he substituted for the Professor of Physics while he continued his law studies; and in 1831 he was sufficiently qualified to enter a local law office and practice his profession. The law, however, was even then an overcrowded profession, which supported very few of its members and which was adopted, therefore, by many of them as a passport to politics. In the same year he stood for public office and was elected to the Municipality as an Alderman, a success which was associated in his mind with another of no less weight. In 1831 he presided over the examination in Physics, which one of his pupils submitted to the Seminary scientists. The two triumphs were not casually coupled—they were the arms of a compass which described his point of view in public life. For a young law student with a bent for physical science, taking his first step in politics, his profession and his avocation combined to provide an excellent education in political science. The facilities which the period offered for investigation and survey were unlimited. The nation was a laboratory of political experiment, and a law student who was also a physicist could discover the principles of self-government by observing daily the action and reaction, computing the natural forces, and analyzing the physical properties by which a new social body constituted itself. The demonstration developed during his student years, at the most propitious moment, with an elementary clarity which made the nature of the process visible to the naked eye.

New nations not being born in the laboratory, but wrested from the bowels of old ones and carrying over the constitution of the parent in the throes of release, the problem was to transform the structure of colonial society into a self-sustaining organism and to create an independent identity and a unified entity out of the heterogeneous mass of raw material, divided by race, color, caste, and class, left over from the paternal regime and molded and cast by the Spaniards for the confusion of their successors. With the consummation of political independence, the internal conflicts generated by its development began to appear. The simplicity of the insurgent movement was succeeded by the complexities of reconstruction; and in the second and creative phase of nation-building the effort of bringing forth a new synthesis of the same elements brought forth at the same time the organic laws governing the creation of any consistent society. Of the hereditary handicaps to genuine independence, diversity of race was the least, all nations being the outcome of a fusion of strains, though the process might require centuries for its completion, and the Spaniards had systematically cultivated cross-breeding for three hundred years. The elaborate caste system which they had created to divide and control the amalgam could be abolished, as it had been, by law, though the prejudices created under it were bound to endure. Ethnic fusion was guaranteed by a common culture, and this was the crux of the question. Social culture and economic interest were synonymous, and the economic interests that determined the formation, the disintegration, and the reconstitution of the colony were the basic obstacle to its complete emancipation from the past.

If human societies were the product of planning and foresight, planning and foresight would be the first instead of the last problem to engage political science and the rational study of self-interest, but being the reverse, the natural order is also reversed, and civilization the continuous process of correcting its origin and revising and unraveling its development. The rule was proved by the exception in Mexico. There indeed nothing had been neglected to anticipate and defeat independence and its inevitable consequences. Planning and foresight distinguished the administration of the colony by the Spaniards, who drained its resources for the benefit of the mother country. Planning and foresight also distinguished the beneficiaries of the independence, who opposed and adopted it, in turn, for the protection of their property and privileges; and planning and foresight were conspicuous by their absence in the Republic, which had done nothing to redeem these liabilities except to borrow abroad without benefit for the economic recuperation and political consolidation of the country. The Spaniards had been supplanted by the Creoles, who preserved intact the structure of colonial society, under a transfer of title to themselves. The propertied and privileged classes, by whose grace a nominal independence had been won for the others, were the arbiters of national development. The wealth of the country was concentrated in their hands and hoarded improvidently and unproductively by a caste without public spirit or responsibility; and this economic autocracy gravitated by natural affinity toward the Church, whose culture protected their common interests, and which was the greatest and most powerful monopolist, mentally and materially, of Mexico. To break that monopoly, to purge that culture, and to recover and control the natural resources of the country was the essential condition of national existence, and political independence carried with it, implicit and implacable, the mandate, the necessity, the physical law of social reform.

Planning and foresight also distinguished one of the students of the

Institute, to whom the destiny of the nation was a topic of burning interest. A Zapotec Indian from the Sierra, who had followed the traditional road to education from Ixtlan to Oaxaca, passed through the Seminary, deserted to the Institute, and joined the staff, Miguel Mendez had made a brilliant name for himself as an agitator of advanced ideas. Endowed with a driving eloquence, which made his convictions contagious, he was in the habit of holding meetings in his rooms, where he held forth freely and feverishly fashioned plans for the future—for he was a prey to consumption—charging his hearers to carry the liberal cause to its logical conclusion and to create a state completely independent of ecclesiastical control. Juarez fell under his influence. On one occasion, according to local tradition, young Mendez, flushed with his mission, impatient for the millennium, and familiar with the capacities of his other disciples, singled out Juarez with the words, "And this one whom you see here, so serious and reserved, this one will be a great politician. He will rise higher than any of us, and he will be one of our great men and the glory of our country."

Foresight certainly, and planning perhaps, were required to divine the coming man of the country in the one on whom Mendez laid his finger and who had barely set his foot on the lowest rung of the political ladder. But Mendez combined the faith of a missionary with the born agitator's insight into men. If time, patience, preparation, and public support were essential to the coming struggle, here was his man, for these were the features that distinguished his chosen messiah at that period: Juarez knew how to listen and to stand and wait, grasping the ladder and biding his time. And it was by way of practical politics, and not by the studied approaches of political science, that the students of the Institute were drawn into the national destiny.

Principles there were none but those of self-preservation to distinguish the two parties—Liberal and Conservative as they called themselves, vinegar and oil as they called each other—that divided the country in the first years of the Republic. The meaning of independence penetrated slowly in Oaxaca, which had barely been touched by the battlers of the insurgent period and had temporized until the turn of the tide, and where the cult of independence followed, instead of preceding, its triumph. In 1828, when Guerrero stood for election to the Presidency, feeling ran high in Oaxaca and nowhere higher than in the Institute, where the fevers of the decade were revived in a fever of retrospective patriotism, and the students turned out in a body to support their hero with a zeal all the more burning for being belated. Bloodshed and rioting marked the primaries—a foretaste of what was to follow throughout the country. Guerrero lost the election; his partisans broke it. One rising led to another: in the south by Juan Alvarez, a veteran of the wars of independence, who came to his rescue; in Veracruz by the governor, General Antonio Lopez de Santa Anna, who followed suit. Marching to join forces with Alvarez, Santa Anna entered Oaxaca in search of support, occupied a convent, and stood a siege without finding any, and was relieved only by the success of another revolt in the capital, where a cowed Congress declared Guerrero President in the autumn of 1829. The success was celebrated in Oaxaca. General Santa Anna was wined and dined in liberal circles, and at a supper given in his honor by a professor of the Institute he met Juarez—without recognizing him as the coming man of the country. Many years later he recalled that meeting bitterly, for he had the flair of an expert politician for names and faces, and all that he remembered was that Juarez was waiting on table at the time, and barefoot. But foresight was not among the faculties of Santa Anna: he was a fortune-hunter, and not a fortune-teller; and being one of the coming men of the country himself, he saw only the feet.

The triumph of Guerrero was costly to himself and the country. By breaking the elections and breaching the machinery of free institutions which they created, his partisans set a precedent by which their opponents profited and on which they improved. Within two years of his imposition by force, he was deposed by the same methods, compelled to flee with a price on his head, captured and killed. The closing scenes of his tragedy occurred in Oaxaca, where he was brought after his capture and confined in the convent which had served Santa Anna as a fortress. Santa Anna deserted him; Alvarez could do nothing; and his sympathizers in the city were a helpless minority of silenced civilians. The public tragedy surpassed his personal fate, for the appeal from ballots to bullets raised a fundamental and recurring issue, to which public moralists—and in that period of political immaturity moralists were in the ascendant—pointed as the coming curse of the country. The imposition and murder of Guerrero made a breach in the machinery of self-government and public confidence in it, opening the way to chronic violence, inveterate lawlessness, and public demoralization. The question of determining the popular will by ballots or bayonets was settled for the moment: justice of a sort had been done— the rudimentary justice of retaliation, which settled nothing for long— and both parties had outlawed themselves, breaking the compact upon which the Republic rested, and leaving power to be disputed without curbs by the parties, and arbitrated by the military.

The moralists were right, as they always are, but not for the correct reasons. More than one moral could be drawn from the facts—for one, whether it was more important for the nation that legality be respected or that the popular will be determined by that revolutionary law which dictates and discards codes, because it is the source of them. That issue had been raised by Guerrero, although nothing more important was involved in his election than his personal triumph. The last of the great trio of original insurgents, he was the symbol of the popular struggle

for independence, and his partisans were determined to repay his services with the Presidency. They claimed power as a patriotic right and
as a token of popular triumph; and when their idol was outvoted, they
flew to arms to enforce their right to self-preservation. These were the
motives, blind and instinctive, sentimental and unreasoning, which
fired old insurgents like Alvarez, loyal to the man who typified their
compromised cause, to take up arms against their class enemies; and
the Conservatives recognized them in a revolt that they repressed with
equal unscrupulousness, as a flare of class warfare that broke the truce
on which the Republic was founded. Like the dispute over ecclesiastical patronage, the minor and ostensible question of the elections fore-
shadowed the larger conflict latent within it. The political moral of the
tragedy lay not in the methods, which were common to both parties,
but in the correctness of the cause that produced them.

Such were the working conditions under which Juarez entered public life. He was elected to office and took up legal practice in Oaxaca in
the same year in which Guerrero was killed there—a conjunction of
circumstances singularly favorable to his political education. The mem·
ory of Guerrero was passionately cherished in the Institute, where he
was honored as the last martyr of independence and as the ultimate symbol of the movement, falling blindfolded before the muskets of triumphant reaction. The firing squad shattered the legal conception of the
State as a social contract and reduced it to something more closely ap-
proximating a scientific demonstration of physical forces. The State
was not a coherent whole to be studied and planned *a priori* even in
theory; in reality, it was a chronic condition of violence, static or active,
of the classes that composed it, a conflict alternately arrested and
aroused, constantly compounded, controlled by the master class and to
be mastered only by correction and experiment. Preconceived concepts
of the State were a theological notion carried over from the Seminary
and only slightly modified by the scientific revisions of the Institute.
Mendez, who had shed the moral bias both of the Seminary and the
Institute, had a clearer conception, perhaps, of the nature of the coming struggle when he put his finger on Juarez to lead it, but both views
were, in fact, academic. Juarez found his bearings slowly in the crude
school of practical politics. His future, and the future of the nation, lay
not with Mendez, but with Santa Anna.

6

FOR Santa Anna was unquestionably the coming man of the country. He was the portent, the product, and the personification of the period. The years that followed the elimination of Guerrero and the old guard from public life were a dreary and static stretch of confusing, incurable, and insignificant turmoil, of governments set up and overthrown by military mutinies, of transient adventurers dogging one another without aim or policy, and so monotonously the same under the ever-recurring ferment of seething instability that foreign observers, and Mexicans themselves, were convinced of the congenital incapacity of the nation for self-government—a verdict based on superficial evidence, for the agitation, shallow and stationary itself, was the symptom of an unlocated infirmity, and if any one phrase could synthesize that age of national colic, it might be described as "the reign of Santa Anna." His was the figure that returned again and again, in one guise or another, through all the veering vicissitudes of those teething times, the constant element in their mutability, the arch adventurer, the persistent opportunist, the perpetual turncoat, trimming his principles to every wind, steering by instinct and without compass, speculating on any program to gain power. Buoyant, ambitious, callow, and self-confident as he was inconsistent, he was the consummate creation of a period which he bestrode like a colossus and straddled like a politician; and because he was both its creature and its creator, he was a social phenomenon.

Antonio Lopez de Santa Anna Perez de Lebrun was the scion of a Spanish family located in Veracruz and Jalapa and established in trade and society by a respectable income: his father was a mortgage broker in Veracruz and a landed gentleman in Jalapa. At the age of sixteen Santa Anna declared for a military career, was sent to the Military Academy, and graduated in time to serve in 1810 and to join in hunting down Hidalgo and his fugitive followers in the north. The culminating year of independence found him still loyal to Spain, but only a captain; for in consequence of a scandal arising out of his gambling debts he had been assigned to chasing bandits in his native state; but thereafter his promotion was rapid. One day in March 1821 he made three grades in twenty-four hours. In the morning he routed a column of rebels and was commissioned lieutenant-colonel; in the afternoon the rebels were reinforced and raised the bid to a full colonelcy; and he declared for independence at the end of the day. The motley was in his blood, but he wore it with epaulettes. Iturbide made a brigadier-general of him, and when Iturbide was overthrown he declared for the Republic. All that he knew of republics at that time was, he said later, what a lawyer in Jalapa had told him, for his education had been confined to barracks; and though he subsequently acquired a nominal acquaintance with political systems, he remained to the end of his life politically illiterate. As opportunities for advancement under the Republic were few, he proposed to liberate Cuba, but found no support for this scheme in Mexico, and after fretting for action and aging in harness for four years, now as governor of Yucatan and now of Veracruz, he seized the first opportunity of resuming his career and revolted in favor of Guerrero.

Up to this point his record presents nothing remarkable—the common career of a pushing young officer bent on reaching the top and indifferent to the means of promotion, whose change of colors betrayed his ignorance of the issues involved, and who tested every cause by its effect on himself. It was not until the individual type was transferred to public life and encountered there the conditions which enabled it to wax and flourish that his career became significant and his promotion portentous. He was the typical Creole, whose mercurial loyalties were the result of his anomalous station under the colonial regime, emancipated by independence but also uprooted by it, for whom his native land remained his adopted country, to be exploited for his personal profit, and whose patriotism remained that of an emancipated opportunist. The motives which impelled him to champion Guerrero were the antithesis of those which fired Alvarez, but they had one element in common—both pinned their faith on popular heroes. In a time of political immaturity, tension, and insecurity, the tendency to look to men rather than principles, and to personal instead of party leadership, was pronounced throughout the country. Here the career of Santa Anna crossed that of the country with contagious effect. Equally indifferent to both parties, but not to the hero-worship which Guerrero inspired and the popularity which he commanded, Santa Anna gambled on Guerrero and won, and a run of political luck was converted into a system which he worked, after the fall of Guerrero, for his own benefit. In the meanwhile he had covered himself with glory by repelling a Spanish expedition sent from Cuba for the reconquest of Mexico in 1829 and had been acclaimed a national hero himself. Thereafter the history of the country was his.

Less than a year after the death of Guerrero, Santa Anna led a successful revolt against the government and, after a short interval, was elected President in 1833. Conscious of his inexperience, he retired to his country estate, leaving the government in the hands of the Vice-President, Dr. Valentin Gomez Farias. Under the provisions of the Constitution the Vice-Presidency fell to the defeated candidate, and as his opponent was a Liberal who had missed the Presidency by a margin close enough to indicate considerable popular support, Santa Anna showed his sagacity in entrusting him with responsibility, while he stood and observed the results.

Gomez Farias was a physician with radical ideas, which he lost no time in testing, with the tacit consent of Santa Anna, who gave him a free hand to experiment. Besides Santa Anna, he had another partner, though an unofficial one, in Dr. Mora, a Doctor of Philosophy who became his mentor and collaborator. Between them the two doctors administered a profound shock to the country by initiating a program of sweeping reforms. For ten crowded months measure followed measure, each more unsettling than the other: education was secularized; the University of Mexico disestablished; civil coercion in the collection of ecclesiastical tithes and the enforcement of monastic vows suppressed; the right of ecclesiastical patronage appropriated by the State; the right to control the sale of Church property claimed; and interment in temples prohibited on sanitary grounds. The invasion of sacred ground by what was no more in reality than a program of civic sanitation was pressed forward rapidly and relentlessly by Mora and Farias and a friendly Congress, but the Reform Laws of 1833-34 so clearly presaged the separation of Church and State that they created consternation among the conservative classes and aroused agitation in the most remote reaches of the country, where the rising generation was provided with a dangerous example of how much could be accomplished, and how quickly, by determination and daring. A halt was called again and again by the offended parties during the ten months; indignation was ignored, remonstrance redoubled, denunciation deepened into the rattle of revolt, and then the situation was saved by Santa Anna, who returned to the capital, dismissed Farias, and restored the confidence of the country in an established order in which such experiments could not be lightly repeated—and lightly they were not.

The reverberations of these events were felt in Oaxaca, where the Liberals breathed freely with Farias in power and elected their best barristers to the local Congress, Juarez among others. Here he distinguished himself by initiating, with two other sponsors, a motion to honor the memory of Guerrero. The motion was carried unanimously, and Oaxaca showed its colors in a solemn ceremony in which the entire community united to make what amends were still possible to the dead hero. A long procession, escorted by troops and headed by the civil, military, and ecclesiastical authorities, wound its way slowly through the countryside to the site of his execution, where the parish

priest pronounced an unqualified eulogy, and the remains were disin-
terred and emptied into a silver urn, which was then brought back in
parade, at the same solemn pace, pausing every quarter of an hour for
a salvo of musketry, to Oaxaca, where it was displayed, amid the booming of cannon and bells, in the Cathedral and, after a Requiem Mass,
transferred to the convent in which he had been imprisoned and sentenced, a trophy of time imposed on eternity. The participation of the
clergy in these rites, as conspicuous as it was politic, honored them, the
only dissenting voices being those of the Dominicans in whose convent
he was laid to rest, and who murmured but submitted.

The participation of Juarez, whose motion was responsible for mobilizing public sentiment, was not forgotten. The gesture by which he extended his hand to this protomartyr of Independence and caught the
consecrating touch definitely placed the young deputy. But where?
About the same time he introduced a bill into Congress to confiscate
the estate of Cortés for the benefit of the State. Both motions were
commemorative gestures linked with the past, and he was engaged in
pious exercises of retrospective patriotism when the country had already
been overtaken by the hurrying call of the future. Farias and Mora,
catching up the heritage of Independence and replacing hero-worship
with reform, had begun their iconoclastic attempt to create that purely
secular state which Mendez had impressed on his disciples as their
common duty; but Mendez was dead, and Mora and Farias were short-
lived, and far away.

The impression which their crusade made on the rising generation in
Oaxaca was remote and faint. Agitation it aroused, but an agitation
confined to scandal, tale-bearing, backbiting, and gossip. A group of
women, signing themselves the "Mothers of Oaxaca," wrote to the papers in the capital, protesting against the corruption to which their sons
were exposed in the Institute; and the conduct of the Institute under
their attack would no doubt have made Mendez turn in his grave. The
faculty met in high agitation to consider whether to ignore or to answer it, elected the latter course, but could not decide how to clear their
good name, whether by a joint statement rehearsing the respectability
of their members and the orthodoxy of their opinions—the venerable
Dominican who had been their first Director, the honorable magistrate
of the Supreme Court their second, the choirmaster of the Cathedral
their third; or by citing the magnificent altar presented to the Virgin
of Guadalupe by the Institute; or by appealing to the neighbors; or by
citing the women to court—and whether to the civil courts or to the
Tribunal of the Faith; or by hiring a lawyer to sue them to expose
what lay behind the tendentious complaints of the pseudo-mothers, for
the charges were certainly concerted and inspired; or—and—if but and
how—until finally, flustered and confused and exhausted, they resolved
to publish the minutes of the meeting as their best defense. The solu-

tion was suggested by Juarez, who sat with the faculty as Professor of Physics.

Six years after its foundation, institutional timidity had fallen upon the house, leaving little distinction between Sadducee and Pharisee, and making it a safe and inoffensive seminary where salvation could be gained by words without works. Fortunately for Juarez himself, however, he had an experience at this time that sharpened and riveted his convictions, one of those saving disgraces which are revelations in disguise, and the value of which he recognized by the extended account he gave of it in his memoir.

"The clergy were still in full enjoyment of their privileges and prerogatives, and their close alliance with the civil power gave them a well-nigh omnipotent influence. The rights which exempted them from the jurisdiction of the common courts served them as a shield against the law of safe-conduct and allowed them to indulge in every excess and any injustice with impunity. The rates of the parish dues were a dead letter. The payment of obventions was governed by the will and the greed of the curates. There were, nevertheless, some honest and upright pastors who confined themselves to legitimate charges without fleecing the faithful; but few were those really evangelical men whose example, far from deterring the bad from their abuses, led to their own censure on the charge that they were 'misleading the people and undermining the curacies.'"

It was with the rule, and not the exception, that Juarez came into contact, since his law practice lay with the poor. A typical case was presented by the villagers of Loricha, who appealed to him for protection against the extortions of their curate. He accepted the case and appeared on their behalf in the ecclesiastical court. "Undoubtedly, by reason of my position as a deputy and because a Liberal administration then governed the state, for this occurred in the beginning of the year 1834, my petition was accepted and the priest was ordered to appear and to answer the charges against him, and was forbidden to return to his parish until the trial was over; but unfortunately a few months later, the administration fell"—and the case collapsed. The accused returned to his parish, secured the arrest of all those who had informed against him, held them incommunicado in the county jail, and obtained orders from the City to imprison the delegation which had made the complaint. "I was then, at the close of 1834, substituting in the chair of Canonical Law in the Institute, and being unable to regard with indifference the wrong done to my wretched clients, I obtained leave of absence for a few days and went to the village of Miahuatlan, where the prisoners were held, to obtain their release." On his arrival he was allowed to communicate with them, but on the following day the local judge started trial against him as a vagrant, and fearful of further outrages he returned to Oaxaca and accused the judge in the

state court. There too the curate had forestalled him, securing a writ
for his arrest on the charge of inciting the people against the authorities. Juarez was imprisoned with another advocate who had been
taken into custody for the same reason. He complained to the Supreme
Court, but it was not until nine days later that he was released on bond,
"and no action was ever taken on my complaints and charges against
the judges who injured me."

"These blows which I suffered, and which I saw suffered daily by
the disabled, who complained against arbitrary acts of the privileged
classes in concert with the civil authority, dimly revealed to me that
society could never be happy with the existence of the former and their
alliance with the public powers, and confirmed me in my determination to work constantly for the destruction of the baneful power of the
privileged classes. And I did so insofar as I could, and so did the Liberal party; but, unfortunately for humanity, the remedy that was attempted at that time was not a radical cure for the evil, for although
retrograde administrations were repeatedly overthrown and replaced
by Liberal ones, the changes were only of persons, while laws and constitutions continued to retain the ecclesiastical and military immunities,
religious intolerance, a State religion, and the possession by the clergy
of that abundant wealth of which they abused to encourage the causes
that cemented their pernicious power. Thus it was that hardly had a
Liberal Administration been established than it was overthrown in a
few months and its partisans were persecuted."

Of such experiences living convictions are made: the curate of Loricha completed what Miguel Mendez began. When Juarez took the
case, he was a professor, a deputy, and a magistrate just appointed to
the bench; when he dropped it, he was a reformer for life. But he was
not yet an active one. Gomez Farias had fallen, the Liberal fling was
over, Juarez was politically out and no match for the ubiquitous curate
of Loricha. "Implacable in his vengeance as the latter was, and as the
sectaries of any religion usually are," he served, however, to put Juarez
on the highroad to Damascus. The results of the "dim revelation" were
long in manifesting themselves, but they had lodged deep in a man
who had the memory of an animal and the patience of an immortal to
wait for an opportunity to strike at the peculiar institution he abhorred.

The failure of Mora and Farias made it clear that they lacked sufficient public support and were still ahead of the times; but their success
proved that they had merely anticipated it and that the attempt would
be repeated; that the opportunity would return was guaranteed by
their wreck, though how and when were unknown terms of the equation. The period between the birth and rebirth of Reform was a long
hiatus, during which the occasional return of a relatively Liberal regime served merely to vary without violating the dominant combina-

tion of Conservative powers, producing the improvisations of persons without jarring the institutions of the privileged classes. Nevertheless, it produced something more than the monotonous intervals of major and minor counterpoint. The *status quo ante* was preserved for another, and yet another, decade, steadily weakened by its very security, before the discovery was made that in political as in physical life an organism that fails to develop tends to decay. Though the succeeding years were filled with the superficial agitations of politics, socially and economically the country remained at a standstill, a prey to the ravages of arrested development. The progressive enfeeblement of national life was abruptly revealed by its first collision with foreign powers, in 1836. What the reforms of 1834 failed to accomplish, the pressure of the outer world and the internal weakness of the nation combined to bring about.

Mora and Farias went into exile, pursued by the execrations of the clerical press. "Yesterday," ran a leader in its loudest organ, "the execrable Farias finally left this capital, laden with the just imprecations of a whole city, the foremost in the New World of Columbus, upon which his frightful excesses will forthwith weigh." An epidemic of cholera, which coincided with the crisis, raged in the oratory of press and pulpit as a divine visitation: "Gomez Farias attracted, like an ominous comet, cholera and misery, immorality and tyranny, treason and espionage, ignorance and sacrilege, the uplifting of criminals and the degradation of honorable men, the triumph of the filthy rabble and the fall of the chosen few, the terror and affliction of families, proscription, mourning, and death under a thousand and more horrible forms," including the death by default of Ferdinand VII—"Ferdinand VII was ashamed to see that his former colonies could produce a monster surpassing him in scandals and terror, and descended to the sepulchre satisfied that his presence was no longer needed on the face of the earth to afflict humanity."

The danger was over, but not the shock, for there was no security that the danger had passed. No revolution is ever lost, however abortive, no reform ever fails completely. Its results may be abolished, but a residue remains. The movement returns pendulum-wise by the very momentum of reaction; and though the reform laws were annulled, they remained on the statute books, a dead letter, blotted, void, overwritten, with erasures, but alive in the popular consciousness, from which they could not be completely effaced. At the opening session of the new Congress the carefully chosen ecclesiastics and Conservatives who composed it were dumfounded to hear one of their own ministers read a memorial on the right of patronage, defending the claim of the State to control it. It was supposed that he had read by mistake a paper dropped by his predecessor, but he persisted in his error and upheld it in the press; and a little later the question of exclaustration was raised by a public scandal, when a nun was abducted in the heart of the capital to the applause of a sympathetic crowd and the approval of some Conservative papers. No less a mouthpiece than the organ which had puffed so hard against Gomez Farias a few months before now declared that "there is no lock strong enough to prevent the progress of the world." Whatever else the reformer had done or left undone, he had left confusion behind him.

But there was always Santa Anna. Convinced by the experience of his colleague of what would not work, but not yet by his own of what would, he jammed the helm hard to the right and filled his administration with Conservative persons and centralist tendencies. This touched off an inflammable issue. Conservatives and Liberals had identified themselves with two mechanical principles, Centralism and Federalism, the former seeking effective control of the country through a centralized administration and the latter ample latitude for local autonomy to preserve their independence in a loose federation that favored states' rights—principles which were of more actual interest to the country at large than social reform at that period when the regional basis of national life was a pronounced feature of its amorphous beginnings. The abrupt reversal excited the centrifugal and separatist forces associated with Federalism and was felt with peculiar acuteness in the remote extremities of the country, where it created other domestic complications. Meeting with active resistance in Zacatecas, the native province of Gomez Farias and a hotbed of reform, Santa Anna led a punitive raid into that state. The agitation spread to the adjoining state of Coahuila and thence to Texas, where it kindled yet another brand of contention in the alien population of the frontier. The American colonists flew to arms to defend the local autonomy guaranteed them by a succession of Mexican governments as their privilege for settling the territory, and the fuse thus lighted developed rapidly into the blaze that ended with the secession of Texas.

The Texan crisis provided Santa Anna, when it began, with a martial diversion from social reform and the opportunity to unite the country and increase his prestige by the suppression of what promised to be an insignificant revolt; but it ended in disaster for himself and a cruel exposure of the condition of the country. In the brief campaign which he conducted against the colonists (December 1835 to May 1836) he displayed his soldiership at its best and worst and fully in both: his organizing ability in putting an army into the field practically without funds; his public spirit in pledging his personal property to raise them; his leadership in the long burning marches across the desert; his gallantry in the capture of the Alamo and his savagery in the slaughter of the prisoners there and at Goliat; his incompetence on the field of San Jacinto, where he was defeated by a beaten foe; his cowardice after his capture and his bravado in recognizing the independence of Texas on his own responsibility, and by a secret agreement, to secure his release. Through every phase of the campaign one factor in his conduct remained constant: he managed the war as a personal enterprise, and the genuine devotion to his adopted country which he displayed when he fought for it was matched by the facility with which he disposed of it when fortune deserted him. Psychologically he was an alien still, sovereign and irresponsible; and while anyone else would have been completely discredited by such a defeat, he returned to Mexico in 1837 and settled down on his estates to recuperate from it.

The disaster to the country was more serious. The inability of the government, with all the material and moral resources of the country at its command, to suppress an insignificant revolt was an admission of weakness which clearly indicated that something was radically wrong with Mexico. What those resources were worth was revealed when Santa Anna was forced to mortgage his own property to outfit an army and to levy forced loans and to resort to makeshifts of all kinds to keep it afoot. The Texas crisis caught the country unawares in its chronic conditions of disorganization and poverty, conditions which went back to Independence and before it. The formation of the nation was from the outset an economic problem which remained untouchable. In 1821, when the colony which Cortés described as containing the most vast and varied wealth ever bestowed upon a single people in a single area declared itself independent, it was cast on its own resources; and after three hundred years of exploitation, which had drawn off all the exportable wealth, prohibited or neglected native production, and forbidden foreign trade, those resources were what might have been expected: they were undeveloped, or disorganized, or exhausted. The mines, which had been worked to the exclusion of every other field of natural wealth, had been abandoned because of deterioration of yield or antiquated methods of extraction, and by the end of the eighteenth century the industry was in a state of chronic slump. Agriculture, in a land whose greatest potential asset was the soil, was unprofitable to the great landowners, in whose hands the largest and most fertile tracts lay idle, because the colonial regime supplied them with no incentive to develop them, and cultivation was confined to the local and immediate needs of a class that was actually land poor and that operated on loans from the Church. It was the threat of foreclosure, when these mortgages were taken over by the Crown shortly before the outbreak of revolt, that eventually led the gentry to join it. Commerce and industry, deliberately restricted by the monopolies of the motherland, were virtually nonexistent.

Everything remained to be done, therefore, when the new nation came into being: roads had to be built, mines rehabilitated, agriculture developed, industry created, trade fostered; but the task was rendered well-nigh impossible by the classes which called the nation into being for their own benefit. With the expulsion of the Spaniards, capital fled the country. Besides capital, economic reconstruction required an initiative of which the native plutocracy was equally devoid. The greatest capitalist in the country was the Church: it was the sole banker, controlling the land-poor *haciendados* by its mortgages, and directly interested in the mines, which built its temples and supplied their treasure; it was rich in its own right, in real estate, in pious legacies, in the accumulated revenue of the centuries; and it was proportionately poor in public spirit. An institution independent of the State, immobilizing one-third of the national wealth in mortmain, it recognized no obligation to contribute to the commonwealth. Theoretically a partner to the State, it took no part in government problems except when they menaced its interests; and in every such crisis the antisocial attitude which it invariably displayed, and in which it was supported by its economic vassals, demonstrated beyond a doubt that the monopoly of the material and moral resources of the country by the Church constituted the greatest single obstacle to the integration of the country.

The new nation began life, accordingly, by borrowing abroad, and to all its other liabilities were added those of a foreign debt which accumulated swiftly and fruitlessly, for the money was dissipated in meeting the running expenses of a government always in arrears. The loan produced none of the economic benefits for which it was made, while the claims incurred by it promoted the infiltration of foreign capital, the appropriation of the natural resources by alien enterprise, and the alienation of the national revenues. Nor were these the only penalties of the failure—the organic and organized failure—of the ruling classes to provide the country with a living. While the overwhelming majority of the population sank to the bottom, submerged in poverty, apathy, and crime, a restless minority struggled to the top and snatched a precarious means of livelihood from the State. The competition for public office produced those furies for which a special word had to be coined —*empleomanía*. Politics for employment attained the proportions of a social obsession in Mexico and reproduced those periodic upsets of the government, led by ambitious generals and backed by hungry bureaucrats, which kept the country in continuous commotion and gave it a bad name with investors abroad. The persistence of these conditions, unimpaired by Reform, from 1836, made them so habitual and accepted that the infirmity they bred was not generally recognized until the collapse of the Texan campaign. Nor was it admitted then, for public opinion was controlled by a conservative press, in the service of a party interested in laying the blame elsewhere, and as far from home as possible.

Trouble with Texas had long been anticipated as an inevitable problem: the problem of a vast stretch of frontier territory, sparsely populated, lying between two countries, one of which failed to settle it while the other was rapidly expanding. Nature abhors a vacuum, and the Americans to the north were a natural people; and as long as the people to the south neglected to make good their claim to the land, their legal title to it weighed as little as an injunction against the law of gravity. Sooner or later the pressure of population was certain to settle the problem. If the question of rights was involved at all, it resolved itself into the right to let a great area of uncultivated territory lie idle indefinitely. One Mexican government after another, recognizing the force of facts, legalized it by allowing that vast outlying domain to be colonized by American homesteaders and sought to assure their loyalty by liberal treatment, nominal allegiance, and loose control of their local autonomy—obligations faithfully observed on both sides, but feeble guarantees against the effects of isolation and virtual independence, the difficulties of assimilation, the proximity of the settlers to the land of their origin, to which they remained bound by consanguinity and easy commercial access, and their remoteness from Mexican markets and the central government. The crisis had long been anticipated, but nothing had been done, or could be done, to avert it, and the result was none the less bitter for being expected. The secession had been foreseen, but so had the secession of Mexico from Spain, and it was the particular time and circumstances in which it occurred that made the inevitable break important. The ease with which the Texans consummated their revolt constituted an indictment of the debility and mismanagement of the Mexican Government, which the holders of power hastened to deflect in another direction—the inevitable direction foreseen by the Conde de Aranda when he pointed to the infant Republic to the north as a focus of infection destined to lead sooner or later to the disintegration of Mexico.

Like their forebears, the Mexicans read the handwriting on the wall. The war in that no-man's-land to the north had not been waged in a void; it had been fought along the frontier, and in the fear, of a neighbor whose shadow had fallen on that territory long before. The first contact between the two peoples established after independence had not been fortunate. Aranda had predicted that the approaches of the other would be made either by propaganda or conquest, and the Mexicans were on their guard against both. The first American Minister to Mexico had made friendly advances, in fact, and had advocated republican ideals with a zeal which antagonized the Conservatives and led to his recall on the complaint that he was meddling in internal politics. The second made himself objectionable to both parties by pressing with all the means at his command—bribery, intrigue, bluster, and cajolery, and in spite of repeated rebuffs—a bid for the sale of Texas and a strip of the California coast; he was also recalled. Thereafter the problem of Texas was allowed to lapse; but when the revolt broke out, in spite of the strict neutrality of the American Government, it was easy to believe that neither its inception nor its issue was spontaneous, and credulity throve on the shadow.

Though the war was unpopular in Mexico, and the upper classes were indifferent at first to its complications, their patriotism awoke with defeat and manifested itself in post-mortem mourning and national alarm. The designs of the adjacent Republic, so plainly advertised by its first two ministers and so suspect after the loss of Texas, were recalled and woven into those of the ruling oligarchy. If the Texan war provided a timely diversion from internal reform when it began, it served that purpose far more effectively when it was over; patriotism covered a multitude of political sins. A pointed comment on the state of the nation was supplied by a famous Mexican who rent the seamless mantle in twain. Lorenzo de Zavala, a disappointed reformer, threw in his lot with the Texans, preferring the prospect of freedom under a foreign flag to the certainty of degeneration under his own—a conception of patriotism that was neither the popular one nor that of the ruling class: theirs was the common variety, springing from the instincts of possession and satisfied with territorial integrity. It was sufficient to cover the loss of Texas with a cloud of popular sentiment, to wrap a republic land-poorer in the ample folds of the national flag, and to nurse mistrust of American ambitions into a fixed idea which deepened with the passage of time. For the secession of Texas remained an unsettled question and a strain in the relations of its neighbors. The independent Republic of Texas, recognized by the United States but not by Mexico, which refused to relinquish and was incapable of enforcing its claim to sovereignty, was too feeble to sustain its position as a buffer state and became a source of agitation on both sides of the border; the strain was sustained for eight years, and in 1845 the inevitable solution was reached. The United States annexed Texas, and the settled question, infinitely aggravated by time, plunged Mexico into an internal and external crisis far surpassing that of 1835, which it reproduced and magnified.

For the Mexican Bourbons had learned nothing from the warning in 1835. The fresh crisis found the country as unprepared as the first, paralyzed by endemic poverty, shiftlessness, and instability. The Conservative forces remained in control of the State, to the accompaniment of those conventional mutinies, revolutionary only in name, which shuffled persons and programs but left the foundations intact. Political ferment was as incessant as it was futile, the bubbling and choking of a stagnant society whose resources, monopolized by the top-heavy and parasitic organizations of Church and Army, made relief impossible. Agriculture was still feudal; mining, commerce, and industry were controlled by foreigners, who exported the country and maintained its governments by supplying their main source of revenue through the customs, which became increasingly crippled with debt service; while government provided the sole national industry for the countless qualified or unqualified unemployed who filled its berths, in a thriving competition of climbers and outcasts taking their turns, on any change of program, to oust one another. A government operated by successive shifts of fortune-hunters, for the protection of the propertied classes, on an ever-deepening national deficit, under the liability of a rising foreign debt and a mounting bill for damages to foreign nations incident to its turbulent functioning—such was still the condition of the Mexican Republic ten years after the Texas war. Yet it was under those risks that the Arandas of Mexico challenged the annexation of Texas as a question of national pride and committed themselves to war with the United States.

But still, as always, there was Santa Anna. During that dreary decade he had gradually recovered from his disgrace of 1835; but it had taken him a decade to do it. In 1838 he lost a leg in action defying a French squadron, sent to collect damages for injuries to French nationals in a riot: the leg was preserved by a grateful country. But he was not yet ready for a political return, and though he served as Acting President for a few months in 1839, he nursed his reputation on his estates until 1841, when he returned and overthrew the government, assuming power as President-Dictator with the support of the clergy. Before long he found it as impossible to govern with the Church as without it—an experience which had ruined most of his predecessors. The reluctance of his backers to foot the bills frustrated and infuriated a dictatorship which could exercise itself only in the ostentation of authority, the persecution of opponents, and an orgy of extravagance and corruption; and in 1843 he was overthrown and fled the country under a storm of obloquy that recalled all the causes he had served, abused, and betrayed. When he escaped to Havana, his career appeared to be irreparably closed, but his buoyancy defied bankruptcy, and his star began to glow again through the war clouds that gathered with the annexation of Texas. The crisis offered a favorable opportunity for another patriotic return. Knowing that a war with the United States was hopeless, he weighed the prospects coolly. Was it not better, was it not the part of true patriotism perhaps, to strike a bargain instead of a blow? Unpopular as such a solution was certain to be in Mexico, it had been contemplated there and abandoned in the face of popular feeling; but Santa Anna had more courage in Cuba, and sent an emissary to Washington with a proposal to sell all the territory north of the Rio Grande and the Colorado of the West for thirty million American dollars. The response was favorable, provided the offer were made by the recognized authorities in Mexico: the agent objected that no government could make such an offer and remain in office and suggested that the proper course, in the opinion of his principal, was for the United States to bring pressure to bear by sending a sufficient force to the Rio

Grande and a strong naval detachment to Veracruz. Upon this basis a preliminary understanding was reached. Santa Anna agreed to negotiate in return for American support, and sent back specific military suggestions for the maneuver. The understanding offered a fair degree of insurance, something to fall back upon in case of defeat, while it left him free to prosecute hostilities in earnest as long as he could do so successfully, and it was merely a gentleman's agreement. Everything was contingent upon his return to Mexico, and his credit was so low there that he was forced to take the first bid from any quarter. The bid came from another bankrupt, Gomez Farias.

During that deadly decade the reformer had not recovered from his defeat of 1834, but neither had he accepted it. "When one has undertaken and started a social change, one must not look back until it is completed, nor halt until one has overcome those who oppose it, whoever they may be. Otherwise one must bear the responsibility for the innumerable evils of an attempt for which a people is made to suffer and from which they derive none of the benefits expected of success." The maxim, coined by Dr. Mora after the manner of Marcus Aurelius but with revolutionary composure, was peculiarly applicable to the past decade in Mexico. The compassionate intransigence, the reasonable ruthlessness, of a classic truism had been repeatedly proved by the patient in that invalid interval and fully appreciated by Gomez Farias. The counsel of the philosopher had not been wasted on the physician, and the prescription had gained a force which compelled its application in 1846. The imminent conflict with the United States roused all the helpless resentment, the patriotic pride, the fear and mortification and confusion, and the desperate resolutions of a country conscious at last of its weakness, to fighting pitch; it also broke the hold of a self-centralized government, and the elements flew apart in wildly careening chaos. In the turmoil the old radical reappeared, determined to recapture power from the bankrupt incompetents who had controlled it so long. Alone, he was too radical to be more than a minority leader; an ally was needed of commanding personal prestige, and such was the poverty of spellbinders in 1846 that the only one who answered the specifications was Santa Anna. Overtures were made and accepted. The risk of such an association was self-evident, but it was no time to be squeamish. In May 1846, two months after the outbreak of war, Gomez Farias raised a revolt against a commander who had employed his troops to capture the government, deposed him, and paved the way for the return of Santa Anna, who slipped through the American blockade by agreement with Washington and landed in Veracruz in July. In December he was elected to the Presidency, with Gomez Farias once more as his Vice-President. Thus twelve years after its collapse Reform reappeared in the persons of the same crippled team, by one of those combinations which sum up a period, and in the teeth of foreign invasion, as a desperate, belated, but supreme effort to save the integrity of the nation. Mora was missing, and so was the game leg of Santa Anna.

It was in the midst of this crisis that Juarez came for the first time to the capital of his country, drifting helplessly toward the vortex of war, bankruptcy, and liquidation. Too late for social cures, some of the principles of the original program were hastily applied to the emergency, and though these measures were not a rebirth of Reform, they were a flare in the dark, a signal of distress that restored the vision of those who had caught it dimly in 1834 and were ripe to receive it twelve years later.

And Juarez was ripe, overripe indeed, for though his vision had not failed, that arid decade of national life had been a barren stretch in his own as well. The failure to advance carried penalties of stagnation in public life from which no one escaped, and least of all those who suffered from shallow living; and his reputation has suffered with posterity for his common share in the miseries of this period. After his brush with the curate of Loricha he eschewed political activity, retiring to private life and the practice of his profession. In the subsequent years he accepted appointments, professional and political, from the prevailing regime, which have scandalized his critics and pained his apologists. One of his clerical critics has tabulated the various administrations which he served to prove the pliability of his convictions and to conclude that he was no better than the vulgar office-seekers of the time; a statistical triumph. The charge, advanced all the more eagerly by his enemies because it was the only one that could be brought against his recognized probity, has been aggravated by his friends who have admitted it regretfully; and it has thus grown into an imputation exaggerated out of all proportion to its importance by a partisan spirit which has reduced critics and champions alike to the provincial scale which the question occupied at the time, and which remains the true measure of its merits.

Whatever political inconsistencies were involved in his conduct were more apparent than real, and were shallow concessions to expediency and temporizing. He had to live—a vulgar motive, no doubt, but sufficiently compelling, if not to his posthumous enemies, to a struggling lawyer who specialized in poor clients and who belonged to an overcrowded profession and a politically outlawed party. Appointed to the bench in 1841, he turned a political favor to public account and served the community well in his judicial capacity. In 1843 he married; and the vulgar motive acquired increased force and perfect respectability. For he married well: from a social point of view, brilliantly; and from a personal one, fortunately. His bride was the daughter of the house in which he had found shelter twenty-four years before as the runaway brother of the cook. The Mazzas ranked among the *gachupin* families of Oaxaca in point of respectability, although they were of Italian origin, and the match was a remarkable example of the freedom from racial prejudice, which was one of the few benefits bequeathed by Spanish civilization to its colonies. His courtship was accepted by society as unquestioningly as by Margarita Mazza herself, and she described her suitor in two words, which honored them both. "He is very homely but very good," she wrote, and the comment conveyed her whole heart, which was conscious of nothing else.

Definitely established in the middle-class world of Oaxaca by his marriage and his professional standing, he now had a position to keep up. Everything tended to reconcile him to the existing order, to make him amenable to its advantages, and, like many another middle-aged idealist, to reduce him to a sensible appreciation of the possible. It was possible, for instance, a year later, to accept a position as secretary to the government, although the Governor was a satellite of Santa Anna, who was then in full blast of his clerical dictatorship. How compromising it was is clear from the satisfaction of his critics, who have cited his signing of an invitation to the unveiling of a portrait of Santa Anna as serious evidence of his political servility. When it came, however, to signing an order from the Governor to the courts directing them to prosecute those who refused to pay ecclesiastical tithes, Juarez resigned. Yet he did not suffer for his stand; he was returned to the bench and seated shortly after on the Supreme Court of the state.

Nevertheless, though the concessions to security and propriety were few and small, they were damaging. A decade of timeserving was deadening, the sands of expediency drove the living springs of faith underground, and the dust continued to accumulate and settle on his late youth. The mere passage of time was a setback: middle age was upon him, not the active maturity of a vigorous prime but the thickening flesh, the slackening fires, the sedentary wisdom of the forties, and he had done nothing to redeem the high hopes with which he had been invested by Mendez so many years ago. Marriage was sobering, his was happy and fruitful, and the birth of children tightened his bonds. In 1845 he was elected to the Departmental Assembly, as the conservative version of the local legislature was called, and universally recognized as a safe man. But new times were at hand. With the coming of war in 1846 the Conservative grip on the government was broken in Oaxaca as well as in the capital. A local mutiny seconded the revolt of Gomez Farias, and a triumvirate of Liberals was set up to administer power provisionally. It was a tribute to his past that Juarez was one of them; but it was also a comment on it that the nomination for a new governor went to one of his colleagues who had been both Liberal and active. Some penalty had to be paid for expediency.

Out of his compromises he was suddenly caught, however, by the national crisis, lifted by the national peril, and swept out of his provincial sphere into the vortex of the struggle for national survival. Elected to the Congress called by Santa Anna to meet the emergency, he arrived in the capital when the nation itself was facing the crushing test of foreign war with the preparation of a backward province.

7

THE "terrible year" of '47, as it came to be known in Mexican annals, was terrible above all as a test of the patriotism of a people deprived of every other resource with which to face a foreign war. When Congress convened in January the war had been in progress for nine months; the invasion had overrun the north and was pushing toward the capital; the Mexican forces had lost one battle after another; Santa Anna was mustering a fresh army, pledging his personal property, conjuring up resources out of nothing: drastic measures were required to produce them. In 1835, under less stress, he had pinched the Church; in 1847, under a national warrant, he was driven to the same extremities, but he delegated the duty to Gomez Farias and Congress while he went to the front, and the actual brunt of the business was borne by the deputies from Oaxaca, who introduced into Congress a motion empowering the government to mortgage a portion of Church property, to the value of fifteen million pesos, for the prosecution of the war. The motion was carried, but it was a costly victory for the government. Six weeks later a crack regiment, suborned by the clergy, rebelled as it was about to leave the capital for the defense of Veracruz, paralyzing the government for three weeks. The deadlock was broken by the return of Santa Anna from the front, defeated, but welcomed as a victor by the clergy and the unruly regiment. He dismissed Gomez Farias and repealed the assessment.

So ended once more the brief chimerical combination of reformer and adventurer, wrecked by the same power and for the same reasons as in 1834, but under infinitely more serious circumstances. The lengths to which the Church was willing to go to protect its property were so cynically revealed by the revolt that outraged patriots pressed the charge further; for on the same day that mutiny broke out in the capital, Santa Anna lost the battle of Buena Vista, missing victory by so narrow a margin that, instead of a familiar blunder, the defeat seemed to be a deliberate foul. Rumors of his treasonable relations with Washington were rife, and suspicion gained a grim plausibility because, in a sense, the whole campaign was a conscious sham. Resistance, as everyone knew by now, was being prolonged to preserve the popular fiction of national honor, and betrayal, more bitter to the sentiment than to the interest of the nation, became a joint guilt and prompted a common defense: so that the most suspicious patriots rejected the rumors of his collusion with the enemy as incredible, and though his proposed deal was disclosed by an American paper, it was discounted in Mexico as enemy propaganda. Denied in one form, the accusation appeared in another.

That a major engagement was lost on the field at the same time that a mutiny in the capital paralyzed the defense of the country was a coincidence which no longer seemed accidental when Santa Anna was welcomed home by the clergy and the rebels and promptly complied with their demands. If it was equally shocking, it was less difficult to believe that the battle of Buena Vista had been lost for the benefit of the Church. After the revolt nothing appeared impossible; and anticlericals could henceforth claim, as they did, that if the nation met the crushing test of foreign war with the preparation of a backward province, it was because the nation was in reality no more than a province of the Church.

The revolt of the *Polkos,* as the devout dandies and dashing ballroom dancers who manned the mutinous regiment were called by an outraged people, was a passing scandal and a lasting stigma that cost the Church more money than it spent on it, for the mutiny was too crude a maneuver in wartime, and the hierarchy hastily retreated from the harsh glare of public opinion and covered its miscalculation by supplying Santa Anna with sums well in excess of those they had refused to Gomez Farias. The cost in moral authority was even more prejudicial to the clergy, for the credit of a corporation that acknowledged no civil obligations sank in public respect past recovery. None of those thwarted by the incident recovered from it completely. Gomez Farias was finished. As for Santa Anna, success alone could dispel his discredit, and victory fled his every approach to it, as he fled the reproaches that pursued his repeated defeats. But the chief sufferer was the country at large. Public confidence called for new leaders, and there were none. Congress presented its customary spectacle of parliamentary impotence, absorbed in an oblivious fury of factional wrangles as if there were no war on the agenda—a morbid condition of which the members were well aware and from which, like sick men or men in a nightmare, they were unable to awaken. As the months passed all the forces that had frustrated national unity in the past were brought to the surface and exposed to public view by the pressure of foreign conquest: the congestion of the two great parasitic bodies at the top, a

Church engrossed in self-service, an Army trained to revolt; a bankrupt government bargaining with both; a minority of hopeless critics below; a demoralized mass at the bottom; and over and above all a Santa Anna struggling to galvanize the whole by personal spellbinding; and the progress of military collapse followed its course spasmodically.

The war was lost at great length, however, and with ample time between blows for reflection. What it meant to an average public-spirited but not party-minded Mexican may be seen epitomized in the running comment on its significant symptoms made by an independent observer, whose correspondence with others of his kind traced the arc traveled by the public mind during the terrible year with the graphic accuracy of a fever chart. The name of José-Fernando Ramirez was generic for a type of mind sufficiently educated, indeterminate, and catholic to be affected by many contradictory influences and to reflect in a sensitive medium the daily zigzags, the broad curve, and the concluding ellipse of the public temper in his reaction to it. For Gomez Farias he felt nothing but impatience. "The most compact, the most organized party is that of Farias, a party of immense basis but small elevation," he admitted; but it was composed of fanatics and had succeeded in antagonizing everyone and attaining the last degree of exaggeration. For the *Polkos* he felt nothing but contempt. "The scapularies, medals, chaplets, and bags of religious relics by the dozen that adorned the chests of the rebels, and especially of the soft and sybaritic young men who form our fashionable class, might have convinced anyone ignorant of our customs that here was a camp of martyrs ready to a man to sacrifice everything for the inviolability of religion"—if it had not been common knowledge that they continued the mutiny only as long as they could blackmail the Church. For the clergy he felt the kind of tolerant contempt of one accustomed to the religious cant with which they sanctioned and subsidized revolt, and a bitter relish when they overreached themselves and were duped by their improvidence. As for Congress, its conduct convinced him of the impossibility of the representative system. Unless it improved, "despotism pure and simple awaits us; that is, supposing that we still have a country." For Santa Anna he had both contempt and pity when he was told that, convinced of his unfitness to command, he proposed to enlist Spanish officers from among the Carlist *émigrés*—the final touch to the countless absurdities of independence. "We have all awakened late, all of us in our various fields, to the hard fact that we are unfit for command! If at least we profit by the discovery, all will not have been lost. What the end of the war will be it is not easy to say, for the sad truth is that no preparation has been made even for peace, but I believe that peace will be made soon, although probably only to renew our old civil wars."

When he was offered an honorable escape from his country—the best post in the diplomatic service abroad—Ramirez refused it. "My pride as a Mexican," he said, "is greater than our degradation, than which no more can be said, and I could not bring myself to represent a people which by its inane quarrels, its puerile petulance, and its senselessness, has been unable to defend itself, inferior in this to dumb brutes."

Counting the months to capitulation, and the dismemberment of the country which he foresaw as its inevitable consequence, he noted the progress of internal disintegration with growing fatigue and comments more and more fragmentary. In April Santa Anna led another army to the slaughter at Cerro Gordo, where "a small number of our troops fought and died heroically; the rest threw down their arms and fled without a fight. We must regard the morale of the soldier as lost, for even his race instinct is at work in the fear he feels of the foreigner." In May Puebla was surrendered by the clergy, the inhabitants having fled as soon as Santa Anna proposed to defend them, and some high dignitaries of the Church declared that, if the Yankees respected their faith and their property, nothing would be lost by the invasion. After the fall of Puebla the American Commander himself was said to be using his secret funds to influence Congress to bring the war to a swift and humane conclusion, but "the first to speak of peace will lose it, and hence none dares to pronounce the fatal word." In June the capital was invested, and a last stand for honor made at all its approaches, amply redeemed at Chapultepec where a score of boys young enough to believe in it bit the dust, and by their elders at Churubusco and Molino del Rey, and by countless feats of isolated courage. The zigzags became more and more erratic and desperate in the convulsive confusion of the culminating battle lost by Santa Anna, whose flight finally relieved a city that had been waiting for weeks to expel the army which it dreaded more than the Americans. Throughout the last hectic phases Ramirez remained there until the day of defeat, the day of delivery, dawned, and after it when the formal war was finished and a private war was waged by the populace against the Americans, whom they lured to death in obscure dives, and against the pest which followed the troops ridden with dysentery and relieving their disease in the sewerless streets.

Then, as peace settled over the extinct but still seething city, he fell to reviewing the past and casting up accounts for the future. He drafted utopias of what he would do, were the history of his country his to rewrite. He cited with approval "an old and neglected political saw which says that it is men rather than systems that determine the welfare of peoples and lend a high renown to nations." Yet that was no solution: the system of personal leadership had been played out by Santa Anna; politics was a science of averages. He laid out plans for reforms, too general to be good, and when he reduced them to cases, he was willing to make any concession for the sake of national unity. He noted the indifference of the people during the ceremonies of Holy Week in 1847 as a feature "which the false philosophy of our revolutionists will hail as a symptom of social progress," but which dismayed him as "one of death and destruction, for when our people reach the point of believing in nothing they will respect nothing." For the sake of self-preservation he was prepared to compound with idolatry and corruption. "I hope that you will do me the justice to believe," he wrote in one of the last and most revealing of his letters, "that when I refer to the reform of abuses, I do not propose to break a lance with the clergy or with any other class of society, as might be supposed from the senseless vulgarities and gross slanders that have been spread against me. The well-founded reputation that I enjoy as an aristocrat should make it clear that that quality is incompatible with class hatred." His conception of aristocracy was superior, but it led him in practice to very ordinary conclusions. Rather than risk a repetition of the penalties of the past, he was willing to return to the past: he surrendered to society, such as it was, his scorn, his disgust, his despair, his dreams of reform, for the sake of peace. He was beaten by his own observations, and in this, though he touched the nadir of nihilism, there is no doubt that his views reflected those of the average Mexican, in varying degrees, after the war.

Such was the conclusion to which Juarez also was driven by the same experience. His comment was quiet but nonetheless emphatic, and he expressed it not in words but in acts. Throughout the war he had played an inconspicuous part in public affairs. By his colleagues in Congress he was remembered only for his "sphinx-like silence," and, in that Congress whose clamorous incompetence was denounced by Ramirez, silence had all the effect of a sentence. Those were the days when a man could make his mark simply by holding his tongue, and it was noticed that Juarez took his seat only to pronounce a laconic yea or nay on the business of the day. He never mounted the tribune, where deputies made a pastime of insulting one another "with the adolescent fury of schoolboys." Silence in the wind—meaning in the mind; and though he left no trace on the public scene, he carried away from it conclusions of his own and a profound sense of the drift of national life, by which he was guided when he finally found an opportunity to act on it.

The revolt of the *Polkos* was seconded by a reflex movement in Oaxaca which captured the local government. With his fellow deputies Juarez initiated a motion in Congress to depose the usurping authorities, and by dint of pressure, parliamentary bargaining, and the influence of a prominent leader, secured its adoption; but as Oaxaca provided the Federal government with a steady flow of supplies and as

Congress had no means of enforcing its decrees, the resolution remained a dead letter until Juarez returned to Oaxaca in August 1847 and joined his friends there in ousting the "intruding authorities." They were successful, and for his part in the push he was appointed provisional Governor in November 1847. With this position he assumed a national responsibility. "The decision with respect to Oaxaca may be of immense importance, depending on the turn that matters are beginning to take at this time," wrote Ramirez when Congress adopted the resolution, for the turn which matters were taking then ran counter to national cohesion. A marked tendency to assert their local autonomy at the expense of the center had appeared among the states during the closing of the debacle, when the Federal powers were, in fact, no more than a conventional fiction, with one honorable exception recognized by Ramirez: "A single state, Oaxaca, has shown itself firm, consistent, and even heroic by providing everything, money and men, amid its own troubles." If the conduct of Oaxaca was conspicuous during the disintegration of the national defense, it was of far greater consequence that it should feed the nation with patriotic example after the war, when the motion of the vortex in reverse, whirling away from center, threatened the country with internal as well as external dismemberment. To counteract that tendency was important, and to begin the work of reconstruction there, preserving the part for the whole and rallying the nation to the example of a pivotal state, was possible, and the only thing possible then for practical patriotism, and it was the course Juarez adopted. He applied himself to his task with the benefit of the experience he had gained in the capital, and in a conservative spirit which would have won the approval of Ramirez, had he noticed it; avoiding controversial issues, superior to class hatred, and proving the truth of the proverb that it is men, and not institutions, that determine the welfare of peoples and lend a high renown to nations. But it was long before the average Mexican recognized the importance of what was happening in Oaxaca.

8

ASSUMING power in the wake of the American war, the first and most pressing test which Juarez faced was the conquest of peace, and the conservative character of his government was determined by the conditions in which it began. After the fall of the capital it was feared that the invasion might spread to the south, and preparations were hastily made for the defense of the state—preparations which gave him the initial advantage of public spirit and spontaneous co-operation, and in which he mustered the full support of the community, including the ecclesiastical authorities, who contributed patriotic sermons from their pulpits and bells from their temples for the casting of cannon. The phantom alarm had not passed when a real one appeared. Santa Anna, fleeing southward, forsaken and disowned wherever he turned, sought asylum in Oaxaca, and, as his approach revived the agitation of the local *Polkos,* Juarez took the precaution of closing the state to that wandering germ of civil war.

Santa Anna never forgave him. Years later he recalled that rebuff as the most bitter of all those which he had suffered because he could not explain it. With the taste still bitter on his tongue, he wrote, rinsing his mouth of the name of Juarez: "He could not forgive me because he had waited on me at table in Oaxaca, in December 1829, with his bare feet on the floor and in his linen smock and trousers. . . . It is amazing," he added, "that an Indian of such low degree should have figured in Mexico as we all know. . . ." Hardened as he was to the reverses of fortune, he was baffled by the unaccountable career of that upstart, except as a freak of fortune. But then Santa Anna never could explain anything, and to the end of his days he continued to wander unknowing through the mysteries of the world and the maze of his Mexican memories—one world which he thought he knew thoroughly, and by which he was bewildered in 1847. Memory, the one faculty which never failed him, and foresight, which always did—the two limitations of the typical Creole—made it equally impossible for him to understand his rebuff by the native in that terrible year. He still saw nothing but the feet waiting on table in 1829 and missed the face waiting on time to clear it. The time had come, the tables were turned, and Juarez had shut one more door in his face. That was all. With the

ground giving under his feet wherever he turned, without a foothold
on his native soil, escaping from it like a volatile gas, Santa Anna felt
this final abuse all the more bitterly because the hunter and hunted of
fortune was unable to realize that fortune was a deity of primitive peoples, that the era of political personalities was passing in Mexico, and
that one in which men embodied forces was beginning to emerge. Like
all tendencies that outlive their time and the needs which they served,
the tradition of personal leadership was long in dying, however, and
Santa Anna waited his turn, trusting to the perennial mutability of his
fortunes, to settle his account with the upstart who, a nobody in 1829,
was everybody in 1847. Santa Anna knew how to return; and life itself knows no more.

Between the beginning and the end of his government in Oaxaca
five years elapsed, and what Juarez accomplished there in that time
was the antithesis of everything that Santa Anna represented and understood. The administration of Oaxaca by Juarez became an example
for the country, in fact, of how much could be accomplished by mere
public spirit, honesty, thrift, and sound management. For it was by
virtue of such qualities, and on his record as a provincial Governor,
that Juarez came to figure "in Mexico as we all know," and the amazing result was accomplished quietly, inconspicuously, patiently—and
permanently.

Beginning under the heavy liabilities of national ruin, he not only
overcame but turned them to account in his own area, mobilizing the
patriotic fervor and fusion of wartime, harnessing their driving power
to the tasks of peace and reconstruction, holding them at high pitch,
and winning the confidence of all classes so completely within less than
a year that when his provisional term expired in 1848 he was re-elected
without question to a post in which he had captured the popular imagination. He took a legitimate pride in the result. "Fortunately," he said
at his inaugural, "neither a faction, nor favoritism, nor intrigue, but
the free and spontaneous choice of the people has placed me in this
position. There is no danger, therefore, that any class will be oppressed
by my government, nor any portion of my fellow citizens." These were
no idle words or conventional pledges: for fortune itself had been reconstructed in his hands, no casual deity or clay fetish, but a rational
force formed and controlled by man. Social conciliation inspired his
policy from the start, and he kept his comprehensive pledge to the end,
despite more than one temptation or provocation to depart from it.

Temptation of a kind to which he was susceptible by nature, the
natural temptation of partiality to his own race, came when his people
tramped down from the mountains for his inauguration and presented
him, together with their congratulations and their small offerings of
fruits, fowl, and corn, their large tribute of trust and a common peti-

tion. "You know what we need and you will give it to us," said their spokesman, "for you are good and will not forget that you are one of us." He responded in kind, assuring them that he knew their needs and had not forgotten his origin. With his promise to do what was good for them he gave them the run of his house, where they spent the night, sleeping on the floor in the corridors; in the morning they tramped back to the Sierra, each with a peso as token payment on his pledge. The Governor's mansion, an imposing colonial building with courts, columns, and suites of rooms of stately solidity, was well fitted to foster delusions of grandeur in his callers, who, remembering that his father, on a trip to market, had died in a corridor of the Municipal Palace, claimed for themselves the son whom they saw installed in the seat of the mighty. The appeal was compelling. Since Independence the native masses had relapsed into silence and submission to an order which, however it changed, remained the same for them; and only at long intervals was their presence felt in a rare voice of protest.

In 1827 a social satirist wrote in his *Political Testament:* "I leave the Indian in the same state of civilization, freedom, and felicity to which the Conquest reduced them, the most notable fact being the indifference with which our Congresses have considered them"; and in later years the grim jest of the satirist was repeated in sober earnest by Dr. Mora, who drafted philanthropic plans of reform for their benefit. But these were the voices of white men, and it remained for an Indian to voice the passionate resentment and repressed aspirations that underlay the apparent resignation of his race. In 1828 there appeared in the back streets of the capital a leaflet bearing the title *The Indians Wish to Be Free, and Will Be Free,* by an anonymous author who revealed himself only in the words, "I am an Indian; for them and with them I propose to expose truths stripped of all foliage," and who rehearsed the grievances of his people as no outsider could do. All their disabilities he laid to the original loss of "our dear earth, which we have never doubted would be restored to us in its full extent: this being the common feeling of all the Indians who populate this vast continent. The Indians are in the most grievous depression and degradation. Our color, our ignorance, and our poverty place us at an infinite distance from those who are not in our condition, and the protection of the laws avails us so little that their effect is negligible." Their communal lands shrinking under the encroachment of the great estates, without property and without initiative, they were an alien element in the country. "Isolated by their language and form of government, which they do not understand because no one takes the trouble to explain it to them, they continue to live within their own customs, habits, and gross superstitions, which are mysteriously maintained in every village by five or six old Indians who live off the sweat of the rest, ruling them with the harshest of despotism. This combination of causes, known to all and by all lamented, preserves them in an inert and apathetic condition of indifference to the future and to virtually everything that does not serve the gross passions of the moment."

Of what they were capable they had shown when Hidalgo raised the cry of "Land and Liberty"; but Hidalgo had fallen, Morelos had fallen, and in 1828 their hopes were set on Guerrero. "Five million Indians rightly look to him alone for their fortune and prosperity. We want no more revolutions for which we, and we alone, pay the cost without any fruit whatsoever. . . . An Indian is, for our good fortune, the first man on this continent, and henceforth all those who govern us will be Indians, because it is just. We shall not appeal to the barbarous arbitrament of revolutions, which are the remedy of the desperate. Let those remain in their posts who now hold them; but let vacancies be filled hereafter by educated Indians, of whom there is no lack. In this manner we shall write an end to those political convulsions, promoted by the very same men who have caused the Nation incalculable evils in the past; in this manner, realize the predictions of our famous men, who foretold the reconquest of this soil by its legitimate masters; and in this manner, finally, fulfill the will of that good God who bade us give unto Caesar what is of Caesar and to God what is of God."

All these high hopes and profound rancors, wavering between racial assertion and social conciliation, between ancestral pride and Christian mansuetude, and so artlessly argued, sank with Guerrero, however, and were heard no more in the land until they were revived in 1848 by the rise in Oaxaca of another blood-brother, about whom his people gathered to claim him as their cacique and to appeal to the atavistic promptings of his blood. The temptation might have been great, had it not been misleading. He answered their plea, precisely as Providence answers the prayers of men, in ways which they do not recognize, not by special favor or land reforms or racial vindication, but by promoting their assimilation into the community, raising the general level of life, and trusting that the benefits would seep down to the bottom and redeem his token peso.

That level was his whole system of government. Education, of which he was so outstanding an example, lay close to his heart, and here he held out his hand to his people. "Myself a son of the people, I shall not forget them," he repeated at his second inaugural. "On the contrary, I shall provide for their education and see that they grow and make a future for themselves and forsake the career of poverty, vice, and disorder to which they have been reduced by men who only in words have called themselves their friends and liberators and in practice have proved their most cruel oppressors." He was as good as his word. Popular education was the branch of government in which he made the most progress, spreading it into the rural districts, adding fifty new schools to the four hundred and seventy-five already in existence, subsidizing the Institute and establishing two branches of it in the back country, and fostering the education of women as an indispensable part of the whole system. "To form women," he insisted, "with all the qualifications required by their necessary and lofty mission is to form the fertile seed of social regeneration and improvement."

That he fell short of the mark, however, he was the first to recognize, and in his reports to the legislature he insisted again and again on the fallacy of considering education as a popular panacea and the cause of his shortcomings. "That cause is the poverty of the people. The man who lacks the wherewithal to feed his family considers the education of his children a very remote benefit or an obstacle to providing their daily bread. If that man had some advantages, if his daily labor were of some little value to him, he would provide his children with solid instruction in some one of the branches of human knowledge. The desire to learn and improve is innate in the heart of man. Relieve him of the fetters which poverty and despotism impose on him, and he will awaken naturally, even without direct protection."

If education was not to be a fetish or a cure-all, what was the remedy? Not revolution, but road building. "I find that the sources of this poverty are easy to destroy. Let us facilitate our communications with foreign parts and with the other states of this Republic, opening our ports and our roads; let us allow fruits and effects of prime necessity, of common utility, and even of luxury, to enter without charge or check, and we shall have accomplished everything." A program of public works was undertaken for this purpose. In this direction his advance was marked by two milestones, the rehabilitation of an abandoned port on the Pacific coast and the building of a highroad to Tehuacan. The latter was abandoned for lack of funds to complete it; but the road to the Pacific was pushed through amid a remarkable display of public spirit. The parish priests co-operated with the local authorities and recruited volunteers all along the way; the peons built the road of their redemption in return for exemption from military service; and prosperous individuals shouldered a share of the costs.

It was a proud day when the port of Huatluco was opened, not the least sign of progress being the presence of the clergy assembled to bless the occasion. Mass was sung in the open, under the heavens overhead and not underfoot, and the official reporter struck a lyrical note in describing the supreme moment when "for the first time in almost three hundred years the Blessed Host was again raised in this place, and in sight of the sea, which in admirable calm seemed to render adoration and respect to the Author of Nature. Jesus Christ Himself made His power to shine upon it." Like pioneers on a peak in Darien, marveling at the illimitable prospects opening before them, the little group of official sightseers surveyed the dazzling scene, and no one noticed what a landmark the Governor had already passed in breaking through the isolation of the Church from civic service. For such works there was no amazement to spare: they were taken for granted. On the same day a church and a school were simultaneously consecrated on the shores of the sounding Pacific, and on his return to Oaxaca the Governor was congratulated by the Bishop and the Chapter on his "characteristic efficiency" in completing an advance with which they gladly associated themselves.

Besides mountains and roadbeds, however, there were other obstacles to be overcome in opening Oaxaca to the world. The antiquated and strangling system of internal customs, dating back to the days of the colony, was one which, despite his repeated appeals for free trade, he was unable to remove. But within the limits laid down by tradition and inertia he continued to persevere, cultivating every patch of the possible. In an agricultural state, paralyzed by the prolonged depression that followed the American war, he introduced rotation of crops, supplementing the flagging staples of cotton and corn with tobacco, and revived the mining industry by the foundation of a local mint, blocked by a foreign concession, after prolonged pressure on the Federal government. His failures and his advances were in the nature of feelers, tentative and groping, which fell short of the goal but which he irrepressibly renewed. The constant attention he gave to economic progress in his official reports testified to his concern with material improvements as the only alternative to social friction; and the most sensitive index of his progress was his financial record.

When he assumed office in 1847, the resources of the state were exhausted; when he retired in 1852, the deficit had been almost extinguished; and a favorable balance would have been shown but for unforeseen charges incurred in suppressing military revolts—the inevitable accompaniment of a return to normal conditions—and in combating an epidemic of cholera morbus. Acts of God and man could be discounted, however, when a government's record is judged by the average, and the average was high. The state was solvent. Corruption was attacked at the root. The plague of *empleomanía* gradually yielded, and something like a cure was insensibly accomplished by the simple device of introducing standards of fitness and efficiency into civil service in place of appointments by political favor. Here he was favored, as he knew, by hard times: the spoils of office lost their lure, because there were none. "In any period but one of transition and trial, I would have declined the distinguished honor with which I am overwhelmed, even at the risk of being branded an egotist," he declared when he first assumed office. "But now that power no longer has the attractions and charms that flatter one's self-esteem in days of peace and plenty, now that the resources of the Treasury are exhausted and the bonds of obedience relaxed by our intestine revolts, the first magistracy of the state is no more than an advance post of imminent peril and a heavy burden, which offers nothing but vigils, fatigue, and bitter fruits."

He had nothing else to offer his subordinates then or thereafter, and economy, discipline, efficiency, were impressed on them by an example which silenced complaint. Punctually at nine every morning the clerks set their clocks by his appearance at the Palace, and the long laborious hours passed in unremitting industry, the whole force keeping pace with the timekeeper. The old casual incompetence of the past, the sociable heel-swinging, the interdepartmental chats, the official idleness which relieved the tedium of official activity, the time out for under-pay, were curtailed to keep in the grace of the taskmaster. A bu-reaucracy reorganized under stiff qualifications and adequate wages acquired a new sense of civil service from a manager who made the machine run, and for the first time in many decades of rule and misrule the community had the novel experience of being actually governed. If he had accomplished nothing else, he would have deserved well of his country, but he would have passed into history as a master bureau-crat. He managed, however, to turn out innovations possible only under a completely nonpartisan administration. His willingness to em-ploy men of all parties was a source of strength, the coefficient of his own weakness in serving any administration in the past. His very timeserving bore fruit: he was a safe man, and as such he was able to rally public support and conduct it toward goals which remained un-suspected until they had been passed. The changes which he intro-duced would have been refused to a professed radical and were not recognized as inroads into established order, for they left accepted institutions untouched and skirted insurmountable obstacles. He at-tempted nothing impossible; but slowly pressing forward what was possible, he steadily enlarged the limits of the feasible.

All this was accomplished by the simplest and most obvious methods. There was nothing radical, or spectacular, or original in the periodic statements which he made to the public on work in progress: nothing but elementary sense and homely morality. Neither his program nor his record was revolutionary, and doctrinaire radicals of a later day have attacked it on that score. In particular, they have been scandal-ized by his relations with the Church. These were of the most orthodox character, as the correspondence that passed between them, stamped on the one hand "Government of the State of Oaxaca" and "Ecclesias-tical Government of Oaxaca" on the other, constantly recognized; and they were governed by the conciliatory policy imposed on him by the nature of his task. Progress, even in the modest measure which he proposed, would have been impossible had he antagonized the ecclesi-astical power; it was greatly facilitated by the collaboration of the Church in every important phase of his advance. The other government responded when he called for cannon and patriotic sermons; it responded when the curates mobilized their communities to build his roads; it responded by sanctioning his seaport and bestowing its blessings on his own; it responded by supplying teachers for his colleges in the Sierra; it responded, above all, during the epidemic of cholera by providing hospital facilities and nursing and shelter for the stricken; it responded, it responded, it responded to all the changes rung on it; and the result was to restore the Church to its original function and to revive something of the faded glory with which it had performed its evangelical mission in the strenuous days of the founding of the colony, before the zeal of sowing civilization had been corrupted by success and forgotten in the fatty degeneration of inactivity and sloth.

The association was of mutual benefit to both governments, and the Church gained in moral prestige by the stimulation of its dormant energies, even when the flush of health was quickened by friction. For friction there occasionally was, and at such times the Governor met the challenge by recalling the spiritual power to its high responsibilities. Provoked by the refusal of a confraternity to permit him to convert an unused wing of their convent into a workshop for convicts whom he wished to rehabilitate, he forced the issue and carried it to the public. "Society," he said, "and civilization will place the blame where it belongs." Society as God, the manifestation of the Creator in the creation of man, was not yet a creed which he professed consciously; but he worked on it consistently, within the limits and with the compromises imposed by social convention. For, of course, there was an obverse to the medal. The co-operation of the Church carried a price—and he paid it. Such concessions as he made to convention were usually of a formal and ceremonial character. When the cholera struck Oaxaca, he led religious processions through the streets and attended solemn services of intercession in the Cathedral—perfunctory compliances with custom cruelly derided by one of his critics as crass catering to superstitious practices; but when religious and sanitary observances conflicted, he set a different example. In deference to one of the Reform Laws of Gomez Farias, forbidding interment in churches—a law nullified "by prejudice to the detriment of public health"—he buried one of his children whom he lost in the plague in the public cemetery. Sometimes, however, he carried complaisance so far as to enforce ecclesiastical censure of a prohibited book. But the most serious of these accommodations was the support which he lent the other government in the collection of parochial obventions, a convention which he justified by appealing to statute and custom and demonstrating, with a great display of Seminary learning, the legitimacy of the claims of the clergy, "since as cultivators of the vine, they must feed on its fruits, and as laborers in the spiritual sphere, they are entitled to sustenance in the temporal." The words literally reproduced those of the Governor from whom he had parted three years before over that very issue; but "a democratic and eminently liberal system, such as that which now governs us," he declared, "is based on a strict observance of the law. Neither the caprice of one man nor the interests of certain classes of society form its essence . . . the most profound respect and observance of the law reveals the character of the true liberal, of the best republican." The publicans approved. The circular stating his position, stamped with the official formula, "God and Liberty," was gratefully acknowledged by the Bishop of Oaxaca, who concurred in all its conclusions, professed his faith in the Federal system, which, "as conducted by the sure and efficient hand of Your Excellency, is capable of leading us to felicity," and repeated his approval of roads and ports, "which I shall second for my part by repeating to the parishes in the mountains my advice to aid in so important a work." If the price was high, so was that of road-breaking.

"In all that has been published under the signature of Juarez from his birth until 1859," says his critic, "there is not one word to prove that his mind projected great social transformations. There is nothing in him that reveals the ideas of a revolutionary, the temperament of a reformer, the philosophy of a missionary of any great cause. On the contrary, following the development of his thought in his writings in Oaxaca (if they are his, for he was never very brilliant), one feels the placid movement of his official ideas, the apathy of his conscience, devoid of all rancor against the past, its monuments and its institutions. For Juarez there is no need of reforms in the State Constitution, nor in Federalism, nor, far less, in religion or the perfect union of Church and State. Whatever exists at that historic moment is good, whatever is rising is worthy of respect. All that the Oaxaqueños need to be happy is to cease their dissensions, to love one another, to unite in the good and the beautiful here and now, and to recognize the plain and easy duty that bids them never to disturb the peace for any reason whatsoever, and to be ready to give their lives when the country is in danger of foreign invasion. . . . Juarez reached the age of forty-six without being more than a good man, an amiable bureaucrat with patriarchal leanings, an affectionate sheep much attached to his wool in the flock of the Good Shepherd. . . . His mind was mediocre, his education insignificant, and hence instead of being ahead of his time he was to be one of its most conspicuous mollusks."

Ahead of his time he was not; he kept pace with it punctually. On the question of ecclesiastical tithes he marked time. That it was a sore point he admitted by arguing it; and that it was a weak one by the reasons which he adduced for his ruling: the "continued complaints" of the curates, the "resistance or sullenness of the flock to pay," and the sanctity of the law, which, if it covered his responsibility as an official, was a feeble defense for moral evasion of a vital issue. While he refused to countenance abuses, he also refused to countenance evasions of the parochial rates, and though he attempted to induce the ecclesiastical authorities themselves to regulate them, he left the correction of irregularities to their discretion. The curates of Loricha triumphed, in fact, all along the line. The battle given and the pledge taken by Juarez over that issue so many years before, the dim revelation of a revolutionary mission awaiting him, the conviction that society could never prosper by the alliance of the public powers and the privileged classes, the resolution to eradicate their complicity when his time came, and the token peso and the promise to his people when he came to power—all were compromised by the triumph of social conciliation, the *status quo,* and superiority to class hatred, which left the system intact and the little foxes free to feed on the vine. And by a cruel coincidence, while he bestowed his blessing on the curates of Loricha who worked within the law, the pulse of the time was beginning to quicken, and his stationary position was sharply accentuated by an incident which occurred beyond the borders of his state and which struck the changing hour.

In Michoacan the same issue was agitated in 1851 by a bitter controversy between a country curate and an ex-Governor of the state, Don Melchor Ocampo. The origin of the quarrel was a small and commonplace incident. The curate refused burial to a body which in life had been that of a penniless peon and in death belonged to a widow who could pay neither the legal nor the illegal rates for interring it; and when it became necessary for sanitary reasons to dispose of the remains, he did so by a bad joke, advising her to salt and eat what was left of her late bedfellow. The case came to the notice of Ocampo, who paid the fees but did not let the offense rest until he had brought it to public attention and made it the base of a petition to the legislature to regulate and reform the whole system of parochial obventions. Thereupon the curate rushed into print. The ensuing controversy went far beyond personal polemics and the bounds of the state, and in the course of it Ocampo made a national name for himself.

So common an instance of clerical callousness and rapacity would have passed unnoticed, had it not excited the crusading zeal of a superior character. Melchor Ocampo was a great landowner and a philanthropist who took a quixotic interest in the living conditions of his peons, and for him it was no small incident that pitted the subsistence of the poor against the subsistence of the priest. The priest took the same view of it; and both carried the dispute to its logical conclusion. The antagonists were ill matched: on the one hand, a pillar of society, a man of property with a distinguished political record as deputy, senator, and governor of his state; and on the other, a country curate. But the curate, cornered and fighting for his livelihood, was more than a match for his opponent in the conditions in which they fought. When the consequences of his little joke became serious, the curate became serious and a pillar of society himself. The reform of parochial obventions was not a minor, nor a local, nor a lay issue: it involved the very constitution of the Church and touched the heart of its organization. A blow to the meanest of its members was a blow to the whole mystic body of Christ, and the curate, hard-pressed and resourceful, rose to the challenge in his corporate character, denying the right of the State to invade the sovereignty of the Church, and raising at once the untouchable question of the relations of the two powers. "Reformers," he wrote, "know very well that the favorite method of attacking the Church is to impoverish the clergy. Away with abuses, they begin by saying, and then away with the ministers, and away with the Church. . . . Let Michoacan see whither Señor Ocampo is unwittingly leading it: to *freedom of faith* and *freedom of conscience,* two programs as impious as they are fatal, and that serve as the standard of socialism in Europe. If, as a scourge of God, they should succeed in settling among us, it is certain that universal destruction would be our end."

Ocampo's curate was of the same genus as the curate of Loricha, but not of the same species. A Liberal before he entered holy orders, he combined the zeal of a convert with the mentality of a renegade and the guilt of a turncoat fighting for his livelihood, and knew how to protect it by playing on the fears of the propertied classes on whom his self-preservation depended. He spread the alarm to the laity, pointing to the danger of a social upheaval in the backwash of the American war, and letting his tongue run to great lengths. "And what shall we say, sir, if it is not the barbarians that rob us, but the hungry masses of Mexicans whom we have among us, and who are the victims of the misfortunes of the country, because of a well-nigh total lack of markets for their former products? These masses may say to justify their depredations: 'Our industry is no more, we labor in vain, and a vain labor must be abandoned, but in the meanwhile we must not perish, the other classes must maintain us, and if they refuse we shall use force. Our methods will be the natural promptings of self-preservation. . . . Hand over those properties, hand over those treasures, hand over those estates. . . . Why is there such inequality in possessions? Why such abundance for some and such poverty for others? Why must our degradation serve to nourish the welfare of the mighty?' . . . These, Señor Ocampo, are but a small part of the pestilential doctrines that derive from your false reasoning."

Ocampo indignantly denied the revolutionary implications of his petition, himself shocked by them. "No one until now has ventured to publish anything so dangerous in Mexico," he retorted. But the appeal to the fears of his class was not lost, and he contributed to them by broadening the scope of the discussion himself and dwelling on the conditions of the peons and the debt slavery which bound them to the great estates as well as to the Church. The inequality of the contest was not on the side of the curate: he counted on the whole weight of the community, while Ocampo engaged it singlehanded. The contest ended in a draw, but it was a test of strength which attracted the attention of the country, and when it was over Ocampo was a marked man —marked by the curate for a bad end, marked by the conservatives as a dangerous crank, marked by the radicals as a man on whom they could rely to fight their battles for them.

The legislature took no more action on the petition to regulate parochial obventions in Michoacan than the Church did in Oaxaca, but the fact that Ocampo raised the issue was sufficient to quicken the pulse of the time. His skirmish with the curate of Maravatio produced a reaction among the conservative classes, whose dread of social disorders following the American war was still acute four years after its end because of the prolonged economic slump of the country, and the word socialism, because of events occurring abroad during that period, increased their insecurity and led them to take precautions for their protection to which, two years later, both Ocampo and Juarez fell victim. The same law, and the same sentence, overtook a marked man like Ocampo and a safe one like Juarez, sweeping together two men widely separated in revolutionary standing and temperament, and the reasons for their common fate were not fortuitous: they were the outcome of the movement of political life during the years following the American war carried to a point where the alternative of revolution or counter-revolution became inescapable, and the middle way was eliminated.

9

THE nation was long in recovering from the shock of the American war. In its wake came not only an economic but a moral depression that was severe and prolonged. Materially mutilated by the dismemberment of its territory, morally shattered by the demonstration of internal debility, the Republic recoiled upon itself in a double defeat; and the second was a worse disaster than the first. The physical liquidation of the war cost the country almost half its original heritage, California, Arizona, and New Mexico being the fine for forfeiting Texas, and the price was paid in national pride. From that shock the nation never recovered: its subsequent history was governed by a morbid complex of feelings—humiliation, hatred, fear, a rankling sense of inferiority, an incurable loss of self-confidence—that settled in the public mind with the force of an obsession and made patriotism pathological. The first effect of this state of mind was a complete prostration of public life; there was a prolonged pause, and it was part of the slow process of readjustment that action gave way to reflection and heart-searching, and the first symptoms of recovery took the form of self-criticism. It was time, it was high time, to stop and take thought and determine the causes of so crushing a disaster; and public-minded men who had tried and failed to make the history of their country turned to writing it.

Two major versions were presented to the public: the Liberal diagnosis of Dr. Mora, whose work, written ten years before, only now began to be generally read, and the Conservative analysis of Lucas Alaman, which was produced under the impact of the American war. Antithetical in their doctrines, there were fundamental affinities, nevertheless, between the ideas of the two historians and a significant parallel in their careers. Each had served a brief apprenticeship in practical politics, followed by a long and melancholy retirement, and each wrote his autobiography in the guise of Mexican history.

As a young man, Lucas Alaman made a brilliant debut in politics as minister and mentor to one of the early presidents of the Republic, but he was turned out of office by the coalition of Gomez Farias and Santa Anna in 1833, and his debut was distinguished by the fact that it was followed by no career. Discouraged by his first reverse, he forsook public life for the study and devoted the next fifteen years to the cultivation of his fortune and his ideas, which, based as both were on the stability of the traditional order, or at most on its slow and peaceful evolution, were repeatedly shocked by the violent developments of the years between the birth of Reform and the breakdown caused by the American war. A veteran amateur in 1833, he was an inveterate one in 1847. In the interval he collected material for a history of his country and began to write it, but the pace of events overtook him, and when the American war threatened to annihilate his subject, the history emerged, under pressure, full grown.

Appearing on the morrow of the debacle, the History of Alaman recapitulated the History of Mexico in a spirit exactly suited to the sober temper and the dull headache of the morning after a long debauch. His aim, he said, was to be accurate, objective, and impartial; but that was the statement of an aim and the delusion of an amateur. Actually his History was colored by conscious class bias, and its conspicuous features were a dominating preoccupation with property, the timidity that derives from it, and an intense search for security. With less reticence than is common with writers of his school, he wrote: "An essential condition for the perfect enjoyment of any possession is the certainty of enjoying it forever." And starting from this premise, he plotted the course of history accordingly. "You ask me what effect the publication of my History of Mexico and the Dissertation has had in Mexico," he wrote to a Spanish grandee whose estates in Mexico he administered. "The effect has been to change completely the idea held, as a result of revolutionary statements, about the Conquest, the Spanish domination, and the manner in which Independence was achieved. The Conquest was believed to be a real robbery, and hence your possessions were regarded as part of the theft, the nation entitled to recover them. . . . All this has been completely changed; you have only to see some of the speeches this year in which the Conquest is presented as the means by which civilization and religion were established in the country and Don Hernan Cortés as a remarkable man, appointed by Providence to accomplish these objects. . . . The advantages to you are obvious, since this has affected the odium with which your name and property were regarded and has secured you in their possession."

Himself a Creole aristocrat and hence not very far removed from his employer, Alaman deplored the course which Independence had taken in the hands of Hidalgo. He had grown up with the movement and was still haunted by the war cry against the *gachupines*—"a cry of death and desolation, which, after hearing it a thousand times in the first days of my youth, still rings in my ears with a terrifying echo!" Hidalgo was an incompetent visionary, whom he scolded for initiating a revolution which he could not control, rousing the rabble with the lure of plunder, and compelling the Creoles who would otherwise have joined it to combine against it, so that "the war became, not a struggle between those who wanted independence and those who opposed it, but the natural defense of those who did not wish to be despoiled of their property, against those who, following the direction which Hidalgo gave the revolution, had no other aim than to rob everyone to the tune of independence. . . . "No!" he concluded. "If independence could not be promoted by other methods, it should never have been attempted."

He preferred to date Independence from Iturbide, but when he scanned the years that followed it, his heart failed him. The grim and unrelenting progress of anarchy and impoverishment which they revealed was too much to stomach; and before attempting an account of those years he gave up and cursed the day on which his country was born. "This terrible Revolution, nevertheless, is what it has been sought to make the Mexican Republic recognize as its cradle," he exclaimed. "Divine Providence seems to have wished to inflict an exemplary punishment for that solemnity when it permitted, in the year 1847, in the very days in which I write these lines, the army of the United States, of that nation to which Mexicans looked in the beginning of their liberation as a natural friend and ally, to occupy the capital on the 14th of September and to wreak, and to allow the people to wreak, a terrible sack on the 15th and 16th, as if in reminder and imitation of the one Hidalgo made in Dolores and San Miguel on that same date." Trusting that a time would come when good sense would prevail over prejudice, and the original begetters of Independence would be recognized as the authors of all the evils of the country, he ended his account of the insurgent period despondently. "In the next volume we shall see other men, of different capacities and greater courage and fortune, follow the career that Hidalgo began with such ill success." But Alaman carried the history of Mexico no further. The next volume was life.

He returned to politics, flushed with the heat of battle among the shadows and insecure of success over the dead, to write the History of Alaman across the History of Mexico in one brief but remarkable page. The case of Alaman was the case of Mexico—an acute attack of heart failure—and he devoted himself to the recovery of his country with the knowledge he had acquired as an historian of their common infirmity. The cure was forecast in the arrested development of Volume One, in his nostalgia for the mother country and the characteristic craving of a class incapable of independence, and worsted by life, to return to the womb; since that was impossible, he could only approximate it in Volume Two. The cure was unpopular, and even the approximation required long and careful preparation; and he laid down the pen with the words: "If my work should have the effect of making the coming generation more cautious than the present one, I might flatter myself that I had produced the greatest benefit that can result from the study of history."

It would be too much to say that Alaman wrote his History to recommend that of his rival, though that was perhaps its most important result; but he did recommend the work of Dr. Mora to his friends, and not merely from professional generosity. After the collapse of his political debut in 1834, Dr. Mora had also passed into eclipse. The next twelve years of his life were spent in Paris, in exile and obscurity. Suffering from every kind of privation, secluded by a poverty that began by being genteel and that became monastic because it could not be bohemian, and that degenerated into such bare need that he begged the Legation for work at the wages of a menial; wasted by consumption and homesickness; subsisting on small remittances from his friends in Mexico; starving for the company of his intellectual equals and refusing that of his inferiors; solitary, proud, and fastidious, he was driven in on his mental resources, which were rich but unrewarding. In 1837 a French publisher brought out the first part of a projected work on *Mexico and Its Revolutions,* and in the following year a small sheaf of his *Collected Works,* both abandoned for lack of sale. These two fragments, which comprised the whole of his literary output, found no public in Paris, where the revolutions of Mexico were as remote as those of Saturn as a topic of popular interest; and none in Mexico, where the phenomena were too familiar to merit attention, save from a small circle of connoisseurs, particularly his political opponents, and above all from Alaman, who gave them the respectful attention due to a member of his class who had deserted it. For Dr. Mora had been born into the Creole aristocracy and, despite his radical views, retained one of its privileges—authority. The critical success which he won in 1838 remained the secret of a coterie, however, until the crisis of the American war led to a general reassessment of the past. Then his work was rediscovered and read as the Liberal antidote to the theses of Alaman and his party.

In their methods the two men had something in common. Alaman set himself an ideal of sobriety and moderation and was determined to be scrupulously scientific and impartial; but in practice his prepossessions violated his principles, and even when he observed them he produced an account of the Independence movement which depreciated and falsified it. The result was tame—a tone of flat and perfunctory justice, devoid of the sympathy and insight essential to the truth, and an estimate based on an obvious fallacy: a dispassionate account of any revolution was bound to misrepresent it. Dr. Mora made no such mistakes. He did not pretend to write history impartially; but he did write it scientifically. His habits of mind were analytical, and his logic, his objectivity, and his conscientiousness gave his work genuine weight and detachment; and his measure and sobriety were the result of judgment and experience, not of a covert desire to depreciate. Of revolution he wrote as a revolutionary, retired but not in retreat, and undismayed by the brute facts that alarmed Alaman; he never forgot that his country was condemned by its very origin to a revolutionary growth. Writing, moreover, against a European background, he brought to bear on his subject a universal perspective, a grasp of historical processes, and a capacity for broad and fundamental generalizations, in overwhelming contrast to the parochial bias that cramped the judgment of his rival. Time and distance had confirmed and sharpened his convictions; but they had also refined and qualified them and made him so discriminating in their application that at times his ideas seemed to touch those of his opponents, and thus it was that he could be read with appreciation by Alaman. A successful antidote contains, after all, an effective dose of the original virus; and the vaccine supplied by Dr. Mora was no exception.

Mora was still the reformer bent on completing the emancipation of Mexico, and his history was a militant analysis of the miscarriage of the Independence movement. Believing no less absolutely than Alaman in the sanctity of property, he deplored the looting and carnage of the uprising, but put them promptly in their place. "The revolution which broke out in 1810 was as necessary for the attainment of Independence as it was pernicious and destructive to the country," he argued, because it was indispensable to interest the popular classes in the insurrection, and this could not be done by the sole promise of remote and unknown benefits to follow, or by abstract ideas of justice. "It was necessary to cater to the prejudices of the multitude in order to secure their co-operation." Hidalgo he judged as severely as Alaman did, because he had failed to plan the result for which he was responsible—the gravest charge that a systematic ideologist like Mora could bring against the first begetter of that chaos which he called his country. What prejudiced the whole subsequent history of Mexico, however, was not the beginning but the end of the movement, which had left the social structure of the colony intact and its correction to future generations, themselves unprepared for the task. Under the name of a republic there had emerged something incompatible with it, or with public spirit, or patriotism, or national life—a corporate state. Whether by accident or design, Spain had bequeathed to its offspring the feudal infirmity from which it suffered—a tendency to create corporations, to accumulate upon them privileges and exemptions from the common law, to enrich them with donations from living or testamentary legacies, and to endow them, in short, with every requisite for independence. Not only the Church and the Army, but the Inquisition, the Universities, the Mint, the *Majorats,* the Confraternities, and even the Guilds, had their privileges, property, and corporate existence; and the mentality which they bred was fatal to national life and prosperity, public peace and morality, and judicial and administrative order. Had Independence been achieved forty years earlier, a man born in the territory would have attached no value to the name of "Mexican" and would have considered himself completely alone in the world, if he had nothing else to support him: his interests and his loyalties lay with the body, or bodies, to which he belonged; and this habit still subsisted. As Mora said, when social conscience or civil authority conflict with the *esprit de corps,* "the principal aim is to vindicate the corporation, to establish its exclusive jurisdiction, and to depress the civil authority. If these purposes can be reconciled with the punishment of the criminal and the observance of the criminal and penal laws, no obstacle is raised to the one or the other, but if, as frequently happens, the course of justice is, or is believed to be, in opposition to the corporate interests, the former will infallibly be sacrificed to the latter." And the damage to the civil authority did not end with moral disabilities, to which men adapt themselves easily. "The greatest obstacle against which the prosperity of nations has to contend is the tendency to interdict, accumulate, and unite lands and capitals eternally. From the day that society allows a given fortune to accumulate indefinitely, with no need of dividing it, it is clear that nothing is needed but the passage of a few centuries for the means of subsistence to become very difficult or fail entirely for the mass. The result is solely and exclusively due to *political corporations,* and a nation in which they succeed in multiplying or, even though they be few, in spreading throughout society, has already broached the abyss in which the public fortune is certain to be lost."

Independence, then, had produced a corporate state which tolerated and controlled the civil authority, and which was the negation of national life. The epitome of the whole system was the Church, which had created a theocratic state within the nominal one, and which Mora indicted, count by count, as an antisocial body by its constitution: because the clergy were composed "of men who are only materially in society and in accidental co-existence with their fellow citizens"; because they were educated to value none but heavenly interests and to identify them with the supremacy of their corporation; because by their celibacy they were without the bond of family, "the first and principal tie of man to society"; because they were forbidden to engage in lucrative enterprises, "and thus are extinguished the love of labor and the betterment of fortune which are the necessary consequence of individual industry and which create the second link with society"; because of their invincible aversion to religious toleration and freedom of thought and of the press, since these principles weaken their hold upon consciences; because of their opposition to legal equality," which eliminates their privileges and hierarchies and the power and consideration which these confer on their class"; because they were a permanent obstacle to the increase of population by defeating foreign immigration, lest it carry the germ of religious toleration; because of the monopoly and sterilization of the national resources, which they controlled and immobilized; and because their monopoly of education was responsible for the ignorance not only of the masses but, more important, of the classes. Here Dr. Mora spoke from bitter experience. He recalled, with the same horror with which Alaman remembered the vandalism of the insurgents, the years of his youth, which he had spent in the College of San Ildefonso. Here he had won honors and knowledge and had seen the effect on the average mind of an education which unfitted the ruling classes for their functions, because its unworldly character debauched them for life. "He who has been educated in a College has seen with his own eyes that, of all that has been told and taught him there, little or nothing is applicable to the uses of ordinary life; that the latter lies under other laws, which are unknown to him, of which no one has spoken to him, and the foundations of which are those common and ordinary needs that are never made the subject of study but are abandoned to *routine*. . . . This is the origin of the charlatanism of Mexico and of the people who have undertaken to govern it, graduates for the most part of our College. Accustomed to talk of improvements merely to display what are called their talents, and never attempting to realize them since they hold them to be ideal and impossible, they cling to the routine which, whether good or bad, is what has served them as a rule of practical conduct."

So, foreshortened, Dr. Mora traced the history of Mexico during his time, but he was not dismayed by his findings. He reiterated the prescriptions of his original program: confiscation of Church property, abolition of clerical and military privileges, diffusion of secular education among the popular classes, suppression of nunneries, absolute freedom of opinion, and equal civil rights for natives and foreigners. But if he retracted nothing and disavowed nothing, he did qualify and refine some of his leading ideas. Confounded himself by the incompetence of his countrymen, which he had so lucidly demonstrated, he found himself asking how far liberty was compatible with equality. "The mischievous meaning given to the principle of *legal equality* has almost always been the source of innumerable disappointments and pernicious results among those peoples that have adopted the representative system. The greatest of the evils caused in our Republic by this dangerous and fateful word has lain in the scandalous profusion with which we have lavished political rights, extending them to the lowest classes of society. . . . To restore the political structure, Congress should determine the conditions for exercising the rights of citizenship throughout the Republic, and these should exclude all those who can inspire no confidence: that is, the non-proprietors. . . . As a general rule, the owners of property alone have genuine civic virtues; beneficence, dignity of person and manners, love of the public good, are virtually the exclusive attributes of property-owners. . . ."

So wrote Mora, and not Alaman. Such a formula for freedom was not very alarming to his Conservative opponents who could read him, as they did, with the calm assurance that, despite his radicalism in some directions, he was essentially sound. And to the Liberal youth who turned to him as an antidote for Alaman it was sobering to find the lifelong enthusiast for freedom reducing liberty to a privilege, available to anyone who could put up a bond for it, and denied to those who lacked the necessary property qualifications.

Nor was this the only sobering conclusion of his History. For the heirs of the Mexican revolution he had some cooling reflections to make on the cost of revolution. Revolutions had their own routine. He drew a didactic distinction between those which arose from a direct cause and produced an immediate effect—"these are the fortunate revolutions: people know what they want, all move toward a

recognized aim, and when it is attained everything returns to rest"—
the English and American revolutions, for example; and those "that
derive from a general movement in the spirit of nations. By the turn
that opinions take, men tire of being what they are, the prevailing
order irks them in every way, their minds become suffused with an
extraordinary ardor and activity; everyone feels dissatisfied with the
place which he occupies and longs to change his condition, but no one
knows precisely what he wants, and everything resolves itself into discontent and unrest. Such are the symptoms of those long crises to
which no direct and exact cause can be assigned . . . and which would
be an endless chain of disasters, revolutions, and crimes if chance, and,
even more than chance, general exhaustion, did not bring them to a
close"—the French Revolution for example—a warning example for
Mexico, which derived its inspiration from it. "An impatience all the
more hasty in its attacks that it is vague in its desires is what produced
the first upheaval. . . . Everyone abandons himself to that sensation
without reserve or remorse. Everyone supposes that the equilibrium of
society is so firmly grounded that nothing can destroy it and forgets
that the interests and opinions of the many cannot be fermented with
impunity." Anarchy, and the natural ferocity of man, make short work
of the brief boast of civilization, "and then it is that fearlessness of
judgment begins to weaken, the dread of deceiving oneself increases,
and the confidence with which one risked everything on the frail securities of human reason ceases. But before these saving deceptions
come, one must pass through all the succession of calamities that *idealism* brings with it."

The brute realities of revolution alarmed him no less than Alaman,
when its scope could no longer be localized, limited, and controlled,
when purpose and plan were dissolved in indefinite restlessness, when
the partial dislocation of society threatened the whole, when the safeguards of reason and the tight system of idealists were swept away by
the relentless momentum of nature, and the revolution became, in a
word, a revolution of Saturn. Then Mora found himself facing a void
in which the heavenly bodies and the celestial corporations overhead,
and the corporate state and the state of nature below, were all beyond
control; and his heart failed him. The very vagueness of his words revealed the vertigo with which he contemplated such convulsions.
Clinging to the confines of his world, he traced with undisguised dismay the phases of the French Revolution in a long downward spiral:
from the philanthropists who began it, to the doctrinaires who followed them, to the cranks repeating "literally and without social modifications what certain books say about 'liberty' and 'equality,'" down
to the parvenus who parroted and the idealists who depraved them,
down to the fanatics and the freethinkers, whose errors were excusable
because they were blind to their spawn, down to the self-seekers, the

cynics, the demagogues, to the Terror, to the Reaction. "When matters have come to this point," the homily ended, "and men have grown weary of suffering, they profit by any favorable opportunity to bring about a change, and then things recede by the same stages but in reverse order. Happy the people that does not return to its point of departure, for then, without having bettered its condition in any way, it will have had to pass through all the horrors of a revolution."

What was this? a caveat or a confession? the morphology of revolutions or of Dr. Mora? Had he carried the History of Mexico as far as the History of Mora could go? Had the clear-sighted scientist finally been baffled by his vision of revolutionary routine, and forsaken the dictates of reason for the promptings of fatality? His counsel was clear, his state of mind ambiguous. The oracular utterance was open to any interpretation, and his work was crowned by the tongueless mask of tragedy. If this was his last word, a Conservative might well mistake it for a retraction; while the Liberals might equally feel that the labors of Mora, like those of Alaman, were addressed to the coming generation as a caution.

But neither man had spoken his last word when he laid down the pen. In 1847, when Gomez Farias returned to power for a few months, Mora was appointed Minister to London. In this war post—for in the crisis of American invasion it was such—he was called upon to defend his country against another foreign danger, the English debt.

This question was as old as Independence, and a growing mortgage upon it. The origin of the nation and of the debt were so closely related, indeed, as to be inseparable: both were the settlement of old scores with Spain. Spain paid for her part in promoting the revolt of the British colonies in North America when her own empire broke up, for British diplomacy was everywhere directed to aiding, abetting, and promoting the movements of secession in her colonies in the southern hemisphere. "I have called a new world into being," Canning boasted, taking a leaf out of Genesis and fanning himself with it. Though he took no part in the emancipation of Mexico, he extended his protection to the infant Republic when it was threatened by the Holy Alliance, and his was the first foreign government to recognize it—favors that were followed by the contraction of the debt. Two loans were floated in London to enable the new nation to begin life and to open a new market and a fresh sphere of influence for English trade, investment, and enterprise. The money sank into the quicksands of Mexican politics. Ten years passed before the mines, into which British capital was pumped, could be restored; trade languished under high protective tariffs, which fostered nothing but contraband; political turbulence and instability cooled the confidence of English investors.

The benefits evaporated, the obligation remained; and the debt accumulated under periodic conversions, which afforded only a fleeting relief to one party and growing irritation to the other, while successive administrations in Mexico ignored the liability, which each passed on to the next.

The first serious attempt to deal with it was made by Mora and Farias in 1834, when they proposed to liquidate it by confiscating Church property—a measure which failed to materialize but which prompted the clergy to liquidate some of their assets in anticipation of its passage: a nervous financial leak quickly dried by the dismissal of the reformers. "Then it was," Mora wrote, "that the depths of the abyss into which the Republic was insensibly sinking began to be suspected. 'Suspected' is the proper word to describe the state of neglect in which the parliamentary tribune, the public authorities, and the periodic press had left matters requiring urgent settlement and a branch of administration of the foremost and most vital importance." No ordinary resources were available: territorial property was bankrupt, the mines had not yet recovered from the slump in which the Spanish had left them, industry was embryonic, commerce was overtaxed, and the national revenues were overhypothecated. The confiscation of Church property was the only alternative to financial collapse and the abyss at the bottom of which lay blind revolution.

Thirteen years later, when Dr. Mora was called upon to deal with the debt again, the problem remained where he had left it, but in the meanwhile it had been aggravated by neglect and improvidence, and the economic debility of the country had been demonstrated in the two collisions with the United States. These conflicts affected the protector as well as the people of Mexico. Along with the commercial empire of Spain, the English had fallen heir to the fears of its former masters, and when the American war defeated and dismembered a country which British capital had transformed into a virtual dependency of the British empire, the bad debt became a matter of official concern in London, where the credit of Mexico, diplomatic and financial alike, reached a new low.

Dr. Mora saved it. He succeeded in negotiating yet another conversion of the bonds, whose accumulation for over a quarter of a century, and with it of periodic lapses, conversions, and defaults, had given his country a bad name and made its future problematical in the financial center of the world. And the feat was accomplished with nothing more substantial than promises. His success was facilitated, however, by the expectation that some part of the millions which the United States agreed to pay Mexico as indemnity for conquered territory would be applied to the British debt. As the British government by no means desired•the extinction of a claim which guaranteed its control of a dependent people, it was possible for Mora and the creditors to come to an understanding—the soundness of nations being rated, like that of individuals, by the amount of indebtedness they can bear.

By this transaction Dr. Mora benefited as much as Mexico. What his country gained was another reprieve; what he gained was fresh confirmation of the necessity of a radical reform of Mexican economy, if the crisis which he had averted were not to recur in an aggravated form in the future. In the counting-houses of London the historian of Mexico gained a better perspective on his country than in his study in Paris. He was now in a position to supply the element lacking in the philosophical sketch which he had begun and abandoned there, and which was indispensable to complete the account of a feudal colony born into the contemporary world of expanding capitalism and compelled to contend with it for national survival. All the weaknesses which he had analyzed in Paris gained fresh point in London, where they carried their inevitable penalty in the growing drain of foreign debt, foreign exploitation, foreign claims, and the risk of foreign complications based on those titles. Henceforth the history of Mexico had to be written internationally: it could no longer be isolated from the world and studied apart from its context. The American war marked a turning point in its destiny. Until then it had been possible to chronicle it partially and retrospectively: from now on it was necessary to relate it to the future and to chart its course scientifically as part of a comprehensive and developing process common to the whole Western world, where the social and political forces active in any one part excited a sympathetic reaction in every other, because the commonwealth of nations was a corporation controlled by the same economic system, and a nervous complex in which the weakest and most vulnerable members were liable to the most violent reactions. As the world went, so would Mexico go, once it was involved in its movements, and all the more readily because of its remoteness, and all the more blindly because of its backwardness. By 1848 that fact was appreciated even in Mexico.

If 1847 was a grim year for Mexico, 1848 was an alarming one for Europe: the year in which revolutions broke out at one point after another on the Continent with a contagious agitation that seemed to presage another of those epidemics that Dr. Mora dreaded—a general movement in the spirit of nations—an indefinite unrest, uncontrollable urges, and universal subversion—another peevish cycle of Saturn, perhaps. In 1848, however, the symptoms were specific and consistent with a definite disorder, which they revealed in various degrees, ranging from nationalism and the insurrection of oppressed minorities in Italy, Hungary, and Poland to socialism and the insurrection of oppressed masses in France and Germany: recognizable symptoms of a period of expanding capitalism whose promises of freedom inspired the movements of national liberation on the one hand, and whose practices of exploitation provoked popular revolts on the other.

The bearing of these events on Mexico were discussed by Mora and his friends with acute concern. "You are quite right in your observation," one of them wrote, "that because of the excesses which the revolution in Europe has committed, we must fear a reaction that will set things far back again; but I believe that will not happen for some time and not without much trouble and bloodshed. When the peoples are not controlled by a religious principle and respect for the higher classes, and aspire to share or possess the property of the rich, they will not readily give ground." The February revolution in Paris, which overthrew the monarchy of Louis-Philippe at the behest of the bourgeoisie which had created it, only to be transformed by the revolutionary proletariat into the insurrection of June against the middle class, alarmed them particularly. "As soon as I saw that the revolution in France, after destroying the monarchy, threatened property and the family," his correspondent continued, "I feared a reaction. And will not the reaction reach us?"

Precisely. The disorders in France were followed, in fact, by a reflex movement in Mexico, all the more dangerous because resistance was weaker and revolution endemic there. "Here the *Santannists* and the *Puros,* who are our socialists, are making extraordinary efforts to bring about a revolution," Mora was informed—a symptom which would have been insignificant but for the troubles in France, which gave irresponsible politicians and inexperienced reformers a pretext to hitch to foreign issues the casual disorders which were called revolutions in Mexico. The danger lay not in a rising of a revolutionary proletariat, since no such thing existed in Mexico, but in the fear of it which had haunted the upper classes there ever since the days of Hidalgo, and of a reaction to anticipate it.

Symptoms of this tendency appeared with the development of a monarchist party, which had begun to emerge before the American war and which gained momentum after it, when the slump favored two fears upon which the propaganda of the party played: the specter of foreign socialism and the dread of another American invasion if the country relapsed into disorder—both fictitious but sufficient to make them look to Europe for support. Mora was warned by Palmerston that bids were being made in Paris for a pretender, and though they were arrested by the February revolution, the movement was resumed under another name, but with the same latent aims, by a group of conservatives whose mentor was Lucas Alaman. The counterpart of the foreign crisis was already discernible in Mexico, albeit in embryo, and both tendencies bore watching in a defeated and demoralized country peculiarly susceptible to the promptings of postwar revolution and counterrevolution. Their morbid significance was recognized by Mora and his friends. "As for our internal questions, all of them founded on the basis of nationality," they warned him, "there are two parties which are fortifying themselves in silence and which tend, one to a foreign monarchy and the other to aggregation to the United States; and what seems incredible, both these parties derive from the same idea, our inability to govern ourselves."

Once again his friends turned to Mora for guidance. His position in London was a post of observation which commanded a broad view of the world and a clearing-house of accurate information where he could detect at once the connection between a commotion on one side of the water and its seemingly unrelated counterpart on the other. But his friends placed him in a cruel predicament. For socialism he had no sympathy; if a reaction provoked by it threatened to set things far back in Europe, how much further would a similar movement carry them in a backward country like Mexico! To press his radical ideas in the treacherous situation prevailing there after the American war, at the risk of foreign complications and an incalculable setback to the progress of his country, was a responsibility from which he shrank; and his friends turned to him for advice in vain. The situation was critical and complicated and called for just such leadership as with his courage, his clarity, and his intimate knowledge of European and Mexican politics he was fitted to give; but the call came too late. History had overtaken him, and he had reached the end of his revolutionary development. Morally he was paralyzed, and physically he was stricken. Consumption, the lifelong companion which had fattened on his years of privation and exile, now compelled him to abandon all his activities. He returned to Paris and entered a nursing home. In his last weeks of life he found himself almost at home under that Second Republic, which with its murky intrigues and multitudinous political combinations seemed to be Mexicanizing France. His friends continued to consult him. They were relieved by the triumph of the liberal bourgeoisie and the Constitution which had been worked out for France under the formula "Property, Religion, Family, and Order," but uncertain of its stability and worried by the election of Louis Napoleon to the Presidency of the Republic and rumors that he was planning a *coup d'état*. But their questions remained unanswered, for these matters were now of very remote interest to Dr. Mora. On July 14, 1850, with the echoes of some sort of a national celebration ringing dimly in his brain, he died.

The last word which Dr. Mora did not live to speak was his legacy to the coming generation. To the liberal youth who looked to him for guidance he left an example of fearless independence and a clear-cut plan of reform, clouded at the last by the difficulties which delay had raised to its application. But where was the coming generation? Where, in 1850, were the liberal youth old enough to embrace his cautious and contracting counsels and young enough to fight for them? That generation had been long in coming and was now middle-aged, and it had produced no outstanding men. Here and there a promising name appeared, and whenever a likely disciple crossed his path the master welcomed him, but few of them were affluent enough to travel and none of them sufficiently formidable to be forced into exile. In 1840 Melchor Ocampo had come to Paris and paid his respects to the famous expatriate, but the meeting was not fortunate and the visit was not repeated. "He is as sententious as a Tacitus," Ocampo wrote home, "as partial as a reformer, and as arrogant as an ecclesiastic." The comment illumined both men. Mora had been subdued too long, perhaps, to the element in which he worked, his mind was steeped in it and his soul dyed by it, and Ocampo had no pretensions to be a reformer himself at that time. Ten years later he modified his opinion, when he served for a few months as Minister of Finance in Mexico, and wrote a sympathetic note to the invalid, dilating on his own difficulties. But in 1850 Mora was a dying man, and Ocampo a beginner. The mantle went begging.

And stature was needed to fill it. The specifications for a successful reformer were laid down by Dr. Mora in a self-portrait. Being modeled on himself, they were exacting and, like everything he laid down, hard to meet: "Cold in his passions and invariable in his designs," he began; a broad culture, above all in the moral, political, and economic sciences, he added; a superior character, independent, disinterested, courageous, unassuming, human—moral aristocracy, in a word. On these virtues he prided himself. But where in Mexico was the man who could lay claim to such qualities and not be buried by them? Mora had written his own obituary. And if the candidate had the vocation, he could claim only half the succession; for who could combine the call, the character, and the training, with the ripe experience which Mora had gained and the mature understanding of cosmopolitan conditions necessary to further the cause of reform after the American war? With Mora the great breed seemed to have died and the cause to have come to a halt. The dead end the nation had reached was manifest in the prostration of public life; exhaustion and war weariness were so general that the succession went unclaimed. The old men, accordingly, continued to rule, despite their tragic incompetence, and the old thinkers returned to the scene.

But the old thinkers returned in a radical role. Alaman was timid by nature, and fear was the foundation of his political philosophy, but fear forced him to take a bold position when he returned to political life, and the apprehension which dictated his activities drove him to adopt an erratic defense of a radical reaction. He became the mentor of a party that was monarchical in all but name. The name was anathema in Mexico; the first propagandist to advocate monarchy in Mexico—a man by the name of Gutierrez Estrada—had been forced to emigrate in 1840; and though the idea had gained some ground since then and had been openly agitated before the war, it still provoked riots at political rallies. When Alaman ran for office, he was abused as an "absolutist," a "Bourbonist," an "antipatriot," an "enemy of Independence," and these epithets continued to be hurled at him despite his denials; for the historian who had written the history of Mexico as an apology for Cortés and a dirge for Independence and closed it with a tribute to Iturbide as the real founder of the nation had shown too clearly where his heart lay to conceal the umbilical vein that made it beat. He denied that he was a monarchist, and truthfully; for after the bids made for a pretender in Paris were nipped by revolution in France, they were dropped in Mexico. The year 1848 was unfavorable to monarchy everywhere, and Alaman adapted himself to the times, following the advice of Mora that "the wisest and surest way of preventing the revolutions of men is to appreciate the revolution of time, and to grant what it demands." He won a seat in Congress, but his party was beaten at the polls and compelled to mark time. The more they gave ground, the more there was to give. In 1851 the first socialist paper appeared in Mexico, and the first strike; the economic slump fermented in a flare of race war, and Melchor Ocampo caught the attention of the country by his polemic with the curate of Maravatio—straws in the wind that indicated the drift of the times to men possessed of foresight and fear. In Mexico they were drifting helplessly with the trend of the times, while in France the feeble figment of the Republic was abolished by the *coup d'état* of Louis Napoleon. "We call ourselves Conservatives because we wish to preserve the feeble life still left in this poor society," they declared in their profession of faith; but how much longer could they do so by remaining on the defensive? how much longer before they applied the caustic touch to tears? With every passing year the choice of revolution or counterrevolution became more pressing, the middle way more difficult, and marking time more dangerous.

Mora and his friends had predicted that the reaction to '48 would not come for some time in Europe, that it would be bitterly contested, and that it would reach Mexico. In the tail of their deductions they were correct. In Mexico the truce lasted as long as the American millions stabilized the government; when they gave out the reaction came. But it came not as a result of any revolutionary upsurge, but as a counterrevolution to forestall it. Promoted by fear and prompted by a state of mind which by no means corresponded to the state of the nation, the effect of the prophylactic was to provoke the actual revolution against which the preventive had been invented. The last word which

Mora did not live to speak was brought forth by Alaman, and it was *Absit omen!*

In 1853 the government was overthrown by a mutiny, and Alaman and his party came to power uncontested. The mutiny would have been insignificant but for the driving forces that rallied behind it. It began as a mere barracks revolt and was already failing when it was adopted by the clergy and the landowners as a protection against their premonitions of a coming wave of reform. They bought into it on a falling market, in a panic so acute that the slightest alarm was sufficient to stampede them, and it was a very small threat that started them. The sponsors were many, but who was responsible for the movement was less important than what—a state of mind that was prepared for any extremities and a wave of panic that demanded strong measures, and strong men, to check it. A plan was drawn by Alaman, but Alaman was an ideologist, and strong men were so scarce at that moment in Mexico that neither the scent of the scholar nor the instinct of the herd could uncover one. But there was always Santa Anna. Santa Anna, accordingly, was recalled from exile to put the plan into effect. The conditions of his return, and the origins and aims of the movement, were explained to him by Alaman in a letter which laid bare the melancholy anatomy of society and the feeble life left in it in 1853.

The responsibility for the reaction was allowed in equal shares to three men. The author of the plan was Alaman himself; the authority to enact it was entrusted to Santa Anna; and the credit for it went to Ocampo, to whose parochial feud with the curate of Maravatio Alaman attributed the whole movement. "The one who really began the revolution," he wrote, "was the Governor of Michoacan, Don Melchor Ocampo, by the impious principles which he developed in matters of faith, the reforms which he attempted in parochial fees, and the alarming measures which he announced against the landowners and with which he aroused the clergy and the proprietors of that state. Once the revolution had been begun by Bahamonde, by a chance accident that of Guadalajara broke out, but it would not have progressed had the clergy and the proprietors not declared for the plan, and from then on one thing conspired with another, as happens in all revolutions when there is great discontent, until it ended in your recall and election to the Presidency in the hope that you would come and put an end to the general dissatisfaction which the whole nation feels. This, and this alone, is the revolution through which you are returning to the soil of your country."

It was in the tone of a master that Alaman explained the aims of a movement upon which he had grafted his ideas, and of which he remained the mentor and the guide. "The first is the preservation of the

Catholic religion, because we believe in it and because, even if we did not consider it divine, we regard it as the only common tie that binds all Mexicans now that all others are broken, and the only one capable of maintaining the Spanish-American race and saving it from the great danger to which it is exposed. We believe also in the necessity of maintaining the cult in splendor and supporting the property of the Church and in settling everything pertaining to ecclesiastical administration with the Pope. But it is not true, as some papers have said to discredit us, that we desire the return of the Inquisition or persecutions, although we believe that the circulation of impious or immoral books should be prohibited by public authority." The creed was adapted to the times: no Inquisition, no persecutions, but also no republican nonsense. "We are against the Federation; against the representative system by means of elections as they have been hitherto practiced, and against everything that goes by the name of popular elections until they rest on a different foundation. . . . We are convinced that nothing of all this can be accomplished by Congress and we want you to do it, assisted by a few advisers who will prepare your work. These are the essential points of our political faith. We have explained it frankly and loyally, for we make no mystery of our opinions, and to realize these ideas we count on general opinion, which is decidedly in favor of them and which we direct through the leading papers of the capital and the states, which are all ours. We rely on the moral force of conformity among the clergy, the proprietors, and all sensible people. . . . We believe that you will be in favor of these ideas, but if not, we fear that it will go ill with our country and even with you. In that case, I beg you to burn this letter and to give it no further thought."

Santa Anna returned and not only conformed, but put the program into effect with a gratuitous force which nothing but the fear of a genuine revolution could justify. There was no opposition; the pseudo-revolution was directed against imaginary enemies, and real ones were invited and created by men who suffered from a sense of persecution themselves and who were endowed with excessive caution and foresight. Measures of public safety were taken, and Santa Anna added his own to them. His first step was to rid the country of undesirable persons: a list of proscriptions was drawn up, but it was short and insignificant, for strong men were few in the ranks of the enemy as well as in those of the prosecution. Only two men seemed sufficiently dangerous to be invested with the mantle of Mora. One was Ocampo, who was expelled from the country without explanation or delay. The other was Juarez.

After completing his term as Governor of Oaxaca in 1852, Juarez had returned to the Institute as its director and to his law practice. His clients were still the poor, and his cases took him into the Sierra. He had just completed one in Ixtlan and started another in an outlying *pueblo* when he was arrested there, on May 27, 1853, and escorted out of the state with a picket of cavalry, but without explanation other than a passport specifying as his destination the town of Jalapa, capital of the State of Veracruz and seat of Santa Anna's ancestral estates. Here he was held under police surveillance for seventy-five days, his arrest still unexplained and his destination still undetermined, baited by conflicting orders to proceed to other points and bluffed by official uncertainties and despotic delays. Despite his repeated protests, the authorities remained inscrutable until the seventy-sixth day, when he was put into a coach by the son of Santa Anna and driven to Veracruz. There he was confined with the same studied mystery in the fortress of Ulua, and after spending twelve days in a cell below sea-level, he was told to pack, handed a passport for Europe, and placed on board the English packet. No provision had been made for his passage, and as he was penniless, the passengers took up a collection and paid his fare to the first port of call. He landed at Havana and made his way to New Orleans; and there he found a little group of fellow exiles ready to reconstitute the country from which they had been driven. In their company Juarez discovered his destination at last.

10

THE designs of Santa Anna were as mysterious as those of Providence; but in the designs of Providence it was reserved for Santa Anna, himself so lacking in foresight and spurred by men oversupplied with it, to determine, in a supreme triumph of improvidence, the destiny of Juarez. The proscription of Ocampo was the logical consequence of his activity as an agitator—he was a plausible peril; but the name of Juarez carried no revolutionary challenge in 1853. He was an inoffensive Liberal known only for his model government of Oaxaca. In his own community he was a man of some consequence, but not until he was deported did he belong to the world and begin to make his way in it as an outcast. He was forty-seven and he had done little to redeem the high hopes with which he had been hailed in youth as the coming man of the Liberal cause; the promise so long deferred had grown dim, and though his faith had not failed, it had lost much of its driving power in the prudence, the timeserving, the compromises with which it had been applied. He was a safe man, and he had reached an age when most men have already revealed themselves and the habits of life have set, and with every passing year the setbacks accumulated: the settled ways of maturity, the satisfaction of a little success, the bonds of family, the claims and the comforts of security, the sedative marriage of the depths and the shallows—everything conspired to dull the slackening fires of youth. Then suddenly the blow fell: picked up overnight and dragooned out of the country, cut off from all his securities and cast into the unknown, he was uprooted and restored to his mission by the implacable memory of Santa Anna.

For if the designs of Santa Anna were mysterious, they were not inscrutable. It was no casual whim but the logical mind of a man for whom politics and personalities were inseparable that drove Santa Anna to settle old scores with the upstart who had expelled him from his state six years before. That motive remained a mystery to Juarez, who attached so little importance to the incident in 1847 that he saw no connection between it and his banishment in 1853. He attributed his proscription to the normal upset of politics and the intrigues of local foes and friends eager to ingratiate themselves with the new shift, "ambitious and vulgar men," as he said, "who made a place for themselves by sacrificing a man whose sole interest in government was to do his duty without injuring them." And it was in a spirit of injured innocence that he bore a blow that he sincerely believed he had done nothing to deserve. "I resigned myself to my fate," he wrote, "without uttering a complaint, without committing a humiliating action." These were not the words of a rebel, and they proved his political innocence.

But besides Santa Anna, there was the party. So far from suspecting that his fate had any political significance, however, he minimized it as a purely personal misfortune. He was known as a conscientious official and it never occurred to him that the combination might be as dangerous as the iconoclasm of Ocampo. How could he suppose that the good government he had made there in a nonpartisan and even conservative spirit might be as menacing to the reaction as a deliberate provocation? He was a sensible man; and it would have required uncommon credulity to believe that so safe an example might be challenging to a party obsessed by its own insecurity, or that so conservative a success would be considered subversive merely because it was achieved by a Liberal. He realized the psychology of reaction so little that he believed himself to be the victim of a political accident instead of a political rule. He had yet to learn that all his years of conformity were wasted, that compromise with reaction was impossible, and that in times of social tension no man was innocuous or inoffensive. That lesson was learned fully and finally, however, in exile, where he fell in with a group of refugees who had suffered the same fate and who were determined to profit by it and finish what Santa Anna had begun. None of them was remarkable minus his misfortune except Ocampo, whom he met there for the first time and with whom he formed a fruitful friendship.

Ocampo was not a rebel by nature. Bred in the closed world of the Creole aristocracy, he had acquired many of the mental habits of his class and the moral bent of a sheltered life before he broke with them. Of a lucifer he had no brand but an obscure origin. He was the adopted or natural son of a lady celebrated under the colonial regime for the great luxury, the great retinue, and the great charity which she displayed once a year, when she drove up from her estates in Michoacan to spend Holy Week in the capital. His father was reputed to be a patriot who found refuge under her roof during the years of insurgency. Whatever his origin, the boy had good blood and honored it at an early age. His mother died before he reached his majority. With her estates he inherited her habits of prodigal charity, and within a few years was so deep in debt that one day in 1840 he disappeared, mystifying his guardian by a wild tale of having been mistaken for a political enemy of Santa Anna, beaten, abducted, and shipped off to Europe. But on arriving in Paris he confessed the truth. "Without means to cover my debts, I was certain soon to appear in my real character," he wrote, "that is, as a lunatic who, partly because of a foolish vanity and partly because of injudicious bounty, had preferred for the past three years to discharge the obligations his prodigal promises had contracted rather than to attend to the sacred ones of his real duty. I had insensibly acquired such a reputation for generosity that not a week passed, nor a day in the seven, when I was not approached with a fresh request. . . . Weak and unable to say no, I could not cure the disease at the root and I could see nothing ahead but bitter mortification, belated remorse, and merited shame. . . . It was imperative to avoid all this in time, and the only means that my overwrought imagination could find was flight. . . ." He ran away with himself no further, however. He vowed to reform and to acquire the habit of work, "which has never been very deep-rooted and which the false prosperity of the last few years had led me to lose," and when he improved, to return to his country and to serve it with what he had learned by self-discipline. "There is no worse torment, sir," he concluded, "than merited self-contempt."

In Paris the young spendthrift spent several months of penitential poverty, steadfastly refusing relief from home lest his critics, as he said, "might take my poverty for a refined hypocrisy and all my actions as so many falsehoods." He practiced his privations, moreover, with a sharp eye on his motives. "Although my need was great," he admitted, "I think that the sense of vanity which prompted me to prove those stories untrue was stronger than hunger, nakedness, and my unwillingness to cause you any further embarrassment." Vanity! the word was always under his pen and the thing under his foot, and though he was always on guard against it, it was elusive and assumed the most protean forms; and when he detected it lurking in his self-denial as he had in his self-indulgence, he broke his fast. A little legitimate income having reached him from Michoacan, he decided to travel. After all, there were other places for self-improvement than Paris and other forms of it than self-mortification, and to waste the opportunities which Europe afforded for a liberal education was the height of improvidence. He made a walking trip through France and Italy, and the impressions which he collected were not those with which young men of his class returned from the grand tour. In Rome he was struck by the universal mendicity which he saw luxuriating there: "The multitude of beggars is amazing, the Pope, the bishops, the priests, friars, magistrates, employees, citizens, all beg alms." The lawlessness of the Papal State reminded him of Mexico—the roads were so infested with robbers that he returned to France by sea. But his observations were those of a casual sightseer, and the principal benefit of his travels was that he returned to Paris sufficiently broadened to be critical of subjects other than himself.

It was at this time that he met Mora. The reaction was unfavorable and significant. He found him opinionated and overpowering, he disliked his dogmatism, he suspected his ardor, he doubted his disinterestedness, and he granted him nothing but intellectual discipline and fluency and eloquence in the expression of his ideas. What he disliked and what he admired were an index to his development at the time. His judgment of the reformer revealed how far he was from being, or wishing to become, one himself. He was too busy reforming himself not to be impatient of any other ambition, and his aversion to the vocation colored his criticism of the man. He carped, and he respected, but he was so far from the author of *Mexico and Its Revolutions,* and from his country and its problems, that he examined his famous compatriot as if he were one more foreign curiosity, and after a single visit he returned to his own corner of Paris, resolved never to repeat it. Never was a decision more defensive. Their proximity was dangerous, for, indeed, they had much in common—discipline, independence, superior character, and a driving conscience—but their affinities served only to accentuate their differences, because those powers, which Mora had always directed to the progress of a people, were still devoted by Ocampo to his own salvation. Conscience he had without a responsibility worthy of it. Although the distance between them was great, it was one not of nature but of degree and development. The reaction of the younger man was negative precisely because the older one was so challenging. Ocampo questioned his authority, suspected his sincerity, dreaded his ardor, resented his domination, and, after finding every professional reason for faultfinding, finally asserted his independence by flight.

After an absence of two years abroad Ocampo returned to Michoacan and the life for which he was born and from which he was only half weaned. He was sufficiently chastened, mature, and master of himself to manage what remained of his estates reasonably, on a reduced scale of living, though he was never successful financially; but he valued property as a moral asset, for the independence it provided, and he economized to preserve it. He came home, however, home to his country, to his kind, to himself, and the prodigal returned to his habits. Carefully as he controlled his failings, he could not curb his charity. Though he learned to say no to a certain class of persons—solicitors, as he said, who "regarded as an undeniable right to be served the mere fact of telling me that they were in need"—he would not harden himself to the others, and the others were all about him, and their necessities nearer and more undeniable than his own. Who was he to say which were the leeches? or how to know that he needed the needy no less than they his help? He ran his estates in a feudal tradition of responsibility for his dependents, and took an interest in the welfare of his tenants and neighbors which became a byword throughout the county. Many were the tales told of his bounty by those who benefited by it, and the favors he bestowed became obligations which insensibly undermined his independence. But for this besetting weakness he would have subsided no doubt into the life for which he was born, cultivating his acres, nursing his gardens, botanizing, browsing among his books, and doting on his three growing daughters, for it satisfied him completely, and he needed nothing of the world but a modest competence to meet his unexacting demands.

Much was expected of him, however, by others. As a landlord, he was expected to go into politics; it was the natural obligation of his class, and his modesty was understood neither by his rich nor his poor neighbors, who were only as modest as their incomes. All kinds of people were ambitious for Don Melchor Ocampo, and it was difficult to deny them and to indulge what he called his Spanish indolence with a clear conscience. Social convention and moral responsibility convinced him that superior people were not what they wanted to be, but what others expected of them; and he went into politics. In a succession of offices, as deputy, senator, and governor of his state, he convinced them that he was not wanting in public spirit. Although he held advanced views on some social questions and was absolute in his library, the measures enacted during his administration of the state were acceptable improvements which met with general approval—prison and financial reforms, schools and roads, the founding of an agricultural college—and he won the confidence of the entire community by applying private philanthropy to public life.

As long as he confined himself to public works and measures of relief which gradually ameliorated the general average, he met the necessities of his own class: regeneration from within was an easy way out
of their dilemma, pinched as they were by a dwindling economy on the
one hand and the approach of reform on the other. But the conditions
of the country came home to Ocampo in practical politics, and the conditions of his class when he fell afoul of the clergy, and his own condition by his encounter with the curate of Maravatio. A casual appeal to
his charity proved his undoing. Plucking up what he mistook for a
mere leech on the poor, he was stung by a nettle with power virulent
enough to inflame and infect the whole community against him; and
though he indignantly denied that he was a dangerous reformer, he
became by stigma and in spite of himself what was expected of him.
What Mora failed to accomplish, a country curate achieved. The curate
drew blood. But it was not until the wild tale of his youth came true in
1853 and he was mistaken for an enemy or two of Santa Anna, expelled from his country and branded a rebel, that Ocampo actually became one.

The man whom Juarez met in New Orleans influenced him in the
only way in which any influence can ever be successful, by quickening
his own capacities. Ocampo was a step or two ahead of him in revolutionary development, and he performed something of the same service
for Juarez as Mora had once rendered him, calling out latent and un-
suspected powers and guiding him toward a destiny of which he was
yet unconscious. By general consent Ocampo was accepted as the leader
of the little knot of refugees, and on the day after Juarez arrived in
New Orleans a meeting was called to consider ways and means of
overthrowing Santa Anna. The undertaking was a large one, since
none of them had any influence or following in Mexico; but being
destitute, with nothing to lose and everything to gain by the attempt,
they were not deterred by such considerations. They counted on a brewing rebellion which had broken out in the State of Guerrero under
Juan Alvarez, and they hitched their activities to his. Alvarez had a
name as a veteran of insurgency and a following of guerrilla fighters
as a local cacique, but like most of the heroes of his generation he was
a soldier without political experience, and they assumed the ideological
direction of the revolt. A political plan was formulated and forwarded
to his headquarters in Acapulco by a courier whose fare they pooled
their resources to pay. The distance was too great and communication
too slow for active contact, but they had a proxy in Ignacio Comonfort,
one of their friends who had joined Alvarez as his lieutenant and
political mentor, and Comonfort was commissioned to proclaim their
plan.
The self-confidence which these steps revealed was the first fruit of

exile. Nothing in their situation warranted it, but they maintained it for several months by the sanguine activities to which of necessity political exiles are prone. The Gadsden Treaty was then pending in the Mexican Senate, and as it involved a fresh cession of territory to the United States the position of the Conservative party, which based its claim to power on the preservation of the remains of the country, was extremely vulnerable. Ocampo drafted an appeal to an influential senator in Mexico to hold up the treaty and stated the terms on which the Liberals would take power. He drew up a profession of political faith and claimed the right to intervene "in the name of the majority of Mexicans exiled in New Orleans." He worried the Mexican Consul with officious communications and, when they were ignored, led a delegation to call him to account. Hot from the interview, he repaired to a hotel to record the result and who had said what. The record was clear, it proved that they were not idle, but it proved little else: it was a record of impotence, all the more plain for the gestures of defiance with which they denied it. The Gadsden Treaty was passed, and the American millions which it supplied Santa Anna provided the dictator with a fresh lease on life.

But there were compensations. Their activities were noticed by Santa Anna's government, and they had the satisfaction of seeing themselves denounced in the official press for more than they had actually done— for engaging in treasonable conspiracies, for directing the revolt in the south, for protesting to the United States Government against the Gadsden Treaty, for hiring filibusters to invade the national territory. At the same time their bid for power was recognized in another quarter: Alvarez welcomed their collaboration and Comonfort proclaimed the Plan of Ayutla, which resembled their own. Thus encouraged, Ocampo moved to the border and settled in Brownsville, where he attempted to prod the governors of the adjoining states into a sympathetic reaction to the revolt in the south.

Juarez moved into his rooms in the boarding-house and into the place which he vacated, for Ocampo had immediately distinguished him as a dependable second. But the removal of the leader left a fading glow among his companions in New Orleans, and the correspondence they maintained with him became a record of flat and uneventful days. There were no more visits to the Mexican Consul, no more professions of faith, no more hours of heady talk, no more consultations and plans to lend them an illusion of activity and importance. The revolt in Acapulco made no headway, and they scanned the papers in vain for support from that quarter.

As the months wore away and nothing happened either in Mexico or in Brownsville, the long ordeal of waiting winnowed the group to its original sponsors. The rest scattered to various points with the coming of summer, for the ravages of the climate were acute and they were

aggravated by an epidemic of yellow fever, and the strength of numbers was reduced to that of conviction. The fit survived—and the fit
were four. When the group first gathered, it would have been difficult
to say which of the names on the roll call were destined to figure in
the future and which were to fall by the wayside; but six months later
the summer soldiers had vanished, and four men knew that they could
always count on one another: Ocampo, Juarez, Ponciano Arriaga, and
José-Maria Mata. But on them too the winnowing process was at work.
Juarez was stricken by the fever, and his life was saved by pure
chance, "since we had no funds with which to care for him properly,"
as one of his friends said. He survived, however, without a medical
bill; and his recovery was proof of a physical fitness no less necessary
for the future than moral stamina; and that other indispensable was
repeatedly revealed in the trials which the survivors underwent.

These were many and severe. Homesickness, despondency, doubt—
against these they were proof, being determined to a man to return to
their country on their own terms or not at all. Snares there were, for
Santa Anna offered an amnesty for the weak, but there was only one
case of desertion, and when Juarez caught wind of it he reported it
with a vehemence rare in his writing. "I have not seen the papers," he
wrote to Ocampo, "but those who have tell me that Sandoval, as if the
humiliation of returning by grace of the tyrant were not enough, is
basely abusing his comrades in exile. Poor devil! who has the talent to
exchange his existence as a man for that of a contemptible reptile upon
whom we must all spit!" Constancy cost them no qualms: they were
marked men, and too important not to be braced by their curse. As
time passed, however, the problem of ways and means of overthrowing Santa Anna gave way to the pressing question of ways and means
of keeping alive. They were proof against poverty. Though they were
frequently pinched by it, it was the least of their trials. Ocampo was
steeled to it by a philosophy that stood him in good stead, when his income was cut off by the confiscation of his estates. Juarez was born to
it and returned to it easily. He received remittances from home, where
his wife had opened a shop to provide for the family, but they were
meager and irregular, and at times, like his companions, he was forced
to eke out his means by such employments as were available to
stranded Mexicans in New Orleans. In lean days Juarez kept himself
in a printing-shop or a cigar factory; Mata worked as a waiter;
Ocampo as a potter. Hovering on the edge of penury and the social
pale, they preserved a precarious existence—as men. But as men they
met the test differently. On the most high-strung the strain was naturally the most trying, and on one occasion Ocampo was reduced to the
verge of complaint. Major trials he bore easily, because they could be
met with pride, but the minor ones that mortified it cut him to the
quick. In Brownsville he found a benefactor in a prosperous Mexican

who served as his banker and through whose assistance he would have been free to pursue his political work—but for the womenfolk. The banker had a wife and daughter as sheltered and guarded as Mexican women across the border, and Ocampo was accompanied by a daughter whom he idolized. Finding her in tears one day, he coaxed out of her a confession that she had been berated in the home of his benefactor because of a bonnet, which had led the ladies to remark that Mexican women who affected such fashions were shameless hussies, whereupon he wrote to his banker, renouncing his aid and severing their relations. "You see how futile a reason has led to results as painful to me as they are prejudicial," he confessed, but "the slur could not be stronger, the offense more direct, nor the words more insulting"—and he felt them the more bitterly because he was unmarried. He recalled others that he had suffered in silence—how he had been rebuked in company for some trifling levity, how an "emancipated woman" had been sent him as a companion for his daughter—trifles, trifles, but trifles were crushing in the life of the exile, where philosophy was a futility and a scratch could destroy it, and his susceptibility to trifles was the final humiliation. The affair was patched up, but not the damage to his pride, which he charged to the account of Santa Anna. From the tyranny of little things, more trying than the oppression of despots, he looked to Acapulco not merely for the salvation of Mexico, but for his own moral rescue.

The demoralizing effects of exile—the petty pressure of poverty, the exposure to mean indignities, the privation of any redeeming activity—were an acid test of character; and as time passed and the revolt made no progress, it became more and more difficult for the proscripts to sustain the self-confidence which they derived from their vicarious share in it. Reduced to their own resources, they were mere refugees with nothing in common but a misfortune which they could not dispute; and with the disintegration of the group they became once more what they were before they met, isolated individuals of no importance to anyone but themselves. The triumph of Santa Anna was complete. A pretense of political activity was kept up, but a pretense only, and they subsided slowly and inevitably into such occupations as they could improvise to cheat their impotence. Ponciano Arriaga, who had no patience with pretense, slipped across the border to agitate in the neighboring states; Ocampo, who had no talent for intrigue, cultivated his garden in Brownsville; and Mata, a zealous disciple with nothing to do, acted as a courier for Ocampo and courted his daughter.

Juarez remained in New Orleans, resting from the exertions of his friends. His days were divided between political work—reading the newspapers and calling at the post office—and the study of Constitutional Law. One day he was invited by an American court to sit in on a case involving a land claim in California, a proud day for his friends, one of whom fondly reported that "his opinion was unanimously approved by the members of the court, he was enthusiastically praised and showered with a thousand attentions to which he was justly entitled." Any recognition extended to one of their number was gratefully appreciated by the whole group. But such tributes were rare, and in the drought of attention from which they all suffered his friends were the last to give him his due. A common mediocrity deadened them all, and a dreary monotony of mutual neglect. As the dead level of life sank to a depth, however, that laid bare his submerged abilities, they began to be recognized in the shallows. During the long draining months of flatness and failure his friends dimly discerned the self-sufficiency which sustained him and of which they all stood in need. One of them noticed "his irreproachable habits and his devotion to study, which he interrupted only to visit some institutions of public instruction or welfare, or to visit one or another of his acquaintances." From five in the morning until eight at night he worked over his books; but there was nothing unusual either in his routine or his studies—Constitutional Law—a lawyer without clients keeping in practice and pursuing his professional interests by himself—unless it was his interest in systems of colonization in the American Republic—the scholarly recreation of an expatriate. Nor was there anything uncommon in the mental independence which he preserved by a routine that defeated adversity; nor in the fact that he was never bored by his friends or by himself; nor in his material independence, which he preserved jealously. Repeated offers of financial assistance from Ocampo and compatriots passing through the city were always declined, and though his consistency cost him some privations, they were noticed by no one but a companion who shared them, and who never forgot that for a time they ate for ten cents in the lunchroom of the Hotel St. Charles, until they found a Negress who fed them for eight dollars a month and a rooming-house for eight more; when they received a remittance from Oaxaca for six hundred pesos and they were both flush. In hardship they were all equals, all Juarez—with one difference which his would-be benefactors and close friends both discovered. His irreproachable habits made him unapproachable. Poverty not only stiffened but exasperated his pride. Ocampo once refused a cigar which Juarez offered him and twitted him with an old saying: "No, sir. When an Indian sucks a cigar, the thief is not far." The reply was sharp and short: "The Indian I cannot deny, but the rest—" And Ocampo undid himself in apologies. If Juarez had not been hypersensitive, and Ocampo mortified by one of those slips to which superior people are sometime liable, there would have been nothing remarkable in the anecdote—and they would not have been friends. But they both bruised easily, and in his susceptibility to fancied slurs Juarez was fully the equal of Ocampo.

The small items of that time that lingered in the memory of the exiles, when trifles loomed large for all of them, would have been trivial had they not revealed qualities in Juarez upon which his companions came to rely and which needed only larger times to emerge and impress them. He was dependable, whatever was expected of him, whether to ship plants to Ocampo in Brownsville, or to walk the levees with Mata, or to appreciate the propaganda sent back from the field by Ponciano Arriaga: he had a knack for nursing the talents of his friends; he analyzed the news with a perspicacity which escaped their attention, but they trusted his judgment, and the event constantly confirmed it. There was a terrible moment when the papers announced the death of Alvarez. Juarez assumed, correctly as usual, that the report had been inspired to discourage the spread of the revolt; and throughout all the fluctuations of their prospects he maintained an equanimity, a patience, a confidence equally proof against undue despondency and premature hope—qualities that surpassed their expression and that passed unperceived by the closest observers. A discerning eye was needed to discover their presence, and a microscopic insight to magnify their importance, in the small chores and plodding services which stunted and buried them; and none of his companions had the talent to dramatize dullness. They were dimly aware of a great self-sufficiency but not of its extent, because it was concealed by an equally complete self-effacement.

Exile was a training school for their task, and its discipline a test of their fitness to survive; and of all its hardships the most trying for the great-minded was the grinding test of dullness, which whetted the spirit or broke it. But it was a necessary groundwork for greatness. The serenity of Juarez was a steadying influence on his friends in days of moral drudgery and pedestrian exercises; but a day came when stamina was not enough, when philosophy was too passive, to compensate for political inactivity.

In Mexico the revolt began to make some progress. Alaman died in 1854, but not before he inoculated Santa Anna with that morbid craving for monarchy which he had disavowed because it was premature and unpopular, but which was the dying breath of his brain; and Santa Anna was well fitted to carry the germ and to acclimate the idea in Mexico. His return to power was accepted, like the seasons, as a perennial but transient phenomenon; but this time his return was marked by an abnormal novelty. He assumed the style of a Prince-President and the title of a Serene Highness, created orders of nobility and a Court of exotic splendor, and consummated the covert ambition of his mentor by a domestic imitation of Louis Napoleon. The trial balloon defied levitation, however. The pretensions of Santa Anna were tolerated for a time and then ridiculed until they could no longer be laughed off.

The trappings of royalty only made the realities of the dictatorship more galling and the Napoleonic precedent more glaring; and in anticipation of another collapse, as normal as his regular returns to power, Santa Anna prepared for his supersession by a foreign prince. Though the negotiations were conducted with due secrecy, they leaked out, for his agent was Gutierrez Estrada. The first man to advocate monarchy in Mexico had been driven from the Republic for plucking forbidden fruit, but he gloried in his fall and ran about Europe, a naked Adam, peddling it to anyone who would bite; but no one would. The only result was to discredit Santa Anna, to weaken confidence in the dictator who was merely warming the seat for another, and to hasten his fall. Popular sympathy with the revolt spread, and Alvarez and Comonfort redoubled their exertions to shake off the yoke.

As the prospects of the rebellion brightened and the fall of Santa Anna appeared to be approaching, Juarez became seriously troubled. "Once the tyrant has been destroyed, shall we have accomplished the triumph of principles?" he wrote to Ocampo. "This is what I fail to see, and what saddens me every day, for, say what we will, there is not sufficient patriotism and enlightenment to win liberty without committing excesses that dishonor it, or to secure it, after success, by setting aside all personal ambitions. It may be that these ideas spring from my bad humor at the moment and that the results will belie them. I hope so, I hope so." But his doubts would not down and they raised challenging questions. Was the revolt to triumph without them? Were they to be mere bystanders of an event they proposed to control? And with that question came another. Could the revolution succeed without them? Was it not their duty to indoctrinate it and prevent it from becoming merely one more of those pseudo-revolutions which perpetuated the chronic chaos of Mexico?

By the end of February 1855 his doubts and his promptings moved Juarez to propose that they proceed in a body to Acapulco, or that Ocampo and Arriaga at least should appear in the theater of war, where their presence would be enough to hearten public spirit. "You see the state of the revolution," he wrote. "It seems to me that a unanimous effort by the few men who have the interests of the country at heart would suffice to destroy the tyrant, and I think that the effort will be made when men of ability and irreproachable reputation set the example." In deference to Ocampo, and to his own modesty, Juarez left the initiative to the natural leader, but his days of retirement were counted. Ocampo decided to remain in Brownsville. The fire which he had kindled across the border began to blaze; a governor revolted, a general volunteered, and he invested his remaining funds and energies in fanning the insurrection in the north.

At the same time came a letter from Comonfort, urging Juarez to use his influence to raise his native state; but the next mail brought

news of reverses in Acapulco, and Juarez decided that the mission
would be a useless expense and remained as modest as his income.
When the call was repeated, however, and Comonfort, in desperate
straits, short of money, munitions, and men, begged Ocampo to send
him Juarez at least and some of the others, Juarez hesitated no longer.
His were clearly the qualities of adversity. Ocampo and Mata constituted themselves a Revolutionary Committee, assuming the functions
of government and issuing drafts on the customs of the disaffected
states, and raised a loan to pay the passage of Juarez to Acapulco. If
there was some presumption in assuming the direction of the movement and coming forward at the eleventh hour, no one could do it
more modestly than Juarez, and even he recognized that his position in
New Orleans, in a boarding-house, in the lee of life, was no longer ten-
able. After eighteen months of exile, his philosophy was no longer passive, or even pensive: he was pledged to a fresh departure, and conscious
of his destination, and crowned with the rings of Saturn. The last to
appreciate his abilities and the first to prove them, he set sail, at the
end of June 1855, invested with the confidence of his comrades and empowered to use his discretion to deal with whatever situation he might
find in Mexico.

II

LANDING in Acapulco late in July, Juarez went directly to headquarters, where, in the absence of the General, he was received
by his son, Colonel Diego Alvarez. The Colonel, according
to a story which he told later and which there is no reason to doubt,
did not catch the name. "What do you want?" he asked. "Knowing
that men are fighting for freedom here, I came to see in what way I
could be useful," was the reply. The volunteer was accepted without
further question and taken to the camp, where the Colonel presented
him to his father as a casual recruit to the cause. Father and son
were both embarrassed by his appearance: shabby, bedraggled, and
drenched by a tropical downpour, he was in urgent need of repair.
"I need hardly say," said the Colonel, "that we did not know what
to do to relieve his pressing need, since we had no clothes for the
newcomer; we had to use those of our poor troopers, a pair of trousers
and a cotton blanket, that is, adding to them a blanket from my

father's bed and a pair of his patched boots, all of which, together with a package of good cigarettes, harmonized wonderfully." What to do with the man they had dressed was the next question: "My father, who was glad to accept spontaneous collaborators in the struggle we had started against Santa Anna, was as perplexed as I, and upon his offering to serve as a secretary and repeating that he had come to see how he could serve here, where men were fighting for freedom, he was given some letters of little importance, which he answered and presented for signature with the utmost modesty." It was not until several days later, when a letter addressed to Lic. Don Benito Juarez was delivered in camp and someone took the trouble to ask his name, that his identity was discovered. Then he was questioned again by the Colonel. " 'Here is a letter bearing your name. Does this mean that you are a lawyer?' — 'Yes, sir,' he replied. — 'You mean that you are the same man that was Governor of Oaxaca?' — 'Yes, sir.' — And overcome with confusion, I exclaimed, 'Why did you not tell me?' — 'Why should I?' he replied. 'What does it matter?' "

The story was not only plausible but significant, for the characteristic self-effacement of Juarez revealed something more important than personal modesty—political tact. When he left New Orleans, the revolution was at low ebb; when he arrived in Acapulco, it was flushed with triumph. A fortnight later Santa Anna abdicated and fled the country. The rapid reversal of the situation, which occurred during the six weeks that Juarez spent at sea, restored his mission to its original purpose: it was not with the dangers of defeat that he had to deal, but with the far greater hazards of success. Arriving at the last moment as the emissary of a group that proposed to direct a movement which had managed without them, he was in reality an interloper who could carry out his mission without incurring the charge of presumption only by the most sedulous self-effacement; and the confidence of his friends was not misplaced. He slipped imperceptibly into his place in the revolution and performed his part as a political adviser with the same consummate inconspicuousness that had distinguished him in New Orleans. An occasion soon arose. As soon as the fall of Santa Anna was seen to be inevitable, a sympathetic movement broke out in the capital, his generals deserted, rallied to the plan of the revolution, and proclaimed one of their number "interim" President. The news excited wild jubilation in Acapulco, and Juarez was instructed to write a eulogistic article for the local paper. The unthinking enthusiasm with which this success was celebrated was a measure of the ingenuousness of a purely popular and indigenous movement. Juarez was obliged to point out to the Colonel that the revolt of the generals was merely a maneuver to save their skins and to falsify the revolution, stealing its fruits from under the noses of the revolutionaries and cheating "the patriots who had flung themselves into the fight to free their country from clerical-military tyranny," and that no common cause existed or could be made between them. The Colonel was convinced, and the article was revised to fit the facts. The facts would have been self-evident anywhere else but in Acapulco; in a jungle full of virgin patriots and political illiterates, the services of an interpreter were needed to decipher them. Thereafter the position of Juarez was secure. General Alvarez confirmed his judgment, having come to the same conclusions himself—he was not above taking advice when he agreed with it. They were both Indians, both born to suspicion as their birthright, and they understood each other instinctively. Juarez was given a seat at the council table when the emissaries of the generals came down to negotiate the recognition of their President. Their overtures were rejected, the jungle was full of eyes and ambushes, and they beat their way back, convinced that their man had no chance. The road being cleared, the army advanced to the capital.

"The whole thing has been a farce to continue controlling the country and to baffle the revolution," Juarez wrote to Ocampo. Of his part in exposing the snare he made no mention. He had put in a word at the right moment, but the same decision would undoubtedly have been taken without him, and the real difficulties lay ahead. Alvarez was marching on the capital to establish a government that would put the Plan of Ayutla into effect and develop the program of the revolution; and feeling himself unable to cope with that situation alone, Juarez urged Ocampo to join him without delay. His own position was still obscure. When the army marched through Morelia, one of his friends there came out to meet him and, after searching the lines of nondescript soldiers straggling by and inquiring for him in vain, found him at last far to the rear, alone, and managing a sorry nag. He was, in fact, a camp follower; he had won a footing in the movement, but nothing more, and his place was inevitably with the laggards. He could not compete with Comonfort, who was the political adviser *en titre,* who had borne the brunt of the fighting, and who was entitled to precedence by the services he had rendered the rebellion. Juarez had gained the confidence of Alvarez, but Alvarez had so little confidence in himself after the battle and recognized his political inexperience so clearly that he hesitated to trust himself among the problems, the pitfalls, the intrigues of the capital, and halted his advance at Cuernavaca. Here he was elected President by a council of delegates whom he appointed, and of whom Juarez was one; but he delegated his powers to Comonfort, who formed his cabinet and became the actual arbiter of the situation. Had he been ambitious, Comonfort might easily have monopolized power, but he was generous and welcomed the collaboration of the latecomers from New Orleans. Ocampo arrived at the critical moment, in time to accept two posts in the cabinet for himself and to distribute the rest among his trusted friends. The Ministry of Finance was given to Guillermo Prieto, a poet who had served a term in the Treasury, and the Ministry of Justice and Public Education was handed to Juarez.

To these four men fell the task of completing the revolution. The Plan of Ayutla, which proclaimed its program, was the plan which the refugees in New Orleans had drawn, revised by Comonfort, and revised downward. When he had proclaimed it in the thick of the struggle, Comonfort had been careful to omit everything that might add to his difficulties and had thinned it down to popular generalities—the overthrow of Santa Anna and the restoration of liberty. These generalities were a vacant mold into which, after the battle, specific meaning had yet to be poured, and liberty was defined by Ocampo as the elimination not merely of Santa Anna, but of the clerical-military tyranny of which he was the creature. In Comonfort, however, he encountered a collaborator who was the incarnation of all the dangers of success. Personally he left little to be desired: he was undoubtedly one of those rare Mexicans ready to forego ambition for the public good; he was disinterested, honorable, high-minded, and sincere; but he was a compromiser.

As soon as they set to work, their differences appeared. The first business to come before the cabinet was the preparation of a call for the election of a new Congress. Ocampo insisted on depriving the clergy of the vote; Comonfort balked. He was overruled, but he freely expressed his regret that the delegates who elected Alvarez and from whom he derived his own authority had not been composed one-half of ecclesiastics—a measure which would have obviated all discussion, but which would have made the revolution superfluous. As for the army, Comonfort would not touch it and insisted on retaining and conciliating the generals of the late regime. After a fortnight in office Ocampo resigned in disgust. "As Comonfort explained to me clearly that the revolution would continue to take the way of *transactions*," he wrote to Mata, "and as I am one of those who break but do not bend, I left the Ministry. The housekeeper called for the keys and I handed them over, since I had no right to keep them. But I very much doubt whether by sleight-of-hand, as Comonfort told me he had pacified Mexico and meant to continue governing, he will be able to succeed. I believe that what is wanted is a hard hand. Time will tell who is right."

Prieto and Juarez remained in the cabinet, the former persuaded by Ocampo and the latter by his own conscience, which was of too practical a cast to be satisfied by a self-righteous gesture of renunciation on principle. "What determined me to remain in the Ministry," Juarez wrote, "was the hope of being able to profit by an opportunity to initiate some one of the many reforms which society needed to improve its condition, and of benefiting by the sacrifices which the people had made to destroy the tyranny that oppressed them." If his choice made him an opportunist, it was for high stakes: an historic opportunity had arisen, and might never recur, to transform a military success into a revolution, and it was in imminent danger of being lost in another re-shuffle: he for one could not afford to be intransigent. Such an attitude was possible only in exile, in a garden in Brownsville or on the levees of the Mississippi, or in the study, or in the empyrean; in Mexico at that moment it was irresponsible. Ocampo grasped the situation and the man at a glance and, foreseeing the end in the beginning, foreshort-ened them in a flash. Comonfort belonged to a breed which he recog-nized with the trained eye of the naturalist, because the characteristics were invariable—the eternal compromiser, which every revolution breeds for its confusion, fatal to himself, his partners, and his cause. To that judgment Juarez eventually subscribed, but at the time he was will-ing to give the beginner the benefit of a doubt—for a doubt there was, though there was little else on which to build. Convinced of the neces-sity of drastic reforms but shrinking from the risks of their precipitate application, Comonfort insisted on consolidating his regime before he attempted them. To temporize was not necessarily to compromise; in his own mind, at least, there existed a saving distinction, and though it was a thin one, it provided a narrow margin, which might spell the whole difference between success and failure. Juarez speculated on it. He understood Comonfort as Ocampo could not, with the insight of sympathy as well as of science: the reluctance to dare, the paralyzing prudence of a little success, the stubborn evasion of controversial issues, the temptation and even the necessity of compromise—Comonfort con-fronted him like his own past, and he had some secret indulgence, per-haps, for his dead self; but he had learned the fallacy of timeserving by hard and bitter experience, and he hoped to guide his alter ego, whom he had outgrown, while he was still amenable to influence.

But the odds were against him. The influences to which Comonfort was amenable were naturally those of his own kind, and he was no sooner in power than he was beset by the enemy. The enemy was not the reaction, routed by the fall of Santa Anna, but the Moderate party, which provided it with cover in days of extremity and whose function as a buffer had often served in the past to ward off revolution and pre-serve the existing order. The reaction, cowed and discredited but not yet beaten, resorted to its usual tactics and blended with that large and influential third party which held a balance of power that, consciously or unconsciously, was always dipped in their favor. To this party Comonfort belonged by temperament and policy; and pressure was brought to bear to wean him away from Alvarez, who was known to favor a purge of the army and the other radical measures implicit in the Plan of Ayutla. Comonfort resisted; his personal loyalty was at stake, and he was, as one of his friends said, "horribly quixotic." Failing to move him by persuasion, the enemy resorted to threats. Manuel Doblado, the Governor of Guanajuato, and one of the leaders of the Moderates, was rumored to be on the point of revolt, and though the reports were denied, the maneuver alarmed Comonfort. Haunted by the fear of a fresh civil war, he set himself to woo Doblado, and for several weeks the cautious neutrality of the one was pitted against the calculated uncertainty of the other in a prolonged duel of doubt; but in so unsettled a period the threat of revolt was too explosive an expedient not to alarm the Moderates themselves, and they held it in abeyance, biding the effect of another and safer device.

Alvarez, who still lingered in Cuernavaca, was induced to take up his residence in the capital in the confident expectation that he would discover his unfitness for office there; and nothing was left undone to discredit him. With him came the army—an army of *Pintos,* as people called the half-civilized tribes of the south, whose war paint in primitive times had given them a reputation for ferocity that clung to them in the civil war; and their appearance created dismay not only among the respectable, but among the popular, classes and produced a political effect by the most primitive of all political devices—an appeal to the eye no less potent with the cultivated than with the illiterate crowd. Lounging in the Plaza, guarding the Palace, overrunning the city, the *Pintos* were regarded as barbarians by the one and boors by the other, and as a plague by both. They were outlandish, they were vandals, they were invaders, and the dread and disgust they excited were visited on the head of their President. Alvarez was derided and ostracized; at a gala performance given in his honor at the theater, the decent people stayed away in droves, and Comonfort was conspicuous by his absence. Every effort was made to dissociate him from such disreputable company and by the most telling means, for he belonged to a genteel family and had never done anything freakish in his life before; but prudery was a slow political process, and his friends fretted under the occupation of the capital by a swarm of pariahs who possessed it like unclean spirits easy to call up and hard to cast out. "I do not know what cursed constellation pursues us," Doblado was warned by one of his political scouts, "and makes us victims at one time of robbery, pillage, prostitution, and immorality, and at others of immorality, ignorance, barbarism, and brutality! Oh! you would have died of shame, as we all have done, if you had seen the hordes of savages who call themselves the Army of the South, and in whose power the Capital of the Republic lies today! I have found myself wishing that they were the hordes of Attila, for then we should be overwhelmed by fierce but valiant soldiers. These are no less brutal and barbarous, but they are, besides, as imbecile and degraded as the Negro! What is to become of us I do not know. If help does not come from your quarter, here it is completely lost!" The time had come to strike, and Doblado was urged to repeat the threat of revolt.

The crisis rose rapidly, but just before it reached its crest a counter-acting influence asserted itself. During those weeks of growing strain and insecurity Juarez had been working steadily against time. Comonfort was clearly slipping, and the only hope of arresting his surrender was to commit him, before it was too late, to an irretrievable step. As the pressure increased, and Comonfort leaned more and more toward the Moderates waiting to board his government, Prieto dropped off and Juarez alone remained at his post. He had prepared the draft of a law reforming the administration of justice, which had been discussed in the cabinet and had met with the approval of his colleagues and Alvarez. Comonfort had not opposed it, though it was highly subversive, for it abolished the judicial *fueros,* or immunities, of the clergy and the army and reduced the members of the privileged classes to the juris-diction of the civil courts and the common law. But Comonfort was cornered. The measure was a challenge which compelled him to de-clare himself, and the more he listed toward the Moderates, the more he recoiled from admitting his weakness to himself or his colleagues, for whatever else might be said of Comonfort, he was not without con-science—it was the curse of the compromiser, indeed, and he was be-deviled by it. He lent his sanction to the measure and authorized Juarez to proceed with its preparation, and on the day when the final version was submitted to the cabinet, he absented himself on the plea of pressing business, leaving his colleagues free to force his hand. To this last conscientious evasion Juarez responded by slipping the measure through with the skill of a conjuror, performing a piece of political sleight-of-hand which, light-fingered in effect, was weighty in conse-quence, and fitted Comonfort's own formula of government. The race against time and intrigue was won by a narrow margin. On Novem-ber 23, 1855—five days after the arrival of Alvarez in the capital and at the same time that the signal was sent to Doblado to rise—the *ley Juarez* was published by presidential decree.

The effect was immediate and far-reaching. The law emerged sud-denly like a dam which caught and clove the swift-flowing current of defeat and sent it swerving and churning in confusion. Even more important than its content was its timing. Comonfort was compromised and braced by it. "Yesterday and today feverish rumors were running in this capital of an imminent revolution," he wrote to Doblado five days later. "The flight last night of General Uraga and the ease with which the enemies of public peace can exploit the recent law on the administration of justice are matters, to my mind, that can encourage the malcontents. To support this law is a duty of the present adminis-tration and to pursue Uraga a necessity." The fugitive general was heading toward a region seething with disaffection, where the Indians of the Sierra had been aroused by clerical propaganda. One of their caciques had issued a call to arms to save "the clergy, deprived even of their rights as citizens, the Church whose property is that of the poor, the army destroyed as a class and prostituted by the entrance into the ranks of notorious bandits and jailbirds, the proprietor whose possessions are unprotected by an unbridled government, and the artisan, humiliated by the presence in the capital of the Republic of the filthy, insolent, and immoral horde which the weakness of a few men has vomited upon Mexico out of the mountains of the south, and which threaten the lives and honor of our wives and daughters."

But it was not from that quarter that the revolt came. Four days after the publication of the *ley Juarez,* Doblado raised the banner of rebellion on behalf of *Religion and Fueros.* He missed the psychological moment, however, and his own friends, who had advised him only ten days before that nothing could save the situation but a menacing attitude on his part, now turned on him in protest and alarm and begged him to forbear. For in the meanwhile something had happened. On the same day that Doblado revolted, Alvarez resigned the Presidency in favor of Comonfort, and the Moderates had accomplished their purpose. In ousting Alvarez, however, they were bound by one stipulation: he resigned on the express condition that the legislation initiated under his brief rule would be inviolably preserved, and they themselves reminded Doblado that the reactionary program of *Religion and Fueros* was not, and could not be, a passport to power. They were shocked by a plan which, as they said, "gives the clergy and the army by respecting their privileges a preponderance to which we Liberals have always been opposed, since it subjects the government to an ignominious tutelage, since it makes any kind of progress impossible, and since its constant tendencies to the *status quo,* which are the same as those of the Conservative party, prevent the liberal from taking the true road of improvement. . . ." This was more than a rebuke: it was a revelation. The *ley Juarez,* lying amid the old rubbish of compromises, expedients, and half-measures, made all the old combinations impossible; it acted like a magnet on the elements about it, compelling them to react according to their true nature; it rallied the Moderates themselves to their real bearings, detaching them from their traditional amalgam with the reaction; and though they captured the government, they were forced to adopt its policy. Doblado recognized his error and retrieved it by dropping his ill-timed feint of revolt and becoming thereafter one of the most dependable and progressive members of the Liberal party.

The hand that raised the dam was virtually unknown in national politics. Only a few days before the law appeared the old politician who served Doblado as a political scout measured the lawgiver as follows: "Today I talked with Señor Juarez. He struck me as a rather circumspect man and, to judge by his vague and general conversation, he will not give us many laws, but only those that are strictly necessary and consulting always the general interest, without disclosing in his measures that party spirit which has been the bane of our poor country." Until the law appeared, Juarez could still be mistaken for a safe man, and so colorless that he was given only a few days more of official life; but he held on to give the nation one of those capital reforms the necessity of which was recognized, and the tonic effect felt, even by tepid liberals. That Comonfort countenanced so provocative a measure was both a guarantee and a surprise. A story subsequently appeared that it had been smuggled through the cabinet without his knowledge, a story that Juarez denied, explaining that his chief had sanctioned the measure before he absented himself. But the correction, strictly accurate as a statement of fact, was something less than the whole truth. A strong suggestion of psychological prestidigitation remained and was emphasized by the speed with which the pass was made; and though it was not manual but moral, it conjured up a Comonfort who was not there before.

Produced in haste, the law was imperfect, as its author admitted. Many immunities of the clergy remained intact, and those of the army were merely pared; but a principle had been established and vindicated, and none too soon. A fortnight after the appearance of the law Alvarez resigned, the Moderates came to power, and in the reshuffle Juarez resigned. The Indian President returned to his ranch in the south, not without recalling in a bitter letter to Doblado the services he had rendered the nation in the wars of insurgency; he belonged to the past and shrank into it; but he lasted long enough to cast over the law of November 23, 1855, which initiated the final phase of Independence, and which was forged by another native hand, the protection, the prestige, the long luminous shadow of 1821.

For Juarez also there were compensations; he was too important a person to be dismissed without them. He returned to Oaxaca as Governor, appointed by Comonfort, and settled down to his homecoming with legitimate pride. The lawgiver retired, the law remained, a revolutionary landmark which justified his satisfaction. "Imperfect as this law was," he was able to say when he reviewed his work in perspective, "it was received with great enthusiasm by the Progressive party; it was the spark that kindled the fire of Reform, which later consumed the rotten structure of abuses and privileges. It was, in short, a challenge flung to the privileged classes, and one which General Comonfort and all the others, who for lack of faith in the principles of the revolution or for personal advantage sought to check its course, compromising with the demands of the past, were forced to maintain in spite of themselves, pressed on by the all-powerful arm of public opinion."

The aftereffects had brought forth light. The law was a beacon which called forth the doubters who had not yet declared themselves and brought them crowding to the fore in eager emulation. Seven months later, on June 25, 1856, came the *ley Lerdo* with which the new Minister of Finance, Lerdo de Tejada, disamortized Church property. This law was, in form, a half-measure; it was not confiscatory, but it abolished the immunity of mortmain and forced the sale of ecclesiastical holdings in real estate and investments, releasing and circulating a large fund of hoarded wealth for the benefit of the nation; and it asserted the right of civil jurisdiction no less absolutely than did the *ley Juarez*.

Comonfort had become a lucifer in spite of himself, and his formula of government had developed overnight into a science in which, by feats of legerdemain, the dead hand of the past was being steadily lifted, and the reaction of public opinion was accurately tested by an active demonstration of the repulsions and affinities, the forces that charged and the properties that composed it; it was no longer a compound of conjecture and jugglery. By the summer of 1856 his government, completely manned now by Moderates, had been identified with two measures, which were both major experiments in political physics: one abolishing the legal *fueros* of the privileged classes and the other the economic *fuero* of the dominant caste. Between these two successful tests several minor decrees had been issued to reinforce their tendency: the expulsion of the Jesuits, the abolition of civil coercion in the maintenance of monastic vows, and the regulation of parochial rates. The Reform movement had been resuscitated and was on the march.

12

THE succession of Mora was no longer vacant; but neither was it filled. Hovering over the head of Ocampo for a moment, settling for a longer one on the hand of Juarez, caught up in turn by Lerdo de Tejada, seeking and finding ever fresh recruits, including even a Comonfort and a Doblado, lighting on one eligible after another with a tentative ghostly touch but fastening on none for the furtherance of its ultimate ends, its direction was never in doubt. The succession was a collective enterprise, not an individual adventure, and the impulse given by a single will had yet to be dilated. The dynamic initiative of Juarez was seconded by a few highly placed persons in power, and the rudiments of a movement could be discerned in the response to it of those widely scattered individuals, many and nameless, who had nursed the vision of Reform during the arid years in silence and solitude, in ineffectual reveries, and in the inertia of complete disorganization. "Unfortunately, the Liberal party is essentially anarchic and will not cease to be so for many thousands of years," Ocampo had written a few years before. "The criterion of our enemies is authority. . . . They obey blindly and uniformly, whereas when we are commanded, unless we are told how and why, we murmur and are remiss, when we do not actually disobey and rebel. For every liberal is one in the degree to which he can and will emancipate himself; and our opponents are all equally servile and almost all equally pupils. To be wholly a liberal requires effort and needs the courage of a complete man."

Whether this psychology was the cause or the result of repeated failure, the unruly and invertebrate individualism of the Liberal party had perpetuated the rule of reaction and made progress impossible until one of their faith raised a challenge that massed and marshaled them. Then the lonely believers, so long separated and isolated by an inbred inability to combine, came crowding forward at a call, all the more potent because it was an individual feat of political prowess; all that they needed to fuse their efforts was a focus, a center, a rallying point, and that they found in the Congress called by Comonfort to endow the nation with a new Constitution.

The most important result of the Congress was not the laws but the men it produced—men who discovered themselves and one another in the common task of reconstituting their country and who would have remained obscure and ineffectual casuals of their time but for that dredge. Few of the delegates had figured prominently in public life. The most illustrious was Gomez Farias, but the patriarch of Reform, old, sick, and long since silenced, took no part in the debates. He was a venerable invalid whose presence, in the absence of Mora, was a symbol of a continuous tradition and a living reminder to the deputies of the fresh departure which, to redeem it, they were bound to make; and his seat, which was rarely occupied, was a pedestal about which his heirs assembled piously on ceremonial occasions and from which they caught the speeding touch before taking off on their lap of the race for Reform. They had the advantage of not being so far ahead of their time, and their prospects were better. A fresh start was about to be made with a completely Liberal Congress, from which the clergy and the military had been eliminated, and in which the only division lay between Moderates and radicals, the former malleable and the latter dynamic. The division, it was true, was not clear-cut, for even in the

Progressive wing there was a sliding scale of conviction and courage, and those who could be accounted complete liberals, according to the dictum of Ocampo, were rare; but the indeterminate were dominated by a small knot of complete men who made up in enterprise for what they lacked in numbers. Of these moving spirits the nucleus was formed by the confederates of New Orleans and a number of spirited newcomers who had known moral exile in their own country. Juarez was absent in Oaxaca; Ocampo took his seat late and left it early in dissent; but Mata was an indefatigable champion of every basic reform, and the boldest of all of them was put forth by Ponciano Arriaga. About them gravitated a group of militant tyros—typical representatives of the generation to which the early reformers had looked to carry on their work, the second, the social, levy of insurgents who had been mustering their energies and maturing their talents slowly against the day of delivery and who arrived with the relay of 1856. Some were ephemeral figures who made their mark in Congress and faded after it, while others outlived it and identified themselves with later phases of the movement. Less than a score in all, these men were the leaven of the Assembly; and in the difficult progress of the movement through Congress the dredge brought out the magnetic properties of Prieto, Ramirez, and Zarco.

For the movement passed through Congress under heavy pressure from many quarters. When the delegates assembled in February 1856 the vibrations of the *ley Juarez* were still in the air, transformed into the reverberations of revolt in Puebla, and for six weeks the attention of the Convention was divided between its deliberations and the progress of the campaign against the rebels. For a time the threat of arms and eviction came so close that the Governor of Jalisco, Santos Degollado, offered the Assembly asylum in his state; but Comonfort crushed the revolt with a speed and energy which stimulated Congress. The Progressives were spurred by it and took the aggressive, and during the first six months the creative forces were in the ascendant. Their advance was stubbornly disputed, however. The Moderates, their *vis inertiae* stiffened by the revolt which provided a running accompaniment to the initial sessions, were profoundly jarred by the very purpose for which they sat. The first proposal laid before the Constituent Congress, in fact, was an invitation to desist and return to the Constitution of 1824. "Let us not run the risk of forming a new fundamental law, gentlemen," the orator urged. "Experience has proved that a nation that varies its fundamental law at every step never obtains the benefits of the Constitutional system, but passes, perpetually vacillating, from essay to essay toward anarchy, and from anarchy to complete dissolution. That is why a political authority has said with truth and profound wisdom that a nation constitutes itself only once."

Even more startling than the appeal was its effect: the proposal was rejected, but by a margin of only one vote. The scale was tipped by Mata, who dropped a magnetic weight into it. Before the motion was brought to a vote he attacked it by a diversion, which outflanked it, moving that Congress, as its first duty, should ratify the *ley Juarez,* a touchstone, he said, which embodied "a principle that had been raised to the rank of a dogma by true republicans and without which democracy would be impossible." The debate called forth a full house on the floor and in the galleries, and the government joined in it. The prestige of the law was so powerful that the author of the parliamentary retreat was reduced to fighting a delaying action, lame tactics against the loadstone, for, far from damming, they merely served to accumulate the torrent of votes that drowned him; and the *ley Juarez* was ratified all but unanimously, over a single dissenting vote. Hailed as "one of the bases of the future Constitution," as its cornerstone, in fact, it served to rally Congress, as it had rallied Comonfort and the Moderates before, and to swing the tide of wavering opinion into a long forward sweep that forced the backsliders to abandon any hope of a Constitution that respected the military and ecclesiastical *fueros.*

The margin of victory was so narrow that the radicals were shocked to their feet and roused to a reckless pitch. When the draft of a Constitution drawn on the most advanced model—that of the United States and including its most liberal features—was reported to the Chamber, Ponciano Arriaga, who was the chairman of the Constitutional Committee, himself rose to denounce its shortcomings. Impatient as always of pretense, he saw little else in any constitution which affected abstract rights and liberties, while the basic right, the economic guarantee of democracy, was ignored. "Ideas are proclaimed," he said, "and facts are forgotten. The Constitution should be the law of *the land;* but the condition of *the land* is not constituted or even considered. Are we to practice popular government and have a hungry, naked, and miserable people? . . . Would it not be more logical and more honest to deny our four million poor all participation in public affairs, all choice in public posts, all active or passive voice in elections, to declare them things and not persons, and to found a system of government in which the aristocracy of money, or at most of talent, will serve as the base of our institutions?" For that was exactly what they were doing. Though some social reforms had been accepted by his committee, "all those were rejected which tended to define and determine the right of property, to procure indirectly the division of the immense lands accumulated today in the hands of a few owners, to correct the countless abuses which have passed into daily practice in the name of that sacred and inviolable right, and to set in movement the territorial and agricultural wealth of the country, arrested and reduced to intolerable monopolies, while so many settlements and laborious citizens are condemned to be mere passive tools of production for the exclusive use of the capitalists."

Arriaga disclaimed any suggestion of communism, or promiscuity, or phalansteries, or universal panaceas, or the extravagances of the utopian socialism of the time. "All these systems belong to the future: humanity will decide whether they are chimerical and whether, instead of pursuing reality, their authors are following a phantom. Under present conditions we recognize the right of property and hold it to be inviolable." Here and now, however, the fact remained that societies were constituted not by lawmakers but by landowners. "In the regions of a purely ideal and theoretical policy, while public men think of organizing chambers, dividing powers, assigning functions and attributes, surveying and laying out sovereignties, other and greater men laugh at all that, knowing that they are the masters of society, that the real power lies in their hands, and that they are the ones who exercise the actual sovereignty. The people are right in feeling that constitutions come and go, that governments succeed one another, that codes accumulate and become more complex, that plans and revolts live and die, and that after all these upheavals and changes, after all this unrest and these sacrifices, nothing practical remains for the people, nothing of profit for those unfortunate classes from whom always come those who shed their blood in the civil wars, who give their contingents for the armies, who people the prisons and labor on public works, and for whom, in short, are wrought all the evils of society and none of its benefits."

In this philippic could be heard the click, and the rattle, and the jolt with which Mexico joined the modern world and was coupled to its progress. While earlier reformers had looked to the French Revolution of 1789 for inspiration, Arriaga drew it up to date. "The Sovereign Congress knows that when the French Revolution of 1848 proclaimed the Republic," he continued, "there arose in connection with the right of property the principle of association, the organization of labor, the lot of the poor, and a thousand other subjects of equal significance, questions so grave that they shook society to its foundation." If the coming Constitution was to lift a country whose history had been revolutionary into line with the contemporary world, and a foreign lever was needed, it must be found in that recent movement which raised the question of property—so hastily settled in favor of the middle class —on behalf of the proletariat. The premises were drastic, but his conclusions were mild. He had often heard foreign colonization discussed, he said, as a cure for the poverty of the land, and had often asked himself if *Mexican* colonization might not be possible; if the fertile and uncultivated lands of the Republic could not be distributed among his fellow countrymen; if it would be difficult, by supplying them with seed and tools, and exempting them from taxation for a term of years, and allowing them to work the earth in freedom, without police, or bailiffs, or confraternities, or parochial obventions, or surplice fees, or notarial fees, or legal fees, or prison fees, or poll taxes, or bridge tolls— if it would be difficult to produce from those immense deserts and dark mountains new, prosperous, and happy populations. People believed, or affected to believe, that Mexicans as a whole were lazy, shiftless, and immoral; but were Mexicans the worst in the world? As a compromise, he recommended that the owners of large and idle estates be obliged to cultivate their surplus acres or to sell them to those who would, planting the reform in a system of small land grants; but whatever solution might be adopted, something must be done. "The reform, if it is to be a real one, must be the formula of a new era, the translation of a new phase of labor, a new code of the economic mechanism of the future."

It is not often that a man lives in history by virtue of a single speech: Ponciano Arriaga was one of those unique figures. Though the solution was so much smaller than the issue, his recognition of the real condition of political progress was sufficient to establish him as a farsighted pioneer, who planted an outpost well in advance of his fellows and towered among them in lonely eminence. For, of course, Congress failed to follow his lead, and the question which he expounded was severely ignored, isolated, and forgotten. His initiative was lost because Congress shrank from the magnitude of the challenge and, paradoxically, because of the support which it received, for it coincided with the appearance of the *ley Lerdo*. Accepted by Congress and incorporated into the Constitutional project, the *ley Lerdo,* which dissolved the largest of land monopolies by liquidating ecclesiastical real estate, satisfied so much of the demand for subdivision and exploitation of idle land, and was so hazardous, as to dispense the Assembly from proceeding further on such treacherous ground and carrying the reform as far as Arriaga proposed. The success of Lerdo de Tajada buried the bid of Ponciano Arriaga—but in an uneasy grave.

The loss of the bid was responsible for the cardinal weakness of the new Constitution, which had no economic foundations and was loaded with top-heavy political ideals that were to prove in practice mortgages instead of assets. Modeled on the American Constitution, it sanctioned existing property rights, as did the original from which it was cast, save in one feature. Reiterating the prohibition of slavery, which every charter after Morelos embodied, it expressly forbade extradition treaties with slave-holding countries and declared that "all slaves who tread the national soil recover their liberty by that very fact." The sole measure of economic relief was an article guaranteeing freedom of labor, or rather—for it had to be read backward—prohibition of forced labor. But the Spanish kings had done as much, only to see their protective decrees flouted by facts. Much was said, on the other hand, of purely political liberties—universal suffrage, the power to impeach, the rights of petition, of assembly, of *habeas corpus,* of trial by jury, and the classic freedom of the press, of opinion, of teaching, of trade, and of conscience, and of these liberties the last carried Congress to the crisis and culmination of its advances.

It was not to be expected that the announcement of an article authorizing religious liberty would pass unchallenged by a Church already invaded in its judicial and economic privileges and unaccustomed to remaining long on the defensive: preliminary protests had been made by the Archbishop of Mexico and the Bishop of Oaxaca, and opinion was tense when the debate opened. The galleries were packed with a dense crowd, hanging over the speakers in a hard white glare of intolerant attention and a focus of murderous appreciation comparable to nothing so much as a Sunday at the bull ring. Nevertheless, as the champions rose and marshaled their arguments, maneuvering with nerve, with skill, and with unfaltering poise and self-possession, the issue obtained a full and fair hearing. "This discussion did honor to the national tribune," the Secretary of the Congress noted on the record. "Good faith, frankness, and civic courage were conspicuous in the addresses of all the speakers, and their sincerity is the best justification of the Congress. The mere discussion of so important a topic is a triumph of good principles. In vain the reactionaries sought out persons to come and insult the representatives of the people. Their intrigues were regarded with contempt. Although from time to time the public seemed excited, and some few tried to mislead it at first, it later gave proof of coolness and preserved perfect order; some jeers were repressed by the dignity of the rest, and the applause which later broke out was entirely spontaneous. It may be said with confidence that many of those who came in a hostile spirit realized that they were not in an assembly of heresiarchs and changed their minds. And to preserve order there were no guards, no police, no precautions. This must be said in honor of a public that has foiled the foolish intrigues of the enemies of liberty."

Under the close siege and support of public opinion, the debate lasted a week and called forth the talents of the Assembly. Their main task was defensive: to place the issue in the proper light and to dissociate the attack on religious exclusiveness from the semblance of an attack on religious faith; and in this the most ardent antagonists united. Prieto, a Christian poet, harped on his piety and harangued the heavens in the hope of being overheard in Mexico; the advocates of freedom of conscience were all apologists, vying with one another in professing their faith and citing Scripture in defense of religious democracy; to a man Congress was composed of devout believers. There was but one exception, and he was by far the most brilliant of its talents.

Ignacio Ramirez was an atheist, the only avowed one perhaps in Mexico. Some twenty years before he had scandalized Prieto and the members of a liberal club, who prided themselves on their freethinking, by denying them a deity. Since then he had gone his way and chosen his own company, browsing among bookstalls, haunting the galleries of Congress, making a name for himself in journalism and pedagogy, teaching but not preaching, suffering persecution and imprisonment for his political heresies, and fascinating and troubling his friends by his religious ones, but always on the margin of public life, in his own eccentric orbit, until he took his seat in the Constituent Congress of 1856. There he occupied a place apart, and a formidable one, because of the devastating intellectual powers which he displayed in defense of every dangerous measure, and on the delicate question of religious liberty his utterance was awaited with dread and dismay. Of what was to come he had already given a hint when the Constitutional project was first broached, and he had arisen, a lean stigmatic figure, and suddenly released his full stature to challenge its preamble. "Gentlemen," he flashed out, "the social pact that has been proposed to us is founded on a fiction. Here is how it begins: 'In the name of God . . .' I well know how much of the fictitious, the symbolic, the poetic, there is in all known legislation . . . but I consider it even more dangerous than absurd to suppose ourselves the interpreters of Divinity. . . . The name of God has everywhere produced Divine Right, and the history of Divine Right has been written by the hands of the oppressors in the blood and sweat of the peoples. And we who think ourselves free and enlightened, are we not combating Divine Right even now? Do we not tremble like children when we are told that, if we discuss religious toleration, a phalanx of old women will attack us, armed everyone of them with Divine Right? If a revolution hurls us from the tribune, it will be Divine Right that will drive us to prison, exile, and execution. . . . Gentlemen, for my part, I declare that I have not come here prepared by ecstasy or revelation. . . . The duty of forming a Constitution is too respectable to begin it by lying."

After that debut Congress was on the alert, but his conduct was more startling than anyone dreamed. To the crucial discussion the firebrand contributed something even more telling than his biting eloquence, his sardonic wit, his towering intransigence, and his scathing common sense—his silence. Save for one brief outburst, he stifled his powers. Lounging in his seat, he tossed no coruscating sarcasms into the ring. Hour after hour, under the most extreme provocation and the most visible strain, he held his fire, his hell fire. One flash, indeed, he could not resist: rising at a critical moment amid clamors of applause and some catcalls, and speaking in "short, sharp phrases that produced a visible sensation," he reminded the House that "in 1824, when the fires of the Inquisition were still smoldering, with one of its ill-quenched

brands an article was engraved in the Constitution of the Republic establishing religious intolerance, and that is the article that we have
come to cancel in the name of humanity, in the name of the Gospel,
and if need be at the cost of our blood." But when, through the tumult
of whistles and cheers that broke out in the galleries, there rose the cry
of *Death to the sacristans!* he raised his hand to silence it. "Gentlemen," he cried, "Jesus Christ never wished to kill," and brought his
speech to an abrupt close. Poised for the thrust and certain of being
awarded the ear, he swung on his heel and strode back to his seat. His
sense of responsibility was greater than his rage; he refused to prejudice the discussion by his notorious views and incendiary genius and
left the trophy to more temperate and conventional men for whom reason was not inseparable from wrath—to Prieto who caressed it with a
loose flow of impassioned and popular piety, to Zarco who cornered it
with level and relentless logic, to Mata who braved it with bloodless
barbs, and to many more who could tame intolerance in that rational
spirit which it was so essential, and so difficult, to preserve.

A high sense of responsibility, indeed, dominated the debate, which
turned not on the principle—on that all were agreed—but on its expediency in 1856. When it was urged that the adoption of religious
tolerance would produce only remote and problematical benefits and
was bound, in a country saturated with Catholicism, to lead to civil
war and the loss of all the other gains of a democratic constitution, the
caution was so obviously sound that it placed a crushing responsibility
on those who denied it; and the most tragic hours of the Congress
were those in which the contest raged between Opportunists and Inop-
portunists on the claim of the latter, which became the taunt of the
former, and the battle cry of both, that the time for this reform had not
yet come. "To those who say that the time is not yet," came the retort
—Zarco speaking—"I put the question, when will it come? When the
people are enlightened, they reply; when there is prosperity; when
there is well-being. But this is to close the question in a vicious circle.
. . . If they wish the reform of society to precede religious liberty, we
have only to consider what Catholic exclusiveness has produced in
three hundred years to abandon all hope. It has produced poverty, ab-
jection, and slavery, it was an element of colonial domination, and it
stubbornly opposed Independence."

Zarco holding his temper was more than the equal of Ramirez holding his peace; but Zarco raged no less insatiably, because his hand was
raised to indite his Divine Comedy and his tongue was tied by the
vision of the vicious circle that forbade his advance. Time! Time! Was
it not high time for a reform long overdue, if so backward and feudal
a country was to survive, let alone to advance, in the modern world?
But he was no match for the Moderates. The timekeepers and the
timeservers swayed back and forth, locked in a long, slow, leaden

match, shifting their grips but unable to break them. The dead weight of wisdom and inertia was a drag against which the vanguard strained in vain, bound by their opponents in a clinging embrace, which hugged them where they were weakest and unheeled them on their own ground. "Make no mistake, gentlemen," they were warned, "the opinion of parliamentary majorities is not public opinion when it differs from the opinion of the people. A majority of this Assembly, if it declares for religious tolerance, will not form a law and much less a Constitutional law. The country will repudiate it and the law will remain a dead letter, as always happens with those that run counter to the national will." Heave as they might, they could not cast the hold of such arguments. The religious wars of the sixteenth century were cited against them to prove at what cost freedom of worship had been won in the Old World—were they prepared to pay it? A robust conscience was needed to face the prospect of Mexico repeating that historical agony to make up for its secular lag in social development. Young themselves, they were cramped by the agues, the palsies, the qualms of time. Worse yet, they were weakened by the very pace of progress. They were belated pioneers blazing a well-trodden trail, long since beaten flat, which led nowhere. It was too late, as well as too early, for freedom of conscience—an issue already obsolete in advanced nations and a burning one in backward countries only if irresponsible doctrinaires decided to make it one. Was it not wiser then, and more humane, and more farsighted, to mark time with the present?

The lowest note was sounded when intolerance was defended by the timeservers as an evil, no doubt, but a necessary one in Mexico in 1856. "Constitutions," they repeated, "are not created or invented; to be good, to produce the social and political results expected of them, they should be nothing more than the portrait, so to speak, of the people for whom they are framed. In the United States, in that pure democracy which is so highly admired, in that liberal Constitution which is so cried up, do we not see the most atrocious principle embedded, the most cruel, the most degrading for mankind—that of slavery? If a people that proclaims itself liberal and democratic to the point of hyperbole rivets into its Constitution an article that dishonors civilization and mankind, will it be disgraceful for us if, before establishing freedom of worship as a right, we wait until it exists among us as a fact?" And the most compromising moment was when democratic dogmas were turned against the Progressives to prove that they exceeded their powers and misrepresented the people. Zarco admitted the charge in a defiant rebuttal. "You forget," he flung back, "that legislators must be superior to their period, that from Moses to the first American Congress reformers and founders of nations have had to overcome resistance."

Between the long and the short view the struggle was highly unequal, and the contemporizers had the advantage. On the short view there was little to recommend religious tolerance, the only immediate benefit which its advocates could adduce being that it favored foreign immigration and would break the monopoly of the Church in the spiritual sphere which sanctioned its monopolies in the temporal; but in reality they were concerned with an ideal of enlightenment so remote as to be academic in relation to present realities. They were, as their critics insisted, tutors rather than representatives of the people, or, as they themselves claimed, trustees for its eventual development: so far ahead of it that they were highly vulnerable to the charge of irresponsible idealism and were forced to fall back, in self-defense, on their faith in the people, their mystic, unreasoning democratic faith in the right instincts of the masses and their capacity to recognize their own interests and those who represented them. The fanaticism and superstition of the populace might seem to belie that belief; but Mata pointed out that when tolerance had been proposed in 1848, it had provoked thousands of spontaneous protests, whereas today, only eight years later, the people had not moved, and, to secure a semblance of opposition, the clergy had been compelled to mobilize the women, "the simple and artless women who have been forced for the first time to appear on the public scene" and to present a handful of petitions, the signers of which candidly admitted that they had been dictated by the parish priest. There was the rate of progress. Neither faith nor statistics swayed the compact mass of the Moderate majority, however, and the contest, strenuous but stationary, would have dragged on indefinitely had not a halt been called by the umpire. The government intervened, and intervened decisively, to discountenance religious tolerance and to signify its disapproval of any more dangerous measures.

Thereafter the radical bloc was steadily driven back and forced from the floor, protesting. One after another its leaders caught and clung to its supreme appeal. "We are threatened with a revolution, sir," Dr. Gamboa challenged the chair. "What would Don Benito Juarez have done when he issued his law on *fueros* if, foreseeing the revolt in Puebla, he had been intimidated by that idea? . . . Don Benito Juarez, sir, saw that he was going to win a principle with his law; Don Benito Juarez feared nothing; nothing deterred him because Don Benito Juarez is a man of heart, and that same Don Benito Juarez tells us today from Oaxaca—reform, tolerance, everything that makes for progress." But the virtue had fled from that spellbinding name. The *ley Juarez,* a beacon six months before, had dropped far behind and became with the turn of the tide a buoy hastily passed by a Congress hurrying to make port. In the rush of retreat the closing bell alone was heard.

The routed made a last stand at the foot of their first pedestal. "To insult the people," Zarco stood and cried, "to call it fanatic, idolatrous, ignorant, and superstitious, is the only weapon our opponents employ to retard the reform we proclaim. Our people is like all peoples. There is no people without superstitions, there is no people of philosophers, theologians, intellectuals, and lawyers. . . . You wise men, you superior souls who see in Mexico a tribe of savages, must blush to have to represent them. If I thought as you do, I would be ashamed to be a deputy. Gentlemen, the past has been evoked here, and here is a man who is a living monument of that period, Don Valentin Gomez Farias, and I am sure that that venerable survivor of 1824 will vote for freedom of conscience." The decision was dramatic. "The most profound silence reigned, the public repressed its anxiety and voting had something grave and solemn, as all the representatives rose and emitted their votes in clear and firm tones. At first each vote was followed by vague rumors in the galleries and marks of approval and disapproval. The article was declared shelved by sixty-five to forty-four. A few deputies left the hall before voting. The result produced an appalling confusion in the galleries, whistles, applause, cries of 'Long live religion! Death to the heretics! Long live the clergy!'"

This session marked the crisis of the congressional labors and their turning point. Disintegration set in rapidly. The little radical group that had dominated Congress for six months, while it had the support of the government, became, as soon as that support was withdrawn, a discredited minority fighting a stubborn but in general a losing battle to save the remaining articles of their creed. They rallied, they closed ranks, they returned again to the charge with redoubled vigor and sharpened vision. One result of defeat was to reveal more clearly than before the indivisibility of reform and the fallacy of neglecting the economic foundations in a backward and priest-ridden country. Abandoning their crusade for freedom of conscience, they bent their effort to securing the other liberties upon which progress depended, and which would eventually prohibit, as they were at present forbidden by, monopoly of faith. On the day after their defeat, apparently floored but merely driven from the top to the bottom and gaining fresh strength, like the mythical hero, from contact with the ground, they revived the discussion of land reforms. The proposals of Ponciano Arriaga in which, as Zarco said, "there is nothing of robbery or pillage or communist fevers," but which had been protested by a body of large landowners, were reintroduced in a bill recommending a reduction of land monopolies. The author—an obscure Liberal by the name of Olvera, but one of those obscurities who noticed what was invisible to the most brilliant—disavowed any ideas more drastic than those of Arriaga. Agrarian reform, Olvera observed, occurred less and less frequently to lawgivers as culture and acquaintance with the rights of man increased; the French Conventionals and Robespierre in particular never resorted to it, although they professed communism, but "wise and prudent as they were, and working for humanity rather than for the gen-

eration to which they belonged, they tried to establish it indirectly by
making the rich contribute to improving the condition of the poor
through education, labor, philanthropic institutions, and the taxation
of articles of prime necessity. And Jesus Christ himself, who was the
communist *par excellence,* what did he ordain? Did he command the
poor to despoil the rich? No, he confined himself to teaching the rich
that it was unlawful to retain their superfluity, because it belonged to
the needy. For more than ten years," he went on, "I have been incul-
cating the idea that the rich themselves, if possible, should direct the
drama by sacrificing a small portion of their substance to save the
whole, instead of wasting it on foolish revolutions and armed resistance, capable at most of temporarily weakening the movement but
never of crushing it; and I firmly believe, sir, that if they had listened
to me they would sleep today with a quiet conscience and in secure possession of their estates. If the government stops short, its head will suffer the fate of Louis XVI and succumb to the execration of all the
parties that represent the revolution."

In words of evangelical moderation but revolutionary omen, Comonfort and Congress were warned that half-measures were futile in mid-
revolution; the enemy would fight the half as implacably as the whole.
The promise and threat of Reform had been carried too far to retreat,
and the most dangerous of all courses was to temporize. "There may
still be time to remedy evils without serious damage to any fraction of
society," Olvera concluded; but how much more obscure must his
voice become to be heard? "Your sovereignty and the government
should reflect seriously on the dangers and the necessity of dispelling
them, and the rich also should reflect on their real interests and aid the
public powers to save the country by the betterment of the poor classes
and by settling definitely a social question that is assuming dimensions
as gigantic as they are menacing." Religion *and* revolution, Christianity *and* communism, their coalition was still possible, but the concessions must not be deferred until they were made by force, and the responsibility for that alternative he placed squarely on the timeservers.
But an appeal that went unheeded before the defeat of religious tolerance naturally fell flat after it, and the warnings of Olvera followed the
proposals of Arriaga into the limbo of unborn reforms.

Religious tolerance was so integral a test of democratic development,
indeed, that the victors were demoralized by their retreat from it, and
compromise and qualification emasculated even those principles of a
democratic society which they were prepared to adopt—so true is it
that moral bodies are subject to the same collective distempers as physical ones. The most elementary rights of self-government were mutilated before they were delivered, by restrictions and retractions dictated, as Ramirez complained, by mistrust of the people. Universal
suffrage was accepted in form but frustrated in fact by the filtering ma-

chinery of indirect elections. Trial by jury was lost; the power of impeachment was thrown out; an attempt was made to refine away the rights of peaceful assembly and lawful petition. Freedom of the press, hedged about with captious limitations, came through thanks to a spirited defense by Zarco. As editor of the leading Liberal paper, the *Siglo XIX,* Zarco rose to the defense of his profession with militant zeal, but it was less by trade-righteousness that he carried the day than by the adventitious aid he derived from a small scandal in which he was then involved. The French Minister had offended the French colony by making a niggardly contribution to a relief fund for the victims of a flood in France, and his compatriots had punished him by a Mexican *cencerrada*—a serenade of pots and pans. The incident had been written up in the *Siglo* by the editor himself, and it was upon him that the nettled diplomat vented his anger, threatening the government with an international incident if he were not promptly castigated. The government had the weakness, or the address, to call a congressional trial, a settlement which Zarco accepted with alacrity and exploited to the full. The case would have been a godsend to the most unskilled publicist, and he was an expert. He converted the affair into a mock trial, regaling Congress with a solemn account of the *cencerrada* and pillorying the victim with a humor, a good humor, a moderation and urbanity that revealed his command of the most admired French qualities, and exploding the international incident with a single prick. "I can only repeat," he concluded after a hilarious day in court, "that to receive a *cencerrada* may be mortifying, but that it can never be one of the official functions of an ambassador. It would be sad to suppose that the conquerors of the East should have to come to our shores to the tune of a frying pan, and that His Majesty the Emperor, and above all the French people, should have to make a national issue of an event that at most will set all Paris laughing." Needless to say, he was acquitted. Under the banter he touched the sore spot of foreign dictation, and freedom of the press was incorporated into the Constitution in a flush of patriotic pride.

But it was only thanks to the unflagging energy of the leavening few that the major principles of democracy came through the thickening pressure of compromise at all. The stamina of Congress steadily weakened as its work approached completion and the verdict of the country loomed nearer. In October a second revolt broke out in Puebla, this time against the *ley Lerdo,* and though it was repressed, the effect on the lawmakers was profoundly troubling. To a few, but a very few, it was a timely confirmation of their contention that half-measures would be fought as implacably as whole ones, and a warning, as one speaker said, "that if you wish to flatter the clergy, it is well to remember that this class will never compromise with liberty." But they were a minority, fighting to hold what ground they had already won. A motion to return to the Constitution of 1824 was reintroduced by a considerable majority and was so nearly adopted as to call all that had been accomplished into question and to cast a long mortal shadow over the final months of deliberation.

Time also told on the spirit of the delegates, and the habits of legislative bodies eager to relax after a heavy meal; after sitting over their work for a year they were determined to bring it to a close at all costs. On February 5, 1857, the Constitution was proclaimed. A solemn unanimity marked the closing ceremony. Gomez Farias presided, kneeling before the Bible and swearing his sanction; a hundred deputies stood and raised their hands, repeating the oath in unison; the volume was handed to Comonfort, who pledged himself to preserve it. The finality of the result was crowned by recognition of its fallibility: a philosophical reflection to that effect was made by Comonfort and echoed by Leon Guzman, the vice-president of Congress, in his reply. "The Congress," he said, "is far from flattering itself with the idea that its work is perfect. It well knows, as you have said, that no work of man is so. It believes, nevertheless, that it has achieved principles of vital importance and opened wide a door through which the men who follow us may develop a just liberty to its ultimate consequences."

Such indeed was the achievement of the Constituents of 1856—prospective. The new Constitution was an unfinished effort, a vehicle for progress, and a compromise between the fundamental and the feasible. Primarily a political rather than a social charter, it represented only a relative advance over the Constitution of 1824: like that counterweight against which it was drawn with so much difficulty, it consecrated, tacitly but no less implicitly, the cardinal principle of religious intolerance, which sealed and sanctioned all the other monopolies of colonial society; and the two anticlerical statutes incorporated in it, the *ley Juarez* and the *ley Lerdo,* originated outside of the Congress instead of within it. The major taboos were respected. But if the social bases of progress were faulty or fragmentary, political machinery of the most approved modern make had been placed within reach of the people, or the conscious part of it, to improve and complete them. The structural principles of democracy were proclaimed—freedom of thought and teaching and the press, of labor, of petition, and assembly, and a faithful replica of the Rights of Man informed a chronically inorganic nation for the first time of its recognized and inalienable birthright.

The features upon which the mechanics most prided themselves were naturally those which contrasted most sharply with the past. A long list of civil liberties, which by their very nature and length recapitulated and indicted abuses that had flourished freely in the turbulent years of tyranny, guaranteed the right of judicial appeal, of bail, of confrontation with the accuser in criminal cases, of access to the material of defense, of inviolability of domicile and private correspondence;

prohibited previous imprisonment for all crimes except those involving corporal punishment, and unmotivated arrest for more than three days, and more than one trial for the same offense, and unusual or excessive penalties, such as whipping, branding, torture, or confiscation of property, and incarceration for debt, and retroactive laws; and instituted as their consummation and synthesis the abolition of class justice by the *ley Juarez* and by a hundred helpmates in the Assembly, of capital punishment for political crimes. Humanity was not among the shortcomings of the men of '57. It was the redeeming feature of their failings and the carnal defect of the partial reforms of incomplete liberals: the parts were not equal to the whole, but the whole was a mosaic of the collective progress of many minds, varying in individual vision and courage but holding a common inspiration of original generosity, which they labored conscientiously to translate into a working approximation of human justice. And that perpetually unfinished effort produced a few workmen ambitious and fit to develop it further.

The crowning achievement of the Constitution was not the measures but the men it produced, and here too the triumph was prospective. The fighting few who dominated Congress during the first six months distinguished themselves by their constancy during the days of decline, and though their ranks were thinned, the survivors were recognized as the national protagonists of reform. Ramirez, the caustic iconoclast; Prieto, the popular sentimentalist; Zarco, the most persuasive of journalists: Mata, the master-disciple; Guzman, the blandest of zealots; visionary realists like Arriaga and Olvera and sensible ones like Gamboa—all displayed what Arriaga declared was "the first requisite of a public man," character; and each in his own way revealed traits of the national character and talent that contributed essential parts to the making of a popular movement. For it was still in the making, and its momentum and continuity could be counted only by its converts.

One remarkable convert was added to the roster of complete liberals when Congress closed. Santos Degollado, the Governor of Jalisco, was a specimen of what the Constitution could produce in the way of men. He had fought with conspicuous courage in the revolution of Ayutla, but to the Constituent Congress he contributed little, and that little either perfunctory or unfortunate, his idea being to go back to an earlier conservative charter. The Constitution exceeded his convictions, but he underwrote it with a loyalty fully equal to the zeal of those who wrote it, and all the more valuable for that very reason. Association in the great collective adventure of reconstituting a nation worked no conversion so happy as the evolution of Santos Degollado. He outgrew his political timidity and overcame his defective vision by virtue of discipline; discipline was the core of his character, and he showed to what lengths he could carry it in an incident which focused attention upon him at this time. After proclaiming the Constitution, Congress remained in session for an epilogue to its labors, of which he was the subject. He had expelled a British Consul from his state for subsidizing a local revolt; the British Legation had protested to the government, and Comonfort had referred the case to Congress for trial. It was a counterpart to the Zarco trial, but a serious one: the British Legation could not be laughed off as lightly as the French Minister, for the Consul was a partner in an Anglo-American bank and had used his *exequatur* to cover a flourishing trade in contraband, and Comonfort sent a special envoy to London to avert an international incident. But the verdict was the same: the issue of foreign dictation was at stake, and Degollado was acquitted. He conducted his defense by waiving it and offered in his peroration "to continue to play the guilty party, if this will lend another service to my country." The words summed up the man: from anyone else they might have been applauded as a forensic appeal, but he was blind to their histrionic effect; for Degollado was as sincere and as artless as an adolescent. He had the vocation of martyrdom and he proclaimed his calling; and it was that quality, or frailty, of the professional reformer that endeared him to the little band of radicals who knew that they would need it as soon as the Constitution was launched. With him their roll call was almost complete. But the absent were not forgotten. Again and again two names were recalled in congressional battle. When Arriaga challenged the government on a wavering issue, "the party of progress," he said, "has the right to ask the government party: what are its reforms? The *ley Juarez,* the *ley Lerdo.* Needless to say, neither Señor Juarez nor Señor Lerdo belongs to the Moderate party." Whenever the battle was dubious, those standards were brandished; wherever the odds were overwhelming, those names were added to the count to make up for the weight of numbers. And after the battle they were needed more transcendently than ever.

13

FOR the Constituent Congress had demonstrated the radical fallacy of attempting revolutionary reforms by parliamentary methods, and the incompetence of the democratic process, where the force of numbers was decisive and negative, to deal with them. Individual initiative was still indispensable to popular progress. As a mold for men, the Assembly had performed an important function, but a transient one. The inspiration which it kindled, the energy which it released, the solidarity which it created, lost their focus as soon as it dissolved, and the few creative spirits whom it mustered were again dispersed and disorganized.

Ocampo left the Congress long before the end and followed its final stages in critical solitude. When the press cited four names—his own, Arriaga, Lerdo, and Juarez—as successive leaders of the radical fraction within a single year to prove its chronic infirmity, Ocampo bridled. "This shows a lack of intelligence," he wrote to Mata. "I say in turn that we Liberals do not like leaders; that any one of us on any given occasion may be the representative (not the leader) of one or many of our ideas of progress, and that the very text of the paper would prove, if it were true, that we always subordinate persons to ideas." He was the first, however, to succumb to the old anarchy of the Liberal clan. He refused to sign the Constitution and retired to his farm, preferring intellectual solitude to active isolation. Heartsick and weary of half-measures—"We are singularly foolish people," he sighed. "The text is long but the preacher is tired"—he studied the progress of compromise and decay with a deepening disgust and despondency, which he concentrated on one man. For it was the influence of one man, steadily curbing the courage of the minority and moderating the mild temerity of the Moderate majority, that Ocampo blamed for the frailty of a covenant which, by seeking security, provided safeguards against every peril but its own debility. "For more than a year now," he said, "all of us who have been compelled to study the present President—a person whom we knew very superficially hitherto—have been able to appreciate his absolute lack of character, his great dearth of convictions, and his more than ordinary want of education. I am not surprised, therefore, that the present system of government is always afraid of everyone and everything. Whence could it draw inner impulse if it is without conviction, physiological organization, and even the instinct of great things? It is sad nonetheless, and all the more so for being expected, that the fine opportunities incessantly offered to Mexico should be lost to such incapable hands."

Of all the personalities called forth by Congress, Comonfort was the last to reveal himself and the most important because of his controlling position and the infirmity of his character: a pivotal figure who confirmed with every passing hour the horoscope which Ocampo had cast of him as an incorrigible timeserver. If destiny meant to do what was expected of one, and every man after his kind, Comonfort was doomed to compromise, to cater to the clergy, and, given time, to undo the Constitution in deference to a class that would never compromise with liberty. The prognostic was calculated on the nature of the man and the character of the time, and Ocampo was not surprised when, shortly before the Constitution was published, rumors began to circulate of an impending *coup d'état* by the President. Ocampo was merely incredulous and contemptuous. "I do not believe in the *coup d'état*," he told Mata, "because those people seem to me too timid for it. They may have the boldness, nevertheless, for what is bad." He prepared himself, however, for the worst; for with the dissolution of Congress there was no further check on the President, and to counteract his weakness there were only a dozen disorganized and leaderless radicals, none of whom was in a position of power.

Of the original group, the only one who still held public office was Juarez. Returning to Oaxaca in 1856 as governor in the first flush of reform, he was authorized by Comonfort to suppress opposition by force, if necessary, but his familiar methods of moderation and firmness stood him in good stead, and though he was branded as the author of the first anticlerical law, he outfaced the hostility of the local clergy without resorting to force to plant the newly won civil rights which he brought home with him and those that followed. The *ley Lerdo* he supported by personal example, purchasing a small property to encourage those who hesitated to take advantage of the benefits of a law nullified in the capital by the ban of the Archbishop of Mexico. Government by example—his favorite formula—served him well as long as he could collaborate with Comonfort, but friction developed when the President refused to abolish the system of Federal garrisons, a system of long-standing which quartered the capital on the provinces and which had guaranteed every arbitrary regime in the past. Abolition of military, as the corollary to clerical, control, was a reform upon which Juarez insisted. To accommodate him, Comonfort consented to invest him with the authority in dispute; but Juarez was not satisfied or silenced by personal favors and pressed for a statutory reform in Congress, where it was eventually adopted. Thereafter the rift widened, and by the end of the year Juarez had quietly shifted his weight from Comonfort to Congress, adopting its acts and incorporating them in a new charter for his state, under the terms of which he was elected governor. The security of his position was strikingly shown when the Federal Constitution was promulgated. He invited the Bishop of Oaxaca to celebrate it with a solemn *Te Deum,* and the Bishop consented without resistance, save for the polite and private expression of certain perfunctory reservations. Such was the ripe autumnal fruit of his collaboration with the clergy in the past and the fallow years of timeserving, which, almost imperceptibly, he had put behind him; but it was his last triumph of that kind. He had taken leave of conformity forever, and he was accepted by the hierarchy, like the Constitution, with mental reservations and provisionally. Their pent-up ire flared up at his inauguration under the new dispensation. The clergy refused to officiate and the Cathedral was closed, for the avowed purpose of provoking a scandal and forcing him to break the strike; but he avoided the trap by dispensing with the religious ceremonies that consecrated the seating of a new governor. He broke the strike with the tradition. The sensation which he caused merely by failing to appear before the great marble façade where the saints in their niches and the sanctity of the solar orb awaited, in graven agitation, the breaking of the ages, was a spectacular triumph upon which he prided himself; nor was it the only one. "Speaking of bad habits," he noted, "there were others that served only to gratify the vanity and ostentation of the governor, such as the custom of having armed guards in their homes and wearing hats of a special shape at public ceremonies. As soon as I assumed power, I abolished this custom, using the hat and dress of an ordinary citizen and living in my home without a military guard or display of any kind, since I believe that the respectability of a ruler derives from the law and right conduct and not from costumes and martial accessories proper only for stage kings. I am happy to say that the governors of Oaxaca have followed my example."

Republican simplicity broke more than one precedent. The reserve with which he always referred to himself colored for a moment with self-consciousness when he remembered himself as others saw him then, and as a portrait of the period preserves him, a familiar black-coated and easily accessible figure, filling out his loose clothes with solid flesh, the sturdy personification of democracy on the march. The age of Santa Anna was gone forever, and the era of the common man inaugurated. It was not the least of his talents as a ruler that Juarez did not neglect the visible truth of an idea, which he brought home to a people abjectly susceptible to visual impressions and invisibly governed by them from time immemorial. And on that note his memoir ends. Autobiography was abruptly broken off by the onrush of events, which swept the pen from his hand in a formidable draught of national and self-effacing life, leaving the sketch that he had begun to be finished by the controversial judgments and partial truths of other minds.

Thereafter his biography became a political treatise, the fragments were fused in the movement to which he belonged, and the parts lost in the whole. Discretion, patience, pliability, and noiseless determination—his tried and trusted methods of progress—had been carried as far as they could go. The movement was fast approaching the point at which progress depended on what Mora called the law of the excluded middle; and like Ocampo, Juarez braced himself for the crisis. How he prepared for it he recorded in his last calm moment of self-accounting. Although he had taken no part in the framing of the Constitution, he had kept pace in mind and act with the little group of men who had striven to remold the face of a nation and in part succeeded—

on paper—but only on paper. The test was yet to come, and he set his house in order against the reaction that was expected to follow the application of the new code. All the precautions which he took during that critical year—the reconstruction of the state, the acclimating of reforms, the abolition of Federal garrisons, the consolidation of his authority—were inspired by a weatherwise presentiment. "It was my opinion," he wrote, "that the states should constitute themselves without delay, for I feared that, because of certain principles of liberty and progress embodied in the general Constitution, a rebellion might break out in the capital or soon form there, dissolving the supreme powers, and it was well that the states should be organized to oppose and destroy it, and to restore the legitimate authorities established by the Constitution."

The calm before the storm was long and unnerving. The storm, it was clear, was not to be one of the usual local squalls, short, sharp, and clearing quickly, to which the country was accustomed in its many changes of regime. It was a profound and complete convulsion, which gathered slowly, preceded by a long and ominous hush, a general but indefinite uneasiness, a dimming of the sun and a growing haziness and unsettling of the atmosphere. The first flares of reaction, promptly dispelled by the repression of the two revolts in Puebla, were followed by a protracted period of recovery and preparation, during which the enemy reassembled his strength and felt out public opinion, that hypothetical power to which the theorists of democracy appealed so confidently. Public opinion was thrown into confusion and ferment by the unwonted importance attributed to it. To the acute distress of a numerous bureaucracy of devout believers and their dependents, the Archbishop of Mexico forbade the faithful to swear allegiance to the Constitution on pain of excommunication, and the bulk of the clergy re-echoed the ban. But the Church itself was divided: even in the upper ranks of the hierarchy there were exceptions, while among the lower clergy there were not a few courageous, public-spirited, and conscientious priests, as usual, to declare from press and pulpit that no doctrinal issue, no religious question, was involved in the controversy. Nevertheless, and also as usual, it was the institutional spirit that prevailed, the solidarity of a corporation which could not be attacked at any one point without bleeding in all and suffering systematically at its sacred heart. Nor was it merely the members of the Mexican Church who rallied as a body. Rome felt the shock, and contracted, and reacted, with a long ultramontane tremor throughout all the reaches of the ecclesiastical nervous system. The Pope condemned the Constitution in secret consistory and declared it null and void three months before it saw the light. The authors of the *ley Juarez* and the *ley Lerdo* were noticed, anonymously but none the less notoriously, by the Pontiff, who placed their sponsoring laws at the head of a long catalogue of injuries to the Faith, singling out for special censure, as the most obnoxious features of the foetus, the proscription of ecclesiastical privilege and the principle "that no one may enjoy an emolument onerous to society," and sentenced them with all the other works of profanation wrought and contumacious decrees contemplated by the Constituents. Pius IX had long since outlived his liberal beginnings and was moving, hard pressed by the times, toward complete condemnation of the independent spirit of the nineteenth century. The development of the modern world, trembling between liberty and license, had everywhere placed the Church on the defensive; and with resurgent nationalism encroaching on the temporal power in Italy, it was no time to tolerate disaffection in Mexico. Far from settling the sedition there, however, the Papal injunction inflamed it, and a furious polemical effervescence ensued. A rash of pamphlets broke out all over the land, the press carried the discussion into every home where thought and the parish priest could both penetrate, and the controversy raged unresolved for six feverish months.

The effects of a semester of agitation were seen in the new Congress elected in September 1857. Of the incendiaries of the Constituent Assembly only one was returned. Ramirez, Prieto, Zarco, Arriaga, and all the other contrivers of lurid light and flickering freedom but Olvera were cast out, and in their places sat a body of middle-men completely subservient to Comonfort, himself committed to half-light and haze. What had happened was clearer than how. If the electorate could be trusted, there could be no doubt that public opinion had repudiated the *Puros;* but could it be trusted? Did the result represent the real verdict of the country? The machinery of indirect elections allowed full scope for manipulation by the government, for local intrigue and fraud, and for pressure by the disfranchised clergy in parishes of political minors. Whatever the reason, the result was profoundly discouraging to those disciples of pure democracy who had so confidently claimed to interpret the right instincts of the people. It converted them overnight into academic theorists, immature idealists, amateur Prometheans of progress. The real, the heart-searching doubt which their failure raised, however, was whether or not a democratic revolution could be carried through by democratic methods, whether, indeed, any drastic social change could be accomplished without an initial period of dictatorship by an enlightened minority.

As a whole, the *Puros* accepted their defeat philosophically and provisionally as the inevitable consequence of the ignorance of the people, the neutralizing deals and ideals of parliamentary bodies, and the unpopularity of a schismatic experiment; but there were some hotheads among them who could not resign themselves to their rout. One of these was a supernumerary by the name of Baz. He was a minor and fanatical figure—one of those fugitive firebrands thrown up by every social upheaval for a brief effervescent moment—in whom a larger idea than himself had lodged. Generally considered a crank, he was a crank equally capable of speeding the operation, or upsetting the machinery, of forces beyond his responsibility or control. He believed, and made no secret of his conviction, that the Constitution itself was an obstacle to social progress, and that basic reforms could be realized only by a personal dictatorship. But, though he buzzed on his obsession, he would not have acted on his belief had he not quarreled with Comonfort. Elected to Congress, he was obliged by the President to resign the position which he then occupied of Governor of the Federal District, the Constitution prohibiting the occupation of both posts simultaneously. Thereupon he became a declared enemy of the President, who suspected him of plotting trouble, without reason other than his reckless and outspoken radicalism.

Comonfort listened with one ear, and Baz would have buzzed out of the other, had not the other been humming with the same drone, but from a contrary quarter. The conservatives were no less disconcerted by the result of the congressional elections. The worst of the radicals had been routed, it was true, but their nest remained. The Constitution itself was confirmed, despite six months of furious agitation, and so plain an index of their failing hold on public opinion quickened their conviction that dictation by an enlightened minority was essential to their self-preservation. But they lacked leadership. For want of their own they turned to Comonfort, whose personal prestige, conciliatory character, and elastic policy provided exactly the kind of cover they needed. Incorruptible, he was not inaccessible. No bait of vulgar ambition, nothing less than his virtues could betray him, and it was through these that the approaches were made. Pressure was applied to discover his weak spot, and expert fingers, feeling their way through the dense tendrils of his scruples, soon located it. He was intensely vulnerable through a habit, uncommon among Mexican men, of consulting a woman on his problems—a habit that tampered with unbroken custom and rewarded the woman for the silent and submissive life of her sex, lending her an influence warranted by her remoteness from the world and her conservative role in it, and affranchising her at the end of her days; for in this case the woman was his mother. He was a devoted son; she was a devout listener; and she had a confidant of her own in her Father Confessor. Father Miranda was the right-hand man of the Bishop of Puebla, who had been banished by Comonfort for inciting the revolts there, and as he was the moving spirit of a secret society formed to combat the Constitution by every means available to a class without political license, he borrowed the voice of nature to soften the heart and turn the head of their persecutor. For a priest whose calling it was to inculcate scruples, it was not difficult to quicken those of a confirmed prey to them, and to insinuate into that congenial mind the advisability of reforming the Constitution and eliminating its objectionable features, or if that proved impossible, the whole mistaken and impractical charter itself.

Thus beset by the same suggestions, right and left, Comonfort adopted an eclectic mean. "Three courses were open to me," he wrote later in defense of his choice: first, to leave everything as he found it, which would have been "a folly and a crime," and second, to introduce all the reforms demanded, which would have been "no less absurd and iniquitous." "To renovate everything suddenly, without respecting any right, interest, or class, meant that I would be doing what great popular commotions have done in other lands in short periods of violence and vertigo; it meant that I would be embarking on a desperate struggle not only with the classes affected by the revolution but with the whole people, equally concerned in preventing such an upheaval," and "that is what governments entitled to the name never do; that is what men who are regarded as just never do, for whatever the modern world may owe to such cataclysms, created by reckless crowds, and notwithstanding that they may be caused by despair and provoked by oppressive governments, they are nonetheless great wrongs and never to be accepted as political systems. . . . Between these two extremes, one as vicious as the other, there lay a prudent and just middle way. . . . This was the adoption of a careful reformatory policy, which would satisfy the demands of the Liberal revolution insofar as they were just, but would not openly clash with conservative principles or the religious habits and beliefs of the people."

In this honest statement of a humane creed Comonfort revealed, no doubt, what was his real ambition: to be numbered among the just— of all the ambitions of men the most delusive and, in a revolutionary leader for whom justice could not be found in his own generation, the most misleading. The very qualities which honored his character in private life disqualified him for public command. In practice the middle way, the way of least resistance, narrowed down into a purely negative course, which yielded under pressure to whatever stress was strongest; and in the interval between the two Congresses, when he was left to himself, it swerved more and more to the right and was strewn with concessions to the clergy. To steer a middle course successfully required a strong hand, and between Scylla and Charybdis there was only Comonfort. While he resisted the extreme drifts from both sides, he was haunted by darkness at noon, and it became increasingly difficult to lay a true course through the haze or to distinguish between conflicting principles and the common solution that both proposed. It only remained for someone to suggest a personal dictatorship to guarantee the golden mean—and someone did.

When Congress convened in September 1857 Comonfort had come

to the conclusion that it was impossible to govern under the Constitution and was determined to obtain its reform—constitutionally, if possible. He sought and obtained, with difficulty, from an accommodating Congress an extension of his emergency powers. A month later he was elected to the Presidency by a sweeping popular majority, which made his position secure. A month before Congress met, Baz sounded him and found him ready to restore the vote to the clergy; a month after his election, Baz sounded him again and found their differences too deep for repair. Baz came away from their conference convinced that the President was preparing to capitulate to the clergy and that there was only one chance of checking him. "On that day," he said, "I acquired the certainty that he would accept the ministry of Señor Juarez, which gave me some hope of a change of policy."

A Moderate Congress, and the overwhelming majority with which he was returned to the Presidency, confirmed Comonfort in his conviction that he represented the common sense of the country; but the elections had one result which gave him pause. Juarez was elected at the same time to the Presidency of the Supreme Court, a position which carried with it the succession to the Presidency of the Republic in case of any lapse in that office. Or the urns, or his undermind, engendered a doubt of his ability to divine public opinion correctly; or his judgment was clouded, or the oracle that confirmed him had been adulterated. So unmistakable a recognition of a prominent *Puro* compelled Comonfort to placate the radicals who had lost confidence in him and who wished to put Juarez in power, and accordingly he offered him a seat in the cabinet. The seat was the most difficult and compromising of which he disposed at the time, the Ministry of the Interior, which gave the occupant command of the police and official responsibility for public security. Juarez accepted and secured for his secretary, Manuel Ruiz, the portfolio of Justice, to the relief of the *Puros,* who now had two representatives in high office whom they trusted. Juarez, the word went, was "absolutely good," and Ruiz at least "relatively good."

When Juarez came to the capital in the first days of November, rumors of an impending *coup d'état* by the President were circulating so freely that they were openly discussed in the press. For this reason, perhaps, they were generally discounted; they had arisen repeatedly before, and currency had staled them. But the absence of secrecy was no safeguard against danger, as many successful conspiracies had proved in the past; it proved the confidence of the promoters, and in this case it was subsequently cited by one of them in his defense. "A conspiracy in which we wrote freely to officials and other friends of liberty!" he scoffed. "A conspiracy that was practiced every day and at every hour of the day in the Palace! A conspiracy that was known to the police and to the Governor of the District! A conspiracy, in sum, that was confided to writing and communicated by mail to high officials with no safeguard but a smear of glue!" The Minister of the Interior assumed his duties at a critical time, and with every passing day his position became more delicate. A fortnight after his arrival, in a conference with the President, Comonfort spoke of his difficulties— the respect which he felt for the beliefs of his mother—his friendly relations with several heads of the army—their opposition and the necessity of his resigning. To these hints, which he noted in his diary, Juarez made a "satisfactory" reply, without realizing their full import. Though they were intimate friends, Juarez was not in the confidence of Comonfort; but he would hardly have made a "satisfactory" reply, if he had not understood that he was being felt out.

Whatever the reply may have been, it satisfied Juarez without bracing Comonfort. The only real danger at that moment lay in the mind of the President, which he made up like his bed in the morning to be undone at night, and what happened there was what mattered. He was worried, he was weakening, he was wavering, unable to decide what to do or not do, and it was difficult to steady him for more than a day, an hour, or a moment at a time. A ready victim of the most obvious form of propaganda, he was profoundly impressed by the immense amount of mail which he received denouncing the Constitution. The brewing unrest of the country confirmed his worst fears; some incipient revolts had broken out here and there; he suspected plots everywhere, and when, several days later, he was informed that one of his ministers, who had just resigned from the cabinet, was attempting to corrupt one of his generals, he decided to investigate before going to bed. Driving out to Tacubaya, he found the minister, Don Manuel Payno, entertaining Baz in his home there and, his suspicions confirmed, invited them both to confer with him in the Palace of the Archbishop, where two thousand troops of a trusted regiment, under the command of one of his cronies, General Felix Zuloaga, were quartered. Payno, without suspecting the purpose of the interview, gladly accepted so favorable an opportunity to reconcile Baz, who was his personal friend, although they differed in politics, with the President. Payno was a Moderate in politics and a peacemaker by temperament.

The conference was held at night, and the account which Payno wrote of it was both obscure and revealing. Closeted in a little room alone with the President, he was surprised—and not a little flattered— when he was confronted with the accusation. The accuser was nervous, embarrassed, and did not know how to begin or end; the accused was calm, with the calm of innocence, for the accusation was false, and Comonfort, apparently accepting his explanations, settled down to a friendly chat on indifferent matters. Then he rose, opened the doors, and called in Baz and Zuloaga, who were both irritated by the length of time they had been kept waiting outside. "He closed the doors again, and we sat down, and Comonfort, with the help of his cigarette, so useful, so essential in all the compromising accidents of the Spanish race, began the conversation. 'Where are we going? What is this revolution? What are your plans? On what elements can you count?'" The questions were flung at Baz and Payno, who were both dumfounded by them. "We looked at each other in silence, each of us thinking that the other had his plan formed and his elements assembled, and the truth was that none of us had any plan whatsoever; but since the President himself had opened the door so wide for an explanation, we did not wish to appear unprepared or completely useless. For my part, I admit that an impulse of vanity made me spread myself in my chair and speak. 'Plan there is none,' I replied. 'We have merely talked of what everyone says of the difficulties of the government. But here is Señor Zuloaga, who can tell you what is happening among the troops, and Juan José will tell you with his customary frankness what he thinks.' — 'Well, *Señor Presidente,'* said Don Juan José Baz before I had fairly finished speaking, 'I need not tell you that my ideas are absolute and that I have been for years a blind partisan of reforms. To my mind, the monks must not be, because their day is over; the clergy must not hold property but apply themselves to the endowment of their curacies; the nuns must be given back their doweries, and the novitiates of both sexes closed; in a word, we must not tolerate in a Republic *fueros,* or hierarchies, or distinctions, or monopolies, or privileges either. Anyway, I have manifested my ideas in the posts I have occupied, and you and everyone else know them, but it is not a matter of that now, but of talking like statesmen. The prejudices of the ignorant crowd are opposed to many of these reforms, which can only be planted with time, and so, although as a partisan I think as I have said, as a person who might influence events decisively, I would have to dispense with some of my ideas and compromise with the clergy, who, in the confessional, the pulpit, and in every possible way, are waging a war without truce on the government.' General Zuloaga listened in amazement to that sermon spoken with ease, with order, and even with eloquence and enthusiasm, and Comonfort listened attentively, doubting whether what he heard was true or a dream or an hallucination."

Small wonder; for if the motives of Payno were inadmissible, those of Baz were inexplicable. But Baz, speaking as Comonfort thought, continued. "'Now I will say something about the Constitution: the Constitution, as I have not been embarrassed to say publicly, is of such a nature that one cannot govern with it. If we mean to follow the way of progress and reforms, it provides such trammels and disadvantages that it is impossible for the Executive to move, because his hands are tied for everything; if, on the contrary, he must make some concessions to the party that has fought the government of Ayutla for two years, neither can he do so, since several of the laws against which the bishops have protested have been raised to the rank of Constitutional rules; so, whatever way he takes, the Constitution is an impediment, and there is no help for it; we must set it aside and, as a necessary step, get rid of the Congress too.' Señor Comonfort, more and more surprised, moved his head, rose, lit another cigarette, and sat down again. General Zuloaga, with his head bent and one finger in his mouth, meditated profoundly. As for me, I should have liked to have been a stenographer to note point by point the peroration of Baz."

He did. The points which Baz was prepared to concede to the clergy were the three laws which had been raised to the rank of Constitutional rules, the *ley Juarez,* the *ley Lerdo,* and the regulation of parochial obventions. Of these the most difficult was the *ley Lerdo,* since so much property had been transferred under its terms that it was impossible to repeal it, but Baz was willing nevertheless to make some transaction with the clergy, "because we have gone as far as we can go." Comonfort, moving his head stiffly but making no comment, asked Payno for his opinion. Payno testified that the Treasury, from which he had just resigned, was bankrupt, that he had always been opposed to the *ley Lerdo* and had only refrained from canceling it because of the complications of property title, and that the Constitution was unworkable. He advised Comonfort to resign. Instead, Comonfort turned to his crony. "And you, *compadre,* what do you think?" General Zuloaga, drawing his finger out of his mouth, replied that he had come to Tacubaya to keep close watch over his brigade. "The soldiers are very unhappy, and to tell the truth, they cannot bear not being buried in holy ground or given spiritual aid at the hour of death." For himself and most of his officers he could answer, but not for the men; he was very much afraid that any night now, when they were least expecting it, they would be seduced by Miramon and Osollo, two young officers who had taken part in the rebellions in Puebla and, pardoned by the President, were very busy close to the Archbishop's Palace. As for the Constitution, he agreed with the other gentlemen, it must go.

The conference was now transformed into a council of war. " 'Well,' said Comonfort, rising as if afflicted and exhausted, but rather with the weight of his own reflections than with the very trivial ones we had made, 'I see that we are in for a storm, and that we must take some course. Let us examine calmly the elements on which we can count; ... but let us make no mistakes. Let us see: in the first place, we must be able to count on Veracruz; this is the most important point in the Republic, not only because of its resources, but because it is a fortified town and has very active people. Let us be under no illusions: in Veracruz most of the people are Liberals. In the second place, the interior.

Doblado is more important than you can imagine; besides, he is a bold and active man and has some military footing that is very well organized; he holds the key to the interior, and as Doblado goes, so will Zacatecas, Aguascalientes, and even Jalisco. In the third place, the Federal District. The National Guard is in the hands of the *Puros,* and it will not be easy to make them all agree to a change.'" Baz promised to secure Veracruz and the National Guard, provided the revolution was accomplished without giving an absolute triumph to the clergy. The others promised to sound their friends, and Comonfort surrendered, with one last attempt to preserve his independence and escape. "'Well, said Comonfort, 'my friends speak to me against the Constitution, and I see that in this they agree with the men of all parties, so I shall not insist on sustaining it; but we must explore the opinion of the nation. If it is contrary to the Constitution, we must not impose it by force; but if the men of influence think that it should be maintained, I shall sustain it at all costs or, in the last event, I shall present my resignation to Congress.'"

The meeting broke up at three in the morning, Baz and Comonfort buckling on their revolvers and driving back to town, completely reconciled. On December 1 Comonfort was sworn in as Constitutional President of the Republic, and a week later the conspiracy was an open secret in the states. Veracruz consented to support it, as Baz promised, on condition that the change of policy would favor the Liberal side and that the clergy and the Conservatives would be excluded from the government; and on those terms adhesions came in from several army men in strategic positions. Doblado came to the capital and in three or four interviews with the President attempted to dissuade him; but his attitude was ambiguous. Agreeing that the situation was compromised and that the Reform movement had been carried as far as it could go, he advised Comonfort to reform the Constitution with Congress instead of against it; if this failed, he would then be justified in dissolving the Assembly. As for himself, Doblado hedged. Having just repressed a reactionary movement in his own state, he could not change face so quickly; but he offered to resign from the government of Guanajuato and leave his resources in the hands of the President. As he refused to take part in the plan himself, however, and his name and influence were what Comonfort wanted, this answer was not satisfactory. Doblado returned to Guanajuato after promising to win over another important cog, the Governor of Jalisco, General Parrodi; and as four other states besides Veracruz had signified their assent, Comonfort felt reasonably satisfied of success.

With Baz, who was the center and spokesman of the radical National Guard, the worst of the Reds had been won over; but one remained with whom the President was obliged to reckon. "The only ones who really knew nothing in the first few days," wrote Payno, and he was no

SANTA ANNA

MIRAMON

COMONFORT

but unavoidable ones under the circumstances. On the most innocent assumption, as on the most disingenuous, he disengaged his responsibility too late to clear it. His position, no doubt, was difficult; politically as well as physically, he was on the mezzanine floor, with the President deserting overhead, and the ground floor giving way under his feet. The governor who gave the alarm did not hesitate, however, and the fact that the responsible minister did, implied a clear neglect of duty. Whatever his motives, they remained his secret, and when the crisis broke he was morally compromised by it.

The next day was recorded in his diary by a blank. The disclosure of the conspiracy precipitated its outbreak, and the accused agents spent the day maturing their plans, unmolested by the police. Payno refused to be arrested and sent word to Congress that he would neither appear nor testify. Zuloaga completed his preparations quietly at Tacubaya, where Baz was busy rewriting a manifesto, which had been altered in his absence, and revising it to fit the original plan. Then that erratic radical buzzed back to Congress to warn his colleagues that they were holding their last session. They sat stunned—"since everyone refused to believe what I said, because of the daily denials made by the government and the assurances which Señor Juarez had given us as a member of the cabinet"—and broke up in confusion. The Plan of Tacubaya was submitted that night to the President for his approval. He read it and sank on a sofa, exclaiming, "I have just exchanged my legal title for that of a wretched revolutionary; but what is done is done, I accept everything, and God will show me the way to take." But he soon brightened and pulled himself to his feet, happy, active, relieved of the weight of indecision at last, and apparently determined to act. At dawn the Zuloaga brigade marched to the Palace, the manifesto was posted on the streets, and the *coup d'état* was accomplished uncontested. The President of Congress and several deputies were imprisoned for effect, and Juarez was arrested as he entered the Palace— an accident that saved his political reputation and transformed him from an apparent accessory to the insurrection into its most conspicuous victim.

He spent three weeks in the Palace, in a little room where he was held incommunicado, in the occasional company of Manuel Payno, who was placed there to guard him against any attempt on his life. Payno thought that possibility improbable. The real victim of the *coup d'état* was Comonfort himself, for instead of consolidating his position, it unsettled and shattered the thin peace which it had been the aim of all his combinations to preserve. The suspension of Constitutional order opened a breach through which the reaction pressed forward, claiming the right of way. They demanded the repeal of the *ley Juarez,* the *ley Lerdo,* and the restoration of parochial obventions. Comonfort resisted, but without support. "Everyone is leaving me," he complained to Payno, and it was true. Seventy ex-members of Congress protested bitterly against his betrayal, and resignations and retractions accumulated on his desk. The states on which he had counted to second the revolution turned against it, and a league of Liberal governors was formed to defend the Constitution. The secession was led by Veracruz, and had Baz been in the capital Comonfort would have shot him, so convinced was he that he had been tricked; but Baz, tipped off by Payno, had skipped. Baffled and confused, Comonfort was completely isolated. All that he had lost—the results of two years of labor, the fruits of the revolution of Ayutla, the blood shed for it—and all that he had gained—the repudiation of all parties, the execration of the radicals, the contempt of the Conservatives, the mistrust even of the Moderates—combined to defeat him, and the end of the middle way was political suicide. He had committed the supreme inconsistency, beyond which lay nothing but collapse, but he floundered on in indecision, doubt, and remorse, blundering and bewildered, without a foothold either of conviction or expediency. He attempted to retrace his steps and retrieve his betrayal. He offered the radicals to restore the Constitutional regime with Juarez at the head of it and to introduce two regiments which they trusted into the Palace as a guarantee of his good faith; but the offer was spurned as a ruse to discover their strength and destroy it. He made advances to Juarez himself, but they were rebuffed with the same independence after the crisis as before it. Of whatever negligence Juarez was guilty before the transgression of Comonfort, he was inexorable now: the issue was declared and the consequences were inevitable—ignominy for the one and glory for the other—and nothing less than greatness could redeem his discretion.

For Comonfort return was impossible; so was advance; and to stand still equally forbidden by the pressure conjured up by his last feat of prestidigitation. Cornered and cramped by the demands of the clericals for his complete capitulation, he managed to keep up a pretense of personal dictatorship for almost a month. For almost a month he inhabited the Palace, a mere wraith of himself. Rising in the morning and retiring at night, rising to the same dilemma every day, he ended his political life competing with his official portrait—a great bust of a man, sitting for posterity in an impasse, but blandly determined to be numbered among the just. "I cannot turn against my own," he told his tormentors. "I cannot banish Juarez and Olvera, I cannot fight Doblado and Parrodi." But he was just Comonfort.

During that month Doblado was the arbiter of the situation. His old friends, the Moderates, urged him to rally to the President and save a situation that was becoming more deeply compromised every day: Santa Anna was reported to be arming in Cuba and the Spanish to be concentrating forces there for an intervention in Mexico. His new friends, the *Puros,* implored him to declare for the League and to save the situation by supporting their program, which was to arm, to accept Juarez as interim President, and to call a Convention, which would elect a Constitutional President as soon as peace was restored. The alternatives were difficult—for Doblado. He was a patriot and a politician. The Moderates, as always, were alarmists, and the terrible consummation of their counsels was Comonfort. The Progressives, as always, were ahead of their time, but for once they were practical; and their best argument was eloquently put forward by Prieto. He hailed Doblado as the coming hero of Reform and made him one. Harping on the weakness of men, the poet derived strength from it. "I have always held and still hold in my heart," he wrote Doblado, "that no one can make a better President than you, but in view of this conflict I believe that legality should be the watchword of the movement, without invoking any name that might arouse jealousy. Power will pass into the hands of Juarez; and Parrodi, Llave, Zamora, and you, and everyone else, will have to follow this moral impulse that is in the popular instinct." The advice was politic, heroic, and compelling; popularity was the prize of abnegation. Doblado hesitated. For a fortnight he held the destiny of Mexico in his hand; for a fortnight he renewed his duel of doubt with Comonfort, waiting to see which way the tide turned, and then, turning with it and turning it himself, he declared for the League.

Holding the key to the interior, Doblado broke the deadlock in the capital. Comonfort consented to take the field against him. But it was too late. Payno, on a tour of the barracks, found a different Zuloaga than the one he had known in Tacubaya. The President's crony no longer sucked his finger; he sulked. "My *compadre* is betraying us," he said; "my *compadre* wants to deliver us to the *Puros,* and we are determined to go our own way." As he went out, Payno noticed a number of familiar faces in the next room. A few days later a second insurrection broke out, this time frankly reactionary. The plan was the same, minus Comonfort. The first had been bloodless, the second was accompanied by some sporadic fighting throughout the city, where Miramon and Osollo stormed and captured several public buildings. A truce was called, and for two days terms were discussed. Zuloaga proposed that Comonfort renounce the Presidency; he would do likewise. No agreement was reached. On January 21 Comonfort left for Veracruz and went into voluntary exile, and the next day Zuloaga moved into the Palace.

In a farewell manifesto, as personal as a private letter, the late President dwelt on his frequent desire to resign the burden of power to the person designated by the Constitution as his successor—and ten days before he shot his last bolt. On the day of the mutiny, he released Juarez.

PART TWO

The Civil War

I

JUAREZ left the Palace on January 11, 1858, with nothing to his name but a liberal education; but that at least was complete. The next day he slipped out of the capital with Manuel Ruiz and made his way across country—walking from farm to farm, sleeping one night in the fields, catching the mail coach to Queretaro—and arriving a week later in Guanajuato. "An Indian by the name of Juarez, who calls himself President of the Republic, has arrived in this city," wrote a local gossip to another in the capital. The words were not merely a sneer; so far as the gossips knew, he had arrived no further than that. Despite his notoriety as Governor of Oaxaca, author of the first Reform Law, President of the Supreme Court, and cabinet minister, a provincial snob could pretend that his name was unknown and his pretension unheard of in national politics. National politics was a collection of unknown quantities at that moment, all of them highly explosive, and all marked "X." No one knew which way the country would turn, anything might happen, and if an Indian turned up in Guanajuato and called himself President of the Republic—well, why not? The head of Hidalgo no longer hung on the Alhondiga.

The gossips were not altogether wrong. One month after the *coup d'état* of Comonfort, Juarez proclaimed his government in Guanajuato against great odds. His legal title rested on an abolished charter, the designation of a deserter, and the good will of a League of Governors sworn to uphold the Constitution that they had agreed to disregard only six weeks before. But his moral title was the burden itself; he came of a race accustomed from time immemorial to bear burdens, and when he composed his first manifesto he remembered his heritage. "Under extremely difficult conditions," he wrote, "the son of Guelatao attained the supreme magistracy." The road from Guelatao had led him far, but by now he knew where he was going, and he arrived in Guanajuato with a liberal education to guide him. He knew that the crisis marked the culmination of a movement that had begun with the birth of the nation and that had repeated for fifty years the abortive throes of a people to constitute themselves freely. Whether they were destined to advance, or to relapse into their insatiable past, was supremely uncertain; but henceforth he stood in lineal succession to Hidalgo and

Morelos, Mora and Farias, insurgents and reformers whose spent lives were invested in his, forbidding him to fail.

The heritage was heavy but bracing; for if the example of his fore-runners who furthered the struggle was spurring, even more challeng-ing was that of those who had shirked it. The closest was Comonfort; his weakness, more than a weakness of conviction or character, was a recurring infirmity in all the revolutionary crises of Mexico, the weak-ness of a man unprepared for his historic task and unequal to it, whose fumbling was responsible, as Mora had once said, "for the innumerable evils of an attempt for which a people are made to suffer and from which they derive none of the benefits expected of success." That in-firmity was common to the whole Liberal family, untrained for their mission and forced to gain their experience at the cost of the country. "The speciality of the Liberals," as Prieto now said, "is the talent for prefaces; the works remain incomplete, but the prefaces are divine"— and prefaces were too costly. The time to finish had come. To redeem the failure of Comonfort was a formidable task; but it was one that Juarez was entitled to claim. He had taken the first step to assume it, in fact, when he had stood aside and let Comonfort blunder to his fall; whether he was guilty of willful ignorance or helpless neglect, he had the most compelling of all motives to retrieve the catastrophe. The heri-tage of his predecessors, the transgression of Comonfort, his own con-duct—everything conspired to crown him with the rings of Saturn. The man who carried such a mandate and who was charged with such a sum of life could not be dismissed as a nonentity; and even the gos-sips knew, when they read his manifesto confidently proclaiming the coming triumph of democracy in Mexico, who Juarez was.

Moral power he had—conviction and character, courage and con-sistency—but his political strength was still uncertain. His historic role was granted to him by the governors, who were the real powers at that moment, and who accepted him provisionally as a compromise be-tween conviction and confidence, until peace could be restored and a convention called to elect a Constitutional President, when it was gen-erally expected that natural selection would favor Doblado. Thanks to the abnegation of Doblado, Juarez was not obliged to reckon with his host as a contender for power; that problem had been settled, so far as such questions could ever be settled, by the foresight of eight other gov-ernors. The triumph of discipline, or discretion, over popularity was the first gain of the Liberal cause in 1858, and a great one; but their choice represented a victory of legality rather than a personal tribute. He was a lay figure of legality, whose principal merit was that his name inspired no jealousy, and an unknown quantity to his sponsors, and even their loyalty to the Constitution was doubtful, as two of their number—Doblado and Parrodi—had been named as sponsors of the late Comonfort's *coup d'état*.

But he had moral power enough, and political magnetism, to attract his own kind. In Guanajuato he was joined by Ocampo and Prieto, who formed, with Manuel Ruiz and Leon Guzman, late of the Constituent Congress, his refugee cabinet; and for this frail skeleton of civil government military support was supplied by the League. General Parrodi, who took credit for initiating it, assumed the supreme command, and with the help of his most active colleagues—Zamora in Veracruz, Doblado in Guanajuato, Degollado in Michoacan, and Arteaga in Colima—succeeded in mustering a force of seven thousand men in seven weeks. The coalition controlled ten of the centrally located states in the Republic—Jalisco, Colima, Aguascalientes, Zacatecas, Queretaro, Veracruz, Oaxaca, Guerrero, Michoacan, and Guanajuato—states so placed that they surrounded the capital and could smother the revolt there by swift and concerted action. The plan of Parrodi was to draw the enemy away from his base by a series of simulated retreats, while his confederates attacked the capital; and in pursuit of it Juarez was persuaded to establish the seat of his government in Guadalajara. When he arrived there in the middle of February, the outcome seemed so sure that he issued a proclamation promising to convoke Congress and call presidential elections, and expressing his confidence in the result by adding that his one desire was to resign power and that he had no wish to retain it one day longer than the brief period of his transient administration required. But Parrodi proposed, and the god of battles disposed otherwise. On March 11 the decisive battle was fought on the field of Salamanca against an army slightly superior in numbers and completely so in generalship. The result was a disastrous rout of the Constitutional forces. Parrodi fell back on Guadalajara with two thousand men and some of his artillery, but Doblado signed a capitulation, which eliminated him, his contingent, and his state from the struggle.

The news was received in Guadalajara two days after the battle. Prieto was impressed by the coolness of the President and the game phrase with which he blunted the shock. "Guillermo," he said, "our cock has lost a plume." But official fortitude would have meant very little if it had not been followed by a proof of physical courage far more apt to catch the imagination of civilians in wartime. Early the next morning a mutiny broke out in the Palace and captured the President and his ministers. This was the first intimation of the gravity of the defeat at Salamanca. The rebels, however, comprised as yet only a single company; the alarm spread, loyal troops occupied the adjacent buildings and laid siege to the Palace, and to swell their numbers the rebels opened the jail and posted the convicts at points of vantage on the roof. One of them, perched in a bull's-eye window commanding the apartment in which the prisoners were penned, trained his rifle on

Juarez and amused himself with a running fire of threats until he was picked off by a stray shot from the besiegers. That particular Conserva-tive produced no impression on the President; nor did those that fol-lowed. The rebel commander, who had been suborned by the local clergy, learning that Parrodi was approaching with two thousand men, offered his captives their lives if they would call off the besiegers. Juarez replied that, as a prisoner, he could give no commands and invited him to do as he pleased, but after consulting his comrades, he consented to a truce, and the transient period of his administration was prolonged. The bugles rang out, a parley was called, and intermediaries met in a neighboring convent. While the discussions were in progress a loyal officer, stationed at some distance from the scene and ignorant of the truce, decided to rescue the government and launched a surprise attack on the Palace. The attack was repulsed, but it produced pandemonium in the Palace—and a page of literature.

Prieto was locked up in a little room to which he had retired to write a manifesto for the President. Deprived of light and liberty, "the darkness in which I was immersed," he said, "magnified everything in my mind." His mind was a sensitive plate, and in that *camera oscura* the uproar was registered so indelibly that twenty years later he could still recall the flickering images that flashed through his vision as he applied his eye to the keyhole: crowds rushing by—racing fragments of a shattered kaleidoscope—convicts slipping from the roof with knives in their teeth—shots and shouts urging him to escape—a combustion of sights and sounds that finally lent him strength to break down the door and burst into the bedlam. Approaching the ringleaders, whom he recognized by a huge priest haranguing them, he demanded to share the fate of the President, and was knocked over the head; a few minutes later he came to himself in his presence. "Juarez was pro-foundly touched, Ocampo scolded me for not having escaped, for he honored me with a tender friendship." Prieto was dimly aware of a great hall with columns and a platform, crowded with eighty other captives for whom time and space had lost their dimensions, for "we had been told that we were to be shot in an hour." On either side of the platform were two little cubicles into which many had managed to retire. "Some, like Ocampo, were writing their wills, Señor Juarez was walking up and down with incredible calm. I went to the door to see what was happening. . . ." And then . . . then . . . Then the breath-less pace of his memories, quickening convulsively, rose to a tremen-dous velocity at which everything blurred but their vertiginous beat. "A tremendous voice, coming from a face that vanished like a vision, cried in the door of the hall, 'They are coming to kill us!' The captives took refuge in the room where Señor Juarez was. Some were leaning against the walls, some seemed to be trying to shield themselves with the doors and the tables. Señor Juarez advanced to the door. I was behind him."

And then everyone knew who Juarez was. "The soldiers entered the hall. . . . The terrible column halted, with loaded guns, opposite the door . . . and without delay, and without knowing who gave the order, we distinctly heard, 'Shoulder arms! Present arms! Ready! Aim!' Señor Juarez, as I said, stood in the doorway. At the word 'Aim!' he grasped the latch of the door, flung back his head, and waited. The fierce faces of the soldiers, their position, the commotion, my affection for Juarez—what it was I know not, but a kind of vertigo seized me, something unaccountable, and swift as thought I seized Juarez by his shirt, put him behind me, covered him with my body, and flinging out my arms and drowning the word 'Fire!' which rang out at that moment, I cried, 'Down with those guns! Brave men are not murderers!' And I talked and talked and talked. What I said I have no idea nor what it was that spoke in me and that made me so strong and so towering, but through the cloud of blood I saw everything fading, and I felt myself subduing the danger, dispelling it, crushing it underfoot. . . . The attitude of the soldiers changed. An old man who stood facing me and whom I apostrophized with the words, 'You want blood? Take mine,' lowered his rifle, and the rest did the same. I gave a cheer for Jalisco. The soldiers wept, swearing they would not kill us, and vanished as if by magic. Juarez embraced me, my comrades surrounded me, calling me their savior and the savior of Reform, and my heart burst in a storm of tears."

The firing squad having been disarmed, parleys were resumed and brought to a successful conclusion. The rebel commander and his company marched out of the city to a point ten leagues distant, and the President and his ministers were transferred to the home of the French Consul. The volubility of the poet rendered an invaluable service to the cause, magnified by the fact that he emerged as the hero of that hysterical hour. In striking contrast, however, to that page of literature, was the laconic note with which Juarez covered the facts in his diary: "On the 13th the Palace Guard rose and I was made prisoner by order of Landa, who headed the mutiny. On the 15th I recovered my liberty." That was all. Of the performance of Prieto he made no mention. No one likes to be rescued, and the President was not impressed by it.

The incident was timely and invigorating in its political value. It met the imperative demand for Constitutional heroes, bestowing on Juarez and his ministers their baptism of fire and the kind of personal prestige badly needed by civilian leaders at that juncture. The steady undemonstrative courage of the President destroyed one disability under which he labored: he was no longer a lay figure of legality; and

it was with no vicarious valor that, two days later, he addressed a proclamation to the army congratulating his followers for "popularizing
heroism, generalizing the sense of glory, and reliving scenes illuminated
by the names of the leaders of 1810." And at the same time, in a manifesto to the nation deprecating the defeat at Salamanca and reaffirming
his faith in the eventual triumph of democracy, he renewed his exhortations and his pledge to continue the struggle in the first person.
"Whether or not we lose battles, whether we perish by the light of
combat or in the darkness of crime, the sacred cause we defend is invincible. The misfortune of Salamanca is but one of the all too common hazards of war. There may be others; we have barely begun the
new campaign, and we may see the groping country become once
again the pupil of 1821, as its thousand times recognized but inept
tutors propose; but democracy is the destiny of humanity in the future,
freedom its indestructible weapon, and possible perfection the goal
toward which we are going," he declared. "With these beliefs, which
are the life of my heart, with this faith, the only title that raises my
humble person to the greatness of my task, the incidents of war are
contemptible: the idea is above the domain of cannon." These words,
which would have been conventional five days before, coming from a
man who had just dipped his faith in the great democracy of death,
carried an accent of indisputable personal authority.

Power, however, was as remote and problematical as ever. On March
18 Parrodi arrived in Guadalajara, followed at a short distance by the
victorious Conservative army, and advised capitulation. The revolt at
Guadalajara was symptomatic of the reaction likely to follow the disastrous initial reverse at Salamanca, and as Landa was only ten leagues
away, awaiting the arrival of reinforcements, it was decided, on the
advice of Parrodi, to remove the government beyond the reach of military operations. With a small escort of ninety men Juarez and his ministers started for Colima the following night. Before the end of the
first day's march they were attacked by Landa at the village of Santa
Ana Acatlan. The presidential party was hopelessly outnumbered, and
though the attack was beaten off until nightfall, it was realized that
when the battle was resumed in the morning, though the idea might
be above the domain of cannon, its exponents were bound to succumb.
Since there was no hope, and no danger, of rescue, Juarez advised his
ministers to make their escape during the night, while he remained behind to share the fate of his escort; but the suggestion was indignantly
rejected, and under cover of the dark the whole party slipped away
across country and succeeded in reaching Colima. There word was received of the surrender of Guadalajara and the capitulation of the Constitutional army, without a battle, by Parrodi. The gravity of the defeat at Salamanca could no longer be minimized: two of the governors
of the League were out of the war, their states occupied by the enemy,

and the whole plan of campaign was altered accordingly. To repair the collapse, two decisions were taken, both of them destined to have far-reaching consequences. Santos Degollado was appointed Commander-in-Chief and Minister of War with full responsibility for the conduct of operations in the interior, and Veracruz was chosen as the seat of the civil government. The choice of this state offered strategic advantages as well as security: a traditional Liberal stronghold, controlling the revenues of the customs, it commanded the approach to the capital from the sea, whence the attempt to smother the insurrection could be resumed; but the civil and military commands were henceforth separated by a distance that made their co-operation difficult and effectively divided them into distinct spheres, virtually independent of each other.

From Colima the refugees made their way unmolested to Manzanillo, where they were to take ship to Panama on the first leg of a long roundabout journey to Veracruz, and there Prieto enjoyed an experience second only to his great day in Guadalajara. By now the ministers were popularly known as "the sick family," from their habit of driving in closed carriages, with the blinds down, and their desperate political plight; and they presented so forlorn an appearance, in fact, that Prieto compared them to a company of stranded actors. But at least they were a family, and as such they enjoyed privileges denied to happier governments. Prieto was actually sick and profoundly depressed by the atmosphere of Manzanillo, which was a dreary stretch of fever-ridden coast with a single store where two or three Germans gathered to guzzle beer, and he pined for a whiff of salt air. He had never seen the sea before, and with nothing to do but wait for their ship to come in, he was already homesick for Mexico. His humor was honored in a way that he never forgot: since his legs would not carry him, Juarez and Ocampo made a seat of their hands and lugged him along the beach—"I riding proud and triumphant, with my soul singing in my breast, happier than on the first throne of the world"—while the official family brought up the rear. Formality could well be forgotten there—and he was the most informal of men himself—but not that phantastic procession, for he was all fancy and effusion and fellowship. Chancing to look back, he was wonder-struck by the luminous traces which his bearers left in the phosphorescent sand, and "my friends and companions, delighted by my amazement, scooped up the sand and flung it overhead, sparkling like a cloud of fireflies." The sick family was not a funereal one yet, and the world was theirs, there by the sounding Pacific.

And for a few weeks more. At Manzanillo one adventure ended and another began—an adventure in friendship that left luminous traces in the mind of the poet during the six weeks of seafaring that followed.

From Manzanillo to Panama the itinerary carried them, across the Isthmus to Cuba and New Orleans, and the interlude which they spent at sea was the happiest period allotted to the Liberal government— long uneventful days, carefree and irresponsible, out of touch with the world, with only an occasional port of call to break the spell, and nothing to do but to discover one another anew daily, as people did in Mexico, and everywhere else in the world for that matter; and Prieto was the proper medium to preserve the memory of those intimate hours. A poet could contribute something important to the making of a popular movement in Mexico, but though he tossed off songs and ballads profusely, he was an indifferent singer; his real gifts lay elsewhere. Sprung from the people, he expressed the popular spirit by his sociable soul and his prodigal talent for friendship. His whole career was a succession of ardent attachments to the protagonists of his cause, and he put all the imagination of which he was capable into the congenial service of commemorating his heroes. An enthusiast who throve on his own transports, born for sentiment and insatiable of it, he gave affection freely to one after another, performing his chosen part by reflecting their personalities in a responsive mind and communicating to others the spell which they exercised over him with the tireless devotion of a complete hero-worshiper.

His collection of idols was a large one. The first was Ocampo, whom he had approached with some trepidation because of the difference of their social stations, but of whom he made a brother. Artificial differences melted away in their common faith, and so did the real ones of mind and temperament, although the poet frequently fretted at the mental discipline of the philosopher, and whenever he was ruffled by the precision of Ocampo would chatter and scold like an irritated bird robbed of its song. Later he lit on Doblado; then on Degollado; and lastly on Juarez. There he settled. Juarez was the last because he was the most difficult to appropriate; but after Guadalajara, Juarez belonged to his savior body and soul. Thus it was that, on the beach at Manzanillo, borne by his first hero and his last, Prieto touched the seventh heaven of his sentimental career; yet something was still lacking. There were years in the lives of his heroes which he had missed, experiences which he had not shared and without which he could not possess them completely—an impossible satisfaction, yet it was vouchsafed to him too. In New Orleans the whole party repaired to the little hotel where Juarez and Ocampo had spent their days of exile, and there Prieto was able to join them without jealousy in talking over old and new times. Once the continuity of their association was restored, nothing could break it again; for the poet it had neither beginning nor end.

To recover the past and retain and perpetuate it—that was his gift as a friend and his power as a poet, and the faculty for which he was remembered himself. He was a medium for whom time had no meaning and who could always recall its flight and repair its transient ravages. His mind was as porous as a sponge, and the impressions he absorbed were imperishable. Many years later, on another trip to New Orleans, he went straight to the spot; but in vain, it had vanished, or his unerring faculty had failed him at last, but he refused to believe his doubts; to forget was to die. One night, wandering aimlessly along the levees with two friends who had known the sick family in 1858, he happened to turn into a dark and sordid alley, and there, amid heaps of barrels, boxes, and sacks, he stumbled on "the half-obliterated letters of what in other times had spelled the triumphant sign of Barranda House." Was it chance that led him into that back alley? A veritable frenzy seized him, and, calling his companions, he met the challenge. " 'Come here,' I cried, 'come here. . . . Here is the room of Juarez. . . . There is Ocampo's. . . . Leon Guzman, Cendejas, and I down that corridor. . . . There at the end Manuel Ruiz spent his time.' And these memories illumined my soul and my voice rose, demanding homage and love for the eminent men who figured in the front rank of the great epic of Reform." Why had he outlived them if not to recall them to the future to which they belonged? And standing there in that grimy dead end, he officiated in the dark and peopled it once more with its ghostly tenants. One by one, they came out of the murky chambers of his mind, magnified again against the background of ignorant time. "Juarez in all his elevation rose in my memory: his clear and serene brow, his black eyes full of sweetness, his impassive countenance, his body of medium height, but graceful and free, and the limp hair falling in loose strands over his forehead like jet—all this I sought to evoke for others than myself. I conjured up Ocampo with his great mane of hair, and his round face, and his snub nose, and his large but eloquent mouth, and his winning speech and his expressive hands. . . ." The hallucination held, and before it faded he hastened to revive the self-effacing presence of one who was always fading even in life. Everyone knew what Juarez looked like in his official portraits, but not how he behaved with his intimate friends. "Juarez, in familiar intercourse, was very gentle, he cultivated intimate affections, his pleasure was to serve others, and he was careful to efface displeasure even in the lowliest servants. He laughed at the right time, he favored jovial talk and, after kindling it, fell silent and enjoyed the conversation, being the first to admire others. I never heard him depreciate anyone and, as for modesty, I have never known his equal." The vein of memories once set flowing welled up irrepressibly; he talked on and on; and standing his ground stubbornly, he faced and outfaced death with indomitable loquacity and subdued it as he had done at Guadalajara, and caught up the dust and breathed on it and brought it to be again, all as it had been in 1858.

The drift of his mind was indiscriminate, and what lodged in the sponge was casual, but everything obeyed a broad trend, and nothing was too small or insignificant to be lost. From that time—but what was time where past, present, and future fused without beginning or end? —he managed to recollect a trifle or two for the end of the journey. The best was the great adventure at Guadalajara, which had become a mere anecdote by the time they reached Barranda House, but in which he figured by his own right; and not the worst was one which owed its weight to his telling too, but which he told at his own expense. When they had boarded the ship for Veracruz, he hung on the rail, lamenting his lost Muse: some lines he had just dashed off to the fading shore were among his weakest. At that moment a woman appeared on deck, and Ocampo, always alert to the sex, nudged him and murmured "the Muse," while Juarez, turning poet and truant too, chimed in with a jingle recalled from his school days:

> The Lady Muse, *Musa Musae,*
> The Master too, *Dominus Domini,*
> Are off to the *templum templi,*
> To hear a *sermo sermonis . . .*

As a prompter of jocularities, the President had so few opportunities to figure in history that the sally was worth preserving, if only as a relief from the solemnity of his official portrait. But the tyranny of the Seminary had still to be broken, the jingle rattled the harness and reminded them all of the end of a liberal education. The sea wind blew, the gulls dropped away, the holiday was over, and the carefree interlude of six weeks was forgotten when they reached Veracruz.

Six weeks far from the field of action were a long period in the life of an untried government—long enough to be forgotten and to die. In his welcoming address Governor Zamora implied that the presence of the President in Veracruz was not indispensable to the cause, although the eagerness of everyone for the coming contest would be the greater with him to witness it. One word more, and the address would have been a sermon; one word less, and it would have seated Juarez on the side lines; but the band blared, the spectators cheered, and the President was escorted to his quarters. There the last of the little incidents that endeared him to his official family occurred. The house was run by a black woman, who laid eyes on him for the first time the next morning, when he climbed to the roof calling for water. Mistaking him for a *mozo,* she put him promptly in his place and bade him draw for himself. He did as he was bidden, and as he had done so often before becoming a public servant, and not until the midday meal, when she saw him seated at the head of the table, did she discover her mistake. She fled from the room, crossing herself, amid the hilarity of the

whole household. Of all the stories told of the President, this was the
most popular; it was repeated in many versions, passing from mouth
to mouth like a folk tale, and meeting the need for a popular iconog-
raphy. Anecdotes were few, he did not lend himself to them, and a
peculiar value attached, therefore, to those that Prieto took the trouble
to collect. Trivial in themselves, they were valuable because of their
scarcity, and they bore, moreover, a singular family resemblance, for
they had one feature in common in their modesty. Whatever the demands made upon the President—and the range was broad, from the
democracy of death at Guadalajara to the democracy of domestic life at
Veracruz—he rose to them easily. His companions came to appreciate
that power—the only one that he actually possessed as yet—in the long
weeks of travel during which they saw him at close quarters and under
all conditions, and the time was not wasted that won him the respect
and affection of his official family; for the family was the fundamental
link in Mexican life and a force more binding than religion or politics;
and this was as true of official as of natural families.

With his arrival in Veracruz the demands upon the President grew.
In that port of refuge his personal life and that of his official family
were fused in the far more formidable adventure of sustaining his
government. Prieto had been right in predicting that, with legality as
the watchword of the movement, power would pass into his hands
and that everyone else would be forced to follow an impulse that was
in the popular instinct; the popular instinct was true, stable, and hom-
ing, and everything that strayed from it uncertain, tentative, and mi-
gratory; and in six weeks that impulse had traveled far and fast. Parrodi and Doblado had dropped out, but the League held fast and
extended its territory to the frontier. Santiago Vidaurri, the Governor
of Coahuila and Nuevo Leon, was raising an army; fresh contingents
were promised by the Governor of Zacatecas, Gonzalez Ortega; and
in Colima, Santos Degollado was promptly seconded in his strenuous
efforts to reorganize and recover lost ground. Not all that·was lost was
bad. Before the battle of Salamanca, it was generally believed that the
campaign would be easy and brief; but after the fall of Guadalajara,
it was recognized that a prolonged and unequal struggle lay ahead. The
first round was lost; the opportunity was lost, that is, of crushing a barracks revolt before it became a civil war; and civil war, long, relentless,
and exhausting, was the penalty of that initial reverse; but an illusion
had been forfeited, and it was followed by a gain in morale, in determination, in strength. The popular impulse, spreading and stiffening,
gravitated about the government that guaranteed, and the President
who polarized, the popular spirit. The turn which the war had taken
put an end to the theory, if it had ever been seriously held, that he was
merely a formula of transition; he was in power for the duration of
the war and indispensable to its triumph; for there was nothing tenta-

tive or uncertain in the initiative which he had provided, and it was impossible to regard him any longer as a purely provisional figure. If he was a substitute, it was not for some popular successor but for his popular predecessors, Hidalgo, Morelos, Mora, and Farias. The demand was exacting, but the fictions that had been exploded cleared the air and supplied him with the support to meet it. He was permanent enough to settle down in Veracruz and make a home for himself there; his wife joined him, walking from Oaxaca with his children, and bringing him an accession of strength that he needed, for she knew better than anyone, and long before his official family, who Juarez was.

2

IN THE first week of May the capacity of the Liberal party to sustain the struggle was highly uncertain; and it was already clear that the burden of proof must ultimately rest on the civil government. The enemy possessed two initial advantages, both of which were decisive factors in the balance of forces in 1858.

The Constitution of 1857, which had called forth the best abilities of the Liberals, also had produced the greatest talents of their opponents in the revolt against it. Those talents were primarily and, indeed, exclusively, military. Politically, they were on the defensive. Plan they had none beyond the abolition of the *ley Juarez,* the *ley Lerdo,* and the recovery of parochial obventions. In his first manifesto Zuloaga frankly admitted that the sole title of his party to power was the sacred right of self-preservation and that it was not sufficient, for he invited advice as to what to do next. But without waiting for the answer, and while the clergy were celebrating the wreck of the Constitution and the restoration of their prerogatives, he started a successful military offensive. From the moment that the warring principles were reduced to the arbitrament of arms, the Conservatives had at their command the preponderant asset of a professional army, abundant munitions and supplies, disciplined troops, and trained officers who practiced the science of war with an efficiency unmatched in the camp of their adversaries. The science was simple and the superiority narrow in the primitive conditions of Mexican warfare, but the odds were sufficient for the Constitutionalists to lose the argument on the field of Salamanca. The victor of that day was Luis Osollo, a young officer not long out of school, who determined the course of history by a single battle. Three months later he died of a disease, but the seminary from which he sprang had ample reserves, and his place was taken by a schoolmate who lived to redeem his promise and to write his name large on Mexican history. Miguel Miramon was an even more conspicuous product of professional talent and training, as the Liberals learned before long to their cost. Born of a breed of soldiers, but weak and sickly as a child, he made himself over in military school and proved his vocation early in life. Distinguishing himself first as a cadet in the American war, and later as a disciplinarian in command of a company of convicts, and constantly as a daredevil in many adolescent adventures, he came to the top with Osollo in the clerical rebellions in Puebla in 1856; and two years later, when at the age of twenty-six he succeeded his senior, he was not so much a youthful prodigy as a natural master of his trade, which was much more important. If emergencies produce the men to meet them, Miramon was that man.

The Liberals, on the contrary, labored under the congenital disability of their party. By definition they were civilians and laymen; militarism was the enemy, and they were not adept at a calling they abhorred. Professionals were few among them, and those few unfortunate (Parrodi was one of them), and, being improvised soldiers, they had to learn their trade by slow and costly experience. Degollado was the type. When he took over from Parrodi, the cause found its fitting champion in a commander who was a professed makeshift and who made no secret of his shortcomings. His first manifesto to the army, in which he appealed to the loyalty and fighting spirit of his men on the basis of their common inexperience, was a document that could not conceivably have been signed by a graduate of the Academy. He was the antithesis of Miramon in every respect except, perhaps, in physique and in courage. In appearance Degollado might have passed for a frail and cloistered scholar, with his slight, bespectacled skull, his peering visionary eyes, his faint, waxen, weightless face, and appearances were not wholly deceptive in his case. He had once served as Rector of the University of Morelia. In that capacity he had enforced academic discipline with conspicuous severity, clashing on one occasion with Ocampo, who was Governor at the time, and who was obliged to overrule him to obtain grace for some students for whom he interceded in vain. This rigidity was significant, for Degollado was himself the product of unrelenting self-discipline.

Who or what he was, was known only by the unbending mystery he became. His origin was obscure. The son, or the ward, of a parish priest, he was painted by his clerical enemies as a prodigal whose gaming debts ruined his guardian, and as an ingrate who left the body of his benefactor to be buried by public subscription. If such were the facts, they deserved to be piously preserved, for no more miraculous conversion was to be found in the *Lives of the Saints*. In manhood the name of Santos Degollado came to be invested with a kind of lay sanctity. As soon as he was known at all, he was known for his immaculate character, his selfless spirit, and his driving conscience, and it was that spur that forced him into a profession for which he had no natural aptitude. Fired by the ideals of Reform, he joined the revolution of Ayutla and acquired the rudiments of soldiering in the course of it; and after the overthrow of the Constitution, he was among the first to spring to its defense. He raised money and men with a speed and efficiency that revealed both zeal and resourcefulness and that designated him for high command; and his character and courage supplied the supreme qualifications. What he lacked in science he made up in morale. Embracing an uncongenial vocation in a spirit of abnegation and faith, he instilled his own spirit into his men, sharing their privations and hardships and heartening them by his indifference not merely to danger, which was easy, but to the slow daily death of defeat and fatigue, which was more difficult. With the raw recruits who made up his ranks he was popular. He had all the elementary virtues that appeal to regular troops, and something more: as the commander of a people's army he drilled them in a primer of ideas as well as the manual of arms and taught them to fight by teaching them what they were fighting for. And it was this slight margin of excess value that enabled the civilian soldier to compete with the professional enemy. In Degollado the emergency also found the man.

To feed the wick that nourished the flame was the vital function of the civil government and the first and most pressing duty the President and his ministers faced when they arrived in Veracruz. Degollado was a makeshift general in the same sense that Juarez was a substitute President; but the morale of an army depended on the resources with which it was provided, and the authority of the Commander-in-Chief on an initial success capable of establishing his credit, rallying the confidence of his followers, insuring the teamwork of the League, and checking the contagion of defeat. When he assumed command, he had to contend with a shortage of money, munitions, and men, and with the steadily deteriorating situation in the interior. The fall of Guadalajara was followed by the loss in rapid succession of four other large centers, Morelia, Orizaba, Tampico, and San Luis Potosi. The ring of states that might have overpowered the capital in March had been perforated at five strategic points by May: everywhere the enemy had seized the initiative, and his expanding gains were supported, moreover, by a permanent advantage of position, since he operated close to his base, while the Constitutional forces, thrown on the defensive and struggling to recover lost ground, were thrust farther and farther back from the capital and the seat of their own government at Veracruz. And in addition to his military superiority, the enemy enjoyed a political advantage, which went far to neutralize the value of Veracruz as a port in contact with the outer world and a position capable of isolating the capital: the Zuloaga government had been immediately recognized by the entire diplomatic corps. Possession of the capital was nine-tenths of the law and more than half the battle on the political as well as on the military front, being the reason, or the pretext, for foreign recognition of the *de facto* authority established there. The handicap thus imposed on the Constitutional government was felt in the difficulty of securing arms and munitions and financial and political credit in the United States, which was the nearest and most available market. Sympathy for their cause existed there, they were informed, but it was not negotiable without official sanction. Their first move as a government, therefore, was to send an agent to Washington to bid for recognition.

The agent was José-Maria Mata, who joined his old comrades to run errands for them once more. He was a novice in diplomacy, but he arrived in Washington at a favorable moment. The American Minister to Mexico was on the point of breaking relations with the Zuloaga regime over a question which was the key to American sympathy and which opened the doors of the White House to Mata. He was received by President Buchanan, who gave his bid serious consideration. After jotting down the name of Juarez and satisfying himself of his political life-expectancy and the term to which he was constitutionally entitled, the American President adverted to a matter with which he was more familiar and in which he was more immediately interested and indicated the lines on which a deal might be struck. They began with the Tehuantepec transit. The right-of-way for an interoceanic route across the Isthmus of Tehuantepec, granted to a Mexican subject in 1842, had since passed by sale to an American company and had become a semi-official American interest. The promoters of the company, Emile Le Sueur and Judah Benjamin of Louisiana, were personal and political friends of Buchanan, and the business passed through official channels because the original title, clouded by conflicting claims and legal complications in its passage through many hands, was subject to the protection of the American, and the sanction of the Mexican, Government. A satisfactory settlement had been reached with Comonfort, and confirmation of the contract was taken for granted by Buchanan as a prerequisite for recognition of the Constitutional government—as the test, in fact, of its legitimacy. Buchanan discussed the subject as a diplomatic contractor, confining himself to technical details, and went on to develop these preliminaries by proposing the concession of another transit for a railway running across the northwestern corner of Mexico from Texas to the Gulf of California.

To both these terms Mata was amenable, and he recommended

them to Juarez with one reservation. Besides a loan guaranteed by the American Government, they assured a political connection that would put an end, he believed, to the revolts in his unhappy country. "I may be mistaken," he wrote, "but I am convinced that Mexico is necessarily bound to this country and that, to preserve her independence and nationality, we must adopt a course based on broadly liberal principles, which will satisfy the reciprocal interests of both countries and allow the two peoples to come into contact, so that, knowing each other better, they may come to appreciate each other better and to lose the spirit of aggression on the one hand and of petty mistrust and suspicion on the other." The only question was how broad and how liberal those principles should be. Forsyth, the American Minister, was a stiff customer and a hard matchmaker. "There is a great desire," Mata added, "to acquire a new portion of our territory by purchase. This was the bait by which Forsyth was induced to recognize Zuloaga. Because of this tendency, which borders on mania, I have felt it necessary to make it clear in each of my interviews that, if we are disposed to make fair and profitable concessions for the development and security of American interests, in no case and for no reason would we agree to alienate a single foot of territory."

But that reservation was the crux of the question, and it produced a prolonged deadlock. So far Mata had enjoyed beginner's luck; but now an expert contest began, a long-drawn contest of patience and caution and angling between the two parties. After his first contact with Buchanan, Mata was kept dangling for months, and his government had ample time to give the proposed terms the serious, the very serious, consideration they deserved; for none but a novice could have supposed that the Tehuantepec transit, the projected railway in the north, and the mania for more Mexican territory could be dissociated; they were inseparable parts of a single whole; and the antecedents of the negotiation were sufficient to measure the hazards with which it was fraught.

The mania for more Mexican territory began with the termination of the American war. Together with the loss by the defeated nation of little less than half its original patrimony, the peace treaty celebrated the birth of that policy of expanding empire to which the victor gave the name of Manifest Destiny. Thereafter every American Minister to Mexico had broached the subject of a further acquisition of territory and had been rebuffed; but mania is obstinate, and mania was undoubtedly the word for an obsession which recognized no obstacle to its satisfaction, and which grew with repression. Mata was a novice, but in 1854, with his fellow exiles in New Orleans, he had protested against the Gadsden Treaty, which contained the whole problem in epitome. By that treaty Santa Anna ceded a narrow strip of territory along the northern frontier—the Mesilla—required by American enterprise for the construction of a railway to the Pacific coast; and the sale of the Mesilla was a minimum settlement: the maximum was mania.

Gadsden had come to Mexico instructed to press for outright sale of the frontier states, and he did so with forcible arguments. "No power can prevent in time the whole valley of the Rio Grande from being under the same government," he assured Santa Anna. "All the sympathies of the Mexican states west of that river must and will be with the state or states east of it, and either western Texas must come back to the Mexican Government or the states of Tamaulipas, Nuevo Leon, Coahuila, and Chihuahua will by successive revolutions or purchase become united with Texas. These are solemn political truths, which no one can be blind to." Least of all Santa Anna. Gadsden offered fifty million dollars for a cession embracing the better part of Tamaulipas, Nuevo Leon, Coahuila, Chihuahua, Sonora, and the whole of Lower California; but Santa Anna was not dictator enough to disregard public sentiment, and on the major bid General Gadsden missed. Failing the territorial line, Gadsden was instructed to secure an eligible route for a railway line running from Texas to California, and on this basis the treaty was signed; but even the minimum settlement was sufficient to shake Santa Anna to his fall. The maximum proposals were not abandoned by the American Government, but they were held in abeyance until a more favorable opportunity arose to renew them, and thereafter attention was concentrated primarily on the question of transits.

This question also went back to the American war. The need of knitting the states acquired from Mexico into the American Union made the construction of a transcontinental railroad a national question, which amply warranted the support given to it by the government in the acquisition of the Mesilla. No one appreciated its importance better than Buchanan, who recommended the projected Pacific railway to Congress, but in accordance with American tradition he proposed that government support should be confined to facilitating the free enterprise of private capital. This was where Benjamin and Le Sueur came in. The national question was also a sectional question, since the route favored by nature lay along the southern frontier and served the interests of the Southern states, and Southern capital was invested in its promotion. Because of financial difficulties, the railway was still unbuilt in 1858, but in the meanwhile the promoters had combined the project with other plans and developed short cuts and substitutes extending far beyond the original domestic purpose of a transcontinental trunk line. The ultimate destination of the Southern Pacific Railroad had been proclaimed, in fact, at a railway convention in New Orleans, two years before the Gadsden Treaty, by a local banker by the name of Benjamin. "This straight line of railroad will stop at New

Orleans, but it will not end there as a line of travel," he promised. "That line carries us straight across the Gulf of Mexico to the narrow neck of land that divides the Pacific from the Atlantic. . . . And when we cross this Isthmus—this Isthmus of Tehuantepec—what have we before us? The Eastern World. Its commerce has been the bone of many a bloody contest. Its commerce makes empires of the countries to which it flows, and when they are deprived of it, they are as empty bags, useless, valueless. That commerce belongs to New Orleans!" Mr. Benjamin was then engaged in floating a company to build a road across the Isthmus, and while the Pacific railroad languished, the subsidiary venture prospered. In 1857 he came to Mexico as attorney for the Louisiana Tehuantepec Company, with the backing of Buchanan, and closed a deal with Comonfort, who recognized his title to begin surveys and construction. The parent project had now become subsidiary to its offspring, and the Pacific railroad, still unbuilt, took shape and ramified in the form not only of the Tehuantepec transit, but of yet another branch line projected to run across Mexican territory from Texas to the Gulf of California, in which Buchanan was also interested.

Government patronage was freely granted to both of them. The offshoots offered more advantages, indeed, than did the original trunk; for a while they satisfied the pressing need for transcontinental communication, the shift to Mexican territory of a network of substitutes and short cuts fell in with the whole line of American policy. Imagination traveled rapidly along those lines, and not even a novice could suppose that, in patronizing these private ventures, an American President was not guided by larger aims of national interest. The northern railroad and the Tehuantepec transit were two sides of a surveyor's triangle, the bearing of which could be read on any map; and lest it pass unnoticed, an American congressman had pointed it out from the top of Capitol Hill at the time of the Gadsden Treaty. "I am glad to be at peace with that nation," he declared. "With an American railroad on her northern frontier, and another through her southern territory, acting like magnetic currents upon her social and political organization, American feeling, American energy, and American mind will be brought into contact with hers. Soothed by friendly intercourse, her opposition to us will relax. She will receive in her veins our healthy blood. She will catch our spirit, accept our views, and become assimilated in character with us, and then the whole question of her future relations toward our Republic will be one of friendly calculation between us." And it was that spirit of friendly calculation that Mata encountered in Washington.

The substitution of a policy of peaceful penetration for one of territorial encroachment was an advance, no doubt, but in the same direction. It was a distinction without a difference. Hand in hand with the negotiations for transits the bids for territory were renewed—the one was the shadow of the other. Forsyth came to Mexico with the same mission as Gadsden, modified only slightly by past experience. He was instructed to negotiate two treaties, one for the Tehuantepec transit and the other for the purchase of Lower California, together with a portion of Chihuahua and the larger part of Sonora; but he fared no better than his predecessor. Forsyth was also a disciple of Manifest Destiny, but less aggressive than Gadsden, and he had good reason to be careful, having been promised in Washington that his name would rank among the most illustrious diplomatists of his country if he succeeded. Loath to begin with the provocative bid for territory, and knowing how much depended in diplomacy on the proper order and precedence observed in presenting key questions, he deferred the more difficult at first, and when, under pressure from the State Department, he finally presented it, it produced the expected reaction. Comonfort declared that he would sooner jump out of the window than consider it. Forsyth forbore and, falling back on the easy minimum of the second treaty, rested his reputation on the negotiation of the Tehuantepec transit.

Forsyth was making progress along these lines when the promoters of the Louisiana Tehuantepec Company arrived in Mexico, armed with the blessing of Buchanan, and to his intense annoyance went over his head and concluded a deal with Comonfort satisfactory to their interests, but not to his or to those of their common flag. "I had sounded the government on the Isthmus question and had ascertained that I could, for a consideration, obtain concessions more ample than those contemplated in my instructions," he complained to Washington; "concessions that would have given a virtual protectorate and military occupation of the transit to the United States." The greatest achievements are always those that are missed, and the Louisiana purchase by Benjamin and Le Sueur being an empty bag, useless and valueless so far as he was concerned, he enlarged bitterly on what the irresponsible conduct, unpatriotic initiative, and semiofficial piracy of private capital had cost their country. "I could, too, have obtained a cession of the right-of-way across the northern region of the Republic, almost on the very line marked out for the new boundary designated by my instructions, with such grants of alternative leagues of land from the Rio Grande to Upper California and to Guaymas on the Gulf of Cortés as would not only have contributed a rich fund for the construction of the road, but would have fenced off and concentrated to American use and, ultimately, to American ownership, the very territory that my Government desired to purchase."

After that slip Forsyth was on the alert to recover his footing. By the end of 1857 the favorable opportunity returned. Comonfort was in political and financial straits, and Forsyth asked the State Department for power to make an irresistible offer at the right moment. Before he received the reply, the occasion came, but he was prepared by then to act on his own initiative. The *coup d'état* of Comonfort and the overthrow of the Constitution he reported as passing irrelevances. "I hold that these events in themselves are of little consequence to the country, are only some of the steps in the inevitable march of Mexican destiny. The State is in a condition of rapid disintegration and decay and is tottering to its fall. . . . I may add that, if Comonfort sustains himself, he will have the power, if he chooses, to dispose of public territory." The conjunction of Mexican destiny and Manifest Destiny was now definitely in sight, for Comonfort approached him for a loan of 600,000 dollars to pay his troops, and Forsyth renewed his bid for territory. But it was too late. "He entertained the proposition and considered it for two days, abandoning it finally because the relief it would bring was too tardy for his purposes. I believe I can safely assure you that if I had had it in my power to make an immediate advance in cash of half a million and to have offered a tempting sum for the territories in my July instructions, I could have secured his signature to a treaty of cession." He was not discouraged, however, for "what was true in this instance is likely to be true fifty times over in the exigencies of the next twelve months. The government, whoever may be at the head of it as the result of the revolution now raging in this capital, is sure to be needy, and, watching the opportune moment, the greatest advantage may be realized by the offer of ready money for a negotiation." Comonfort had no sooner fallen, therefore, than Forsyth began to sound his successors. In the kaleidoscopic changes of Mexican politics American policy remained the one permanent and stabilizing factor.

The government of which Zuloaga became the head was, like every Conservative administration, intensely anti-American, but it fell heir to the pecuniary difficulties that made every Mexican government alike in the eyes of the American Minister, and Zuloaga and at least two of his cabinet were sufficiently amenable to his advances to induce him to grant their claims to immediate diplomatic recognition. But he relied, above all, on the clergy, who had the most powerful reasons, as he explained to Washington, to lend him their aid and influence. The government depended on the Church for revenue, since all the coasts and customs houses were controlled by the Constitutional coalition, and the Church had lent its credit to the amount of a million and a half Mexican dollars. This security was difficult to negotiate and was currently discounted at fifty per cent, Mexican capitalists fearing to risk the stability of the government and expecting a Constitutional triumph to be followed by the confiscation of Church property. It was clear, consequently, that the only real security for the Church, certain of being ruined at a single blow by the Liberals or slowly bled by its defenders, lay in filling the public treasury from abroad. "I have had this idea sown in the minds of several of the leading friends and advisers of the clergy," Forsyth informed the Department, "and it has germinated in a way fully equal to my expectations." Both the Archbishop of Mexico, "the purest man in the powerful body of which he is the head," and the Bishop of Michoacan, who managed its finances, entered warmly into the scheme, and within six weeks Zuloaga and his cabinet had reached the point of unanimously recognizing the necessity of a territorial cession. Nevertheless, Forsyth bided his time, for "while the government admits that these measures should and must be adopted, it lacks the courage to do so"—and he at least could afford to wait.

The battle of Salamanca was fought and won, and the bracing effect of that triumph was manifest in the Palace. Forsyth was invited to submit his proposals, and he did so promptly, but after prolonged study they were rejected in what he described as "a paroxysm of political cowardice," for the Liberal government had just landed at Veracruz. The fortunes of war failed to affect the confidence of Forsyth, however, for it was based on the long view of Mexican history and the short term of Mexican governments. "Mexican administrations are short-lived, and the present one already exhibits unmistakable signs of decay. Indeed, I think the rejection of the treaty sealed its fate," he advised Washington. "I already see the visible elements of an early change, and a change of an interesting character for the United States. The time and the occasion are not quite ripe for a communication on this subject. I may only add that, if no untoward event occurs to mar this new development, I have taken measures to master the situation and that the whole must result in making our country the undisputed arbiter of the destinies of Mexico, if our government chooses to accept that office." The measures to which he alluded were no secret in Mexico. A Liberal conspiracy was then afoot in the capital, and one of its leaders, Lerdo de Tejada, had found asylum under his roof.

The conspiracy failed to materialize, however, and so did the collapse of the Clerical government, and the American Minister turned to a short cut. As a last resource there remained but one way of cutting short the vacillations or the existence of any Mexican government, and he recommended it to his own. "You want Sonora? The American blood spilled near its line would justify you in seizing it. You want other territory? Send me the power to make an ultimate demand for the several millions Mexico owes our people for spoliations and personal wrongs. . . . You want the Tehuantepec transit? Say to Mexico, 'Nature has placed the shortest highway between the two oceans, so necessary to the commerce of the world, in your keeping. You will not open it yourself nor allow others to open it to the wants of mankind. You cannot be permitted to act the dog in the manger. . . . Give us what we ask for in return for the manifest benefits which we propose to confer upon you for it, or we will take it.'" Frankly exhausted by two years of fruitless labor, Forsyth reverted to type and the arguments that had failed Gadsden; but it was unnecessary to use them. Zuloaga sent for him again, declared himself insolvent, and promised to eliminate from his cabinet the one member who still opposed a territorial cession. On the following day Forsyth waited for a message announcing the change, and learned, instead, that Zuloaga had changed his mind once more and chosen to cheat fate by another forced loan; and when the forced loan fell on an American citizen, who was banished for resisting it, Forsyth exploded and called for his passports.

It was at this juncture that Mata arrived in Washington. The time was ripe for a shift of recognition to the Constitutional government, but several months passed before Forsyth could bring himself to consummate the break or to abandon the scene of a defeat which he still doubted, and he was in no haste to recommend a new match. "My experience has taught me," he wrote when the alternative was weighed in Washington, "that all parties and all changing governments in Mexico are so much alike, that I do not believe that whatever Mexican policy our government may see proper to adopt should be varied in its essentials, whether Conservatives or Liberals are in power. The only difference should be in the manner of insisting upon it. If the present government should stand, nothing but force would accomplish the purpose. If the Liberal should come in, persuasion might answer the purpose. . . . In either case, determination is indispensable." Such advice naturally cooled any inclination to confer recognition hastily, and after his first welcome at the White House, Mata was allowed to cool his heels in Washington for six months—a highly effective form of persuasion. By the end of that time he was thoroughly convinced that the preliminary question of transits which Buchanan had explored with him was merely the superficial reef, the partial outgrowth of the main, the submerged, the continental mania for land underlying it, and that the imaginary line which he had drawn between the one and the other was indeed the delusion of a novice. Nevertheless, he was ready to risk the negotiation. Mata, no more than Forsyth, was satisfied with the mission of running a fool's errand. He was young, intrepid, and sanguine; during the American war he had distinguished himself by running the blockade and smuggling money and arms into Veracruz; and he believed it possible to repeat the feat in 1858.

For six months the Veracruz government gave the question of transits the serious consideration due to a deal that made the permanence or the transiency of their cause depend on Forsyth, Buchanan, Benjamin, and Le Sueur. The connection of those two questions, one bordering on mania and the other bearing on Mexico, placed the government in a trying position and left them in a deadlock of conflicting claims. The indefinite postponement of recognition prevented them from adequately supplying the army, the revenue derived from the customs was crippled by the immense mortgage of foreign debt secured by those resources and the partiality of the creditor powers to the recognized government in the capital, and the forces in the field had to shift for themselves.

Fortunately the course of the campaign showed a favorable balance in the summer and autumn of 1858. In June Degollado laid siege to Guadalajara, but was forced to raise it by the approach of Miramon, who pursued and attacked him while his men were crossing the bottom of an immense ravine; the battle lasted eight hours and ended in a draw and a retreat on both sides. The drawn battle of the Barranca of Atenquique was followed, however, by a number of uncontested gains for the Liberal flag. In that same month of June San Luis Potosi was recaptured; in July Durango was occupied; in August Tampico was retaken. In September Santiago Vidaurri, leading an army from the frontier into the interior, was defeated and routed by Miramon; but the effect of his fiasco was effaced by Degollado, who returned to the siege of Guadalajara in the first days of October, stormed and captured the city, and scored his first resounding success. But these victories had an obverse side: they were won without the aid of the constituted authorities, by forces that operated independently of them and that lived on the land, improvising and extorting their own resources. Credit and popularity went inevitably to the military command, with a corresponding paling of the civil power that threatened to eclipse even its moral authority, and with the passage of time the demand increased for some major and material contribution to the cause to raise the prestige of the government and prevent it from being relegated to the side lines and the rank of a noncombatant.

Failing American recognition, there remained one alternative, which Prieto urged upon his colleagues. In the cool of a little village to which he had retreated to escape the fever season at Veracruz, he applied his imagination to finance and drafted a program for the end of the war based on the nationalization of Church property. Here was a constructive measure capable of raising the political and financial credit of the party and destroying that of the enemy at a single blow, of supplying the sinews of war, of extinguishing the foreign debt, and of providing something even more important to Prieto than material resources— the reputation of those who initiated it. It was not only as a war measure that he planned it; he was thinking of the future and of the place which its authors would occupy in Mexican history; and what recommended it above all in his eyes was that it would complete what the *ley Lerdo* had begun, and begun badly, in 1856. "The eminent Dr. Mora and Espinosa de los Monteros and Quintana Roo and the whole pleiad of sages, in short, who illumined the future of democracy in our country since the glorious administration of '33, conceived the law of disamortization on the following bases," he wrote to Ocampo. "This whole reform, immense in its consequences, started from the principle that property is national, subordinating the clergy to the government, dispersing the funds in various hands, and abolishing the clerical *clientèle* which gives them the prestige of political power. Lerdo falsified these principles, mutilated the idea like a plagiarist, erected it on a falsehood, set two doubtful proprietors face to face with indefinite titles, and for the sake of the petty collection of internal customs exposed abundant wealth to waste, leaving the clergy their *clientèle* and power; and after so many absurdities all that belongs to him is the glory, enviable no doubt, of having been the first in our country to set his hand to the great work of revindicating the civil power. I think that our conduct today should be confined to restoring to the law the ingenuous expression which it had in the administration of Farias." Partial to his own heroes—and Lerdo was not one of them—he was jealous of their fame. "It is true that we shall not have the merit of originality, but we should not aspire to patents of invention but to the title of good rulers. . . . Look up the works of Mora, read, discuss the matter with our Benito, and give me your opinions," he concluded, "because it will be to our honor to have thought of this even amid our troubles and pains."

Putting his talent for hero-worship at the public service, Prieto accomplished his function in the movement with crowning devotion. The idea was not novel, but it was still nameless and needed a brow to bear it broad enough to merit the succession of Mora. Ocampo was in complete agreement, for it formed part of a comprehensive program which he was preparing with Juarez for the end of the war. But when would that be? Could they afford to wait? And was it not visionary to be so farsighted at that time? These questions were raised when Prieto learned, to his dismay, that his bolt was in danger of being blunted, before it was shot, by the enemy. A group of prominent speculators in the capital, meeting in secret conclave, offered the Zuloaga government three million pesos on the security put up by the clergy. Whence so much courage suddenly? Prieto had the answer. "Father Miranda, who is the soul of this business," he warned Ocampo, "attended the meeting and informed them that he wished to wait merely until December when the United States Congress meets, and that he would find money there, either through the sale of California or through the Tehuantepec transit. He said that Mata was swimming beneath the current, meaning that he knew nothing of the maneuvers of the Padre and that the Yankees were merely looking for the best market. You will see that the padres will nationalize their property. . . ." It was October; the time was short, the danger was pressing; whether the clergy ceded sacred property to the speculators or national territory to the United States, some step should be taken to forestall them; but his warning went unheeded, for besides Ocampo he had to convince Juarez, and Juarez was not to be hurried.

The advantages of confiscating Church property were self-evident; but so were the risks. It was important not to play a trump card prematurely, and there was a distinct risk that such a measure, produced by a government without the strength to support it, would miss fire and recoil on its authors; the challenge would be met by the enemy with every means at his command, and among those means there was one to which the Veracruz government was extremely vulnerable at that time. The unanimous recognition of the Clerical government by the diplomatic corps was a factor that weighed heavily on their councils, for it meant that foreign opinion was officially enlisted in favor of the reaction, and that the great creditor nations whose claims were secured by the customs could at any moment favor the enemy by bringing pressure to bear in the collection of the debt service at Veracruz. As a seat of unrecognized government, Veracruz was a highly exposed position, and a strong hint of such possibilities had been given its guardians that summer by the visit of a British squadron in that very connection. Prieto was panic-stricken when he heard of it. "The business of the English vessels," he wrote to Ocampo, "seems to me extremely serious and no sacrifice too costly to ward off that danger. I do not know why I see in this move a machination of Mexican capitalists, who figure among the bondholders, and whose lives and fortunes are engaged in the present struggle in favor of the clergy. Behind this squadron I see Barron, Iturbide, Jecker, Mier y Teran, and others who will take advantage of the British hand to distract us while they strike us in the back." The British Minister was an avowed partisan of the Clerical government, the British debt was the largest lien on the customs, and the fact that it was held in large part by Mexican bondholders made it necessary to reckon with the British flag as the ready ally of the black flag of reaction. And besides the British Minister there was the French one, whose partisanship was pronounced and aggressive. M. de Gabriac was credited with active complicity in the second *coup d'état,* he was the acknowledged guide of Zuloaga and mentor of his British colleague, and he bore watching in the autumn of 1858 because the expropriation of Church property was a burning topic at that time in France, where the Emperor had announced a decree of nationalization that divided public opinion sharply in Paris. The Orleanist, Republican, and Imperialist press and the peasantry supported the measure ardently, but before the outcry of the Clerical and Legitimist press the Emperor recoiled and suspended its enactment, though it was predicted that, as his popularity was waning, he would not miss the opportunity of refreshing it by issuing the decree eventually. If so seasoned a politician as Louis Napoleon found it necessary to hesitate, Juarez could hardly be blamed for biding his time and observing the effect of the trial balloon abroad. Every move made or contemplated in Veracruz had to be calculated in relation not only to its domestic consequences, but to the position of foreign powers; and before so provocative a measure could be attempted by a weak and unguarded government with its back to the sea, it was necessary to determine to what degree M. de Gabriac represented or misrepresented the bias of the French Government. The value of the measure depended on its timing, and that faculty of which Juarez had given such memorable proof with his pioneer law in 1855 had not forsaken him in 1858.

So the mantle of Mora still went begging: a moth-eaten garment which Prieto tried on for a moment and, finding it too large and too loose for himself or his companions, reluctantly laid away once more on the shelf. "When in doubt, do nothing," was sounder advice than any he could offer his friends, and it was the course which Juarez chose to pursue for six months. But six months were a long stretch in the life of a fighting government, which was on trial before public opinion and which had made no recognizable contribution to the war. It was on the defensive, and the conservative and negative course imposed on it by the dictates of self-preservation did nothing to raise its prestige or to meet the exacting demands and legitimate expectations of the country; and while the problems, the alternatives, the dilemmas that beset the President and his ministers in Veracruz required careful calculation, they met them with a caution indistinguishable from inaction. For six months they made no other mistake. They succeeded in prolonging their period of impeccability to the end of the year; but the situation could not continue indefinitely. Prudence and temporizing were neither popular qualities nor practical securities; when fresh reverses occurred in the field, it became imperative to break the spell of inaction by breaching the diplomatic blockade that created it; and gradually, insensibly, under the strain, every other consideration was subordinated to the value of securing American recognition.

In December the first approaches to a decision were made by the American Government. In his annual message to Congress, Buchanan devoted a significant passage to the situation in Mexico. Abundant cause existed, he declared, for resorting to hostilities against the government holding the capital, because of injuries suffered by American nationals incidental to the civil war, and all hope of a peaceful settlement would expire if that government overcame its opponents. If the latter prevailed, there was some reason to hope that it would be animated by a less unfriendly spirit; and but for that expectation he would have recommended that Congress grant him power to take possession of a sufficient portion of the remote and unsettled territory of Mexico to be held in pledge until the injuries in question had been redressed. The passage exactly paraphrased the prescription of Forsyth. With the Zuloaga government the only possible argument was force; with the

Liberal, persuasion might serve the purpose; and the purpose of combining a threat to the one with a qualified tender to the other was plainly to prepare public opinion in the United States for the application of pressure upon both.

A few days later Forsyth called upon Mata and offered his friendly services to favor a loan and recognition by the cabinet. After spending six months in Washington for no purpose, apparently, but to wear out his patience, Mata accepted the tender with some reserve, but little encouragement was needed to revive his flagging hopes, and he called upon the President, confident that recognition would now be promptly accorded. Buchanan, however, was not to be hurried. It was necessary, he said, to *go slow*. There was a hitch, and, Mata, who had been swimming under the current for six months, was stunned by the pressure he encountered at the last moment. Buchanan was halfhearted, Mata informed his government, because emissaries were on their way from the Clerical government "with proposals very favorable to this country (the sale of the states of Chihuahua and Sonora), and it was proper to wait and see what advantages could be drawn from the indefinite situation in our country. This one trait will suffice to describe the man with whom we have to deal and also to make you understand my position." Mata was weary; he was bored, he was bluffed, he was baffled by Buchanan. Whether the emissaries were a fact or a fiction he was not sure; they might be an invention of the diplomatic corps, which had done everything in Washington, as it had in Mexico, to prevent recognition. He was in Washington, he was in the dark, and he transmitted the facts for whatever they might be worth, together with the despondency which colored his reports and which was worth a great deal at that moment.

If a decision had not yet been reached at the White House, a long step toward it had already been taken. Buchanan himself admitted the meaning of his message, and public opinion in Mexico was prepared for the application of pressure. Two days later a confidential agent of the State Department left for Veracruz to survey the ground for recognition on the spot.

The psychological moment was well chosen. The capture of Guadalajara in October had been a transient triumph; Degollado was not strong enough to sustain it, and by the beginning of December he was forced to abandon the city by a converging offensive led by Miramon from the south and by Leonardo Marquez, his ablest lieutenant, from the north. On the 24th Miramon occupied Colima, and on the 27th he met and defeated Degollado at San Joaquin, capturing three hundred prisoners and all the artillery and munitions. The Constitutional army, broken and demoralized, disbanded and fled in disorder into Michoacan. The political effect of this victory checked, at the same time, the first symptoms of fatigue and discouragement in the Conservative party. Two generals, within a week, revolted against Zuloaga on the grounds of his complete ineptitude and discredit, both declaring for a return to some form of reformed Constitution and both claiming the Presidency for themselves; but both were snuffed out by the success of Miramon, who discountenanced any split and insisted on the solid prosecution of the war to an end that was no longer distant or doubtful. In a proclamation that he issued on New Year's Day in Guadalajara he reviewed the events of the past twelve months and claimed for himself, as the best of the booty, the word on which the Liberals prided themselves, but which rightly belonged henceforth to his flag. The year just ending had raised in Mexico, he said, the banner of progress, "and that word, which is already so hackneyed in revolutionary language and is used to deceive the people, is as stale as it is noxious in democratic parlance, because it produced the Law of dis-immunities, and the spoliatory Law of disamortization, and the Law on parochial obventions, and the ridiculous steal of the Law on Civil Registry; because it led to the discussion of the Agrarian Law, and the Law on religious tolerance, and the Law sanctioning the dissolution of marriage; and lastly, because all classes of society have been abused, and the defenseless population sacked with impunity, by that word." Discussion was down and out. And who was to gainsay his boast? Juarez?

3

WITH the opening of the new year all the elements of action which had remained suspended for twelve months began to develop, and the Liberal government was forced to rise to its responsibilities. Immediately after his proclamation Miramon returned to the capital, ousted Zuloaga from the Presidency, assumed his functions himself, and announced, as the next move, a campaign against Veracruz to bring the civil war to a close. This warning was accompanied by another, which warranted his confidence. The vulnerability of Veracruz was forcibly brought home to its guardians early in January by a joint demonstration of French and British warships, which called to collect arrears in the debt service and to demand satisfaction for forced loans levied on their nationals by commanders in the field. The demands were peremptory and were presented under threat of shelling the town; and the brunt of defending it diplomatically fell upon Ocampo, who occupied the key post of Foreign Affairs.

Like Prieto, Ocampo was convinced that no sacrifice was too costly to avert the danger, but he managed to muzzle the guns with a very small sop. He accepted the allied demands and settled for damages of eight per cent on the customs tolls, with a further raise to ten per cent for the British when the French claims had been fully satisfied. It was his first important negotiation and he was properly elated by the result; for he had scored a point over an adversary who was neither Commodore Dunlop of the British fleet nor Admiral Penaud of the French, but the formidable M. de Gabriac. Writing to a friend, he dilated gaily on "the unfathomable profundities of diplomacy," and invited him "to exclaim like St. Paul, *'O altitudo divinae scientiae sapientiae Dei! Quam incomprehensibilis sunt juditiae ejus et investigabilis viae ejus!'* Our ranchers in Michoacan," he explained, "have made a free, a very free translation of this passage, which runs, 'The high judgment of God not even the Devil can understand!' The text would lend itself to long comment, I believe, if it were applied to M. de Gabriac. M. de —— is so deep in diplomacy that poor M. Penaud, knowing nothing of the facts, tangled himself in such a rigmarole of claims that all I had to do was to yield to his demands. Behold how clever they were! Where they were already entitled to fifteen per cent for a single article, they demanded eight for several." This bungling was the best proof, if any were needed, that the move was purely political; but none was needed: M. de Gabriac was not incomprehensible; the god in the machine, descending too soon, had become entangled in his own wires and remained suspended in mid-air. As a result of the settlement there developed a controversy between the French Minister and the French Admiral which had to be referred to Paris. Already famous, unfortunately, for the *cencerrada* which he had suffered in 1856, M. de Gabriac was destined to be the victim of that indignity again, for his hand was not only recognizable, but exposed, at the most opportune moment for the Constitutional cause.

The fact that the move was made on the eve of the impending siege by Miramon was a matter of concern to all the interested parties, and next to the Liberals themselves, the most interested party at that moment was the American Government. The attempt had long been expected in Washington. Two months before, the American Consul in Mexico City had reported the arrival of a French fleet at Veracruz, at the call of the French Minister, and had predicted that Admiral Penaud would serve certain pecuniary demands on the recognized government in the capital, which it would be unable to meet, that he would then offer to put it in possession of the ports, and that some maneuver would be undertaken for that purpose. The accuracy of the forecast was confirmed by the event, and though the maneuver miscarried, the gravity of the threat was fully appreciated in Washington, where the designs of Gabriac had recently been denounced by Forsyth.

One of the last reports of the retiring American Minister was devoted to a colleague in whom he found a competitor, and of whom he filed an itemized record in the diplomatic rogues' gallery. "This gentleman from the beginning of the revolution of Tacubaya has been the open and active partisan of the Zuloaga party. . . . He spends a large part of his time *daily* in the Palace. . . . He is disliked by all foreigners and intensely hated by the French. . . . He is a schemer, very ambitious and quite unscrupulous. . . . His head is filled with dreams of a European protectorate, to be followed by a Mexican kingdom or empire, and these senseless visions are industriously instilled into the brains of the fanatics and imbeciles who now constitute the government. . . . He is intensely anti-American and has been heard to exclaim with great heat that he was determined to defend Mexico against the Yankees. . . . There is no doubt that he is the regular counselor of the Government. . . ." Nor did Forsyth forget to mention the famous *cencerrada* of 1856, which he emulated. The accumulation of counts testified to the helpless hostility of the American Minister toward an interloper whose influence with the Clerical government he was unable to dispute; and it was one of his main arguments, in fact, for breaking relations, that he expected to succeed to the same favored place with the Liberal government. But the portrait testified to something of far more consequence. Forsyth magnified the importance of the man on whom he focused his professional microscope.

M. de Gabriac was important. Germs are important. The senseless visions of a European protectorate were seriously contemplated by Zuloaga. Six months after his accession he sent for the French Minister and settled his succession with him. He might last for another twelve or eighteen months, he said, before the Liberals triumphed; then Juarez and his friends would come in; but they would be ousted in turn by the Conservatives; the Conservatives would return to power, but would not be able to retain it; and the country would continue to turn "in a circle of anarchy" until the day when the United States took it over. He proposed, therefore, to raise a loan, secured by Church property, to buy four or five warships with it, and to engage a corps of ten thousand French troops under the command of a French general, who would "put everybody in his place"—"beginning with myself," he added—because authority was indispensable, and no one in Mexico was capable of exercising it. The proposal was forwarded by Gabriac to Paris, where it produced no effect. The loan was the least difficulty, Rothschild's offering to float it at a reasonable discount (twenty-eight per cent); but the French Foreign Office was not interested. The Quai d'Orsay was a peculiar institution, a department apart, aloof, independent, self-sufficient, unaffected by changing regimes, and governed by the aristocratic routine of a gentleman's club; and in that stronghold of entrenched tradition bankers were not diplomats, and it was not the custom to encourage them. French commercial interests in Mexico were negligible and too insignificant to outweigh a time-honored rule; politically the idea was also beyond the pale, the accepted attitude toward American affairs being one of complete indifference unless they related to Europe, which was the only proper sphere for *haute politique* and the development of French influence. The department was run, moreover, by Walewski, the Emperor's cousin, who was averse to adventure of any kind and committed to the English entente, which was the basis of the Napoleonic policy; and the English cabinet, when it learned of the scheme, frowned on any suggestion of intervention in Mexico. To have overcome such a combination of obstacles would have required more influence than M. de Gabriac possessed; for he was not as big a man in Paris as he was in Mexico. He was not even M. "de," but plain Gabriac, who assumed his title from his birthplace in Brittany.

His real importance lay in his insignificance. A restless and irresponsible intriguer, incapable of carrying his government with him, but able to fire the imagination of foreigners, he provided a conspicuous example of the latitude that diplomats of his stripe allowed themselves in out-of-the-way corners of the service like Mexico. He was dangerous because he was dreaded; the fears which he excited were unfounded, but they were sufficient to alarm the American Minister, who magnified them in the advice that he pressed on the State Department. "It is not safe for statesmen in the United States," Forsyth insisted, "to ignore the fact that other nations besides our own have their eager gaze fixed on this rich and superb country. Whether Mexico maintains her personality or falls to pieces, we have a deep-seated interest in her future and should secure an influence in her councils. If she cannot stand without the aid of some friendly power"—and that was self-evident —"who should occupy the commanding position of benefactor and friend? If the United States refuse, others must. What if it comes in the form of a French prince supported by ten thousand French bayonets? Or of British gold effecting a floating mortgage on the territories which we decline? Believe me, sir, we cannot play the dog in the manger with our Monroe Doctrine. . . . I can see a multitude of contingencies that will make Mexico the battleground for the maintenance of American supremacy in America." Fears are facts in politics; and if M. de Gabriac had not existed, it would have been necessary for Forsyth or any other disciple of Manifest Destiny to invent him. But he existed; he existed very definitely, independently of the imaginations he irritated; and for a brief moment he played his part in history. The demonstration at Veracruz in January 1859 would have been inconsequential if his hand had not been seen, or suspected, behind it. As it was, it was perfectly timed to serve the party it was designed to cripple. The agent sent by Buchanan to survey the prospects of the Liberals arrived in Veracruz just in time to witness it and to include it among the reasons that he recommended for immediate recognition.

The decision to recognize had been taken in Washington before the agent left, subject to his judgment on the spot, and his judgment was formed rapidly. There was little that he could add to the arguments of Forsyth save some minor matters of detail, such as the composition of the government, an element with which the Department was still unfamiliar and which, however irrelevant to the consummation of American policy, seemed to him to merit some notice. "It may not be improper or uninteresting that I tell you of the President and his cabinet," he wrote after a fortnight of close observation. "President Juarez is a man of some forty-five years, a full-blooded Indian, well versed in the laws of his country, a prudent and sound jurisconsult but a distrustful and timid politician, stern and incorruptible, yet of a mild and benignant disposition; in his intercourse, modest like a child. He has a voice in the council and is listened to with respect, but he has no influence over his ministers and is unconsciously, perhaps, under their most absolute and unlimited control." Discounting the nominal head of the government, therefore, as a mere figurehead, the Constitutional government could be reduced to two ministers. "Ocampo is a gentleman of great native intellect, and of considerable parts and learning, inflexible in his resolves, peremptory in his views, rather prompt in discourse and impatient of contradiction, but high-minded and, like his chief, incorruptible." The other minister was not unknown in Washington, Forsyth having sheltered him in the Legation in Mexico City, whence he had recently escaped to Veracruz. "Lerdo de Tejada (who is in the cabinet at the suggestion of your Agent) has all the brilliant qualities of the other two, is as pure as they, but possesses more of the practical habits which constitute a mind turned toward the actualities of life rather than toward its dreams. He is the most popular man in his party and is deservedly considered the master spirit of the cabinet. His tendencies are all American. . . . We should look up to him as the man most reliable in his preferences for us, frank, open, and always ready to approach a question and to assume responsibility."

One novelty indeed distinguished the activity of the advance agent —speed. The celerity with which he formed his judgment was in striking contrast to the dilatory tactics of the Department; but he had good reasons to jump to conclusions. The situation was satisfactory and the prospect excellent in every respect but one. The impending siege of Veracruz he discounted in advance, as did the Liberal government, which was confident that it would fail and prove the undoing, military and political, of Miramon, provided the menace of foreign intervention were removed. But that was the hitch. Once that factor had been eliminated, the balance of forces would automatically right itself and incline in favor of the Constitutional government, for which public opinion had declared in sixteen out of twenty-two states, and which would already have established itself but for the lack of material resources. It was remarkable, he noted, that troops raised without coercion should have remained in camp for many months without reward of any description, without sufficient clothing or provisions, relying solely on the justice of their cause and their faith in its final triumph, and in this instance it could not be denied that the Mexican people had exhibited a fidelity to the principle of Constitutional government scarcely to be expected from their past history. Something uncommon had certainly occurred in Mexico when an army in which the superior officers received two pesos a day, the subordinates one peso, and the men twenty-five centavos—when they received it—and who were induced to desert before battle by Miramon, who threatened to shoot without fail all those who did not and advertised a schedule of bounties for those who did, and who were repeatedly beaten, flocked back to its banners after every defeat. His respect for such tenacity prompted him to remind the Department that "no obstacle that could be presented either in the mantle of diplomacy, which sometimes covers destruction, or in open discountenance, had been spared the Liberal party, and that powerful foes had recently given aid and comfort to Miramon by crippling their meager resources in the guise of demanding only just compliance with the terms of a former convention." Surely, therefore, the time for protection had come. "The present condition of affairs in Mexico," he concluded, "affords the best, and it may be the last, opportunity that will ever be presented to the United States to form a treaty with this Republic that will secure to them not only sovereignty over a country which recent disclosures and the most authoritative accounts respecting its soil and mineral resources represent as being even more valuable than Upper California"—the long annex, that is, of Lower California —but also the transits. "In my opinion, then, although it may be an experiment, we have no alternative left but the immediate recognition of the Juarez government. The occasion is one which should be improved without the intermission of a single hour of unnecessary delay."

In support of these promises he forwarded a memorandum, approved by Ocampo, covering the points suggested by himself as suitable stipulations for recognition and indicating the willingness of the Foreign Minister to negotiate upon them affirmatively, including the cession of Lower California. This advance was no mean triumph for a minor agent; where Forsyth had failed, a political scout had succeeded; and supposing that his services would be officially recognized in Washington, Juarez favored his nomination as the regular Minister. But the name of William B. Churchwell was not destined, any more than that of John Forsyth, to rank among the most distinguished diplomatists of his country. Forsyth himself had been worsted too often to want the job; a fresh, unspoiled, persuasive talent was needed; and immediately upon receipt of Churchwell's report Buchanan appointed a senator from Maryland, Robert McLane, as his Minister to Mexico. He was still hesitating, however, and accepted Churchwell's advice under pressure from the cabinet, but with misgivings, and at the last moment, alarmed by reports that the siege of Veracruz had begun and that the government he had been hurried into adopting might no longer be in existence by the time his representative arrived, he reconsidered the question with the cabinet. The move, so long weighed and so hastily made, was never more of an experiment than when it was finally settled, and as it was still a step in the dark McLane was granted discretion to confer or withhold recognition, as he saw fit, on his arrival in Veracruz.

The seat of the civil government now became the center of the civil war. All the forces upon which the solution depended—the military ability of Miramon, the menace of foreign intervention, and the support of the United States—were focused there, and the civil government became an active belligerent, forced to defend itself simultaneously against its domestic foes, their diplomatic allies, and the advances of its American friends. Of these forces the least formidable was the first. The city was well fortified by nature and science, and by all the rules of the book in which he was schooled Miramon was bound to fail. The manual of military science offered four possibilities of success, and no more. The first was a siege by starvation, which required control of the seaways, and he lacked it; the second, a siege by pressure and approach, which was impossible because of the sandy terrain and the deadly climate; the third, a siege of nerves and demoralization, which called for a constant and crushing bombardment, and he was short of munitions; the fourth was a siege of assault, which demanded a reckless waste of lives, and his manpower was limited. He tried them all in turn, and the events confirmed the book. Arriving before Veracruz in the first days of March, he spent a month in conducting a field class for six thousand pupils and a masterly demonstration of what not to do with the inadequate resources at his command. The experiment was conclusive, and on March 29 he broke camp and beat his way back to the capital. The foreign fleets remained neutral, biding the outcome of the dispute between M. de Gabriac and Admiral Penaud.

The enemy melted away; the friend remained. On April 1 McLane landed in Veracruz; five days later he accorded recognition; on the sixth he presented his credentials; and on the seventh he sat down with Ocampo to talk business, and the real contest began, and began badly for both parties. McLane perceived immediately that a long diplomatic siege lay ahead of him. Ocampo, he reported, "manifested great uneasiness as to several of the points suggested as proper subjects for adjustment when intercourse should be established between the two governments, especially in relation to Lower California." McLane read him the Churchwell memorandum, "but I carefully avoided any intimation that he, the Minister of Foreign Affairs, himself had signed the memorandum," preferring to treat it, not as a written commitment, but as a gentleman's agreement, since he was dealing with a gentleman whose embarrassment was visible and vulnerable. Ocampo "continued reluctant to engage himself in any actual cession of territory, but I held him to his implied obligation to give us Lower California if we desired it," an approach against which Ocampo guarded himself with an offer to negotiate transits and trade favors in the most liberal spirit. McLane forbore to press the point at their first interview, since he could afford to wait. "It must be acknowledged, however," he admitted, "that the depressed and bankrupt state of the National Treasury is the main impulse that will excite him to action."

Contact had been established, but nothing more, and both men were in an awkward position. To what extent Ocampo had engaged himself by his understanding with Churchwell was not clear; but Churchwell had arrived at a favorable moment and had benefited by the discouragement that preceded him. "I found them rather dispirited on my arrival," he had noted. "They had been made to believe that the United States would not take any decided course, but now they seem like new beings and manifest sincere and earnest friendship"; and the tonic effect of his fillip was labeled Lower California. The dilatory tactics of the Department and the depressing reports of Mata had done their work, and he was able to touch on the topic of a territorial cession and to come off not only without rebuff but with encouragement. What he had gained, however, was a loose pledge, "a willingness to negotiate affirmatively," which had been given before the siege and which Ocampo was obviously reluctant to acknowledge after it. The tonic had worn off and compunction had set in by the time McLane arrived, but to disavow his lapse was even more difficult for Ocampo than to commit it. Evasion exposed him to the charge of having misled the American advance agent by an implied promise made to obtain recognition and meant to be forgotten after it, and Ocampo was not enough of a professional diplomat to pride himself on the tricks of the trade. But his embarrassment was due to something more than the odious constructions to which his conduct was open. The cession of Lower California, far from being a diplomatic feint, had been so seriously considered in Veracruz that Mata, who had begun his mission in Washington with an uncompromising refusal to entertain the idea in June, had accepted it as inevitable by February and had reached the point of discussing what it was worth—twenty million dollars in money—with Ocampo, who had been softened up by then more than he was willing either to admit or to deny.

The American Minister was in a scarcely less awkward position. He

had accorded recognition on the assumption that the Churchwell memorandum had been accepted in good faith and that it represented a
working agreement between the two governments; and the speed with
which he acted now required strong justification. The considerations
which he adduced in explaining his haste to Washington were less
compelling than covering reasons—the very large interests, political
and commercial, already involved in the Tehuantepec transit; the
knowledge that this right-of-way was the subject of decrees by both the
warring factions; and, lastly, "the fact that commercial relations between the United States and Mexico, embarrassed beyond all precedent, seemed to demand imperatively that the representative of the
United States should be heard and his influence respected at a moment
when the fleets of Great Britain and France are at anchor in Veracruz
harbor, exacting the performance of conventions contracted with governments not only not now in existence, but which existed, it would
seem, no longer than was necessary to destroy the independence of the
country and insure the humiliation of all future governments that
might succeed to the direction of public affairs." Of these reasons the
last was certainly the strongest; whatever the war might mean for Mexico, it was a trade war for the foreign powers. The liquidation of the
British Convention bonds was one of the stipulations, in fact, suggested
by Churchwell, who proposed that a portion of the purchase money for
Lower California be applied to their extinction. That point was as important in Washington as Lower California, and the best justification
for its cession by the Veracruz government. But all these reasons were
embarrassing to McLane. Knowing that he was open to criticism for
the promptness with which he had granted recognition, he determined,
after his first interview with Ocampo, to go slow. It was evident, he
wrote, that "extravagant expectations had been excited in regard to negotiations of loans for money, arms, and ammunition in the United
States on the strength of such recognition"; time would cool them.
Ocampo was as impressionable as McLane. "It was not difficult to perceive also," he added, "that he counted somewhat on the brightening
prospects of the Liberal cause as lessening the value of recognition of
the Juarez government by that of the United States"—and the fortunes
of war were fickle.

Within a week the brightening prospects of the Liberal cause were
overcast. The siege of Veracruz had left the capital exposed to attack,
and Degollado had taken advantage of the opening to concentrate all
his available forces against Mexico City. After his disastrous defeat in
December at San Joaquin, he had managed to muster fresh volunteers
in Michoacan, but he suffered from the same shortage of resources that
now prevented Miramon from taking the offensive successfully, and
though he led an army to the gates, his advance died there. Hovering

on the outskirts, he succeeded merely in menacing the city by sudden feints and lunges, shifting concentrations, and swift demonstrations, designed to draw off the investment of Veracruz, but destined to have a deadly outcome. Miramon had left behind him a mate who came up from the rear to strike the feint and to make his name suddenly famous. Speeding from Guadalajara by forced marches to the relief of the capital, Leonardo Marquez fell on the Liberal army and inflicted a crushing defeat on Degollado in the two-day battle of Tacubaya (April 10-11). The result was a rout: the Liberal colors were scattered to the four winds, and the very shirt of Degollado was flown among the trophies over the doors of the National Palace. The disaster was a terrible demonstration of the folly of attempting large-scale operations with the inadequate resources and inflated tactics of guerrilla warfare.

The extent of the disaster was immediately recognized in Veracruz. Ten days later McLane was able to report progress with Ocampo. "The Minister of Foreign Affairs," he wrote on April 21, "avows the readiness of President Juarez to cede Lower California to the United States, but doubts whether the Congress that is to be elected next October could be induced to ratify such a provision in the treaty that is now the subject of our consideration." To meet this objection he recommended to Washington that two treaties be drawn, one for the transits and the other for Lower California, a method that would facilitate the negotiation without impairing its security, since he counted on the consent of Juarez as the best guarantee of success, and the confidence of the President was undashed by the defeat of Degollado. "Should this Constitutional government be established in the City of Mexico before the next Congress is elected, and it certainly will be, for no Congress can be elected to assemble in the capital until that government is inaugurated there," he explained, "a period of some months will elapse during which the Executive branch of the government will be authorized to ratify as well as to negotiate treaties, and in this contingency no difficulty will be experienced in the ratification of the entire treaty." On this assumption he was willing to be accommodating and to separate the easy question of transits from the difficult one of cession.

He was a little too willing, however, to be easy with Ocampo and with himself. The concession was opposed in Washington. "I will tell you," Mata wrote to Ocampo, "what are the two great obstacles to separation. The first is the idea they have of us here as treacherous or astute in diplomacy, and they believe that the proposal to separate the treaties arises from the intention to refuse the one relating to California later. The second is that the President is bent upon distinguishing his term by some piece of big business that will produce great results, to make himself popular and his re-election probable. This is the key." Mata promised to insist on separation, but, knowing Buchanan, with so little hope of success that he proceeded to draft the terms of a contract by which, in return for twelve million dollars in bonds guaranteed by the United States Government, Mexico would mortgage the territory of Lower California for a period of six years, at the conclusion of which, if capital and interest had not been redeemed, title to the territory would be forfeited to the United States.

If the negotiation had been conducted in Washington, Buchanan might have gained more from Mata than McLane did in Veracruz from Ocampo, whose idea it was to divide the treaties; but the fact that it was formulated by two ministers both obliged to retrieve an initial indiscretion affected its development. The separation of the light and heavy matter was a convenient diplomatic device by which each benefited, McLane adopting it to make headway and Ocampo to gain time. For the Mexican a few months of grace were a bright prospect at that moment when there was no other, and McLane was confident that the catch was hooked and that he could afford to play out the line. Time was a coefficient in both their calculations, and a gain for McLane whether he conducted his diplomatic siege by slow starvation, by pressure and approach, by nerves and demoralization, or by direct assault; but time was a partner on which neither could count long, and both were building on loose and shifting ground.

Sinister though it was in its military effects, the battle of Tacubaya was important only because of its aftermath, for it was followed by an atrocity that defeated its political value. Returning from his fiasco at Veracruz, Miramon entered his own capital on the morning of April 11 just in time to witness the triumph of Marquez. He rode out to the field, inspected the results, and returned to the city; a few minutes later an orderly galloped back with an order for Marquez to shoot his prisoners. This had become common practice since the beginning of the war, when a Liberal officer from the frontier had slaughtered his captives on sight and had set a precedent which Miramon adopted by way of reprisal and upon which he improved to induce desertions from the ranks of the enemy. But on this occasion, according to Miramon, the order was limited to deserters from his own ranks and was warranted by military law. As it was executed by Marquez, however, it became an indiscriminate massacre, in the course of which the wounded lying in hospital in Tacubaya were dragged from their beds and butchered together with the physicians and medical students attending them.

It was this feature that gave the day its undying celebrity: Miramon and Marquez sought to escape it by blaming each other for a criminal blunder, the former maintaining that his order had been abused, the latter that it had been obeyed but had miscarried; and by the light of their subsequent records the benefit of the doubt belongs to Miramon, whose career was marked by a fairly consistent respect for those niceties of his profession that constitute its melancholy ethics, while Mar-

quez continued to repeat the same mistakes and the same excuses and
to distinguish himself by the ferocity of a born criminal who had never
gone through military school. If the massacre was an accident, Marquez was not. "The Tiger of Tacubaya" he was called after that day—
a name that clung to him and that was confirmed not only by the flair
of the hunted but by the reek of the hunter, who showed his contempt
for the technical refinements of war as long as he remained at large.
Neither Marquez nor Miramon made any defense of their conduct,
however, until they were called to account for it many years later; at
the time the massacre was condoned as a normal excess of civil war,
and none of those responsible for it was brought to book. In explaining
his failure, which by his own standards was a serious one, Miramon
pleaded the difficulty of disciplining a successful general in the full
flush of triumph; fresh from defeat himself, he was forced to be prudent, but he sacrificed his reputation to his popularity, and the names
of Marquez and Miramon were henceforth linked in fame and infamy.

Personal responsibilities were of passing importance, however, for
the atrocity was no accident. It was a symptom of the rising fever of
civil and religious war. Excesses had been committed on both sides and
justified as retaliations for previous license in a futile and unending
dispute that merely served to press the responsibility further and further back, where it belonged, resting its accumulated weight on the
original warmakers who had kindled the conflict and incurred all its
innate and inevitable consequences. Excesses were the salaries of strong
convictions and unruly ranks, and the Liberals had their share to extenuate. After the capture of Guadalajara in 1858 fatalities fouled their
flag. Two criminals long wanted for the murder of a retired Liberal
governor were hanged before the Episcopal Palace by a mob, while
Degollado stood by, helpless to preserve his authority. More serious was
the assassination of the captured commander of the city, who had surrendered on condition that his life be spared, and in this case Degollado broke the responsible officer, though he subsequently restored him
for services rendered to the cause. In both cases authority was the victim; the precedent provoked the reprisal, and the excuse the crime.
Nevertheless, the fatalities at Guadalajara were forgotten, while those
at Tacubaya were remembered. Why? Why should the one be forgotten and the other remembered, or either singled out for stigma, the
whole of human history being written in dried blood, clotting as
quickly as shed? Was it not absurd to moralize war, neatly to weigh
guilt against guilt, and to regulate the law of nature? But human history is human precisely because of the struggle of mankind to master
nature, to moderate aboriginal brutality, and to cheat necessity with
choice. Between the massacres at Guadalajara and those at Tacubaya
there was at least one saving distinction: the former were not perpetrated against noncombatants nor countenanced by a responsible com-

mander, and though the margin was small, it was enough to make the difference damning. The 11th of April marked a crisis in the mounting tension of civil war beyond which lay the abyss. The breach made in the conventional rules revealed the real nature of a struggle that craved and found its own law, and that broke the feeble restraints under which men like Miramon conducted it as a gentlemen's affair. The bottom emerged, and the inhuman truth came to the top, and Marquez was its man. His rise was equally ominous to his friends and his foes; for where a hundred other outrages were overlooked, the horrors of Tacubaya were noticed and denounced by the world.

The slaughter of the sick and wounded and of physicians hallowed by their calling provided just that jot of excess value necessary to tip the uncertain sympathies and tolerant neutrality of the outer world: a transgression of fair measure that surpassed all precedents and all limits, that was more than custom could stomach, and that revolted public conscience in the tender nineteenth century. It was a detail, and it was a disaster. The outcry was quick, and it was lasting, for it was not allowed to die. The Liberals concealed in the capital exploited their martyrs. Before their blood could cool, an anonymous pamphlet appeared that baffled the police. Arrests were made right and left, and always the wrong ones; copies were smuggled into Veracruz for export abroad; the tale was picked up by McLane and found a platform in the next message of Buchanan to Congress. But no propaganda was needed: the sensation was spontaneous and far-reaching, and many Conservatives, shrinking from the crying shame of publicity and driven beyond the pale by the government that was guilty of it, rallied to the Liberals as the lesser evil. Against this rising reaction the Tacubaya government found no better guarantee than to distract public attention by raising a clamor of its own.

A topic lay at hand, inflammable, blinding, and infallible in effect. In a concerted attack through all the organs of publicity they controlled, the colleagues of Miramon denounced American recognition of the Veracruz government, published the letters of Forsyth, and protested in advance against any treaty involving a cession of national territory. The blast began on April 21, and by May 1 the American Consul in Mexico City felt it necessary to warn McLane that the outcry might well favor the velleities of intervention already manifested by the British and French Ministers. Mr. Otway and M. de Gabriac were dangerous organs of publicity, even though they were mere windbags, for both had long favored foreign intervention and "have always held up to their governments, as an excuse for these acts, 'the dangerous designs of the Colossus of the North.' The publication, therefore, at this time of the correspondence between Mr. Forsyth and the Mexican Minister of Foreign Affairs is particularly indicative of what is to be the burden of the despatches to be sent forward by the English and

French Ministers. . . . However wrong these gentlemen may be in fact, their despatches must have some weight with their respective governments, until such time as they are refuted by events. . . . The French Minister will, of course, move violently to the same purpose. Mr. Otway will unquestionably join his French colleague in forwarding orders for the taking of a hostile position against Veracruz immediately—no matter whether his instructions justify the step or not. I am told that he has declared his determination to avail himself of the first opportunity of crushing the government recognized by the United States. . . . Although I believe that the tone of the instructions from the English and French Governments due by this mail will be pacific and that the game between Gabriac and Penaud will stand drawn, still it is to be feared that the next mail will bring advice and instructions for the French and British Ministers to enforce reparations for the outrages committed upon their subjects; and notwithstanding that those outrages have all been committed by the generals of the clergy faction, the Ministers will be too glad of the opportunity of seizing Veracruz and thus dragging their governments into the first step for bringing about European intervention. I consider the event much to be feared, as I know it to be an important feature in the program of Gabriac. I think, if it is possible, that our government ought to take strong precautionary steps." Specifically, he suggested the occupation of the fortress commanding Veracruz harbor and "the hoisting of the Stars and Stripes there at the earliest possible moment."

Of this advice McLane took the better part. The strongest precautionary step was to change the subject. The blast leveled against the Veracruz government was met by an answering clamor and a joint defense. Ocampo lost his temper in diplomatic language and rejected the protest against the pending treaty in a long and impassioned philippic in which all the resources of rhetoric were employed to paraphrase the old retort of the kettle calling the pot black. McLane joined the war of words with a defense of Forsyth and American policy, remarkable alike for its courage and its reticence and the embarrassment it betrayed by its very verbal ability. He also seconded Ocampo in denouncing the atrocities of Tacubaya and demanding, on the ground that the head of the hospital had once been an American citizen, the death penalty for the responsible parties. The mouthpiece of Miramon, Foreign Minister Bonilla, retorted with a pointed allusion to the practice of lynching in the civilized South from which the American Minister hailed. A sharp cross-fire of mutual recriminations ensued between the three Ministers, the only result of which, when it died down, was that the American Minister had been personally antagonized to the point of becoming an outspoken partisan in the civil war. The strongest precautionary step, after changing the subject so often, was to drop it. The charges raised by the Tacubaya government were still unrefuted, the

letters of Forsyth could be belied only by the event, and the best way
to lay the accusation, obviously, was to let it rest until time answered its
presumption. It was no time, with international complications pending, to discuss Lower California; and that part of the treaty, consequently, remained in abeyance.

What could no longer be held in abeyance, however, was the crying
need for material aid and the crying demand after the disaster at Tacubaya for the Liberal government to raise it. Degollado was undismayed. Rallying his routed forces in Morelia, he set to work with unbroken spirit and unflagging faith to repeat his customary miracle of
recuperation. He had lost a battle, he was confident of winning the
war, but in that battle he had lost a large part of the reputation he had
won in a year of trial and error. Elementary mistakes had been made:
in his haste to reach the capital he had left an army hanging on his
flank and had been surprised and laden with the haunting trophies of
Tacubaya; and in some quarters, close to headquarters, his resignation
was expected to follow. His conscience and his pride forbade him to resign in the hour of defeat, when his peculiar gifts were indispensable,
and he defended his misfortune by insisting that he had risked defeat
to protect Veracruz. But his popularity was impaired, and even that
phoenix of a soldier could not repeat the resurrection that he had
wrought a year before without a helping hand. After vainly attempting
to rise from the ashes, he abandoned the field and made a flying trip
to Veracruz, in the last days of May, to lay his case before the President.

Crippled, discredited, but indomitable, Degollado brought a powerful appeal to bear on his government. His very appearance in Veracruz was a reproach, and it coincided with private advice that the President received from a trusted correspondent in the capital, an elder
statesman who ventured as a patriot, a partisan, and an experienced ex-
minister to act as his political guide. This expert also laid the situation
before Juarez with a pressing force not far from friendly reproach.
Degollado was not to blame; he had done what he could with the elements available, and by blocking the capital he had assured the security of the civil government in Veracruz. To repair the disaster at Tacubaya was, therefore, the undeniable obligation of the government, and
the means of doing so were within reach. Miramon was bankrupt and
making the most ruinous deals, selling the principal properties of the
Schools of Arts and Sciences, Medicine, and Agriculture to the bank-
ing house of Jecker & Co., and these institutions were on the point of
closing. Education was the first concern to be sacrificed to survival; the
next was to be ecclesiastical capital. Miramon demanded a million
pesos to continue operations; he threatened the clergy with nationalization of their property, and a shake-down was impending in the cab-

inet; but such shifts would not be necessary—"they will consume the property in mortmain little by little by little by mortgages and sales in which the principal party will be Jecker." The question arose, therefore: why should a banker be the one to benefit by the pinch? Why Jecker? Why not Juarez? "I believe that it is time for you to decree the complete nationalization of all property held in mortmain. This will prevent waste, and the clergy themselves will not be surprised by a measure which they consider inevitable. I remember that you have already studied plans by Señor Lerdo, and it would be useless, therefore, and foolish, for me to say anything further. What I will say, however, is that the opportunity should not be lost, since there is no further reason to defer a measure that has so long been expected."

Failing the confiscation of ecclesiastical capital, there was only the American treaty, a resource the writer weighed very carefully. "Setting aside the declamations, insults, and slanders of the reactionary press on account of the reception of the American Minister, I cannot deny that the publication of the notes exchanged between Forsyth and Cuevas in reference to a new treaty has produced very serious fears, since it is supposed that our neighbors will entertain the same pretensions as they did then. . . . Unfortunately, all that has been said about our inability to hold our northern deserts to the benefit of the world is quite true, but above these questions of material interest stand those of honor and dignity and the melancholy memories of the Treaty of Guadalupe and the sale of the Mesilla. . . . These reasons lead me ardently to hope that the government will not consent to any cession of territory or to the settlement of claims as proposed by Forsyth." The caution was accompanied, however, by encouragement. "On what bases, then, are we to deal with the United States, it will be said, if we reject these two capital points?" A great opportunity had arisen for Buchanan to initiate a disinterested policy of good neighborhood and to make his mark in American history. "If the United States really wish to inaugurate a generous and continental policy in America, if they wish to protect the other republics and to serve universal liberty, they do not need to acquire some few leagues of land for that purpose, at our expense. . . . More glorious advantages, and more practical ones, can be obtained on this continent if they raise their views a little above immediate material interests. I who have seen the world accept as legitimate and even profitable, in the opinion of many, the pact known as the Holy Alliance, which was the compact of the thrones to protect one another at the cost of the peoples and to deprive them of all liberty—I believe it legitimate and advantageous for the peoples to unite to consolidate their institutions and to prevent their destruction by anarchy and despotism. If peace, order, and prosperity prevail in the republics of America, advantages will result not only for them, but for the entire world, and nothing can be said against the government of Mexico should it be

fortunate enough to ensure the future of the country. Such an advantage can be obtained only by great concessions," and short of a territorial cession he was prepared to approve of any. The transits and trade
favors were a small price to pay for a holy alliance in the democratic
interest; "the United States will obtain incalculable advantages that
Europe will envy but will not be able to dispute, and we can count on
immediate resources and a rich and flourishing treasury in the future."
In conclusion, he apologized for proffering officious advice, because of
"the interest which, as a Liberal and a personal friend of yours, I feel
in your good name. I know only too well your abnegation and patriotism, I know that you will spare no effort for the Republic, and I know
also that we have a great guarantee in the intelligence and keen honesty of our friend Mata. All this has encouraged me to speak with perfect frankness and, wishing you the utmost success of your labors, I
shall never be the one to censure the concessions that you may have to
make to imperative necessity."

Between these alternatives Juarez hesitated no longer: he had hesitated too long, indeed, for his own good, and the frank prompting of
his friend left unspoken, though it hinted at, facts too familiar and too
painful to bear explicit statement. Discontent and impatience were
growing among the fighting Liberals, whether they fought with the
sword or the pen, against the passive conduct of their government.
What were the President and his ministers doing? Were they doing
anything at all? The war was over a year old, desultory and disastrous,
succeeding spasmodically, failing consistently, and what had the civil
powers, safely entrenched in Veracruz, to show for their share in it?
Were they supplying the sinews of war or the fat? Were they doing
even their ideological duty and providing the party with revolutionary
leadership? These questions were heard with increasing force and
frequency and could no longer be muffled or shunned in 1859. Degollado and the elder statesman spoke for Mexico. Even in the United
States the press of all shades of opinion was urging material support
for the Constitutional government, yet Mata was no further advanced
than on the day he arrived in Washington. Churchwell had offered to
secure him a loan in Wall Street in anticipation of the pending treaty,
but the negotiation had failed for want of security; temporizing was
repaid in kind, and the market value of recognition was falling. Buchanan now took the position that no indemnization was due to Mexico for the transits, since this would amount to paying for benefits bestowed on the country by American development, and that whatever
price McLane might agree to pay for them would be pure bounty; the
deal depended, and his re-election into the bargain, on the big business
that remained in abeyance. Mata was resigned to returning Buchanan
to the White House from Lower California. But not Juarez. Between
the alienation of national territory and the nationalization of Church

property the choice was promptly made; and the President met the demand imposed on him by the quick and the dead, recognized the mission for which he had been elected by history, and, rising to his secular responsibility slowly but firmly, like a man laden with years without age, finally promulgated the Reform Laws.

4

THE first of the Reform Laws, and the foundation of all the others, appeared on July 12, 1859, in the form of a presidential decree nationalizing Church property. The rest followed in close succession: the separation of Church and State (July 12); the exclaustration of monks (July 12); the establishment of civil registry for certificates of birth, marriage, and death (July 23); the secularization of cemeteries (July 31) and of public holidays (August 11). Religious liberty, the logical outcome and the crown of the others, was reserved for a later date, but was announced in the program proclaimed on July 12, an epochal date in Mexican history. Conceived as a whole, the Reform Laws were a sweeping proclamation of emancipation of the civil power, which fulfilled the promise and corrected the omissions of the Constitution of 1857 and gave the party of progress a future that revived its fighting faith.

The word "progress" was wrested from the enemy and restored to its original owners; the discussion that Miramon had closed six months before was reopened by Juarez on July 12 with dynamic effect. And on July 12 Miramon issued a proclamation of his own in which, anticipating that effect, he pledged himself anew to destroy the ley Lerdo, the ley Juarez, and all their corollaries, and to champion "the interests of the Church, vigorously sustaining the prerogatives and independence of that institution"; but at the same he frankly admitted that, despite the incontestable victories which he had won, no advance had been made by his cause and no one knew when or how the war would end; and he appealed to the country to rally to "the fair name of Reaction" in which he glorified—the word "progress" was dropped.

More significant than this admission of weakness was the invigorating effect of that word on the Liberal party. The weary, the fainthearted, the disabled, the defeated, recovered their fighting spirit overnight. Doblado returned to the battle and offered his sword to Degollado

and a defense of his previous conduct to his party. In a manifesto
to the people of Guanajuato he rehabilitated the perennial summer
soldier successfully. He denied that he was a deserter; he had never
doubted his duty but only where it lay; if he had hesitated, it was from
conscientious and honorable motives, fearing first to precipitate, and
then to prolong, a ruinous struggle that would split the country and renew all the horrors of the period of Independence. When he had capit-
ulated, it was to spare the proprietors and proletarians of his state unnecessary suffering; but his discretion had been wasted, and he was
now convinced of the ineluctable nature of the struggle, the inexorable
necessity of finishing it at all costs, and the right of reprisal which the
atrocities of the Reaction had given "the Liberal party, which is the
national party, to advance once and for all on the road of reforms, af-
fronting definitely all those that were indicated long ago as the radical
cure of the inveterate evils bequeathed us by the Spanish domination."
The apology of Doblado, like the declamation of Miramon, was a reflex action that testified accurately to the mercurial virtue of the Emancipation Proclamation.

But bracing though the effect was on the party, Juarez himself benefited very little by it. When he finally rose to his revolutionary mandate, the bolt was belated and the thunder stolen by a combination of
circumstances that dampened its thud. Party politics were excited by
the first momentous act of his government, and the credit for the Reform Laws, though it was collective, was widely attributed to the initiative of Lerdo de Tejada, who came to Veracruz determined to finish
the reform he had begun, if not badly, mildly and tentatively, in 1856.
The reasons for this partiality were not far to seek. When Lerdo joined
the government he brought with him two assets—a radical program
and a commanding personality. The program he showed to Churchwell, in confidence, as his handiwork, and it confirmed his reputation
as an enterprising statesman, which the American agent accepted as
unquestioningly as he did the assumption that Juarez was a timid and
mistrustful politician and Ocampo a difficult idealist. All these conclusions were hasty and founded on hearsay. Placed in the cabinet at the
suggestion of Churchwell and on the strength of his pro-American
sympathies, Lerdo disappointed his sponsors. McLane found him "very
averse to a territorial cession, as he is to any new and enterprising policy connected with the foreign affairs of the country." A new and enterprising policy in domestic affairs, on the contrary, was what he
pressed on his colleagues as the only compensation for the American
treaty and as the best guarantee against its risks. He pressed against an
open door, for their ideas were identical with his. Nevertheless, differences developed between them that more than once threatened the dissolution of the government.

The last of these crises occurred just before the adoption of the program. With sanction assured, Lerdo suddenly resigned and laid the responsibility for his decision squarely on the President. "You and I," he explained, "are making an effort which can be of no benefit to ourselves or to the cause. You are working against your ideas, and hence I lack the confidence necessary to enter fully on the difficult course that, in my opinion, we must adopt. How can anything good come of such a start in so thorny a task as the radical reform of a society like ours? It is a thousandfold better that I retire and that you follow your own inspirations. This is bound to happen in the end and sooner than we think, and it had better be before we compromise the situation by a course that is not in conformity with your ideas." In reply, Juarez discounted the idea of any difference between them, declared himself at a loss to explain it, and, implying very plainly that the misunderstanding was deliberate, induced Lerdo to withdraw his resignation. A week later the program appeared, after a rapid reading in council, with a precipitation as conspicuous as the judgment that awarded it to the influence of Lerdo.

What those differences were was never revealed, but they were thinly veiled and easily guessed. The strain that developed within the government from the day that Lerdo joined it was visible to the naked eye. They were differences not of principle or policy, but of personality and pace. The Reform Laws had been adopted in principle long before Lerdo appeared in Veracruz, but the test of the policy was its timing, and that faculty to which Juarez had proved his title was called into question by his long delay in enacting them. The reasons were deeply rooted in his temperament and training, and Lerdo had neither the time nor the patience, if he had the wish, to appreciate them. What he encountered was the deliberation of a mind that was judicial before it was revolutionary. The expropriation of Church property, prepared by Prieto a year before, had been reserved for a propitious moment, and before Juarez was convinced that it had come, he had to overcome scruples and hesitations and lifelong habits of mind, which, to a practical politician or a professional revolutionary, were merely the subterfuges of political timidity. To the jurist, the measure was a violent spoliation of vested rights; to the statesman, its expediency was doubtful in drawn battle; to the provisional President, his Constitutional right to decree it without congressional sanction was questionable; and to the revolutionary, to postpone it until the end of the war was preferable. His caution was finally overcome by a combination of compelling circumstances—the distress of Degollado, the necessity of raising resources at all costs and of anticipating the enemy's use of the same methods, and the hope of eluding the pressure of American diplomacy. With these considerations the recommendations of Lerdo coincided; but the facts, and not Lerdo, dictated his decision.

Their differences did not end there. When Lerdo joined the govern-

ment, he did not join the family that composed it. He was a distant
relative who arrived on the scene at a trying time to direct public affairs, to mend an administration that had been notoriously neglected
and mismanaged, and to patronize its members. Such at least was the
impression he produced on his partners. There were times when they felt
themselves treated like poor country cousins. His self-confidence made
collaboration superfluous, his independence was hampered by it, and in
spite of his punctilious courtesy he could not conceal a casual attitude toward his colleagues and even toward the President—particularly toward
the President. Juarez had the moral superiority to ignore it, but his
friends were profoundly outraged. Ocampo, the closest of them, suffered
in silence as long as he could, but when his tongue was finally loosed, he
recalled bitterly "the superiority with which Señor Lerdo regarded us,
an affectation that led him sometimes into incivilities incredible in a
person of his breeding; as, for instance, in failing to attend appointments
with the President or the summons that he sent him. So determined
was I to preserve our unity that I bore from Señor Lerdo what I would
not have suffered from anyone under other circumstances." The antagonism between Lerdo and Ocampo, himself of a peremptory temper
and impatient of contradiction, developed into a repressed feud all the
more bitter for being buried by discretion and duty. Small mortifications were remembered because they excited a deeper and more impersonal antipathy between the two men. What Ocampo really resented
was the intrusion of a personal element, which had hitherto been successfully excluded from the government, and with which neither he
nor Juarez could cope. They were not politicians and could not contest
the superiority of Lerdo in that respect. He was a master who had the
supreme gift of concealing his art. Unconsciously perhaps, and imperceptibly certainly, he contrived to cast his colleagues into the shade by
anticipating their intentions, appropriating their ideas, monopolizing
their virtues, and attracting attention without appearing to court it.
Against that unsettling influence Ocampo was helpless. The philosopher who had always protested against the cult of leaders and insisted,
in his innocence, that anyone in turn could be the representative of a
ruling idea, now found himself confronted with the fact of a dominating personality that appropriated a program to which no one could
claim patent or priority. And as Lerdo did not deny the flattering imputation, and as his colleagues, in the interests of solidarity, did not
contradict it, the assumption gained general currency at the time.

And it was a time when personalities were important. The rise of the
revolutionary temper aroused by the Reform Laws demanded a figure
to personify the idea. In radical circles Lerdo was accepted as that man,
and the stature of the President suffered by comparison. The positions
of the two men who had started their revolutionary careers together
were now completely reversed: the initiative Juarez had given the

movement four years before had passed so patently to Lerdo that, in 1859, instead of leading, the President appeared to be led; and among the Lerdistas he was rated a dead weight and a drag on the progress of the revolution. In advanced circles it was common to speak of his irresolution and apathy and to complain—in print—that "to all the blows of fortune he opposes the indifference, the fatalism, the inertia characteristic of his race." And that complaint, under its transparent prejudice and partisanship, raised the real question of whether a member of a subject race, however far he had risen above it, could ever outgrow its bonds and transcend its secular limitations, mounting above the prudence, the patience, the beaten virtues of his people to the commanding position and the enterprising qualities which his responsibility required. At the very time when he issued the laws that answered that challenge and assured his place in history, Juarez himself was the most disparaged member of his party.

His friends suffered in silence and referred the verdict to posterity— the test of the measure was still its timing. By the standards of practical politics the Reform Laws were a war measure, produced to meet an immediate emergency, and as such they were a forced birth. Immediately after their delivery Lerdo left for the United States to raise money in the open market on the security of Church property. The political credit he reaped from the whole program rested, in fact, on the financial credit that the confiscation of ecclesiastical capital promised to provide, and his reputation as a financial expert was unquestioned when he left for the United States. But he reckoned without his host. By the same packet a communication from McLane to the State Department sped him on his way. "Should he succeed in negotiating a loan in the United States with the Church property as a lien or security," the Minister pointed out, "it is not likely that either he or his colleagues will be disposed to cede Lower California in the present condition of the Constitutional government. On the other hand, if he fails in this negotiation, I am satisfied that he will no longer oppose, but rather advocate, its cession." Needless to say, Lerdo failed.

The political strategy of the Emancipation Proclamation was sufficiently self-evident to make that result a foregone conclusion. The value of the Reform Laws as a timely expedient was their least attribute, however, in the eyes of Juarez. "I take great pleasure in sending you the decree I have just signed," he wrote to a friend on the momentous day of July 12. "The most important things that it contains are, as you will see, the absolute independence of the civil power and religious liberty. For me these were the capital points to be won in this revolution, and if we succeed we shall have the satisfaction of having rendered a service to our country and to humanity. I also enclose the program I have published, in which other measures have been voted that are certain to improve the condition of this society." The nationalization of Church property was one of those "other measures," but it was not the cardinal one. For Juarez the initial law, basic as it was in subverting the economic strength and political power of the clergy, and profitable as a source of immediate revenue, was merely the material lever that raised, released, and supported the ideal structure of a secular society; it was a means to an end, and his mind was trained to the long view. But the two aspects were inseparable, and the element of timing affected his timeless fame as well, for most of the capital points of the program had been anticipated by militant leaders in the field, acting on their own authority. Santiago Vidaurri had not waited for sanction to confiscate Church property in his territory; nor had Gonzalez Ortega, who confiscated Church property spontaneously in his state and introduced civil registry there without consulting Veracruz; the dissolution of monastic communities had already begun in Michoacan. Wherever the war spread, it secularized the society it destroyed; so that the action of the Federal government came as an anticlimax and appeared to be merely a belated ratification of an accomplished fact and an automatic response, or even a surrender, to pressure from the ranks. Such was the way in which a sure-footed lawgiver would guide his people, and it was a proof of his political instinct that, before rushing in where the Constitution-makers of '57 had feared to tread, Juarez waited for some popular prompting to force and strengthen his hand; but his sense of pace could be appreciated only in historic perspective, and his chronic caution alone was noticed at the time. To wait for the rising tide was a mark of democratic statesmanship, but before it could float the leader it swamped him. The policy was too slow, too sound, too unspectacular, to have any popular appeal, and the result was that when he produced the measures that consummated the movement, the vanguard of the party had already passed him by and looked on him as its most backward representative. As a measure of popular progress, this was a healthy sign and encouraging to anyone who could observe it disinterestedly, as he did; his philosophy condemned him, however, to be consumed by his political offspring. Conceiving of his function as a medium for popular forces, he identified himself with his office and sank himself in it with the detachment of a genuine public servant. And so literal a practice of the democratic ideal set a lonely example far ahead of his time and impractical in a period of violent transition. Democracy was a distant ideal to a people who had no experience of its discipline, and whose whole history had been controlled by the collective anarchy of personal leaders; and his reserve, his self-effacement, recognized and respected as they were in his private life, were negative virtues in the public man and encouraged the notion of his nonentity.

Now, this was not a negligible matter; his personal prestige was more than a personal disadvantage; the depreciation of the President reacted in turn on the movement, fostering the inherent anarchy of the Liberal party and producing serious disaffection among the leaders in the field. An incipient urge to secede from Federal control began to stir here and there in the summer of 1859. In Guerrero the press complained of the lawless guerrillas that wasted the state and held the President personally responsible for their outrages. "Don Benito Juarez has neither sought nor been able to moralize the revolution; to prevent it from being detested, he lets the good and bad have their way alike, without a thought for the evils caused by his apathy and complete ineptitude," the complaint ran. "It is high time that the legislature of this state sever its relations with a government that produces nothing but harm." The local Red club recommended that the governors of the League be circularized with a petition demanding his retirement. "We acknowledge no other sovereignty than that of the states, which must delegate it to able hands of recognized activity. Don Benito Juarez is able to wait without suffering, but incapable of working and sacrificing himself; he is not the man of the revolution but of the counterrevolution." The severity of the censure was aggravated by the fact that it was signed by Ignacio Altamirano, an ardent revolutionary and a fellow Indian, who vindicated the reputation of his race by the energy with which he belabored Don Benito Juarez.

Democracy was no substitute for personal authority, and the murmurs that ran through the harvest of the summer of 1859 were not long in taking shape. In September Santiago Vidaurri seceded, in effect, withdrawing his troops from the field and his support from the Juarez government on the ground that what the country needed was a progressive dictatorship; and though further defection was checked by the prompt action of Degollado, who drove the deserter out of the country, the incident indicated to what lengths impatience with the President could lead.

The one quarter, perhaps, where the reputation of the President was safe was in the hands of the enemy. The enemy gave him a tremendous press. The enemy had a long memory and laid the Reform Laws to the original evil of the *ley Juarez,* which in turn was "merely a reworking of the French laws of '93," and since profane history was nothing but a repetition of proven errors, predicted that "the result would be the same, a social ferment exploding in a deadly detonation that caused the downfall of the impious and brought them to death on the gallows that they themselves raised over a mountain of ruins." The enemy gave him no quarter. The enemy exulted in the dissensions of the sick family. The enemy gave him his due and denounced him as the "Constitutional despot." The enemy buried him under a mountain of abuse. The enemy called him a socialist, a traitor, an American, and of all the epithets hurled at him the last was undoubtedly the deadliest,

for the enemy immediately seized the connection between the Reform
Laws and the American treaty and, realizing that American recognition supplied the security for the Emancipation Proclamation, fell back
on patriotism as a last refuge. This line was propagated with a zeal so
persistent that for generations to come devout and unknowing Mexicans were taught that the reformer who despoiled the Church with
one hand sold his country with the other.

The failure of Lerdo to raise a loan in the United States now made
the conclusion of the treaty imperative. Before Lerdo left Veracruz,
McLane had sounded him once more on the cession of Lower California, and in their final conversation the strenuous opposition which
Lerdo had always shown to it—unless at an exorbitant price and at
some future date when, as he said, his direct influence and control over
the government might be greater than it then was—was materially
modified. Warned by McLane that he could not reasonably expect any
pecuniary assistance except for a cession of territory, Lerdo proposed to
his colleagues to reconsider their position and to cede Lower California
for fifteen million dollars. With the departure of Lerdo, however, the
opposition remained, and McLane found himself confronted by a force
in the cabinet which he could not identify and which was so inflexible
that he was reduced to echoing its views. "The cession of territory is
the gravest and most important act of sovereignty that a government
can perform; it is questionable, therefore, whether it should be performed at a moment when it is in conflict with another government
for the possession of empire," he advised Washington, "and this consideration is as important to the party purchasing as to the party ceding
the territory." Without waiving the territorial claim, Washington consented to reserve it while McLane negotiated the subsidiary question
of transits; but from that day the claim was abandoned in fact. The
compliance of Washington, at the very moment when the quarry was
cornered, was remarkable but not inexplicable. Besides the agitation
aroused in Mexico and the risk of precipitating foreign intervention,
two other factors made it impolitic to press the claim at that time. One
was the rise in the United States of sovereign sympathy for the Liberal
cause; one of those forms of popular intervention, springing from disinterested motives, that sometimes upset the plans and force the hands
of statesmen, the pressure of popular sentiment obliged Buchanan to
make an involuntary concession to Veracruz. The other was the Reform Laws. The confiscation of Church property promised to provide
the bankrupt faction with a source of revenue sufficient to dispense
with the American loan and to elude a territorial cession; and of all the
factors that combined to block Buchanan this was the most foiling.
The Reform Laws, appearing at the most favorable moment to produce

their maximum value, demonstrated the political instinct of Juarez and vindicated his uncanny faculty for correct timing.

With the elimination of Lower California from the agenda, the negotiations entered their decisive phase. The reduction of the treaty to transit facilities compelled McLane to compensate for the defeat of the major claim by driving a hard bargain on the lesser; and he was on his mettle. The remaining forms of persuasion were employed for all that they were worth. Financial pressure was still worth a great deal, for the confiscation of Church property was accomplished more quickly by a stroke of the pen than the collection of such tribute could be effected in fact. The most valuable ecclesiastical capital was concentrated in the territory controlled by the Clerical government, and in the outlying provinces the Constitutional authorities had to contend with the moral effects of expropriation. The masses were shocked by the plundering of sacred buildings: paupers themselves, but as pious as proprietors, they were doubly wounded, in their sense of possession and superstition, for the churches were the palaces of the poor, and the poor were deprived of a delusion of splendor and a life of phantasy, which they prized more than the comforts of the flesh. The prosperous classes were reluctant to defy the ban of the Church against the purchase of ecclesiastical spoils and were as poor in spirit as the inheritors of Heaven; and the liquidation of the great asset was slow and insufficient to relieve the insolvency of the government. Pecuniary pressure, diminished but not forfeited by the Reform Laws, still provided a working margin on which McLane was able to operate effectively.

Nevertheless, another six months passed before the treaty was concluded. Even in its reduced scope McLane encountered constant and stubborn impediments. The character of the Minister with whom he had to deal was one of them. With the departure of Lerdo, the master spirit whose practical mentality made him naturally pro-American was eliminated from the cabinet. Ocampo was also pro-American, but for precisely the contrary reason, and whether to emulate Lerdo or to redeem a wrong start, he too was on his mettle. Improving on the pregnant suggestion of the elder statesman, he proposed to convert the treaty into a general alliance between the two Republics for the support of republican institutions in America, an ambition, as McLane dryly observed, "that evinced so little appreciation of the relative condition and power of Mexico and the United States that I have not felt myself encouraged to expect any practical result therefrom." For such a holy alliance to produce mutual advantages more glorious and more practical than a few leagues of land, large compensations had to be made; and those which Ocampo could offer were not sufficient to bribe the American Government to be great. When that delusion had been dispelled and the discussions reduced to their proper scope, the regulations of the transits gave rise to practical difficulties that produced further delays. The most important of these was the right, claimed by McLane, to police the transits with American troops. The demand was warranted by the disturbed state of the country, but it excited national susceptibilities which the most pro-American Mexican could not ignore, and after weeks of fruitless conversation it was clear to McLane that he and that difficult idealist could never learn to speak the same language. Their differences ended in a deadlock; Ocampo resigned, but his successor was equally adamant. McLane paid a flying visit to Washington, and on his return Ocampo was again in the Foreign Office; and McLane used his last argument. An American citizen having been murdered by Marquez in the meanwhile, the American Minister adopted Ocampo's proposal for a general alliance, but in a unilateral sense, and recommended to Washington a punitive expedition by American troops against Miramon, with or without the consent of the Juarez government. The argument convinced Ocampo, the deadlock was broken, and the protection of the transits, under certain express conditions, was granted. "It has been with much difficulty," McLane informed the Department in plain English, "that I induced the Constitutional government to recognize its obligation to seek the aid of the government of the United States when it is unable to perform with effect its proper functions as a government, and it was only when I represented that sooner or later the government of the United States would act without reference to it or to any other government or authority in defense of its treaty rights and to protect its citizens, that I was able to come to any conclusion satisfactory to myself on this point." On December 14, 1859, the negotiations were finally concluded, and Ocampo signed the treaty that was to prove his political and physical death warrant.

Several days previously the *New York Herald* had published a summary of the treaty. The capital points secured to the United States Government perpetual right-of-way across the Isthmus of Tehuantepec and the projected railway bed across the northwestern corner of Mexico, together with the right to police them with its own military forces, with the consent of the Mexican Government or, in cases of emergency, without it. In return the Mexican Government obtained the promise of two million dollars in cash, two on credit for the settlement of American claims, and a bad name. The outcry was immediate and immense. The Miramon government led it with scathing denunciations in the press and a formal protest to Washington against an invalid contract drawn with an irresponsible party. "The Veracruz government," it declared, "in approving the treaty has arrogated to itself titles and powers that it does not possess even by the charter it invokes, and should it be successful, its partisans, in order to establish some regularity in its affairs, would make it expiate by an exemplary punishment so great an offense against the national sovereignty." The charge was true, and the Liberals, galled and angered by their inability to refute it, passed the same sentence on the treaty and condemned their government for transgressing its Constitutional limitations and compromising the national sovereignty. The protests, beginning with attacks in the press, resignations from the militia, and placards posted on the house of the President, swelled into a party scandal, which, far from abating with the passage of time, grew into a standing reproach to the Juarez government. Party lines were effaced in a common patriotic panic; the verdict was unanimous; and the damage was not confined to the domestic effects of the deal. *The Times of London* noticed it as an historic event of mournful significance: "The news of Mexico arriving today from New York is of extraordinary importance for bondholders, for if the treaty that is said to have been concluded in Veracruz should be definitely ratified, Mexico will pass from that day forth virtually under American control. All the northern part of the country will be opened to American colonists, who not only have the privilege of introducing their effects free of duty, but will be able to summon the troops of the United States to their assistance in any difficulties that may arise with the native population. . . . Under such conditions the absorption of the Mexican Republic can be accomplished gradually without provoking the fierce and futile resistance which more direct methods would entail."

In Paris and Madrid, where the dread of American advances was no less acute, political capital also was made of their progress. But the sharpest shock was the behavior of public opinion in the United States. Nearly all the Mexican correspondence in the press was concentrated in the journals of New York and New Orleans, and as no regular correspondents were maintained to cover Mexico, information was supplied by volunteer contributions colored by partisanship and adapted to editorial policy, which made those two poles of propaganda foci of infection for the rest of the country. With one or two exceptions, the press in New York discredited a convention that held no commercial benefits and many political perils for northern interests; but it was in New Orleans, in the home of the Louisiana Tehuantepec Company, that the treaty received its worst press. The *Daily Picayune* appreciated its value in terms that depreciated the loser; the sum of four million dollars, it declared, was "certainly very little to pay for such extensive and valuable concessions. For the right of transit across the Isthmus of Tehuantepec alone, the Polk administration, about twelve years ago, authorized the offer of fifteen million dollars. We bought the valley of the Mesilla a few years ago and gave more for it than is asked of us now, only to secure a route of transit through our own territory and to find that the best trade route remained within the territory of Mexico. We now hold the right-of-way through Tehuantepec and a control over two other routes as complete as if we had bought the territory. In fact, we cannot say whether it is not better to hold the right-of-way with unlimited power of protection than to have obtained a territorial cession. We need be in no hurry to acquire territory in those parts, and it may be assumed that we shall have it as soon as it is useful or needed." The contempt for Mexican incompetence implied in those lines was emphasized by an appeal to the Mexicans to "trust the loyalty and good faith of the United States with respect to the use which they will make of the powers granted," and an appeal to the Americans to "abstain from abusing such concessions, avoid all cause of friction, and reward the liberality of the Progressives in Mexico by aiding them actively and effectively in their undertaking." The alliance thus proposed was precisely the kind of trade favor that the organ of the Catholic diocese in New Orleans had in mind when it wrote with a contempt that was neither implied nor palliated: "Mexico may be destined to lose its nationality, but we would have wished that it might at least lose it nobly. It remained for Juarez to degrade the nation the more easily to destroy it, and to drown the spirit of independence in the foulest of slime." The reflection cast on the national colors was the historic revenge of the party that had lost the last of the Three Guarantees of 1821. The government that was guilty of the treaty was red, it was green, but it was no longer white; the hue and cry of 1859 called it yellow.

For the moment the Reform Laws, of recent memory, were forgotten in the clamor that greeted their price—a clamor so universal and unyielding that it drowned any hope of defense. No dissenting voice could be raised at the time, and least of all by the Liberal government. A fair judgment of the treaty was impossible without some knowledge of the concessions refused as well as of those accorded, and the public remained in ignorance of the demand for a territorial cession, which had been successfully lost in the shuffle, though the presence of the ace in the pack was suspected from old precedent and scented in the privileges actually granted. Of these the most compromising was the protection of the transits by American troops. On that delicate point Ocampo and McLane had reached a reasonable agreement, which confined the privilege to its ostensible and legitimate purpose, the security of public thoroughfares running through sparsely settled and lawless territory, and provided the proper safeguards for Mexican sovereignty even in cases of special emergency, when it was stipulated that the right of intervention was limited to the preservation of order and lapsed with the passing of the crisis, the end of which was to be determined by the Mexican Government. So far as legal safeguards could secure the future, they had been supplied, but it was obvious that legal safeguards weighed very little against the laws of economic progress and imperialist expansion; and when the limited privilege was applied to rights-of-way acquired in perpetuity, it was inevitable that the inference should be one of indefinite servitude and that the prospect of American troops passing over Mexican territory should suggest a lane of laborious ants traveling eternally, and with unerring instinct, toward their Manifest Destiny. Moreover, a supplementary article extended police privileges to the frontiers of the two countries and made it obligatory upon the government failing to maintain order to seek the aid of the other in the event of any of the stipulations of existing treaties being violated, or the safety of citizens of one country endangered within the domain of the other. The latitude for intervention which such co-operation allowed was limited only by the good faith with which it was defined; but good faith or aggressive designs were in reality irrelevant; war and peace were both phases of the same process, which the best intentions, the most honorable observance of treaties, could not prevent, once they had been concluded. The lines laid across the southernmost and northernmost margins of Mexico traced a magnetic triangle destined, as had long since been announced, to act as a penetrating current on the people they enclosed, permeating, mollifying, Americanizing them; and as the course of history was determined by trade routes and the flag followed the market, the concession of transits was a more dangerous inroad on the integrity of the nation than the outright cession of a remote and unfrequented stretch of territory would have been. The objectionable feature of the treaty, in fact, was not the protection of the transits, but the transits themselves.

The difficulties under which the Liberal government labored might have been urged in defense of the terms under which it closed with the friendliest of its antagonists. Military defeat, financial need, diplomatic pressure, social reform, the fear of foreign intervention—the treaty was the mean resultant of a combination of overpowering forces; but they were equally irrelevant in the final verdict. The treaty was condemned both on its text and context, and the internal evidence of compulsion, which it bore so plainly on its face, aggravated the offense. Fear that the concessions would be abused and mortification that they had been imposed combined to unite Mexicans of all parties in the morbid psychology begotten by the outcome of the American war twelve years before and in raw repudiation of a treaty that published to the world so palpable a proof of their besetting sense of inferiority. There lay the unforgivable sin. The avowal was, by common consent, a deed of servitude and an indelible stigma on the government guilty of it.

In the storm of obloquy that burst about the heads of that government none escaped unscathed, but the brunt was borne, of course, by Ocampo. How much of human flesh goes to the making of public documents was exposed in the strands of himself that he left in that

leonine bargain. By a grim incongruity it fell to the intransigent idealist, whose whole political skill was to resign as soon as he disagreed, to
conduct a negotiation that he mistrusted profoundly and that compromised him irretrievably; but he performed his inglorious part to
the end and sacrificed his reputation to necessity. The treaty was no
sooner signed, however, than he retired from office, a marked man, in
search of an obscurity which he had forfeited forever. Understanding
friends there were, here and there, to assure Ocampo—in private—that
he was a prey of partisan criticism. The best of them, perhaps, was a
kindred spirit on the staff of the Legation in Paris, who, judging the
effect of the treaty from a distance and in broad perspective, hailed it
as a piece of practical and farsighted statesmanship. Hot from a dispute
with a fellow Liberal, this apologist wrote: "He knows as well as I do
that, even were European diplomatic agents to intervene in Mexico,
what you least wished to do was to give the United States a hand in
our politics. You have fought stoutly to avoid the fatality of the treaty,
as he well knows and as do all those who hate democracy, but what
they pretend not to know, or really do not know perhaps, is that the
treaty, disadvantageous as it seems to be, averts any pretext for the
Yankees to take possession of Mexico, in case the theocratic-monarchical
faction should triumph, on the grounds of indemnization or incom-
patability of policy. Even were we to lose our action in the Republic, even were the saints to triumph there, the treaty already settled and
accepted, avoids the danger of monarchy on the one hand and that of
a *protectorate* and a conquest on the other." But it needed a trained eye
to recognize the ultimate purpose of the treaty as a dam, and connoisseurs were few, and their consolations akin to excuses.

Discredit was the first effect of a treaty which inflicted on its authors
a diplomatic defeat more disastrous than the military reverses it was
designed to relieve. In the chorus of abuse, however, one detail was
unanimously overlooked. The deed had not been consummated, and
the validity of the treaty depended on two conditions, which were
taken for granted in the haste to denounce it. One was the approval
of the American Senate, and the other the ratification of Juarez.

5

THE benefits contemplated by the treaty were not pecuniary alone; they were also political. A virtual alliance was implicit in it—not indeed of the visionary kind contemplated by Ocampo, but nonetheless capable of development as a working partnership, and the ground had been laid for it by the right granted to the United States to intervene in support of their treaty rights and the security of their citizens. The use of that right was urged by McLane, even before it was accorded, in a stream of despatches to Washington recommending that the President seek authority of Congress to employ the military forces for domestic duties in Mexico, preferably with the consent of the Constitutional government, but if it were "unreasonably withheld," without it. Consent was a question of diplomatic courtesy rather than of mutual consequence. On this advice Buchanan acted, reproducing the suggestions of McLane to the letter in his annual message to Congress of December 1859. Though the treaty had not yet been received in Washington, the President anticipated its provisions for a political scoop. After rehearsing the events leading up to the constitution of the Juarez government—"General" Juarez, Buchanan called him, not being very familiar himself with those events—he stressed the necessity of sending American troops into the interior for the protection of American citizens. He observed that, since this involved passing through territory controlled by the Constitutional forces, the most acceptable method of securing the object in view would be to act in concert with their government, whose consent and aid might be obtained; but, if not, the duty would be no less imperative. "Such an accession to the forces of the Constitutional government," he added, "would enable it soon to reach the City of Mexico and extend its power over the whole Republic." If this involved intervention, the chronic anarchy prevailing in Mexico warranted an exception, he believed, to the wise and settled policy of the United States Government not to interfere in the domestic concerns of foreign nations. "If we do not, it would not be surprising should some other nation undertake the task and force us to interfere at last, under circumstances of increased difficulty, for the maintenance of our established policy." He asked, therefore, for a law authorizing him to employ a sufficient military force to enter Mexico for the purpose of obtaining indemnity for the past and security for the future. Intervention was warranted by considerations superior to the consent of General Juarez—by the necessity of preventing intervention by other powers and by a general historic warrant for the arrest of General Miramon.

The force of these suggestions was heightened by their context, for they were raised by Buchanan against the background presented by the state of the nation in December 1859. Materially, the American people had never been in better condition, the harvests had been unusually plentiful, the health of the country was excellent, peace and prosperity smiled on the land, and there was every reason to believe, he said, "that we have enjoyed the special protection of Divine Providence ever since our origin as a nation. We have been exposed to many threatening and alarming difficulties in our progress, but on each successive occasion the impending cloud has been dissipated at the moment when it appeared ready to burst upon our head, and the danger to our institutions has passed away." A cloud had arisen, however, with the hanging of John Brown at Harpers Ferry. "I shall not refer in detail to the recent sad and bloody occurrences at Harpers Ferry," he continued. "Still, it is proper to observe that these events, however bad and cruel in themselves, derive their chief importance from the apprehension that they are but symptoms of an incurable disease in the public mind, which may break out in still more dangerous outrages and terminate in an open war by the North to abolish slavery in the South." The state of the nation and the state of the union presented a grim contrast, and the premonition of approaching disaster could not be minimized as lightly as the neck of John Brown. To dispel that cloud something more was needed than the intervention of Divine Providence; intervention in Mexico might prove equally providential. An ounce of prevention below the border was worth a pound of cure above it, and the veiled invitation to relieve domestic tension by a foreign diversion was an inspiration of far-reaching statesmanship —a scoop that brought up the vitals of both nations. The prescription passed unnoticed, however. To the prompting of the President, Congress turned a deaf ear in 1859, as it had done in 1858, and withheld the sanction he solicited for policing Mexico, and the treaty came up for consideration in the Senate only two months later.

Within the limits of the Executive power Buchanan continued, nevertheless, to pursue his own policy. The conclusion of the treaty and the duty of enforcing it created obligations to protect and cooperate with the other party to it, the exact degree of which was determined by his agent in Veracruz, and the opportunities became pressing with the opening of the year 1860. Five weeks after signing the treaty McLane advised Washington that Miramon was preparing to besiege Veracruz again, and among those preparations he included the recent conclusion of a convention negotiated in Paris by the Spanish and Mexican Ministers, Mon and Almonte, by which diplomatic relations between Spain and Mexico, suspended for several years because of a dispute over the debt, were restored, with full recognition of the Spanish claims. The opportunity thus afforded for another raid on the Veracruz government called for corresponding precautions, and McLane sought specific instructions as to the manner in which he was to conduct himself when the city was exposed to siege and assault; and he made suggestions. "When Texas sought admission to our Union, as soon as the Congress of the United States gave its assent to such admission, the President (Mr. Polk) gave directions to the United States naval forces in the Gulf of Mexico to act as if Texas were an integral part of our country and to defend it if assailed— though the Texan Congress had not yet accepted *the act* of admission. With the spirit of these instructions it would harmonize, I think, to direct me to act as if the Treaty and Convention recently concluded by me had been ratified by the Senate of the United States—but this is a view which I did not think it proper to suggest in my official despatch." If this involved intervention—well, the Executive power might well be stretched to protect an investment. "Were the Treaty recently concluded by me with the accompanying Convention duly ratified by the Senate of the United States," he repeated, "it would be the obligation and duty of the authorities of the United States in the port of Veracruz to act in concert and conjunction with the Mexican authorities at that port to protect the lives and properties of citizens of the United States residing there and to enforce existing treaty stipulations"—a course for which there were ample precedents in the conduct of the French, British, and American authorities in Shanghai in 1854, "and each of these governments respectively approved the conduct of their naval officers to the extent of justifying their forcible intervention against the duly recognized authorities of China as well as in concert with them, against the revolutionary movement that then disturbed that part of China." And such was the course adopted when the crisis came.

After the first siege of Veracruz, Mata had been promised that the United States fleet would be ordered to the Gulf to protect his government against the presence of the French and British squadrons stationed there and to insure the negotiation of the American treaty. The unsettled fate of the treaty in February 1859 made it inadvisable to advertise American protection by a large demonstration, but a token force was located in Veracruz to lend assistance to the local authorities or the American Minister in case of danger.

The second siege of Veracruz began exactly a year after the first, lasted just the same length of time, and fared no better, but in one important respect it differed from the earlier attack. Profiting by his previous failure, Miramon made an attempt to complete the siege by sea. Two small transports were purchased and outfitted in Cuba, and four days after the bombardment on land began they were sighted off port, carrying no flag, and making for the roadstead of Anton Lizardo several leagues down the coast, where they unloaded munitions and cast anchor for the night. Their appearance was expected, and in preparation for it the Constitutional government had declared them pirates and requested the American authorities to pursue and arrest them. The invitation was accepted by the senior naval officer—McLane having absented himself in due time. Shortly after dusk an American man-of-war, towed by two small steamers recently leased by the Mexican port authorities, passed the French, British, and Spanish squadrons riding in the roads of Veracruz harbor and, without answering their salute, disappeared down the coast, captured the transports, and brought them into port in the morning. During the night the towns-people had crowded to the roofs, lured by the flash and sound of gun-fire to the south. The commander of the Spanish squadron protested against the American right to police the seas, but he was not supported by the French or British, and after several days of imprisonment the piratical captain and crews were sent with their craft to New Orleans and placed at the disposal of an American prize court. The court found against the captors and released the captives after prolonged litigation, which led to a flurry in Congress and an interpellation of the President, who admitted that the American naval officer had acted with his knowledge and consent.

The Conservatives dated the decline of their cause from the incident at Anton Lizardo. They caught at any straw to account for it. The military value of the captured vessels was negligible: they were engaged in arms running and could not have invested or shelled the town without embroiling the foreign squadrons stationed there. Their political value lay in testing the freedom of the seas, and their power of provocation gave them a considerable nuisance value; but whatever the threat, the theory of a siege by sea was thwarted by American intervention, and the breach of international law was acknowledged too late to alter the effect. For another three weeks the bombardment continued by land in a deadly demonstration of impotence. The fury was sufficient to drive foreign residents to their ships and to provoke a protest from the British Commander against the useless slaughter of civilians, but it did no other damage. And promptly at the end of March, when the sickly season set in, Miramon raised the siege and returned to his capital to prepare another campaign in the interior. No one else, perhaps, could have failed twice in the same attempt without a fatal loss of prestige, and his was seriously impaired. His last appearance as a star had been made the previous December, when he returned to the scene of his triumphs in Guadalajara and was welcomed by the clergy with a special liturgy composed in his honor and sung in the Cathedral, likening the sacred name of Miguel Miramon to all the politicians of the Old Testament in turn, hailing him with each swing of the censer as their heaven-sent savior, and hallowing with obsequious eulogies his popular nickname of "the young Maccabee." Thereafter his star waned swiftly. After his return trip to Veracruz his credit fell so low in the capital that Zuloaga reasserted his right to the Presidency and announced his resumption of office. The forgotten man of the civil war was promptly arrested by Miramon, who effaced him without raising more than a finger to his mouth. "I will show him how Presidents are made," he said, and carried him off as a hostage on his campaign. Thereupon the diplomatic corps met and announced that there was no longer an effective government in the capital and that their presence there was required only for the protection of foreign nationals.

American intervention was of doubtful service, on the other hand, to the Constitutional cause. The government, already discredited by the treaty, was further compromised by the one benefit that it produced. The fears excited by the treaty itself were inflamed by an incident that demonstrated to what length one party was prepared to go to protect it, while the readiness of the other to accept such protection added a fresh provocation to the national pride. Designed as a dam against foreign intervention, the treaty was serving, in fact, as a sieve for it, and what it raised was the question of how far the co-operation of one party would carry the other.

That question was of acute concern to the American partner as well. Referring in his first report after the siege to "the rage of the Miramon government against all foreigners, and particularly against Englishmen and Americans, the latter being more bitterly denounced than all the others," McLane observed that fortunately very few of his countrymen remained in the Republic, "otherwise the malignant resentment so constantly manifested against them would involve the two countries in a war of conquest." The working alliance with the Liberal government had broadened the scope of the civil war and brought it to the brink of an international conflict. It was high time to cry halt, and the British Government was already doing so. "The British Government has communicated to both parties its desire to see the country pacified," he continued. "I need only refer in this connection to the opinion heretofore expressed that foreign intervention is the last and only hope of those who desire to establish the reign of law, and that intervention to be effective must, if necessary, be enforced by the presence of the military power of the nation intervening. Such intervention will sooner or later, and I think at no distant day, be offered to the Miramon government, perhaps to both governments, and if so offered, acceptance,

if not cordially and promptly manifested, will be enforced by a demonstration of naval forces in the Gulf of Mexico that neither of the governments contending for the possession of power can resist. This intervention may at first assume the character of a demand on both
governments for the due execution of existing conventions in virtue
of which nearly seventy per cent of the gross revenue from the customs
in this country is due to the holders of a certain portion of the public
debt known as the Convention debts of Great Britain, France, and
Spain, but it will speedily assume larger proportions, and the European
element will under its influence recover its ascendancy, extending perhaps to the Central American States." To anticipate these developments it was imperative, therefore, to determine how far the American
Government was prepared to go to protect the Monroe Doctrine. "I
submit these reflections certainly not for the first time," he concluded,
"in the hope that the President will be encouraged to persevere in the
policy he has adopted in relation to this country, renewing at the same
time the expression of my opinion that if Congress does not confer
upon him the necessary power to enforce it, this Legation should be
withdrawn and our countrymen in Mexico duly notified that it is not
in his power to afford them adequate protection, for the failure of
Congress to act is generally regarded here as evidence that the government is not sustained in the exercise of its legitimate and Constitutional discretion, and that either from the intrinsic nature of the
opposition it encounters in Congress, or in consequence of some sympathy felt for the Miramon government in the United States, it may
rely upon continued forbearance while it pursues a policy marked by
atrocious cruelty and inhumanity in war, and by every species of
spoliation and exaction."

The protection of the Monroe Doctrine was more important than the
protection of the Juarez government, but the complications created
by the pending treaty made the one inseparable from the other, and the
fears of the American Minister were not unfounded. The war in
Mexico had reached the stage at which party principals were identified
on both sides with patriotic interests. About the treaty, as a pivot, both
factions swung toward their natural spheres: while the Liberal was
drawn into the American orbit, the Conservative turned to the European to counteract its effect, and the rotation reopened the momentous
question of Mexican independence. To that question the foreigner was
no more indifferent than the native. Driven back to the origin of the
nation by American pressure, and reverting to their congenital bias,
the Conservatives were now clambering up their genealogical tree in
search of support; and there, in their extremity, they were reaching for
the first principles of national independence proclaimed in the Three
Guarantees of the Plan of Iguala—union of Europeans and Americans,
a Mexican monarchy, and supremacy of the Church—as their last hope

of self-preservation. Correspondence intercepted at Veracruz revealed the desperate efforts that the Clerical faction was making to secure European protection by the offer of a Mexican throne to a French or Spanish prince; and it was high time to cry halt—but to whom? To Miramon? Or to the meddling of France and England? And how? By withdrawing the American Legation and abandoning Juarez to his fate? Or by backing him against a possible coalition of European Powers without the support of Congress and public opinion in the United States? That was the hitch. Buchanan had gone too far to back down, but he could not pursue his personal policy any further because of the opposition it encountered in Congress; and McLane had to reckon not only with the reaction to the treaty in Mexico, but with the equally strenuous reaction to it in the United States.

There the opposition was composed of many factors, all of which excited the national interest and exhibited the national character very crudely. The treaty was a bone of contention between the two parties in office and out of it, and the Republicans seized on it for their own purposes and made political capital of its occult designs. The *New York Tribune* led the attack in an article which called the President's hand without mincing words. "The whole country should understand the question in all its bearings before the government commits itself to the proposed radical change in our relations with that huge, rotten mass of slunk civilization. Whether the consequences in store for us under the proposed new adjustment of our international relations with that country shall be the annexation of its comparatively unpeopled provinces falling to us in disintegrated masses, as fast as we may be able to spread slavery over them, or whether they shall come in the shape of a ready absorption of its area that is already covered by a priest-ridden, mongrel, dwarfed, and semi-savage population, is alike unimportant to us in a national point of view. Either arrangement would be alike mischievous and pregnant in evil consequences. . . . We do not want to get into any Mexican quagmires or Dismal Swamps. If we are after Sonora, let us say Sonora. If it be other provinces, let us name them. If it be all Mexico, let us say so. Let the people understand exactly what the government aims at. We protest against doing things by stealth and under false pretenses. As things now stand, the Free States must fight for their share of new territorial acquisitions. We demand that they shall know when anything of this sort is going on, in order that they may, as Mr. Calhoun used to claim for slavery in California, 'have a chance to get in.' If we are going to take Mexico or any part of it, the people of the North want a chance to get in."

Strenuously as the *Tribune* protested against the stealth of the government and the false pretenses of the treaty, there was some ambiguity in its own motives for undertaking the attack. The leading organ of the Opposition was willing to get in, provided there was anything for the Republican party to get out of the deal. On the day after the attack the treaty was submitted to a preliminary test in a secret session of the Senate, which was fully reported in the columns of the *Tribune* the next morning. The discussion was opened by a Republican senator, Mr. Mason, who was expected, because of his party affiliations, to oppose the prize project of a Democratic administration. But Mr. Mason could not make up his mind. He did oppose it, reluctantly, as a departure from the settled American policy of non-intervention in the domestic affairs of other nations, which he would never consent to sanction; nevertheless, in view of the state of anarchy existing in Mexico, he was willing to make the experiment. "In regard to the objection urged, that Juarez does not represent the regular government, he supposed that he was as much entitled to that recognition as the other faction; and though he now exercised authority over a small district of the country, he believed, though unable to give any positive assurance to the Senate, that the ratification, with the aid which we would render, would establish the liberal cause in power." But none of the speakers behaved as they were expected to do. While Mr. Mason was open to persuasion, Mr. Wigfall, who followed him, was not. His mind was made up and, although a Southern Democrat, he "denounced the whole scheme as utterly unworthy of countenance or toleration. There was no government in Mexico capable of making a treaty, or of carrying out its stipulations if made. We did not want Mexico or her mongrel population. Juarez and his Indian crew could not govern themselves and if brought into contact with our people would contaminate them." Party positions being thus reversed, the next speaker preferred to overlook the political aspects of the treaty altogether. "Mr. Pugh objected to some of the commercial provisions as favoring certain interests over others, but was willing to make the treaty if amended in those particulars." Mr. Pugh spoke for Republican interests, but another Republican denied them altogether. "Mr. Simmons closed the discussion in one of his strong, conclusive, practical arguments, exposing the sophistries of the alleged commercial advantages. New England has no interest, immediate or remote, in this treaty, but exactly the reverse. It is substantially free trade with Mexico, which would require us, under the clause inserted in every commercial treaty for the last forty years, of admitting each nation on an equal footing with that of the most favored nation, to claim similiar privileges, and would result in destroying our revenue and compelling a resort to direct taxation. This point, and others equally forcible, produced much impression." The discussion was adjourned until the following day, when Mr. Seward promised to take the floor, but the eloquence of the Republican whip was not needed, the treaty being, the *Tribune* reported, "as dead as Julius Caesar." The credit went to

Mr. Simmons, who made it clear that there was nothing in it for the Republican party, and to Mr. Wigfall, who did as much for the Democratic; nor could anyone attribute the verdict to party affiliations, since several Democratic senators, "who yielded to the persuasions of the President and were prepared to conquer prejudices," could now be counted adversely, and the main body of the Republicans, if not all, were pledged to kill the corpse.

The test was by no means final, and the administration was undeterred by a straw vote; but the publicity given to the secret session of February 28, the tirades of the *Tribune,* and the general and open interpretation of the treaty as an option on Mexican territory, made the position of the American Minister extremely delicate. In the face of such feeling in the American Senate, how was he to defend the personal policy of his President and to protect his Mexican partner against the imminent threat of foreign interference? For now, to add to his difficulties, the position of the American Government was directly challenged by the British Government, which assumed the right, as a neutral, to act as arbiter and call a halt all around.

Four days after McLane wrote his warning to Washington, European intervention in Mexico began in the form he had foreseen. Ignoring the opposition in Congress, the European Powers were guided by the general trend of American policy advertised in its discussion in the press and the necessity of checking their predatory tendencies in time. The warning raised by the London *Times* was followed by a move of the British Foreign Office to forestall the pacific absorption of the Republic by an offer, equally peaceful and equally forcible, to terminate the civil war by diplomatic mediation. The support of the Quai d'Orsay was secured, but the lead was taken by British diplomacy, and the offer was communicated simultaneously to the warring factions and the American Minister. The British Minister, Mr. Otway, having been recalled for indiscretion, the note was written by the Chargé d'Affaires, Mr. Mathew, and it gained greater weight from the fact that it came from a minor official who merely transmitted the instructions of Lord Russell. Mr. Mathew notified McLane that Her Majesty's Government would see with satisfaction an armistice of six months' or a year's duration and the election of a National Assembly impartially chosen to determine the future government; though there was no intention of prescribing what that government should be, it should be one that would give some guarantee of stability and order, and hence some advice was in order. "A general amnesty should be proclaimed, religious and civil toleration should be declared, for unless some mercy is shown by opposing parties there can be no hope of internal peace. If this advice intended for the good of Mexico is not accepted," he further explained, "Her Majesty's Government will

have no other course than to demand from both parties sufficient reparations for the wrongs British subjects have suffered."

To such terms no reasonable objection could be raised by the
American Minister. They were inacceptable to the contending parties
and were rejected by both, Miramon ruling out religious liberty and
Juarez insisting on unconditional recognition of the Constitution; but
their objections were beside the point. The British proposals were addressed to the only party that counted, and they were heavily biased in
favor of the Liberal creed as a bid for American support; and as a
further inducement, the French plan reproduced the British, differing
from it only in omitting any mention of religious toleration. Nevertheless, McLane fully approved and supported the refusal of Juarez
to consider any settlement short of his own terms. Four-fifths of the
states, he informed Washington, would have refused to acquiesce in
a compromise, and the almost unanimous sentiment of the Liberal
party would have condemned Juarez for abandoning his functions as
a Constitutional President. The working alliance had now reached the
point where the preservation of one party was essential to the self-
preservation of the American partner, and betrayal would have been
a criminal blunder, and McLane insisted sensibly that the only hope
of pacifying Mexico lay in the zealous and rigorous prosecution of the
personal policy of Buchanan. He deemed the situation serious enough
to send a message of his own to Congress. "I submit that before Congress adjourns that body should be fully advised of the present aspect
of the Mexican question," he repeated, "that it may appreciate how
imminent is the danger of a government based on the ultramontane
and monarchical principles of the Plan of Iguala." The British had
served notice that they meant business, and having been rebuffed by
the Liberals, they were quite capable of courting the Clericals to force
a compromise. McLane temporized, and for three months he managed
to maintain, without support, an uncertain truce with the British
Legation.

Such were the conditions in which the treaty came up for final
consideration in the Senate on the last day of May, 1860. They were
adverse in every respect, for in the meanwhile it had been subjected
to a searching and thorough discussion in the press, which threshed
out every aspect of the question save the one in which the American
Minister to Mexico was interested. Foreign competition was completely ignored. The Mexican question was debated for its bearing, not
on foreign policy, but on the domestic issue that dominated it, and the
treaty was involved in the slavery question and grafted to the growing
threat of disunion in the United States. Upon one premise all arguments agreed—the underlying assumption that the treaty involved the
annexation of Mexican territory. "If a new treaty, of straightforward

stipulations, giving us unencumbered commercial advantages and clear grants of land, could be made, we might well hold a complacent attitude in view of its ratification," the *Tribune* conceded, "provided we first had a Homestead bill. The slavery extension party should be met by going ahead rather than by holding back. Let us have the vacant territory south of us and fill it with colonists, and thus overslaugh slavery therein. Mexico is falling to pieces, and we shall soon have an opportunity to obtain the fragments we need on our own terms." Warming to the idea immediately after the defeat of the treaty in the straw vote in February, the *Tribune* appropriated and adapted it to the demands of the Abolitionist party. "If we could run a tier of free states straight across the continent, on the southern line of Texas, we should let in an amazing flood of light on the slavery question in the process. Such a cordon could not be jumped by slavery, and Lower Mexico might fester and putrify at leisure, with comparatively small danger of spreading her contamination upon us. As things now stand, and they would be even worse under this hybrid treaty, we have no security against a peon slavery being established and gradually ligatured on to our southern extremity, to be followed by a weltering process, making our southern limits more vague than the tail of Milton's Satan."

While Horace Greeley's paper was now frankly in favor of an aggressive policy in Mexico, the *Atlantic Monthly,* entering the discussion at the same time, found some strong arguments, however, for holding back. "The people of the United States have to choose between the conquest of Mexico and non-intervention in Mexican affairs. There may be something to be said in favor of conquest, though the President's arguments in that direction—for such they are, disguised though they be—remind us strongly of those which were put forth in justification of the partition of Poland; but the policy of intervention does not bear criticism for one moment. Either it is a conquest veiled, or it is a blunder the chance to commit which is purchased at an enormous price, and blunders are to be had for nothing, and without the expenditure of life and money." But as Buchanan was bent on committing the blunder and was appealing personally to leading Republicans to set aside partisanship and co-operate in perpetrating it, stronger arguments were needed. The divergent objections to the treaty had one common denominator in the intense and outspoken aversion of the American to the Mexican people, and the *Atlantic* proceeded to examine the contaminating consequences, both for the Free and Slave States, of the proposed conquest. "The final cause of the absorption of Mexico by the United States will be the restless appropriating spirit of our people; but this might leave her a generation more of rational life, were it not that her territory presents a splendid field for slave-labor and that, both from pecuniary and political motives, our slaveholders are seeking the increase of the number of Slave States. There is not an argument used on behalf of the rigid slave codes of several of our States that would not be applicable to the enslavement of the black and mixed Mexicans, all of whom would be of darker skins and less enlightened minds than the slaves that would be taken to the conquered land by the conquerors. How could the slaves thus taken there be allowed to see even their inferiors in the enjoyment of personal freedom? If the State of Arkansas can condescend to be afraid of a few hundred negroes and mulattoes, and can illustrate its fear by turning them out of their homes in mid-winter, what might not be expected from a ruling caste in a new country, with two and a half millions of colored people to strike terror into the souls of those comprising it? Just or humane legislation could not be looked for at the hands of such men, who would be guilty of that cruelty which is born of injustice and terror. The white race of Mexico would join with the intrusive race to oppress the mixed races; and as the latter would be compelled to submit to the iron pressure that would be brought to bear upon them, more than two millions of slaves would be added to the servile population of America, and would become the basis of a score of Representatives in the National Legislature, and of as many Presidential Electors; so that the practise of the grossest tyranny would give to the slaveholding states, *per saltum,* as great an increase of political power as the Free States could be expected to achieve through a long term of years illustrated by care and toil and the most liberal expenditure of capital. The Indians would fare no better than the mixed races, though the form of degradation might differ. The Indians of Mexico are a race quite different from the Indians whom we have exterminated or driven to the remote West. They are a sad, a superstitious, and an inert people, upon whom Spanish tyranny has done its perfect work. Even if it should not be sought to enslave the Indians of Mexico, that race would not be the less doomed. There seems to be no chance for Indians in any country into which the Anglo-Saxons enter in force. A system of free labor would be as fatal to the Mexican Indians as a system of forced labor. The whites who would throng to Mexico, on its conquest by the Americans, and on the supposition that slavery would not be established there, would regard the Indians with sentiments of strong aversion. They would hate them not only because they were Indians—which would be deemed reason enough—but as competitors in industry who could afford to work for low wages, their wants being few and the cost of their maintenance small. . . . The sentiment of the whites toward the Indians is not unlike that which has been expressed by an American statesman, who says that the cause of the failure of Mexico to establish for herself a national position is to be found in her acknowledgment of the political equality of her Indian population. He would have them degraded, if not absolutely enslaved, and degradation, situated as they are, implies their extinction.

This is the opinion of one of the ablest men in the Democratic party, who, though a son of Massachusetts, is ready to go as far in behalf of slavery as any son of South Carolina."

The arguments of the *Atlantic* agreed with those of many Southern Democrats who were deserting their leader, convinced that the acquisition of Mexican territory would be unprofitable because of the risks of introducing their peculiar institution there and aggravating the growing race problem of the South. But imperialism would be abandoned only when it proved to be unprofitable; and race prejudice being its badge, it could still be made to repay cultivation. A religious appeal to race prejudice was made by the Honorable Frank Blair, who, speaking at Cooper Union in New York on behalf of American Catholics, represented the Mexican question as a race war in which the whites, menaced by the overwhelming numbers of Indian and colored races, were saved from submersion only by the influence of the Church. "Mr. Buchanan has leagued himself with the Indian Juarez in this war of religion and caste; leagued himself with the chief who has by edict confiscated the property of the Catholic Church and will exterminate its defenders of the white race in order to possess himself of the spoils," he concluded, skillfully confusing the most popular prejudices of his public. "The Dred Scott decision, having already overthrown our free institutions, would carry slavery into this new conquest, and the system of peonage, the hereditary servitude of debt, would still more readily become assimilated to the peculiar institution. Inexorable indeed is the demand for the extension of slavery, when it compels Mr. Buchanan to league himself with an Indian in a war of caste and religion—a war against the proprietory class in Mexico—and to confiscate the estates of that Church whose members in this country elevated him to the Presidency." The translation of the Mexican question into American terms was applauded as heartily in New York as if the speech had been delivered in Dixie or, for that matter, in Mexico City.

Opposition to the treaty came from conflicting sources, but the contradictions of interest combined to create a catholic antipathy to it. Any cross-section of public opinion revealed the knotted motives that militated against its adoption. When the question came up in the Senate in May, they were all summed up in the words of one speaker, who contended that "the ultimate acquisition of Mexico, which the treaty was intended to initiate, would be the forbidden fruit which Mr. Calhoun has described when speaking of Cuba; and while it might tend to the dissolution of the Union, he could not see how the South was to benefit by the addition of that mongrel population. Hence he was opposed to it." Republicans and Democrats were ranged on both sides of the fence, or on it, in a conspiracy of cross-purposes that was perfectly consistent in its seeming confusion, because the forbidden fruit had lost its power to tempt. Falling afoul of the sectional issue which was already dividing the Union, it was rotten fruit for both parties, and rotten fruit matured rapidly. The warmongering maneuvers of Buchanan, annually ignored by Congress, were definitely doomed in 1860, even as a contraceptive to domestic insurrection, for the cloud which was no bigger than a man's hand in December had grown ominously larger by May, and the lengthening shadow of approaching civil war in the United States could no longer be diverted by a dying adventure below the border. The administration mustered its strength, however; the treaty was defeated by nine votes (27 to 18), and the count being close, a motion to reconsider was introduced just as the Senate was about to adjourn and carried in the confusion of the moment. "Thus ends this farce," the *Tribune* reported. "The Mexican treaty was nominally reconsidered and thereby goes over until the next session." Since only three senators, and all of them Republicans, voted to "galvanize the corpse," it could be counted out. "Juarez," the obituary added, "will probably be in exile before the treaty is again considered, if present signs may be trusted."

No one was more bitterly disappointed by the defeat of the treaty than the correspondent of the *New York Times* in Mexico. Though he wrote for Seward's paper, Edward Dunbar was not a politician, nor even a professional journalist, but an American businessman who used the columns of the *Times* to contribute his knowledge of the Mexican question to the discussion, to protest against its manipulation by professional politicians, and to bring about a sympathetic understanding between two liberty-loving peoples—the one interest which had been consistently neglected by Congress and the press in the United States. "Does anyone doubt," he wrote, "that if the administration had, at an early date, marked out an intelligent, decided, and just policy with Mexico, *the result of convictions based on knowledge,* and enforced this policy with that moral power which intelligent and honest convictions always command—does anyone believe, I ask, that this treaty, wrought by an honest and capable public servant, could not have been carried even against the destructive opposition of the Republicans and fire-eating politicians who united to destroy it? And does anyone believe that the Republican party in Washington evinced any *honest convictions based on knowledge* relative to the Mexican question, or any sentiment higher than that of a determination to achieve success in their own thoroughly selfish political purposes, no matter by what means, or at what cost to the country at large?" As a symptom of this spirit, he observed that "There is probably no instance on record where the simple diplomatic efforts of an American envoy to establish friendly and profitable relations with a foreign power have been attacked with such bitter malignity and rude violence as in the case

of Mr. McLane. . . . Had he been a very dolt in diplomacy, as corrupt
as the vilest politician, and a blackhearted traitor to his country, he
could not have been more heartily abused than he has been in his
efforts to sustain the American name and character abroad and the
cause of liberty in Mexico, and to create permanent relations of amity
and commerce between the two countries. Whether such extraordinary
conduct on the part of the American people and Congress, so contrary
to their professions and the spirit of the age, arises from apathy,
ignorance, partisan feeling in politics, or the lack of anything like
real sympathy with freedom in other countries, time alone can determine. At the present moment we are united with despotic agencies
to smother the new-born hopes of freedom in Mexico and cast the
people back into darkness and despair. The United States now occupy
the meanest position toward Mexico that it is possible for a powerful
and free republic to hold toward a weak and despairing neighbor—a
position that will prove a sin and a shame to us in the future."

He was bitter because his country suffered from the reflections that
the Mexican question cast on American character. The failure of the
treaty was due to its manipulation by party politics, but in the final
analysis the ultimate responsibility lay neither with the Democratic
party, which adulterated a liberal policy toward Mexico with predatory
designs, nor with the Republican, which, progressive at home and
reactionary abroad, was equally lacking in moral power, but with the
American people, who had no more moral power than their politicians,
because they had no knowledge of the Mexican question, and hence
no convictions; and their ignorance was due, fundamentally, to their
indifference to the Mexican people. For this apathy he found what
excuses he could. "Much of the indifference, and we may say aversion,
felt toward Mexican affairs generally are doubtless owing to the peculiar character of the correspondence from Mexico that appears in
the public journals," he admitted. No paid correspondents were maintained there, the reports of volunteers were irresponsible and biased,
and his own were an exception to "the manner in which every sound
argument and every statement of fact in favor of the Liberal cause in
Mexico has been opposed throughout those countries called Christian
and enlightened, especially the United States. No sooner has anything
of this nature fallen upon the public eye than perversions, false statements, or flat denials have sprung up in all quarters, and for the time
being truth has been overcome by error." But the press was only
partly responsible for the misrepresentation of the Mexican question.
The prevalent errors of public opinion were fostered by other forces.
In the first place, there was Prescott, who had done so much to
popularize an erroneous conception of the ancient history of Mexico
by faithfully following the exaggerations, inconsistencies, and palpable
errors of the early Spanish historians. "No one has done more to cloud

the perceptions of the present generation, or to throw obstacles in the
way of a just comprehension of the Mexican people, their present condition, and the nature of the conflict now raging in that country, than
our own favorite historian. Prescott's well-known honesty, industry,
and singleness of purpose, combined with his ability as a writer, have
given his *Conquest of Mexico*—which is nothing more than a beautiful high-wrought romance—all the weight of truthful matter-of-fact
history. Prescott concedes the Christianization of Mexico and his
writings are eulogized by Spain. On these premises alone it is safe
to conclude that our standard work on the Conquest is unreliable as
history." Prescott had never visited Mexico; Prescott had drawn his
material from the first Spanish Minister to Mexico; and Prescott, moreover, was temperamentally unfitted for his task: he was "of too gentle
a nature, too delicate and feminine in his mental composition, to write
the true history of the Spanish Conquest and rule on the American
continent." The danger of good writing was never so well demonstrated; for on the basis of Prescott's literary conquest of Mexico there
had grown up the flourishing fallacies that still misled public opinion
—the common belief that Christianity had ever prevailed in Spanish
America because the Church had prevailed there, and the current mis-
interpretation of the Mexican question due to the almost exclusive
possession of the means of manufacturing public opinion abroad by
the Church and the retrograde parties in Spanish America. But
neither Prescott nor Catholic propaganda were more than minor
causes for the callousness of the American public toward the Liberal
struggle in Mexico: the primary one was race prejudice.

As propaganda flourishes in proportion to the affinity of a people for
it, all these causes were poor excuses for the American people; and it
was no better apology for race prejudice to point out, as Dunbar did,
that that motive was equally prevalent in Europe. It was the favorite
argument of reaction everywhere. In France the groundwork for it had
been laid by the Comte de Gobineau, whose voluminous *Essay on the
Inequality of Human Races* was known, however, only to a small
number of initiates, and a popular application of his thesis to the
Mexican question had just been made by the *Revue des Deux Mondes*
with material supplied by M. de Gabriac, and by the *London Satur-
day Review,* which vulgarized the same doctrine across the Channel.
According to the English weekly, disturbances in Spanish America in
general, and in Mexico in particular, were due to the Indian element.
"Many of us have the impression that Juarez, Vidaurri, and Degollado
are as actual Spanish gentlemen as Sartorius, Narvaez, and O'Donnell"
—the leading Spanish politicians of the time—"yet the truth is that the
three persons named, who are all Mexicans, generals, and Constitutionalists, are neither more nor less than full-blooded Indians, and are
therefore much nearer relations of the Ojibbeways who were exhibited

in London a few seasons ago than of any *hidalgo* in Spain. It need not be said that this circumstance entirely destroys the importance of the Spanish revolutions as precedents." For the benefit of those who had missed the Ojibways, however, the article went into detail. "The difference between a European and an Indian leader is well illustrated by the history of the rival Presidents of the Mexican Republic. Juarez, the so-called Constitutional President who was lately besieged in Veracruz, is, as has been stated, an Indian of unmixed blood. Miramon, who has been styled President of the Church party, is, on the contrary, a Frenchman by the father's side and a Spaniard by the mother's—in other words, a European, descended from two of the finest races in Europe. Of the merits of the contest in which these two leaders are engaged we shall say only that it has been grossly misapprehended in the United States and England. It turns on the confiscation of Church property, and this circumstance has caused some degree of mild favor to be extended here and in America to Juarez, who is the champion of the anti-clerical faction. The Mexican clergy are certainly indolent and ignorant, according to European standards, but with all their defects they alone prevent the Mexican people from relapsing into the beliefs and practices of savage life. The Haytian negro, when the destruction of the whites relieved him from the control of his priests, went straight back to his Obi, which he scarcely deigns to overlay with a thin varnish of Christianity, and the Mexican, whether Indian or mongrel, can scarcely now be kept by all the vigilance of his spiritual pastors from throwing himself into sorcery and fetish worship. The cause of the Roman Catholic Church in Mexico is, therefore, for once the cause of civilization; and if the truth were known, it would probably be found that Juarez, who is panegyrized by the American papers as the liberal and enlightened antagonist of spiritual despotism, is simply the foe of priests because he prefers some private enchantment of his own to the celebration of the Mass."

The virulence of race prejudice abroad could not compare, however, with its vulgarity in America, where it was common to all parties, native to the national character, and indigenous to the arrogant ignorance of the American people. How easily the most vulgar of all the vices of human vanity could be manipulated for political purposes the discussion of the Mexican question in Congress and the press proved. The dense indifference to the Mexican people had been turned into deadly aversion by lumping the Mexican question with the abolition issue in the United States, and for this result Dunbar held the Republican party primarily to blame. "Because the Indians, the aborigines, the *natives* of Mexico, who have for centuries writhed and groaned under the heel of their oppressor, are, according to the best of their ability, endeavoring to achieve freedom, they are abused and denounced from one end of Christendom to the other," he wrote. "And who are foremost in thus denouncing the Indian race of Mexico and doing their best to crush out the aspirations for liberty in this race, because it is *Indian* and has a *dark skin?* Why, they are those who call themselves the leaders of the great Republican party in the United States—leaders who are fairly screaming into the public ear their hatred of oppression, their love for their *black brother* in bondage, their determination to give him freedom at all hazards and to place him on an equality with his white brother at the earliest possible moment! What a fathomless depth of cant and hypocrisy this glaring inconsistency reveals! . . . If ever a great measure of general and vital importance to the whole country came before the United States Senate without the negro in it, we believe it was the McLane–Ocampo treaty, but the negro was lugged in, and of course the ruin of the measure followed."

Dunbar smarted, because for him the first and greatest of the national interests was the national character, and he wrote to defend it. Whether the defeat of the treaty was due to apathy, ignorance, partisan feeling in politics, or the lack of anything like real sympathy with freedom in other countries, the result was profoundly disappointing to his faith in American democracy. The majority was against him, and in democratic theory the majority was right. In practice it had rarely been so wrong; but his efforts to interpret the Mexican question truly and to bring about a just understanding and alliance between two liberty-loving peoples would have passed unnoticed had they not earned him a caustic comment in an American paper. "Mr. Dunbar deems it legitimate in discussing questions of Mexican policy," wrote the *New York Journal of Commerce,* "to arraign and to praise and condemn, giving to his *Mexican Papers* a wide scope and range, and tending, we fear, to involve him quite as deeply in American politics as in the affairs of Mexico." The danger of acting as an interpreter of the Mexican question was that it developed the ability to see it from both sides; and Dunbar was forced to finish what he had begun. "The criticism of the *Journal* is just and to the point," he replied. "Nothing could be more so. I am an American citizen, born and bred, and have the right to vote. I am, according to the theory if not the practise of democratic institutions, one of the people—the masters, who send their servants to Washington to attend to my interests. I find that those national servants in Washington do not attend properly to my interests as a private American citizen, engaged in lawful and legitimate business. Therefore I very naturally claim the right to 'arraign and to praise and condemn' pretty much everybody connected with the government, according as, in my opinion, they deserve, and to investigate the causes that carry individuals so notoriously unfit for their position into power. Not being a disappointed or expectant politician, I feel a glorious independence in being able to apply the knife to *both* of the great political parties, whose politics, as I conceive, are of a destructive character to my own lawful and legitimate interests, and who have brought the whole country to the condition and position so correctly stated by Mr. Seward in his recent Detroit speech: viz., universal dissatisfaction at home and our institutions a hissing and a by-word for all creation abroad. The discussion of the Mexican question *inevitably* involves the discussion of American politics, and of those vital interests in the United States over which the politics of negro politicians have been so long allowed to maintain their destructive ascendancy."

He had the presumption to defend the national character single-handed, because he knew and spoke for the genuine American people, so generous, friendly, fair-minded, and ready to respond to their kind everywhere, but so ingenuous also and easily blindfolded by the theory of their free institutions and the practice of their professional politicians. The Mexican question called up all the devils of American democracy without casting them out—the spirit of liberty perverted by the spirit of imperialism; the unclean spirit of race prejudice; the incubus of plutocratic power and the succubus of popular sanction; the feeble spirit of independent public opinion and the superstitious spirit of majority rule. The majority, if not right, was mighty, and authentic Americans were one in a thousand; and the real damage of the defeat of the treaty was that it drove men like Edward Dunbar first to challenge, then to question, and finally to doubt the virtue of American democracy.

The damage went deeper than that in Mexico. There the only possible defense of the treaty lay in its fruits, and they were bitter. The benefits evaporated, the odium remained. Delusion could hardly go further; but the dregs remained to be drained. The barren bond remained to plague its authors, and Juarez, condemned for the attempt and not the deed, had now to contend with the aftereffects of the ill-fated contract. Though it was not consummated, it was not dead, and the abortion infected the country with fresh complications by its very miscarriage.

The narrow margin by which the treaty was defeated encouraged the friends of Buchanan, and they planned to reintroduce it before the coming presidential election in November; but as the six months provided for ratification had expired, an extension of time had to be secured from Mexico, and after the discussion in the United States had disclosed the real nature of the contract and the close call by which Mexico had escaped foreclosure, consent from that quarter was so improbable that one American paper buried the treaty and both its beneficiaries in the same sneer. "When it was thought that a political object could be promoted by extending aid and comfort to the mongrels and mixed breeds of Mexico, who, under the name of Liberals,

were seeking possession of power but unwilling to fight for it as brave
men should do, the President was prompt enough to recognize the
Indian Juarez, who knows as much about liberty, in its high sense, as
he does about the Koran," wrote the Philadelphia *North American
Independent*. "It turned out like most of his experiments, and the 'Constitutional President of Mexico' has not been able to survive the partiality of his friend in the White House." Though the announcement
was premature, the end of Juarez was imminently expected, and by
no means improbable, since the abandonment of the treaty also begot
beneficiaries who had long been preparing, and who were now free, to
enter the battle.

The shadow of foreign intervention under which the civil war had
been fought for two years thickened in the third year. It was no longer
cast by a pair of officious ministers—the recall of Mr. Otway for indiscretion was followed by that of M. de Gabriac for the same reason—
but by governments directly concerned in extinguishing the civil war
for the security of their national interests. Such was the ultimate result
and actual consummation of the McLane treaty, which, by introducing
into the magnetic field of Mexico a foreign object that excited the
activity of all the others embedded there, virtually reduced the country
to the colonial status which it was struggling to overcome.

The final phase of the civil war began with the British effort to
mediate. A prolonged diplomatic duel ensued between Mathew and
McLane, seconded by Miramon on the one hand and Juarez on the
other, and throughout it the American Minister extended a steady and
decisive support to his partner which foiled all the attempts—and they
were many and persistent—of the British mediator to initiate his
maneuver. Rebuffed in his first approaches, Mathew renewed his peace
offensive in the summer of 1860, but as the failure of the treaty had
relieved international tension and facilitated a more conciliatory approach, he modified his tactics and relied on the force of persuasion
alone. Following the old diplomatic rule that the easiest way to control
a competitor is to side with him, the British Government was negotiating with Washington for joint mediation in Mexico, and Mathew
sought the support and co-operation of McLane on those terms. Searching for some common ground of agreement, he deplored the stubborn
attachment of the American Minister to the Constitution and presented the case on its practical merits. Since the contending parties
were irreconcilable on the question of principles, the sole possibility of
compromise lay in a sacrifice of persons. "Concession of every sort
has been refused by Señor Juarez," he observed. "On the other hand,
the occurrences of the past two years—the utter incapacity of his
leaders, his own want of energy—preclude any expectancy of a party
triumph under his guidance. Indeed, they give consistency to a current

belief that Señor Juarez and his Minister of Foreign Affairs, conscious that the establishment of the Constitutional government in Mexico would reduce them to deserved obscurity, are far from desiring peace. That such is to some extent the feeling on this side—that neither General Miramon nor any member of his government nor any leader of his forces wishes for a termination of the war, unless it be by a conquest that would maintain them in office and command—I feel well assured. Under these circumstances, I feel we have no hope of peace unless by mutual conciliation, arrangements the result of Foreign intervention, or the substitution of a more energetic and capable person as the leader of the Constitutional party in lieu of Señor Juarez." And he produced a candidate: Comonfort. Provided he guaranteed religious liberty, he was the most eligible and, indeed, the only available leader. "I am inclined to think that at the present moment he might unite the suffrages of the Allied European Powers, if the influence of the United States were exerted in his behalf at Veracruz," Mathew continued. "I confess that I cannot but doubt the success of Allied intervention, unless it is supported by some show of force. The United States naturally possess the dominant influence with the government they have recognized, and it might be more easy for them than for any other nation to induce the leaders at Veracruz to acquiesce in a diplomatic settlement and arbitration. Would not, however, the best mode be the adoption by the United States and the Allied Powers, in the exceptional case of Mexico, of a specific form of government—say for eight years—and a demand for its unconditional acceptance by both parties?"

The termination of the civil war by the return of Comonfort would have been a grim judgment upon Juarez and a terrible atonement for supplanting him, had the idea been adopted; but it made no sense in Mexico, and no impression upon McLane. That it was seriously advanced by Mathew would have reflected on his judgment, had the notion originated with him; but he was not the umpire. He merely followed the instructions of Lord Russell, who was himself the proxy for the Prime Minister; to Lord Palmerston there was nothing exceptional in the expedient of compulsory arbitration, nor to his agent in the choice of the arch-compromiser to make it acceptable to Mexico. The solution was eminently British and eminently reasonable in London; and it was the duty of Mathew to produce the evidence to support it. He performed his part industriously, and his findings confirmed, and contributed to spread, the current detraction of the Constitutional President whose elimination was a necessity of British policy. Thus reputations are made and unmade. The weakness of Juarez was indispensable to the success of British policy in Mexico; but knowing that that was the weak point in his argument, Mathew hacked away at his supporters and used a better one to suborn McLane. "Unless I greatly err in judgment," he argued, "the sole object and desire of the United States is to see established in Mexico a government upon the best and firmest basis upon which commerce may thrive and from which foreigners may enjoy perfect religious liberty and due protection and justice. I have imagined, therefore, that the question of a federal or central constitution was wholly unimportant in their eyes." Moreover, he added, he had taken pains to ascertain the sentiments of the Constitutional leaders in the interior, and his investigation gave him good reason to believe that "Señor Juarez greatly errs in supposing that any attachment exists among them to the Constitution of 1857, beyond the broad principle it embodies of civil liberty"; while very little could be said, he suspected, with regard to the claims of *legality,* that word being used on both sides for purely personal ends. Since the Constitution meant nothing to the Mexicans who were fighting for it, what possible importance could it have for foreigners? The tenacity of Juarez in clinging to that bone of contention amply warranted his removal. "He makes no concession for the sake of peace, or in deference to the advice and just demands of foreign Allied Powers," Mathew complained, "but expects a *party triumph* by negotiation, which the most glaring incapacity and want of energy have hitherto precluded his attaining by force of arms, though supported by the most powerful ingredients of success."

The motives of Juarez he could understand, but not those of McLane in supporting him. The just demands of foreign Powers for law and order, stability and trade, religious and civil liberty, met every reasonable demand of democracy. What more did the American Minister want? Surely they could come to an understanding in Mexico; they spoke the same language of capitalist democracy, the British compromise covered their combined interests, Juarez himself meant nothing to his sponsors, and Comonfort was just the man to justify his elimination. So far Mathew was right. What he refused to recognize, however, was the obvious fact that McLane was committed to support the Constitution together with the government he had recognized, the treaty he had negotiated, and the working alliance he had established with the party whose success was essential to the security of American interests; the validity of all his titles was involved in its legality. But George B. Mathew had an uncommon capacity for being baffled by the obvious. It was also obvious that the Constitution could not be discarded without sacrificing the basic right of self-determination, which was indispensable to any kind of democracy; and this point at least he recognized as an obstacle that could be overcome only by foreign intervention, a show of force, compulsory arbitration, and the imposition of a government by the Allied Powers.

But Mathew was no match for McLane. The American and the Englishman spoke the same language, but not the same dialect; and the dialectical difference defeated Mathew. If there was any aspect of the Mexican question which all Americans understood, it was an argument, and undoubtedly the best, that Dunbar advanced in favor of the Liberal cause. "A strict regard for historical truth," he wrote, "compels me to state that British diplomacy in Mexico has from first to last, next to the Church, been one of the chief obstacles to the progress of liberal principles in that country. In this matter the British Government has acted on a false conception of political necessity and commercial interest, namely, opposition to the spread of the institutions and interests of the United States on this continent." Against that national prejudice, which was stronger than all the others and provided the best protection for Mexico, no amount of persuasion could prevail; and all the arguments of Mathew were lost on McLane. He could not do better than Lord Palmerston. Lord Lyons, the British Ambassador in Washington, presented an official invitation for joint intervention, which was declined. More, the American Government asked Paris for explanations of a paragraph in a London paper, announcing joint intervention by England and France, and received satisfactory assurances that the intervention contemplated was purely moral—satisfactory, that is, because a crisis had arisen in the Near East and military intervention by England and France in Syria was imminently expected.

But another Power had now to be reckoned with in Washington. The Mon–Almonte Convention, which McLane recognized as the counterweight to his treaty, became active with the arrival in Mexico in the summer of 1860 of the Spanish Minister. The partiality of Señor Pacheco for the Clerical government to which he was accredited was advertised by the activity, as industrious as it was indiscreet, with which he sought to bolster, singlehanded, its failing fortunes; and within a few weeks of his arrival he was embroiled with its adversary. A Spanish vessel having been embargoed at Veracruz for arms running, the commander of the Spanish squadron, acting on order from his Minister, threatened to bomb the town and blockade the coast unless the prize were promptly released. The demand was ignored, and tension ran so high that the Juarez government consulted the American Legation on the possibility of securing American aid in the event of a war with Spain. McLane was in Washington at the time, consulting his government, and the incident dramatized the question that he had come to discuss. How far was American protection of the Constitutional government to be carried? Great Britain, France, and Spain, he repeated, were certain to intervene sooner or later, either jointly or severally, and unless it were in the power of the President to anticipate or counteract such intervention, the position of the American Legation would be humiliating. He advised that the Legation be withdrawn in anticipation of such a contingency, unless the naval forces of the United States could be employed to avert it. The President was reluctant to accept either alternative until the fate of the treaty had been finally settled; but the adverse vote in the Senate obliged him to act with circumspection. A repetition of the naval demonstration in March was out of the question in August; and Buchanan, unwilling either to back down or to become embroiled, directed McLane to continue to lend the Constitutional government moral support, but to offer no opposition to bona fide intervention for the redress of legitimate wrongs.

The qualified support with which McLane returned to Veracruz therefore placed the burden of averting intervention on the Constitutional government itself. The only alternative being a military triumph of the Liberals, Mathew renewed his peace proposals, but this time he adopted a different approach. He addressed an appeal, *ad hominem,* to Juarez himself. In a personal note, offering him some friendly advice, he informed him that Miramon was about to take the field with a force of six or seven thousand men and added, "This in no way alters the position of the Constitutional government as to the peace proposals, which, in my opinion, that government should make and publish, but it greatly aggravates—morally—the position of a Republican President who commits the crime of shedding the blood of his fellow countrymen and of the nation that is hostile to him." But he did not moralize unmercifully. "I shall not conceal from you, sir, that the best advice that I can offer you is to accept, *without a single day of delay,* the services of an auxiliary corps from the United States, insisting, however, on keeping their employment secret until a proclamation announces their landing as a Republican legion composed of men of all countries coming to take service under your government, to join your troops, and to fight for Mexican freedom."

The notion of engaging a corps of American volunteers had been debated often and bitterly in the cabinet and the country, and whenever and wherever it appeared Juarez had opposed it. Coming from a diplomat bent on eliminating him as an obstacle to mediation, it received no more consideration, therefore, than was due to a snare that would insure his political suicide. The note was written in French, a language which Juarez understood as well as the ruse of his British friend. The tongue of the tempter would have been recognizable in any language, and Juarez replied in his own, thanking Mathew for his proffered friendship and mentioning in passing, as a matter that merited no further attention, that "as for the forces of the United States, I must tell you that in my opinion there is no need for them. We have sufficient forces in the country."

If Mathew expected Juarez to compromise his cause and discredit himself by accepting intervention in the form of a foreign legion, and to commit the American Government surreptitiously, the advice was uncommonly artful but uncommonly credulous. After failing to dislodge him by way of McLane, the man deserved credit no doubt for so bold an attempt to make him a party to his own undoing. But there was nothing Machiavellic about George B. Mathew. He was simply at his wits' end.

The confidence of Juarez in self-help and the ultimate triumph of his cause remained to be proved, however, and the burden of proof rested on him. With intervention imminent, speed and activity were needed to anticipate it; and at that moment he was faced with a collapse of morale in his camp that marked the crisis of the civil war.

6

THE case for intervention rested on the stalemate into which the war degenerated after two and a half years of strenuous but inconclusive struggle. The fanatical pitch to which the Reform Laws wrought it intensified the bitterness and the obstinacy of the battle, but not its efficiency. In every corner of the country the hum of an implacable hatred could be heard, in harangues, in sermons, in pamphlets, in public rallies and political clubs and private homes, but the maddening drone of the dynamo produced nothing but a monotonous momentum without material issue or moral relief; the driving power vibrated with tireless impotence, finding spasmodic vent in violence without power, in the sputter of persecution, in the polemics of pillage, in the fuming of an interminable feud, in all the by-products of war short of military triumph. Victories and defeats were equally indecisive, and by the summer of 1860 the war had become a conclusive demonstration of the inability of either faction to prevail over the other, which amply warranted foreign intervention to put a merciful end to the convulsions of domestic dissension. More and more Mexicans succumbed to that conviction, and the capacity to resist it became the decisive factor in the final outcome.

When the contest reached that point, the advantage lay with Miramon, who had succeeded in maintaining the morale of his party and his troops by a series of spectacular if fruitless and fugitive triumphs, marred only by his repeated repulses before Veracruz. Degollado, on the other hand, was still "the hero of defeats," and though his powers of recuperation were unimpaired, a long succession of disasters had fostered demoralization among his subordinates. The respect which he commanded was pathetic or perfunctory, and limited to his staff; the malcontents formed their own clique, relieving their feelings in complaints of his incompetence and consoling themselves for their loyalty by professional backbiting. Santos Degollado was still a name to conjure with, but the spell had worn thin, and what it conjured up was faith without hope, loyalty to a cult, and sneers without charity. Lip-service was paid to the cult, but the hero was profaned behind his back. He was "the little saint," "the sacristan," "the Jesuit," "the hypocrite," to those who were surfeited with defeat; his failure to resign was indelicate, indecent, shameless shamming, and to hasten his exit he was discredited by hearsay. He was said to favor hiring American volunteers, and predamned for the one weakness that would confirm all his failures. To the relief of his critics, he left the army for a few months in February to act as Minister of Foreign Affairs in Veracruz—the first real service, they declared, that he had rendered his country—and as he signed the note inviting American intervention there, his days appeared to be counted. However, he returned to the army undaunted, and his detractors resigned themselves sullenly to the cult of incompetence.

In the ranks a thorough reorganization and a strong infusion of professional competence were required to repair the influence of persistent defeat. General Lopez Uraga, a trained soldier who joined the Liberal colors and won a battle for them about this time, described the conditions he encountered in a candid report to the President: "Our troops, accustomed to defeats, are shy of fighting and ready to retire at the first shot. Their leaders and officers, ill chosen, capriciously appointed, and easily promoted, try to drag out the war and to avoid exposing themselves and are the first to quit. No section leader subordinates himself to his commander; if he joins him it is in obedience to some combination which is never carried out and which divides when it should most unite them. Here today and there tomorrow, by dint of isolated efforts, the enemy escapes when he ought to be caught and succeeds when he is weakest. The General of our army, with none to second him, must be everything himself, gunner, mule-driver, quartermaster and division commander; he must fight in the open and direct his columns and attend to his artillery and even to his munitions, for if he does not he will be beaten, and if he does he will be killed, and then, as on the 24th in this city, there will be no one to continue the victory that he had assured, and it will be turned into defeat." Such, in short, was the inside history of two and a half years of Liberal disasters and the condition with which Degollado had contended in vain.

"We are ruining the richest elements, the best personnel, and the justification and idea of our cause by disorder, indiscipline, pillage, and the lack of order and centralization in our operations," the report continued. "I do not believe that an honorable general, who tries to serve the government conscientiously and to do his duty, can miss being killed in the first or second show of arms. I myself should have been killed at Lomas Alta, and I announced my fate to my friends for the second action." Short of a radical change in the constitution, structure, and personnel of the army, he saw no hope of breaking the deadlock. On that condition, however, the elusive chimera of victory and defeat could be tamed, the equation split, and "the campaign will be over, despite all our difficulties. Otherwise, the total destruction of the country is certain, and though the Liberal party will not perish, it will never triumph." That Degollado was able to take the field under such conditions was a remarkable proof of his mettle and the loyalty of his men; but it was no longer enough. He had given them everything of which he was capable: organization and discipline, which had melted away; resources, which had been consumed to no purpose; inspiration, which had drugged and deluded them. The one thing that he could not provide was success, and a tremendous premium had been placed on success by the pressure for foreign intervention in the summer of 1860.

A great reward awaited the man who could break the stalemate. Many had tried and failed, and the season for approximation and experiment had passed; and when a promising figure appeared in the person of Gonzalez Ortega, who won two victories in succession, the first on the field of Penuelas in June and the second at Silao in August—the latter against Miramon himself—it was generally believed that the coming man of the Liberal cause had been discovered at last. A wave of fresh unwonted hope ran through the weary ranks; it seemed as if the balance had been finally tipped; but it had dipped so often that foreign observers discounted these tentative triumphs. The decisive blow had yet to be struck by a co-ordinated campaign and a crushing conclusion. The prospects, however, were favorable; the territory controlled by the enemy had shrunk to three great strongholds—Puebla, Mexico City, and Guadalajara, and Guadalajara was chosen by Degollado as the next point of attack, and Gonzalez Ortega as the man to master it. Trusting to the talent and fortune of his lieutenant, he mustered all his remaining strength to support him; and the strain produced one of the great personal tragedies of the war.

At the outset the campaign was paralyzed by the perennial want of money to move and maintain the troops, and the shortage was so critical in September that Degollado consulted Ortega on a question of conscience. "Our terrible want of money and absolute lack of resources," he wrote, "make me think that, in order to save the country, it is legitimate to appropriate 200,000 pesos from one of the *conductas* of Zacatecas or Aguascalientes that are leaving for Tampico. Give me your opinion by return courier and with due secrecy." The risks were self-evident. The *conductas,* or mule-trains, that carried silver from the mines to the sea, were entrusted with property for the most part of British ownership, and it was no time to embarrass the civil government with foreign complications. Marquez had resorted to such methods, and his example was enough to condemn them, for he had been court-martialed by his government, and though he had since been restored to service, the money had been returned and his conduct disowned. Nevertheless, necessity was inexorable and the risks had been carefully weighed by Degollado before he consulted a confessor.

Two weeks later he was relieved of his dilemma, but not by Ortega. Doblado confiscated a *conducta* on his own responsibility, and without consulting anyone. "I realize," he reported to Degollado, "all the disadvantages and all the consequences of so grave a decision, but I am also intimately convinced that if we do not resort to such expedients the revolution will be indefinitely prolonged and the whole country will sink into poverty and anarchy, losing at last its very nationality. In the situation of the Liberal party today, we must choose between two extremes of this terrible dilemma: either to waste three years of bloody sacrifices, and this when we are approaching the end of them, or to seize such resources as we can find, whatever their origin. The alternative is hard but unavoidable: either we authorize the disbanding of the numerous troops that are now at our command, or we supply them with the means of subsistence, which, by preserving morality and discipline, will place them in a position to conclude the operations of the war. In the whole extent of the Republic only three cities are still held by the Reaction. One month of campaign and they are ours. Are we to lose a situation won by dint of blood by refusing to appropriate funds, the return of which to their owners is a matter of a few days? If it were possible to calculate arithmetically what the country will lose by the continuation of the war, it would be easy to prove that what we take today is a trifling sum compared to what the people will have to pay if a war that destroys and annihilates everything were to last unfortunately one month longer."

The trifling sum was something over a million pesos. But an even more compelling argument was added by Doblado: he offered to revoke his act and to stand trial for it if it were disapproved. That inducement was irresistible; he addressed himself to the right quarter, and by exactly the right method, to secure absolution. It was no longer a temptation with which Degollado was faced, but a challenge, a challenge to equal and surpass a subordinate, a challenge to his most susceptible instincts—chivalry, courage, self-immolation—and he rose to it recklessly. The decision of Doblado altered the whole problem, and Degollado accepted the accomplished fact and assumed full re-

sponsibility for it—but with a significant difference. The tentative
approach to a temptation, which had dismayed and fascinated him two
weeks before, was transformed by the cool resolution and robust conscience of Doblado into something which the prompter could not
divine and to which the principal was peculiarly liable—the temptation to accept the fact as a personal fatality and the tragic consummation of his unfortunate destiny. The difference was tremendous; and
the decision, which had been deliberate and unsentimental with Doblado, cost his superior a moral conflict that had incalculable consequences in his subsequent conduct.

Writing to his government, Degollado repeated the argument of
Doblado and added to it an accent all his own. "I have taken on
myself the complete responsibility, and I am at the disposal of the
government, so that with my head, if need be, it may avoid any international conflict." He would have served his country better, perhaps, had he kept his head, but Doblado had turned it, and beyond the
government he appealed to the nation in a manifesto that revealed his
state of mind even more clearly. The dedicated spirit spoke the tongue
of the doomed. "From the height of that moral scaffold which opinion
erects to immolate a man implacably, when he looks back and sees an
obscure but stainless life and his consecration to a sacred cause, regardless of his family, or his rest, or his fortune, or his self-esteem, or
any of the things that men most cherish, and in a moment, by a fatal
vicissitude, faces the loss of everything and finds himself ranked among
malefactors, that torment is greater than martyrdom, for in martyrdom the generous hand of glory gives some relief. With my eyes on
my cause, with my heart upheld by hope and faith, after every defeat
I have risen like a promise of triumph and my cry has been a call to
battle and a summons to patriotism. . . . I had given everything to
my country; I had preserved, with miserly severity for me and mine,
a pure name to leave to my children, some of whom I have left without
education and deprived others of my presence in their last moments;
yet necessity came knocking at my door and demanding, in the name
of my cause, my reputation to deliver over to malediction and contempt, and after a horrible agony I slew my name and closed my
future, and plead guilty. In the profound conflict that tortured me in
the solitude of my soul, I asked myself: And what of the national
name and honor? Cold reason replied then, and repeats now, that the
national name suffers far more from the prolongation of the struggle,
and that with the loss of independence all will be lost. I conjured up
also, as a painful contrast, the conduct of Miramon with Marquez;
and it told me that those wrongdoers have made of the wealth which
they call God's their treasury, and of His conniving clergy a powerful
banker, and that we have no resource but to open the veins of the
people and to ask them for their blood. . . . And for this reason I have

offered my name and assumed the responsibility that I might have evaded by the generous determination of Señor Doblado to bear it. I have not sought to vindicate myself or to elude my destiny by subterfuges of any kind, or even to win the sympathy of those who are fighting the battle. I am accustomed to having my own devotion to the cause described as a fatal obstinacy and my misfortune as a crime, to the point of not being allowed to die for my cause on the battlefield."

Seldom has a public document been put to such intimate uses. The whole man was exposed, not only exposed but exhibited, his moral anatomy revealed and his motives laid bare: his genius for self-mortification, his infinite capacity for sacrifice, his unflinching courage and disinterestedness—and together with these qualities, his acute appreciation of them. Self-consciousness did not detract from his sincerity— pain is self-conscious and suffering is sincere—but it was the inevitable defect of his qualities, and neither the compensation of self-pity nor the vaunt of self-abnegation lessened the power of his apology. With the complete candor of despair, he appealed to the world without reserve or relief, out of that solitude of spirit in which he was aware of himself alone, because he felt himself severed from the world and morally isolated in it. Henceforth he was a man set apart by his own choice for a foreordained destiny—misfortune, misunderstanding, disgrace, defeat, death—and transfiguration. For every calamity has its compensations. The manifesto was a shroud in which he wrapped himself for a living death and through which shone the transparent stigmata of a spiritual triumph. No soldier could have signed it; it was the effusion of a saint, and the danger of waging war with a saint for a soldier was revealed in the rapture of a man who had found his true vocation at last and who discovered himself to the world exactly as he was, destined for martyrdom and resigned to receive it in its most ignominious form.

How far Degollado was isolated by a fever of soul that magnified himself and his offense in his own eyes he was the first to realize as soon as the inflammation subsided. Writing to Juarez a few days later, and enclosing a copy of the manifesto, he added: "In deference to the truth, and to my great surprise, I must tell you that neither the foreign consuls nor the interested parties have made me any reproach, and that they have spoken to me with the utmost consideration. By what I see and hear, I am led to believe that the necessity of this measure was in the public mind, and all the natives and foreigners who have spoken to me have said that they would consider themselves compensated if the Liberal party triumphs." Emerging from his nightmare into the broad light of day, he was dazed to discover that, instead of a pariah, he was a practical man; but the relief was brief. As his brain cleared, he was appalled by the hazards he had incurred and took steps to check their damage. He restored 400,000 pesos to the British in the belief, he explained, that the next packet would bring British recognition for his government and in the fear that, if he did not, the Gulf ports would be closed by the British fleet. In his haste to protect Juarez, he came to his senses with fresh compunction; his misdeed might be a mere peccadillo in the eyes of the world, but the moral damage to himself could not be undone, and the only effect of his belated caution was to weaken his self-confidence yet further. Of the remaining funds he set aside 600,000 pesos to buy the garrisons of Guadalajara and Mexico City, "and some further pecuniary sacrifices," he added, "may spare us the shedding of blood, put us in possession of munitions, armaments, and supplies of far greater value, and place us in a state of complete peace." Peace! Peace at any price! An intense craving for the end of a struggle to which he had immolated the best of himself, a weariness unreasoning and irresistible, beset him; he was exhausted.

And now came another collapse. The responsibility of success, after the robbery of the *conducta,* was too crushing for a man hounded by misfortune and dogged by defeat, and at the very moment when he had won the means of concluding the war at so cruel a cost to himself, his faith failed him. The moral sacrifice he had made for it was more than a man so constituted could bear; and with the loss of self-respect went the loss of self-confidence. The perversion of heroism violated something too vital to be abused with impunity, and nature—*his* nature—avenged itself for the excessive demand he exacted of it by an inevitable reaction. The urge of self-sacrifice which sustained him was suddenly transformed into the urge of self-destruction; from the dizzy height that he reached in his effort to surpass himself, he slipped downward in a desperate confusion of the suicidal impulse that possessed him; and the first forfeit was followed by a second and far more serious one.

Less than a week after reporting the robbery of the *conducta* Degollado wrote to Juarez, enclosing a copy of a letter he had written to Mathew, the acting head of the British Legation, on his own responsibility, inviting mediation and submitting peace terms, which he proposed at the same time to his own government. To Mathew he advanced them, subject to the approval of the President, but to Juarez he recommended them with finality. "If you approve them," he wrote, "I believe the triumph of the Liberal cause to be infallible; but if you disagree, I hope that you will be good enough to accept the resignation which I presented when I was in Veracruz and which remained pending, inasmuch as this is a pledge of honor that I have contracted. Señor Gonzalez Ortega agrees with the bases I have indicated, and Señor Doblado will do whatever the government decides." The bases indicated by Degollado were to be laid down by the diplomatic corps, together with two representatives of the contending parties, and included religious liberty, supremacy of the civil power, nationalization of Church property, the principles embodied in the Reform Laws, national representation in a freely elected Congress, and the appointment of a provisional President, chosen by the diplomatic corps to serve until Congress assembled and decreed a new Constitution. "The war that I have maintained for these three years has convinced me," he explained, "that pacification cannot be attained by force of arms alone, and I am prepared to sacrifice the form of persons, provided the principles sustained by the Liberal party are preserved and perfectly secured." If both sides rejected his terms, he was resolved to "retire completely from the political scene of my country," but if the enemy alone declined them, he was determined to prosecute the war to the end—a provision that saved his loyalty at the cost of his consistency and raised the question of why the proposal was made at all. The confusion of the scheme was equaled only by its futility. The terms were substantially the same as those that Mathew had repeatedly presented, and that had invariably been rejected by both sides, and the purpose of renewing them at that moment was inexplicable on purely logical grounds.

Upon learning of the robbery of the *conducta,* Juarez had immediately given orders for the return of the money and the trial of the officer responsible for it. He refused to believe that Degollado had countenanced it until the evidence confounded him; and before he had decided how to handle the scandal, he was confronted with a second misstep, which completely nullified the necessity of the first and which created a far more delicate problem. What had induced a man who had just committed a crime for his cause to commit another against it? For such was the verdict at Veracruz: Degollado had deserted. The connection was close, though obscure; but it was not with the psychological problem that the government was concerned. The erratic conduct of Degollado was a political aberration, which could be explained only on the assumption that he was not his own master. The logical deduction was that the return of British funds had appeased Mathew only partially and that to buy him off completely Degollado had consented to promote his peace plan at a highly embarrassing moment for the Liberal government, and some color was lent to this assumption by the admission of Degollado that he was committed to the proposal by a pledge of honor. A pledge of honor, supported by the approval of Ortega and the acquiescence of Doblado, to force the President to accept foreign mediation—this at least was a reasonable explanation of the ransom of a saint by a sensible man who knew exactly what his soul was worth. The result of the robbery was, apparently, a piece of diplomatic blackmail. In any case, the connection between Degollado and Mathew was clear; and so, within a few days, was the real purpose of the plan.

Mathew himself presented the same terms and urged Juarez, if he felt it his duty to reject them again, to retire in order to avoid the dangers that threatened him. The mysterious warning, the liberal conditions, the entire notion of a negotiated peace—Juarez dismissed them all in a reply that accepted nothing but the recognition of his constancy and his consistency. A week later he received another letter from Degollado urging him to resign, and the eloquence of the appeal showed how shrewdly Mathew had chosen his medium. "By sacrificing yourself and saving the country, you will become greater and greater in the eyes of the world," wrote Degollado in words that might have applied equally well to himself. "With your hand on your breast," he adjured Juarez, "place yourself before God, the whole world, and the Mexican nation which is watching you, and let your conscience decide in this difficult matter." Degollado was no longer the accused but the plaintiff, and he appealed to his judge on terms of equality. The mania of sacrifice was upon him; he expected as much of others as he exacted of himself, and in the intoxication and solitude of his own abnegation he felt entitled to dictate. To prove his disinterestedness, he added an article to his peace terms, stipulating that neither he nor Miramon should be eligible for the provisional Presidency, and he challenged Juarez to emulate his generosity and placed him in a position in which it was painful to decline competition. But what he found in Juarez was something more important than generosity: justice. Placed in a position as false as it was embarrassing, the President was forced to emerge from his customary self-effacement and to state the case in its true light; and he did so with an absence of heroics and a cool dignity that reminded Degollado no less solemnly that the issue was not and could never be a personal question.

"I am informed that you felt it necessary to address this letter to Señor Mathew," Juarez wrote after an impressive delay, "because your duty to your country so dictated, and because of circumstances, which you do not describe but which, you tell me, I shall learn later. As your proposal is so firm and decided that you have authorized Señor Mathew to publish it; as you tell me nothing, except that you reserve the powerful motives that have obliged you to adopt a resolution as unexpected as it is perilous to the cause of freedom, the dignity of the nation, and the future of the country; and as until now it is not public opinion, but your own and Señor Mathew's that indicates that I should abandon the Constitutional banner, leaving the settlement of the public administration not to the judgment of the Mexican people, who have shed their blood for almost three years to defend their fundamental law, nor even to the reactionaries who are, after all, Mexicans, but to a foreign body, which, because it helped the rebels of Tacubaya ever since the fatal betrayal of Don Ignacio Comonfort, has been interested in seeing the revolution end by a compromise by which the existing Constitution should be sacrificed"—for all these reasons he repeated what he had already said to Mathew.

To Mathew he had explained, with patience due to a diplomat, the self-evident and elementary reasons that governed his conduct. "If the war had a personal object, that is, if the question were whether I were to remain in power or not," he pointed out, "the decent and dignified course would be for me to retire from the post I occupy; but it is not so. . . . If I were to abandon my post, destroying the legality sustained not only by the city of Veracruz but by the majority of the Republic, I would descend voluntarily to the level of the rebels, deliver my country to the most appalling anarchy, and be as criminal as Don Miguel Miramon, and that at a time when the Constitutional party is fortified by its recent victories and is about to crown its efforts and sacrifices by a definitive triumph that will establish peace. It is not mean personal interests, therefore, that retain me in a power that has no attractions. . . . I remain at my post as a matter of duty and with the noble object of co-operating in the conquest of peace for my country. And I hold the profound conviction that peace will be stable and lasting when the general will, expressed through law, reforms the Constitution and appoints and removes rulers, and not an audacious minority such as that which revolted at Tacubaya in 1857."

To Degollado he repeated himself with equal patience, but in a tone of stern temperance, and concluded: "Since these reasons still exist and circumstances have not changed save in a manner favorable to the Constitutional cause . . . I believe it superfluous to seek to dissuade you from the decision you have taken, and I shall confine myself to replying that I in nowise approve your plan of pacification, and that, on the contrary, in fulfillment of my duty, I shall employ every legal means in my power to oppose it. . . . I trust that you are in good health and repeat that I am your friend."

Forbearance could go no further. In that reply Juarez wrote himself as broad and plain on a sheet of paper as Degollado had done in his manifesto; and he could copy himself indefinitely without weakening his reserve power, for the supply and the demand were unlimited. What Degollado had forgotten, among so many other lapses of judgment, was that the President was the incarnation of a cause; and what the President impressed on him, with such memorable common sense, was that his conduct could not be dictated by motives as irresponsible, as insignificant, and as histrionic as personal heroics. There, for his own part, he let the matter rest, and there it would have ended, had it been a private issue. But Degollado had authorized a public test of his proposals, and forbearance was impossible because of the effect which his defection produced on his fellow troopers.

To a man, the government rallied about Juarez. Within the official family the desertion of Degollado was greeted with consternation, indignation, and dismay. Old friendships were strained or broken, and the moderation of the President was in striking contrast to the bitterness with which Degollado was rebuked by his bosom friends. Ocampo, who idolized him, found not a word to say in his defense, and Prieto, who adored him, found too many to scourge him. "I do not know how to begin," he wrote, "so stunned am I by your decisions both as to the end of the war and the money restored to the British subjects. The former might have ruined us, and it has done you more damage—I say it, baring my soul—than you can imagine. The idea of intervention by the most ignominious of all means, the anomalous representation of foreign ministers to perform acts depriving us of national sovereignty, the evidence that after this infamous request on our part foreign arms will come to realize it, and all this from you, the democratic type *par excellence,* are things that leave me confounded; for I believed that a suicide like that of Comonfort would be unique in our history. On the eve of success to set aside the banner that has led us to it; to repudiate its power when we owe to it the triumph of the idea; and this during a siege, in the midst of enthusiastic leaders; to agree with the enemy to abjure the Constitution on the field of its evolution; to make of the barracks deliberating bodies; to depose Juarez, the benefactor, the friend, the comrade—I cannot explain this, and I am overwhelmed because you have disinherited us of our glory with the atheism of a believer, with the despair of a man of constancy, well nigh with the apostasy of the living incarnation of political society. I cannot, I will not, believe it; I want a denial to dispel this nightmare of shame that makes me weep blood. I told Doblado frankly that I did not understand what had happened, but today I learned it fully; the board met and held the trial and reached the verdict to which you resigned yourself in advance. It is clear that you must withdraw from the scene. I who believed that our greatest misfortune, our most irreparable defeat, would be your absence from the command; I who joined your circle because I felt myself more honored there than anywhere else; I say that you must leave the command; and God grant that you do not leave us weakness, anarchy, and the horrible prolongation of the civil war! As for the money, in refusing to return a single penny, there was a breadth of view; to restore it is to flatter the mighty and to become the hangman of your unhappy countrymen, whose advocate and conscience you were. . . . This substraction by fear, this course which makes the whole crime mean—I do not know what has happened or what I am saying. I offer sympathy to my country for the emasculation of one of its most eminent men and to myself for the death of my purest illusions. Your brother and grateful friend hugs you to his heart and begs you to command him as you will, as always. Your brother, G." The poet, so sensitive to the spiritual secrets of his friends, was completely blind to those of Degollado in his downfall because he was then serving as a liaison agent between the government and the camp, and the factor that made forbearance impossible was the reaction in the army.

The generals assembled for the siege of Guadalajara met and decided unanimously to condemn the proposal of the Commander-in-Chief. Though Degollado had resigned himself in advance to the verdict, coming from that quarter, he regarded it as a betrayal. With complete candor he wrote to Juarez: "I am sorry to tell you that Señores Doblado and Ortega assured me in Guanajuato of their absolute approval of the idea which I disclosed to them then and which they have now opposed with as much heat as little good faith. This merely proves that I am an impediment to the interested aims of the men who figure in our political scene." In the conduct of the generals there were secrets as well, and not spiritual ones—secrets lying so close to the surface that they were visible to the naked eye, and Degollado was not so nearsighted as to overlook them. Discontent with his leadership, long brewing in the camp, had been repressed in the interest of union, but his authority was respected by his subordinates only in form and ignored in fact, and the demand for his removal persisted in insubordination and intrigue. The power of suggestion was an insidious influence during the period preceding his fall. Only a few weeks before there had arisen a serious crisis between him and Doblado, smothered by the exertions of peacemakers and settled by the promise that Doblado should be appointed second in command. The opportunity to oust the impediment by the capture of the *conducta* and encouragement of the peace proposals was obvious—so obvious that one observer imputed the inspiration of both those missteps to Doblado. Degollado did not go so far, but he intimated that he was the victim of trusted advisers. Whether the offer of Doblado to bear the responsibility of the robbery was made in good faith or as a shrewd appeal to his chivalry, Degollado had no doubt that he had been misled both by Doblado and Ortega into believing that they sincerely supported his peace proposals. Disowned by them both, he discovered that he had walked unaware into a trap, and he found himself tripped and floored by the very men from whom he had borrowed confidence to transgress. For him this was but one more drop of gall; but for the government it cast an ugly and dangerous light on the whole situation. The admission of Degollado that he had concerted his backsliding with his subordinates, and that he had conceived it before the robbery of the *conducta* brought on the brain storm which was his best excuse, made it necessary not only to censure but to punish him.

Therefore the justice of Juarez went further. Degollado was ordered to Veracruz to stand trial. His friends were later to complain of the severity of this step. His resignation was indispensable, and he had offered it; was it necessary also to pillory him? And on what charge? Treason? The construction depended on the intention and the effect. Technically he was guilty of indiscipline in initiating a political proposal without previously consulting his government, but the degree of the offense could be determinted fairly only by the purpose and interpretation of the plan. On the face of it the plan was impractical and could have only one result—the prosecution of the war; and such was the defense, in fact, that Degollado put forward as soon as he came under attack. "My idea, supposing it to be bad, was imposed on no one by force. Its action would have gone no further than a confidential discussion. Approved, it would have been a powerful weapon for the quicker and more complete triumph of our cause. Rejected, it would have been nullified in its effect, to my regret, but it would never have served to favor speculations detrimental to the national cause." The resignation of Juarez was contingent on "the remote event of our enemies admitting" mediation. "What I expect, naturally, is that the Clerical party will stubbornly refuse, but in that case we shall be able to defend the Constitution of 1857 and your government," he assured Juarez, "with full vigor and with the support that the whole diplomatic corps, minus Pacheco, will lend us, and our triumph will be infallible." Consequently, the plea concluded, "we shall continue fighting with better right, since we shall have exhausted the proofs of abnegation of the Constitutional government."

The resignation of Juarez, in other words, was to be a mere gesture, and the purpose of the plan a spectacular play to the gallery; one of his friends, in fact, borrowed a word from the bull ring to describe it— "a new and prodigious *faena* for the Liberal cause within and without the country." But this version of the plan merely reduced it to the puerile level of a flourish and added frivolity to its futility and mock heroics to its manifest folly. A better defense was put forward by the same friend when he explained that it was dictated by fear of forcible foreign intervention at no distant date. "Will it be time then and will it be possible to set conditions? The mediation that may be friendly today, will it not be an armed and violent intervention then?" This was a motive to which the government might be expected to be sympathetic, since it was the same one that governed the conclusion of the McLane treaty, of which the misconduct of Degollado was the final result and the obscure retribution. A standing reproach to the government was involved in all Degollado's apologies. "By reason of that infallible law of compensation, each advance and every crime of our enemies has produced its inevitable reaction," he had declared in his manifesto; "the idea of a treasonable protectorate, that of a continental policy, reprehensible also under the form of protection; the connection of rapacious speculation with a prostituted clergy has begotten the hatred of those powers; the gold of the faith, employed as a blood value, has justified crimes against property. . . ." The failure of the government to provide funds had forced him to rob the *conducta;* and its efforts to do so by "a continental policy reprehensible under the form of protection" had bred intervention and his peace plan; and after being neutralized by contending impotences, he was crushed by them. But the best defense of his plan was not rational; it was the internal evidence that it bore of fatigue and confusion and cross-purposes that made the whole idea self-defeating, the feeble and pathological production of a mind profoundly unsettled and divided. The long strain of the war and the stress of a moral crisis had clearly unbalanced the judgment of its author, and because of his previous record it could be claimed that he was entitled to be treated as a sick man and spared the stigma of public disgrace and indictment. Revolutions, however, are lost that way.

For there was much more at stake than the fate of Degollado himself. Rational explanations might minimize, psychological excuses might extenuate, his offense, but both accepted the incontestable fact of a surrender of national sovereignty to foreign arbitration, and it was on that count that he was brought to book. In that state of mind in which he was obviously not his own master, he had become the mouthpiece or the dupe of another. The master mind was Mathew's, about whose aims there hung no shadow of doubt; and behind Mathew there was Comonfort. The civil war was to end in the return of the renegade, who was to reap the fruits of his betrayal in the waste of three years of fratricidal strife and the reward of the prodigal. Nor was this prospect a hypothetical peril, for Comonfort, after wandering abroad like a lost soul, had settled on the border and was conspiring with his friends in the interior to cross it. One of his agents had felt out Doblado and had pushed audacity so far as to approach Gutierrez Zamora, the Governor of Veracruz. Incorrigible blindness? By no means. Comonfort, his agent said, had reformed; he was no longer the irresolute man of other times; his travels and sufferings had convinced him of the necessity of "embracing a system with all its consequences"; he had no intention of increasing the conflicts in his country and would return only if he could bring peace. The best guarantee of a Liberal triumph was Veracruz; if he could count on Gutierrez Zamora, he would embark immediately; the support of the diplomatic corps, who would never recognize Juarez, was assured, and intervention was imminent.

To all these arguments Zamora replied with quiet contempt. After some reflections on the nature of turncoats, whose ideas were as flexible as their characters, he remarked that "we know what peace Señor Comonfort would make and we prefer war," and he improved the occasion to explode the great argument that authorized every betrayal. "The diplomatic corps will submit to the decision of the country, whether they like it or not," he added. "Neither do I agree that you can be certain that the United States mean to take possession of our territory. . . . As I do your ability and education the justice they deserve, I cannot but believe that the use you make of these vulgarities is the result of the necessity of finding arguments to vindicate your bold undertaking. In the present condition of our country, nothing would be easier for the United States than the conquest you suggest. They will not attempt it," he concluded, "because it is not to their advantage, because it would prejudice the balance of their interests, because it would introduce further complications in the racial question, dangerous enough as it is in the neighboring Republic, and for many other reasons that you know very well."

Comonfort had been judged once and for all in Mexico; the just are judged only once in this world; and justice was done to Juarez at the same time by his guardian angels. But the coincidence of these intrigues with the blunder of Degollado, though both remained abortive, placed Degollado's conduct in too dangerous a context to indulge any tenderness toward his trespass.

Indiscipline, indiscretion, imprudence—however his conduct might be qualified, it could not escape public correction. In lending himself to a maneuver that, whether it failed or succeeded, could breed only disintegration and defeat, he was guilty of demoralizing the movement he had inspired. The focus of infection had to be cut from the living tissue it contaminated; and the penalty was as exemplary as his previous record had been. So long as he had faith and hope, all his failures had been forgiven; when he lost his evangelical virtues, he forfeited the right to charity as well. This was revolutionary justice, and Juarez satisfied even the radicals who belittled his leadership by steering the movement through a treacherous crisis with the unbending will, the basic insight, and the drastic severity of the genuine revolutionary.

But revolutionary justice is rough justice. In strict equity Gonzalez Ortega was equally guilty of debauching the movement, not only because he was privy to the intent, but because he had intended a similar transaction on his own account. Before beginning the siege of Guadalajara he negotiated with the commander of the town for its surrender and proposed a peaceful settlement of the war, without consulting either Juarez or Degollado, on terms which included the resignation of Juarez and the sacrifice of the Constitution, without saving reservations of any kind. The negotiations came to nothing, and the only censure he received came from Degollado, who reprimanded him with an inconsistency which had become inveterate and reminded him that "neither you nor I can depart from our legal faculties, which are the maintenance of the Constitution and the legal government, without appearing to be traitors and disloyal to those from whom we derive our mission."

Copies of the correspondence exchanged in this negotiation were sent to Juarez by Degollado himself, oblivious or indifferent to the light which it cast on his own responsibility. Juarez filed them with the reference, "Degollado and Ortega exhort the President to forsake his post," as further evidence of the contagion undermining the camp. The duplication of disaffection was merely a detail in the dreary routine of recording its spread. The independence of the military power was a danger which had been exorcised for three years by the moral influence of Degollado, and with his collapse the check disappeared. Yet the fault for which he was disgraced was condoned in Ortega. The difference, however, was obvious: Ortega was a success; and, to make the moral more glaring, he succeeded Degollado as Commander-in-Chief. The justice of Juarez was tempered by a sense of expediency no less essential to the triumph of the movement, and the promotion of Ortega was vindicated by victory; Guadalajara was captured within a month, and a swift and unbroken succession of triumphs followed. But the discretion of the President gave his detractors an opportunity, which they did not neglect, to accuse him of catering to the strong and scourging the weak.

Juarez was not insensible to the inconsistency, and though his attitude toward Degollado remained unchanged, it underwent certain subliminal but perceptible modifications with the passage of time. In the heat of the crisis he remained cool. "A government whose duty it is to set the most complete example of morality, and which must in any case obey the laws and enforce them, has merely to judge by those laws any and every delinquent, whoever he may be," he wrote to a friend in defense of his justice. "Hence it is that, in spite of the services lent by Señor Degollado, and although he was one of the persons whom the central government trusted and on whom it conferred a large part of its ample powers, now that that person has departed from the path traced by the spirit of the present revolution and has sought to nullify a law, he has been called to trial as he deserves." The action of justice was automatic, impersonal, and impartial, and the sympathy of Solon perfunctory. A month later, however, reverting to the subject when the crisis had subsided, he wrote: "Like you, I regretted the false step of Señor Degollado, for I shall never be able to forget his previous good services, but he has wronged himself by repudiating a revolution such as Mexico is pursuing and was completely disabused when he discovered that not a single commander seconded his ill-conceived plan. That is why the event has produced no unpleasant consequences, and why our leaders today, stronger and more united than ever, are bearing down on the capital of the Republic with a terrible prospect for the Reaction." And that was why, the danger having passed, it was possible to temper justice not only with discretion, but with mercy. The trial of Degollado was suspended and the case quietly dropped. But though the President contemplated his justice and weighed his triumph without sentimental qualms, the mercy meted out to Degollado was a compromise that satisfied neither the coroner nor the casualty. Degollado suffered from it acutely: suspended sentence condemned him to a living death and embalmed him in the hardening fluid of a clouded reputation without the possibility of clearing it in court; and since some compensation was due him for the indulgence shown to Ortega, the government relented again, permitting him to return to active service on the staff of a subaltern and to redeem his name in the closing weeks of the war.

7

THE Degollado affair was the turning point of the war. The steadying hand of the President during the crisis was heaped with a great reward after it. The removal of the loose gut, the rise of a successful commander, the fall of Guadalajara, restored the flagging morale of the army like the lifting of a curse; and as Ortega bore down on the capital and the Liberal flag surged forward for the final thrust, the pressure for foreign intervention relaxed.

Two weeks after the fall of Guadalajara, Miramon declared a state of siege in the capital and rallied his followers in a manifesto that proclaimed to the most fugitive reader that his days were numbered. But a more patent admission of his desperate straits preceded the manifesto. On the previous night Marquez raided the British Legation, broke the seals of the Convention bonds deposited there, and extracted 660,000 Mexican dollars. The choice of Marquez for this chore was the only feature of the affair that suggested any political sagacity; for while the Constitutional government, rocked by the Degollado scandal, was righted only by the strong hand of Juarez, nothing but the strong arm of Miramon sustained the waning credit of his party, and he forfeited it completely when he counted his days in British bonds. The diplomatic corps protested as a body, led by Señor Pacheco himself; and so glaring an avowal of the extremities to which he was driven dealt the final blow to the confidence of his party, already war-weary and ready to capitulate. By a reckless use of muscle, and for the sake of six hundred and sixty thousand pesos, he sacrificed the initial advantage with which his faction began the war and converted the solid diplomatic support, which had buttressed it for over two years, into complete isolation at the very moment when the last hope of his cause lay in foreign intervention.

By that act Mathew was driven into the Liberal camp. He had long been moving toward it, and the nature of his peace terms made his destination inevitable, but he approached it reluctantly, searching step by step for a formula of mediation that was not to be found. The plunder of the British Legation ended his quest. He suspended relations with the Miramon regime. As he was not authorized to go further, however, he took up his station at Jalapa, halfway between Mexico and Veracruz, to await the end of the war and the decision of his government to recognize the victor. This was a purely formal compromise. Actually he had already gone the whole way and favored the winner by forbearing to press the claims created by the robbery of the *conducta* and granting a request of the Veracruz government to use the installment then due on the British Convention bonds for the termination of the war.

The capitulation of Mathew marked the triumph of McLane, whose unswerving refusal to countenance mediation or compromise had acted like a magnet on the shifting field of foreign intervention and closed the forbidden ground to trespassers. The steady support and legitimate protection which the American Minister lent the Liberal government during the long diplomatic siege to which it was subjected constituted the real benefit of his treaty; the treaty, in fact, was the loadstone that had drawn Mathew into the fold and defeated him, and in the hands of McLane it had revealed the virtue of the philosopher's stone. Nevertheless, at the very moment when Mathew swung around to the Veracruz government, McLane began to veer away from it. For him the philosopher's stone had lost all its value. The service which he had rendered his partner was contingent on the validity of the treaty, and though he had not abandoned hope of its passage in Washington, the opposition it encountered in Veracruz was insurmountable—and it was the opposition of one man. The entire cabinet, with a single exception, was in favor of extending the time for ratification; but the dissenting member was sustained by the President. The force that had constantly frustrated the American Minister and that he had refused to recognize was now admitted to be none other than Juarez himself. "He will adhere to this disposition to avail himself of the failure of the Senate to ratify the engagements within the time agreed upon, unless some extraordinary pressure is brought to bear upon him," McLane notified Washington, "precisely as he resisted originally the actual conclusion of the same."

Precisely. For two long and lean years McLane had worked on the assumption he inherited from Churchwell and adopted himself, that the President was a timid and mistrustful politician wholly under the influence of his ministers; for four and twenty fruitless months he had attributed the difficulties he encountered to every reason but the real one, to sundry ministers changing places but not policies, to the interference of the frontier states affected by the treaty, to the friends of Comonfort, to systematic opposition within the party, only to realize at last that the one factor with which he had failed to reckon was the responsible statesman who had borrowed proxies and pretexts to prolong and control the negotiation until it had served his purpose, and whose powers of resistance he had seriously underestimated. The President, who had always eluded him, now escaped him completely; and McLane was nettled to discover, and mortified to admit, that the only result of his mission was that he had placed himself and his government in the awkward position of having granted recognition on a memorandum and sustained it for two years on a promissory note, while Juarez quietly eased himself out of his engagements without a claim to hold him, and with incontestable legitimacy. They were both honorable men; but one of them felt abused.

"The final determination of President Juarez will be much influenced by the degree of pressure," he repeated, "that may be brought to bear on him and the actual prospect of his party in the pending civil war"— but what kind of pressure could be applied with the end of the war approaching and the weight of foreign intervention weakening? After standing by the weaker party through a period of extreme stress, McLane frankly regretted the support he had extended to it, now that it was the winning party. "Under these circumstances," he warned Washington, "our relations with this country will be as unsatisfactory as they could well be, and instead of finding any fault with European Powers for supporting with armed forces their respective demands for redress, we will only have to reproach ourselves with failing to provide the same means for pursuing a like policy—and that, too, when a treaty has been concluded that enabled us to enforce our intervention with the consent of the recognized government. . . . I trust, therefore, that the President will not modify in any degree the views he communicated in his last annual message—and it is now more necessary than it was at that time that his recommendations be presented in the double aspect of acting with or without the consent of the Constitutional government, for it is impossible to foresee what difficulties will be encountered in securing that consent, in consequence of the failure of the Senate to ratify the treaty concluded in December 1859." In November 1860, however, it was not easy to outwit Juarez. Duped into playing a purely disinterested part and forced by circumstances to pursue a superior policy in Mexico, the Senator from Maryland was surfeited with superiority and galled by the glorious role he had performed there; and he hastened to retrieve himself at the eleventh hour. He had presented his views, he concluded, from the first day that he had recognized the Constitutional government; and he now presented his resignation.

His resignation was accepted, and so was his advice. Buchanan transcribed it in his message of December 1860, deploring the blindness with which Congress had failed to empower him to send a punitive expedition below the border and harping on the dangers, suspended for the moment but still latent, of European intervention there. But it was too late. The message was his valedictory to Mexico and to his own people as well, for the policy which he had preached so persistently was subject to the results of the presidential election that had been held in November. James Buchanan had begotten Abraham Lincoln, and the end of civil war in Mexico coincided with the crack of secession in the United States.

If the best defense of the treaty was its fruits, this was their final measure, and they were gathered in all their abundance by Juarez in December 1860. As the threat of intervention subsided on all sides, the timing of the long-drawn deal, which redeemed its dangers and reaped its rewards, amply vindicated the dilatory tactics with which he had handled it. Never had his political instinct been exercised to greater effect; never had timeserving been employed more successfully. Merely by temporizing, and on the strength of a prospective bargain, he had managed to secure American recognition, and thereby to break the diplomatic blockade, to facilitate the issue of the Reform Code, and to derive every benefit from an ostensible alliance that neutralized foreign intervention until the independent triumph of his party was assured. For a beginner in international diplomacy, who had baffled both Buchanan and Palmerston and broken the grip of the ruling powers within the country, it was not a bad start. Tortuous, his policy was called by his critics, tactless, and contrary to the popular will, but he had pursued it with an unerring sense of direction, making minor concessions to avoid major forfeits, and brought it to a clear and triumphant conclusion. If the result was due to deliberate strategy, it revealed consummate statesmanship; if it was accidental, the result was no less remarkable, for the risks were as high as the rewards, and he narrowly escaped the penalties of foreclosure and failure; and if, as is likely, it was a compound of both, an expedient imposed by necessity and evaded by determination and delay, a shifting equation daily adapted to changing conditions, a devious improvisation directed by flexible chance and immutable aim, the outcome was equally incontestable: by gaining time the timid politician and incorruptible magistrate of

Mexican destiny had won against overwhelming odds. But he cleared the mark none too soon.

Though the political race had been won by the slow, popular recognition and acclaim went to the speed with which the military campaign was wound up by Gonzalez Ortega. After the fall of Guadalajara he advanced with swift strides, and by the first days of December the capital was isolated and its fall so near that the Veracruz cabinet issued a call for Congress to assemble there and published the long-awaited decree of religious liberty that crowned the Reform Laws. The progress of Ortega guaranteed both steps. With the Constitutional armies closing in for the kill, Miramon had barely life enough for one last lunge. Sallying from the city, he surprised an advance detachment of the investing forces at Toluca and returned with two generals among his captives, one of them Degollado; but this was the death rally. Mustering the mere reminiscences of victory and the ragged regiments that recalled it, he issued once more in force and met Ortega at the village of Calpulalpam where, on December 22, he was finally crushed. On Christmas Day the Constitutional armies entered the capital in undisputed triumph. Contrary to the fears which the dying regime had excited as its last line of defense, the occupation of the capital was accomplished without reprisals or disorders; not a cry nor an act of vengeance marred the occasion on either side; the crowning victory was the triumph of moderation and discipline, which transformed the day of reckoning into a day of reconciliation, and the alarmists were routed by the enthusiastic welcome that the army and its commander received from a city that was both conquered and converted. Many were the spectators, waiting for the vandals against whom they had been warned and watching the troops filing by, who were gratefully surprised by their gallant bearing and who realized gradually that it was given to them to witness the triumph of truth in their time and to recognize the progress of law and order with the return of legitimacy. The magnanimity which the Commander-in-Chief displayed toward a vanquished foe was widely acknowledged and extolled; and so was the chivalry which he showed to a fallen friend. Catching sight of Degollado among the bystanders, he halted the parade, called him out and, handing him the flag, embraced and hailed him as the man who had made that day and that gesture possible. The gesture was greeted by a tremendous ovation from the crowd; the hero of defeats, his disgrace forgotten and his services alone remembered, was swept along by his comrades, and revolutionary justice was submerged by a parade of plain, human, popular justice.

Such triumphs occur, as a rule, only once in a lifetime. The capital was so completely converted, however, and its conquest was so popular, that, by general request, the performance was repeated a week later, and with unabated success.

Word of the battle of Calpulalpam was received in Veracruz while the President and his family were attending a gala performance at the theater. The house was full, for the bill was *Les Huguenots,* and the political value of an opera celebrating the religious wars in France in the sixteenth century was a drawing card by which the impresario profited. Just as the tenor and chorus swung into the heaven-storming air which was the cue for an ovation in Veracruz, the drama was transferred to the President's box. A courier stumbled in, and Gonzalez Ortega stole the show. Juarez rose, the orchestra stopped, and amid a breathless hush he read aloud, in a low voice, a bulletin announcing the victory of Ortega and the end of the war. The house rose as one man to the man who had made that message possible, and then and there the world knew him, as well as his wife had known him always, for what he was. Standing there in the penumbra, silent, self-effacing, retiring, and obscure, his sober mien, his somber skin, his dark eyes shrouded in the shadow of his own spirit like transparent reflections of steel, a statue of a man whose reserve suddenly became obtrusive in the glare of public attention, Juarez triumphed in his turn. The singers swung into the "Marseillaise," bedlam broke loose, the performance ended in an uproar for Ortega and the President, and the audience poured out into the streets on a full-flowing tide of sound that surged through the sleeping city, waking the dead.

But that was in Veracruz. A fortnight later the President left for the capital, and his appearance there, after popular acclaim had twice been tapped by Ortega, threatened to be an anticlimax. The capital had still to be conquered by the civil power. The culminating moment had come, in fact, when the co-operation of the military and civil arms, so severely strained by the war, was essential to secure the peace. The triumph of the movement inevitably dramatized its leadership and excited personal comparisons between the soldier and civilian, which were hardly in favor of Juarez, and a test of their relative popularity then and there was a fair measure of the degree to which the war had actually been won. Who really knew who Juarez was? How many recognized the services which he had rendered his country or knew him better by the end than the beginning of the war? Who could say how the man who had chosen to supplant Comonfort and substitute for Hidalgo, Morelos, Mora, and Farias had made good his promise and won the historic salvation of Mexico and himself? He had redeemed the permanent promise of things to come in things undone; he had kept faith with his forerunners and brought about the indivisible reunion of then and now; he had become the man of destiny who consummated the emancipation of his country, and the result spoke for itself. But who could divine the workman in the work? Two versions of his character and conduct were current, one picturing him as the indomitable champion of a lost cause who had rescued it from Comonfort and carried it with unflagging faith and constancy to a successful conclusion, the other as the merely nominal leader of a movement by which he was himself carried to a triumph that would have been won with or without him. The first was drawn in the broad strokes of a poster, the second in the small digs of partisan design, and it had the advantage of wide circulation in political clubs, military circles, and diplomatic propaganda. Ortega, on the other hand, was the operatic figure of the hour, favored by talent and fortune and a late entrance on the scene, and featured by the spectacular triumph which brought the war to a close. The active and passive agents of victory, as they then appeared to the casual observer, were called forth for public recognition in a critical test not only of their personal stature, but of the capacity of the public to judge their respective services, and few could be sure, when the President left for the capital, whether he would not be welcomed there as he had been welcomed in Veracruz in 1858, as an accessory to the struggle and not as the arbiter, in fact, and indispensable guarantee of its triumph.

But the encounter with the capitaline public dispelled any doubts that the war had indeed been won. Gonzalez Ortega met the President on the outskirts of the city and postponed his entrance for twenty-four hours until the final arrangements for his reception had been completed. Then, on January 11, 1861, Juarez drove into the city that had twice celebrated its conquest with a national solemnity unequaled, as the press said, since the proclamation of Independence in 1821, and for over eight hours he was welcomed with an ovation which, as the press also said, "has just been repeated now with the same spontaneity, the same enthusiasm, the same outpouring of hope and joy, on the arrival in the capital of the Constitutional President of the Republic." The last phenomenal triumph had been accomplished; for Gonzalez Ortega himself had guaranteed that the third and final command performance should be no everyday event.

PART THREE

The Year 1861

I

IN THE lives of nations certain years stand out singly more important than entire periods, because they compress and epitomize them. Such were the years 1821, 1847, and 1861 in Mexican annals, and the last was the most momentous of all. Eighteen sixty-one was the year of the comet. Beginning with a triumph that was rightly hailed as the culmination of four decades of struggle to redeem the False Independence of 1821, it ended in a portentous demonstration that the battle was only half won. The triumph was not permanent; it was merely a pause in the march of the Reform movement and the development of the national destiny. The false start had been corrected, the corporate state had been shattered, but the fact that the victory was won in 1861 instead of 1821 was itself a setback, for the conditions were infinitely more adverse, and the delay was reckoned not in calendar, but in social, time. No revolution could be won locally in 1861: independence meant emancipation not merely from the mother country and the social mold of the colony, but from the whole family of nations of which the misbegotten member had become a vital, vulnerable, and invalid part; and at the very moment when it broke the mold in which it was conceived, it became involved in a far more formidable conflict with the civilization to which it aspired and embroiled with the modern world as the penalty both of its past and its progress. By its origin and its growth alike, it was predestined to produce a foreign as well as a domestic contest between the forces working to reclaim it for feudal exploitation on the one hand, and the powers pressing forward to claim it for capitalist culture on the other. What the victory of 1861 won was merely a brief and breathless respite in the same relentless process. The first phase ended and the second began simultaneously; the transition was swift; and within twelve months the nation, exhausted and divided by three years of civil war, was called to defend its independence again against a coalition of forces and under conditions that canceled the reversal of 1821 and recalled the far more pregnant anniversary of 1847. For four decades the throes had repeated the toils under conditions that became ever more complex and portentous, the periodic return of the years of the comet magnified their fatality, and if 1847 was remembered in Mexico as the *annus terribilis* that first brought the country into foreign conflict and to the brink of collapse,

269

1861 eclipsed it. Terror was the keynote of those twelve months; and it was struck from the start.

At nine in the morning of January 11, when Juarez drove into the capital, the final ovations of victory were ringing in his ears; at nine that evening he sat down with the cabinet to its realities. A fortnight before, Gonzalez Ortega had proclaimed in an eloquent manifesto the disavowal of vengeance, proscription, or persecution of the enemy, but the first fine raptures were over: the magnanimity of victory, the easy promise of reconciliation or forbearance, the bounty of triumph, and the discipline of the army by no means corresponded to the sentiments of the rank-and-file of the party. The war was not a bad dream from which they awoke overnight; it was a nightmare knotted in the entrails of the nation, a sick and feverish infection that raised implacable passions and imperishable losses, which cried aloud through the press, the political clubs, and all the organs of public opinion for retribution, for primitive justice, for blood. The day of reckoning had long been foreseen and accepted as a necessary purge of civil war by the Conservatives themselves. Expecting no quarter and giving none, they had painted it in apocalyptic colors to prolong their defense, and the very peacemakers who attempted to avert the catastrophe in time evoked it no less violently than the infallible prescience of the vanquished. Two years before, a priest, pleading with his party to compromise before the passions it had excited became the exclusive right of the Liberals, wrote: "Unbridled as they now are, what prestige will be sufficiently powerful, what power will be able to prevent them from running to excesses that will be greater because more general and deliberate? Will the magic names of Juarez and Ocampo and the Constitution of '57 control them and make them vomit the blood from their mouths and spew the venom from their hearts? Wholesale proscriptions and confiscations will be enacted, and the same bandits who rob and kill today will perforce be the leading authorities in the towns, which will become the scenes of the worst crimes, under the protection of barbarous laws befitting a reign of terror." And he predicted the worst because he allowed for the best. "Supposing that Señor Juarez is President then, on what force will he rely to bring the robbers to heel? What balm will soothe those hearts athirst for vengeance? Will they return to work and morality overnight and obey orders which I wish to believe will be issued in a spirit of moderation and justice? He who attempts to stem such a torrent will be declared a traitor." Precisely. The phantom fears that had nourished the defeated for two years were allayed by the conduct and prestige of Gonzalez Ortega, but only for two weeks; after a fortnight of soft peace the public temper turned, soured by an overindulgence in fine sentiments, and the morrow brought up the vindictive dregs, the hard sediment of civil war. Padre Valdovinos had predicted the truth, and the fictitious truce

was over when Juarez arrived in the capital to face the exactions, together with the ovations, of victory.

Juarez, no less than Padre Valdovinos, was prepared for the truth.
Before leaving Veracruz he had mapped his course with the cabinet
and Ocampo, who joined it for a last exacting duty before retiring to
private life. The pacification of the country required some degree of
appeasement of popular passion; to ignore it was impossible, to cater
to it craven, to trifle with it frivolous and foolhardy; and it was decided
to prosecute the ringleaders of the Reaction, to banish the bishops who
had backed them, to expel their allies in the diplomatic corps, and to
couple these examples with a decree of general amnesty. But these
measures, taken in the spirit of moderation and justice that the Padre
expected of Juarez and Ocampo, were treason to the party in the capital, which had been thwarted for two weeks of the thorough house-
cleaning which it demanded. If Juarez had forgotten the circumstances
under which he fled from the capital exactly three years before, his
party had not, and on the night of his homecoming a test case arose.

The ringleaders of the Reaction had escaped after the battle of Calpulalpam, Marquez and Zuloaga into the interior and Miramon to
Veracruz. There the "Maccabee" found refuge on a French warship,
where he defied pursuit not by his own countrymen alone, but by the
British naval commander, who demanded his surrender to answer
for the plunder of the Legation. From his sanctuary he gave out an
account of his escape, which was published serially in the press of
the capital and which further exasperated popular feeling there. His
brother-in-law and principal minister, Isidoro Diaz, was caught, however, and on him the full fury of baffled justice was bent. Word of his
capture reached the capital as Juarez was holding his first session with
the cabinet, and orders were immediately despatched for his trial under
martial law and summary execution of the sentence; but a few days
later, on the intercession of his family, the President consented to com-
mute the sentence to banishment, and on the following day the storm
broke.

"A grave, an alarming rumor is spreading. If it is true, it will mean
the discredit of the government and the ruin of the country. It is said
that a pardon has been granted to Don Isidoro Diaz, and that an amnesty will be issued in favor of all the reactionaries." The alarm was
raised by the most powerful paper of the party, the *Siglo XIX,* and led
by its most eloquent tribune. Zarco, who had spent the civil war in the
capital, returned to his post at the head of that forensic organ to wield
the scourge with the fury of a baffled civilian. "If this happens, farewell
freedom, farewell justice, farewell all public order! There will be no
end to the series of mutinies and revolts, and the country, desperate
and disappointed, without hope or faith, will recant its exertions, curse
its sacrifices, and lose itself in the convulsions of anarchy," he protested.

"The country will not tolerate the amnesty that is announced because it wants justice, because it craves peace, order, morality, and because it cannot consider as political crimes the perjury and betrayal by the authors of the *coup d'état* or the mutiny of Tacubaya or the whole series of robberies, assaults, snares, sacks, assassinations and conflagrations perpetrated by the Reaction. . . . It is true that justice can be administered with mercy, and that our Constitution gives the Executive the right to pardon; but that pardon must not be a scandal or a crime against society as a whole." The scourge was brandished by a good friend, for when the pen of Zarco gave the cue, there were no lengths to which the hue and cry would not run, and the fate of Diaz and the amnesty, blindly confused, became a test of the strength of the government. The real ruler of Mexico at that moment was neither the civil nor the military power, but the press; and the warning was heeded. The government retreated, canceling the pardon of Diaz and holding him for trial in the civil courts; and no more was heard of the amnesty, though its provisions were quietly observed in fact. The cabinet was also recast to appease public opinion, and the three most popular tribunes of the hour were induced to join it. Zarco succeeded Ocampo as Minister of Foreign Affairs, Ignacio Ramirez took over the Ministry of Justice, and Gonzalez Ortega the portfolio of War.

The tension of public feeling ran so high, however, that every concession made by the President was interpreted as a sign of weakness and an admission, not a correction, of error. The press was a jealous and exacting master, the irritation aroused by the amnesty did not subside when the measure was dropped, and even the decrees that met the crying demand were challenged. The banishment of the bishops was approved with one breath and withered with another, and the President was censured for expelling them by decree and permitting them to pose as victims of political persecution instead of holding them for public trial as rebels under the laws of their country. "The banishment of the bishops, for all its appearance of energy, is nothing but a proof of real weakness and a violation of the Constitution," the *Siglo* declared; for though Zarco had been dislodged from his editorial chair and caged in the cabinet, he had left a whole flock of avenging angels behind him, and a chorus of caviling echoed the complaint. The lesser press pursued it and demanded that justice be wrested from the hands of the Chief Magistrate, who administered it feebly and arbitrarily, and restored to the courts and the nation—to the capable and aggressive grasp, that is, of Ignacio Ramirez.

Amid this wrangling the real issue was neglected. The banishment of the bishops was a symbolic sacrifice to the *vindicta publica*. They were convicted on suspicion and sentenced by acclaim, and as the evidence of clerical treason was always elusive, the one certain result of a public trial would have been a domestic scandal and a foreign sensa-

OCAMPO

PRIETO

ZARCO

RAMIREZ

tion; and the latter was a consideration to which the government gave more weight than the press. Before leaving Veracruz, Juarez had been advised by McLane to observe all reasonable forbearance in the pacification of the country; and the new French Minister, M. de Saligny, also had urged him to propitiate foreign opinion—officious advice, but well meant in both cases, for the prevailing prejudice abroad against the Liberal party and its Indian leader was only waiting for a case to prove and provoke it. In the case of the prelates the method adopted was the one least apt to prejudice foreign judgment, but for that very reason it was denounced by a press writing to read the world a lesson and to declare the emancipation of Mexico from foreign influence; and the President was allowed no latitude for discretion.

Foreign hazards, however, were a serious consideration in the expulsion of three members of the diplomatic corps—the Papal Nuncio, the Minister of Spain, and the Minister of Guatemala—whom the government singled out as examples on charges of notorious complicity with the Reaction. Here the government and the press were in complete agreement, and the most captious found no fault with the President. Reprisals against the foreign enemy were recognized as a measure of public safety, and there was no dissent as to the necessity, or the justice, of purging the Republic of its avowed opponents. Nevertheless, the step was provocative and the policy questionable. Ocampo, who signed the letters of expulsion—it was his last official act before resigning to Zarco—was careful to state that the censure they conveyed carried no reflection on the governments represented. The Spanish Minister refused to admit any distinction between his public and private character and replied stiffly to that effect, and one member of the cabinet at least thought it impolitic to antagonize him: Gonzalez Ortega, carrying discretion one step further than his colleagues, called on the irate Minister on the night before his departure, deplored their hasty decision, and announced the visit of Zarco to accommodate the affair. Señor Pacheco was perfectly willing to be wooed, for he was loath to believe that he was simply *persona non grata,* and he stayed up all night awaiting the peacemaker; but the night passed without any further approaches, and in the morning the escort appeared promptly at the door, and he drove away unreconciled. He made the journey in company with the prelates, and at Veracruz, where passions ran even higher than in the capital, the party was received with a riot. The carriage of the Nuncio was stoned, the bishops were pelted as they alighted; the Nuncio found refuge in the parlor of the French Consul, the bishops made for the nearest home with lace curtains, and there they were held in protective custody by the police until their ship sailed and they could be safely spirited away. The addled Spaniard was not molested, but his parting impressions of Mexico were highly inflamed; and he was no sooner out of the country than he sent a detailed account of the outrages which the whole party had suffered to his French colleague, to whom he bequeathed the protection of Spanish nationals.

Not until the outcasts were well on their way did the press notice the effects of their expulsion; and then not very seriously. The *Siglo* regaled its readers with a flippant account from its correspondent in Cuba of the appearance of the Spanish Minister and Miramon flocking together in the fashionable promenades of Havana and attending the Opera, where they attracted some attention from the curious but none from the Captain-General, who alone counted. Later references to the affair were relegated to the gossip column. It was difficult to take Señor Pacheco seriously; the only impression he left on Mexico personally was that of a figure grotesquely inflated by gout, obesity, and self-importance, and his political stature was gauged by the parting glimpse of Minister and General parading their misfortunes together amid the indifference of the official and fashionable worlds of Havana. As for the bishops, they were mere ghosts.

The influence of the Church on foreign opinion had already been tested. The efforts which the Clerical party had made to secure foreign intervention had come to nothing, and it was clear that they would come to nothing unless the Church could identify its interests with those of the great Powers; and that danger was a remote contingency in 1861. The victory of the Liberal party and its program were the best guarantees for the interests of the great Powers, which were completely independent of those of the Church, if not diametrically opposed to them.

Abundant evidence of that fact was provided by the experience of Mgr. Labastida. Banished by Comonfort in 1856, the Bishop of Puebla had spent four years abroad in search of support, and although he was an active and energetic churchman, he had traveled the apostolic path to final resignation. His correspondence with Father Miranda told the whole tale. During the last six months of the civil war, from a villa in Viareggio, he followed its development with a detachment remotely resembling that of a disinterested observer. The decline of his cause was accompanied, month by month, by his own moral progress. In July he still saw some grounds for hope. One was Señor Pacheco, another the defeat of the American treaty, and a third the new French Minister, M. de Saligny, who was the likeliest of all, for M. de Gabriac was still working for them in Paris, and "the substitute shows good ideas and intentions and promises to do great things for Mexico, beginning with his passage through New York where he has good connections, particularly with Mr. Benjamin, who has influence." To base his faith, however, on someone who had connections with someone else who had influence, was to rely on second- and third-hand hopes. American capital was still on the wrong side, the European Powers were temporizing, England was weakening, and hence Louis Napoleon as well, and he trusted only in Spain and in Spain only with the help of God. "Spain alone is firmly resolved to favor us. May God give her strength and wisdom, which are needed even to do good!" But Spain could do nothing without England and France; England and France had the strength and the wisdom, but not the need, to do good; and gradually he lost hope in any ground-given god.

By August he was completely despondent. "It is useless to exert ourselves to obtain peace by ourselves," he confessed. "We struggle, but without sufficient strength. The intervention or mediation of Europe alone can afford us some respite, but will it be made? Europe is very much troubled by its own situation." Whatever the prop to which he clung, he fell by it. "I see very clearly," he concluded, "that the sacrifice of ecclesiastical property, its ruin and certain disappearance, are inevitable. But I tremble for the fate of those property-owners who regard it with indifference today or who favor it jealously. Sooner or later their possessions will suffer the same fate. They think to save them, and they destroy the buttress that protects them in that wretched society." Without power enough either to protect or be protected, the Church was doomed. One melancholy reflection leading to another, his mind veered to divine intervention or self-help, which, as the adage would have it, were one and the same thing, and in September he preached that sermon. But he had no faith in it himself. His last hope was Miramon, and that was the faintest of all, for "to sustain it some foreign bayonets would be needed," he added, "and they are not to be had." Hard on that postscript came October and Ortega. In November the British Legation was plundered and everything vanished—intervention, mediation, Miramon, and Miranda; and by December Mgr. Labastida abandoned whatever idea he still entertained of returning to his diocese. So, culling simples all the way, he came to the end of it completely disabused but grateful for four years of exile, which left him exactly where he was, but which cured him of the world, "after having made a trip entirely useless for the Church and the State, though of great mortification for your affectionate Prelate, P.A., Bishop of Puebla." No other P.S. was possible, and the case of the Bishop of Puebla provided a fair enough test to discount in advance the banishment of five more Mexican bishops.

The expulsion of the diplomats was more serious, however, for here the blow struck the professional *esprit de corps* of a caste capable of retaliating and accustomed to an immunity in meddling with the domestic affairs of the country that had never been questioned before; and it was not allowed to pass unchallenged now. The first reaction came from the French Minister, who immediately protested the expulsion of the Nuncio and went so far as to declare, in a heated altercation with Ocampo, that the Emperor of the French would consider it a personal affront. His expostulations were ignored. Before long, however, both the government and the press awoke to the fact that the new French Minister was a man who meant, and who deserved, to be taken seriously. Pacheco and the prelates were phantoms, forgotten as soon as they vanished. But M. de Saligny was the comet.

2

THE successor of M. de Gabriac deserved attention indeed, and soon received it, as an even more portentous specimen of the partisan and irresponsible diplomat that flourished so freely in Mexico, and as a consummate example of the license that the genus had come to enjoy with time and impunity. When he arrived there, he had already been ignored too long for his own good or that of the government to which he was accredited. Neither his antecedents, nor his connections, nor his sympathies, were auspicious. Pierre Elizodor Alphonse Dubois de Saligny was a diplomat *manqué*. After a promising start in the service, he had been placed on the inactive list and had vegetated in semidisgrace, for reasons unknown but that may have had something to do with his peremptory temper, soliciting employment unsuccessfully for ten years until he was suddenly recalled for a mission which linked his professional future with the destinies of Mexico. In May 1860 he was appointed to represent his country in the joint mediation by which France and England proposed to extinguish the civil war. The mission was important because of its bearing on the expansion of American influence in Mexico, but his departure was delayed, and the war was over when he arrived in Veracruz in December 1860. For a man who had been shelved in mid-career and for whom the future had just reopened, this was a setback, but he was prepared for it, for whatever else he may have been, he was not a fatalist, and he set to work with redoubled zeal to attract the attention of the Foreign Office and to win the good graces of the Emperor in what remained of his mission.

When he left Paris the end of the war was foreseen, and he carried contingent instructions covering the protection of French interests and outstanding claims created by the war—debts and indemnities—which he was directed to settle before recognizing the government. Since communication was slow and the normal delay of three months in the exchange of diplomatic despatches hampered efficiency in the discharge of his duties, he had requested and received permission to use his discretion and initiative in these routine transactions; and the latitude and confidence thus invested in him were employed not only to settle public debts, but to pay private ones. He owed his appointment to the recommendation of M. de Gabriac and inherited the friends, the clients, and the obligations of his sponsor, and when he was approached by the Mexican clericals and expatriates for whom M. de Gabriac was working in Paris, he accepted their commissions as a matter of course. He promised to do great things for Mexico, and he kept his word. The confidence of the Bishop of Puebla was not misplaced, for it was precisely through such private commissions that M. de Saligny was able to restore to his mission the importance which it had lost by the untimely end of the war. The confidence of the Quai d'Orsay allowed him ample latitude to operate on margin, and how far he was prepared to stretch it he proved when he protested the expulsion of the Nuncio and honored his obligations to his clerical friends, at some risk to himself, for it was stretching discretion very thin and initiative very far to include the championship of the Church in the protection of French interests and to commit the Emperor to that position. Such was the view that the Mexican Government took when it ignored him, but its security was based on his public character, and it was only on better acquaintance with his private character that it discovered that the distinction between them was as imaginary as in the case of Señor Pacheco.

Several weeks later the government ordered the Convent of the Sisters of Charity to be searched for a deposit of money and valuables concealed there in violation of the law nationalizing Church property. "It was the stormy period," wrote an eyewitness, "when the Liberal party plunged into turbulent agitation, concerning itself incessantly with public affairs, supervising all the acts of the administration in the press and the clubs and attacking those which it considered feeble or deficient and anything that appeared to be a compromise with Reaction." As word of the raid spread, a crowd collected about the convent. Apart from the rioting in Veracruz, no anticlerical demonstrations had disturbed the pacification of the country as yet; the turbulent temper of the capital effervesced in rhetorical agitation, the terror was confined to talk, and the crowd that mounted guard about the convent was curious, watchful, but orderly, no resistance was offered, and the lawbreakers were women. The Sisters chatted amicably with the soldiers, and the investigation would have passed off without scandal if the *Visitadora,* who was a Spaniard, had not protested against the presence of Mexican troops at her skirts and, when they broke down a wall and located the treasure, hurried off to the French Legation to demand protection. M. de Saligny, having taken over the protection of Spanish nationals from Pacheco, espoused her protest and forwarded it to Zarco, who was obliged to choose between Agustina Zuazua and Francisco Zarco. The soldiers were not withdrawn, and on the next day M. de Saligny repeated his remonstrances in his own name and on behalf of his government. As he had not yet presented his credentials, he had no official standing, but technicalities did not prevent him from indulging in personalities and raising his voice and losing his temper. "So!" he ejaculated in a furiously informal note, "your government is determined to drain my patience and break with France? I am forced to think so, when I see it persisting in the incredible outrages of which the establishment of the Sisters of Charity has been the scene for the past six hours. Despite all the recommendations which I addressed to you yesterday, the establishment is still occupied by a coarse and brutal soldiery that indulges in every form of insult to the Superior and the other Sisters. I shall no longer be a witness to such a spectacle, which is a direct and premeditated offense to the government of the Emperor, under whose protection these holy women have been placed in every part of the world. Unless you withdraw your soldiers, whose presence nothing can justify, immediately, I shall send you a protest today, renouncing the renewal of relations with a government for whom, I am forced to say, nothing is sacred."

No government could submit to such an ultimatum without forfeiting national sovereignty, and no responsible minister could retreat from so peremptory a position, but the notice was unofficial, and an informal accommodation of their quarrel was made. The soldiers were withdrawn when they had completed their duty, and the incident was apparently closed, but a few days later, on a new denunciation, they returned to the convent for another search, and the scandal flared up afresh. M. de Saligny mounted his high horse once more and protested, this time with an obscene insinuation, against the orders of the government "to carry out a search and Heaven knows what kind of investigations" and a breach of agreement which he could only explain as a mistake. "Be that as it may, I am sending you this so that you may put a stop to what is happening. Otherwise my orders are so imperative that I cannot but obey them, and I shall be obliged, to my great regret, to break all relations with your government and to leave the capital." Again the soldiers were withdrawn, but the government made its position perfectly clear by publishing a statement in the press that "the establishment of the Sisters of Charity is to continue to lend its service to suffering humanity and needy children under the inspection of the government, and is never to be subject to the protection and refuge of any foreign government."

The press glossed over the incident very lightly, suddenly aware that, however untenable the position in which the French Minister had placed himself, he was a man to be handled with care. The *Siglo,* all amenity and official optimism, nevertheless read him a lesson. "Unfortunately, and we venture to say so because it has passed into a common saying, the generous character and tendencies of the French nation have not been properly personified in Mexico in recent years, and the majesty and prestige of the Empire have served to cover mean and personal connections. The general clamor of the French residents in Mexico proves how its most respectable interests have been sacrificed to the alliance of the French Minister with the Clerical party. . . . The general version of this incident does not agree with the high idea that we hold of the new representative of France." Far franker was the rebuke of the French colony: "The right of the government to control alone and directly the temporal administration of the Mexican Church cannot be denied," it declared. "Is this the end or the continuation of the deplorable conflict between the Cabinet and the Legation of France? We believe that it will be the end."

The end it was not, but it was a halt. Saligny was silenced for the moment, but he had gone too far to draw back, and he referred the dispute to Paris. His position was weak. His formal instructions explicitly forbade any interference in the internal affairs of the country, and had he been requested to produce the imperative orders under which he claimed to be acting, he would have been hard put to attribute them to the French Government. The Order of St. Vincent de Paul, to which the Sisters of Charity belonged, enjoyed the protection of the Emperor, it was true; but the exercise of that pretension had been admitted in only one country in the world, Portugal, and in Mexico it had been consistently denied even by the Zuloaga government. As for Napoleon, who was engaged in supporting the Vatican with one hand and the Italian liberation movement with the other, his clerical policy was equivocal and depended on preserving the balance at home and abroad, and there was no reason to suppose that an attempt to tip the scales in Mexico would succeed. That M. de Saligny was willing to risk a rupture under such circumstances and on so flimsy a pretext revealed so much assurance that the government was obliged to take him seriously, at least until the degree to which he was supported in Paris could be determined. Realizing that the man was serving more than one master, Zarco temporized, but he would have been spared worse difficulties had he accepted the rupture, for the tradition established by M. de Gabriac was unbroken. The persons changed, but not the practices, and the incident acquired a peculiar gravity because it coincided with a negotiation which the French Minister had just initiated with no less nerve, which was equally irregular, and in which there was no doubt that he enjoyed the authority of his government.

This negotiation, of which the public had not yet caught wind, was an affair destined to attain international notoriety under the name of the Jecker bonds. In 1859 the Miramon government issued bonds to

the amount of fifteen million pesos and gave the agency to the firm of
Jecker, Torre & Co., one of the leading foreign banks in Mexico, in a
desperate attempt to reconvert its debts and restore its credit. The market was so low that special inducements were offered to float the issue.
The first, and most important, was the privilege of paying twenty per
cent of the customs duties with the bonds—a feature designed to interest the foreign merchants, and it was to that public that the appeal was
primarily addressed. The Miramon government, it was true, did not
control the ports at which the customs were collected, but it had established an inner ring of its own, and the actual value of the reductions
was considerable, as the bonds could be picked up at a thirty-five per
cent discount. A circular stressing the selling point was sent to all the
foreign Legations, and as the principal consideration for Miramon was
the political value of interesting the foreign colonies in the triumph
of his faction, M. de Gabriac was able to obtain a decree extending the
privilege to include all tax payments, by which the French colony benefited to the extent of ten million francs a year.

The second inducement was the signature of the bank, which guaranteed one-half of the interest for five years. This security was not
very sound. J. B. Jecker was a Swiss financier who had speculated recklessly for years in many forms of Mexican investment—mines, iron-
works, the mint at Guanajuato, public lands in Sonora, claims at
Tehuantepec—before he took a flier with the Miramon government.
His family and partners abroad considered his scale of operations
altogether too American and had repeatedly warned him against over-
expansion, and in 1859 the firm was in difficulties. At the time that he
underwrote the bonds, however, they were merely a small turnover
between a reputable international banker on the one hand, and an insolvent government on the other; but the relative positions of the two
parties were soon equalized. In May 1860 the bank failed in Paris.
Liquidation was suspended pending a settlement with the creditors.
Among the assets were the Mexican bonds, of which only an insignificant fraction had been sold, worth exactly 700,450 pesos, and on these
Jecker continued to meet the interest regularly to protect his title to
the unsold residue, which amounted to over eighty-six million francs,
and to prevent a contract between a government and a bank, both of
them bankrupt, from becoming extinct.

As the value of the asset depended on the issue of the civil war, and
as the prospects of the Miramon government declined rapidly after
May 1860, the relatives of Jecker in Paris and Switzerland began to
interest themselves actively in insuring the contract. By October his
brother-in-law, Jakob Elsesser, who knew nothing about Mexico, but
who was reading a serious German book about it, could see that the
future was black, and he busied himself borrowing advice wherever he
could. "I must tell you about the bonds," he wrote to a confidant in

Paris from his corner in Ponterrey, Switzerland. "A learned philologist here is busy translating the decrees, the full explanation of which I shall send you later." But even had they been written in a dead language, Elsesser would have understood them without engaging a scholar to decipher their meaning. "Although these acts emanated from a government then recognized by England and France, and the bonds were held in considerable amounts by the merchants of both nations, I have no doubt that once the Liberals come into power, as they soon will, the bonds will be put out of circulation. M. de Saligny has assured me, however," he added, "that the recognizing governments and even the United States would support them, because of the benefits which their nationals derive from them by paying heavy customs duties with paper that they buy cheap."

The services of a Saligny were worth more than those of a philologist, and Elsesser secured them at less cost, merely by unbosoming himself freely to the Minister; but the comfort he derived from consulting him was secondhand, like the encouragement which the Bishop of Puebla drew from his connection with Mr. Benjamin. Valuable though that connection might be for both his clients, what M. de Saligny had to offer were hopes, not guarantees, and gratuitous services were worthless anyway. The assurances of a diplomat who had been so long out of circulation himself, and who had barely been floated again, were valueless without official backing for the bonds, and Elsesser had none. But he set to work and worried what friends he had in Paris, and connections were established there that carried the business into the inner circles of high finance and won a friend at Court in no less a patron than the Comte de Morny, the Emperor's brother, who consented, for a commission of thirty per cent, to promote the affair and to guarantee that the bonds would be honored by the Mexican Government.

Besides the private backing of M. de Morny, the official support of the Quai d'Orsay had also to be secured, however, and this was more difficult because of the guarded attitude toward bankers observed there. The favor of the Foreign Office did not follow automatically from that of M. de Morny, whose indiscretions had embarrassed the Emperor more than once, and as Walewski no longer presided over the department, a different approach was needed to induce the new Foreign Minister, M. de Thouvenel, who was personally incorruptible, to play host to so compromising an affair. The difficulty was adroitly turned, however. The failure of the bank had ruined a number of French depositors, for the most part small investors and charitable institutions whose rights were respectable and whose distress was pathetic, and on their behalf a petition was addressed to the Foreign Office to protect their claims and indemnify their losses with the Mexican assets of the firm. Presented in this light, as a legitimate credit and a national interest, which offered, furthermore, appreciable privileges for French commerce at the customs, the plea was accepted, and the Jecker bonds were included among the public claims which Saligny was instructed to settle with the Juarez government before recognizing it. M. de Thouvenel was an accomplished diplomat and a schooled courtier, and without examining too closely the premises of the amphitryonic affair, he covered himself with a provision that Saligny was to satisfy himself of the legitimacy of the claim before he pressed it. Legitimacy was an ambiguous word in the lexicon of diplomacy, but the services of a philologist were not needed to define it. The interpretation was left to M. de Saligny, and the application to his discretion, and he was empowered to impose recognition of French claims globally, if necessary, by a display of force—one of the usual naval demonstrations employed by creditor nations, of which M. de Gabriac had availed himself in the early days of the civil war—a plain indication that M. de Thouvenel understood the difficulty of negotiating so raw a bit of business.

The deal with M. de Morny was not closed until January 1861, but the affair had taken shape before Saligny left Paris the previous September, and he had contributed to its promotion. M. de Gabriac had made a tidy fortune of his own from his mission to Mexico and lost it in the failure of the bank, and his substitute was in duty bound to help his patron recoup it. *Noblesse oblige* was the more binding upon M. de Saligny that he was a genuine nobleman upon whose title none of the doubts that darkened that of M. de Gabriac could be cast. The Marquis was a man, moreover, of many and enterprising ideas; besides those which he shared with M. de Gabriac, he had his own. In addition to the bonds, the assets of the bank included several other possibilities which opened a large field for French enterprise—the gold mines of Sonora, which caught the fancy of M. de Morny, and the claims at Tehuantepec, which might attract the attention of the Emperor, whose interest in cutting a canal through Central America dated from his youth and was still an unrealized ambition among so many others of Louis Napoleon. By a fortunate coincidence, the Louisiana Tehuantepec Company had fallen into financial difficulties, Mr. Benjamin had come to Europe in 1860 to secure foreign backing for it, and M. de Saligny displayed his political flair in a memorandum that he addressed to the Foreign Office recommending, among other original ideas, that the French Government buy into the American enterprise. With a wealth of combinations at his command, he was in a position to make his connection with Mr. Benjamin serve the interests of France, of the bank, of M. de Morny, of Napoleon III, of the Mexican clericals, and of the Marquis de Saligny all at once; but this embarrassment of riches was purely mental, and his ideas still tentative, when he left France. The bonds were but one among many combinations, but they were the lever to move the others, and the omnibus business on which the success of his mission depended.

The hands of M. de Thouvenel having been washed, and those of M. de Morny greased, the final shaping of the affair rested in Saligny's hands. Between the ways of force and skill, his preference was pronounced, and no small skill was needed to handle a negotiation which not only saddled the debts of the vanquished on the victor, but transformed the agent of the bonds into their owner. For such was the assumption upon which the credit was founded. What began as a conversion of the public debt of a government that had fallen, ended in the conversion of a bank that had failed into the holder of a diplomatic claim against the legitimate government that raised the public debt of Mexico by eighty-six million francs. Baldly stated, those were the facts, and very light fingers indeed were needed to pick the pockets of Mexico publicly. The delicacy of the question was betrayed by the delicacy of M. de Saligny. Promiscuity was his sole asset, and on his passage through Veracruz, he discussed the general claims of his mission with the government; and finding its members, much to his surprise, moderate and reasonable men, he reported to Paris that an understanding could easily be reached with them. Agreeably surprised, he was accommodating in turn and deferred the main question. On his arrival in the capital he received a petition from five hundred bondholders soliciting his support for their claims; he advised them to be patient and to give the government time to settle itself; but he was not allowed to temporize long. In January the deal with Morny was closed in Paris, and in February he received orders from the Quai d'Orsay to act. He broached the question with Zarco, demanding recognition of the bonds in principle and leaving the amount open to discussion and adjustment. The principle that the debts of one government were binding on its successor, regardless of the origin either of the government or the obligation, was sanctioned by international law, both deriving their legitimacy from their recognition; but from the outset he met with a resistance no less firm for being polite and evasive, and snags in what were merely preliminary sparrings tried his skill and his temper severely.

It was amid these initial difficulties that the incident of the Sisters of Charity occurred. Addled by the difficulty of hatching the Jecker affair, and heated by the offense to the Sisters, he exploded. His interference in favor of the nuns was unauthorized and his hectoring sheer bluster, but he was in a huff and, infuriated by opposition on both questions, he applied to the one the arbitrary powers with which he was empowered to handle the other; and the result favored his negotiation with the government. The effrontery with which he browbeat Zarco on behalf of his clerical clients fostered the presumption that he was acting with the same license in championing them as in defending the Jecker bonds, and that in both cases he enjoyed the support of his government. The deduction was deceptive, but one thing was added to another, and though two and two make four in arithmetic, in the science of inference they usually make five. The temper of the public was highly impressionable, and the Legation of France was regarded as the center of all the intrigues and conspiracies against the Constitutional government; and henceforth Saligny was treated not merely with the seriousness due to a suspect, but with the respect due to a diplomat who apparently held two of the controlling forces of his country in his hands, as indeed he did. The interests of the bank and the Church were distinct, but he was able to combine them, and the combination of clerical protection and a financial offensive was a powerful form of pressure to apply to an unsettled government; but suspicion not being an exact science, the sum of the two still made four and their confusion five.

Benefiting by that misconception, the Minister pressed his advantage, but he made small progress in the financial offensive after the alert sounded by the press for his protection of the Sisters of Charity. Suspicion spread, and the attention which he attracted by that scandal shifted to the Jecker transaction, of which the public now became aware. The press was silent but watchful. A discreet warning was raised by the *Siglo,* which changed the subject for the worse and featured the Mirés scandal on its front page. This affair involved the ruin of a Parisian financier cornered by the rival firm of Rothschild, and with him of so many of his highly placed protectors that the Imperial Government was rocked by revelations of corruption close to the Throne and compelled not only to prosecute him, but to appease public opinion by restoring the right of criticism to the Corps Législatif and a measure of free speech to the controlled press. While the *Siglo* spoke in parables, and Zarco in adjournments, it was not easy to crack the Jecker question, and nothing had been settled when, in mid-March, Saligny again became reckless and lost his head in an excess of discretion. He recognized the Juarez government without a guarantee to guard his judgment, much as McLane had done when he took the same step in 1859 led on by the belief that the sale of Lower California would follow, and with no different results. Far from facilitating the negotiation, official recognition deprived the Minister of a normal form of pressure, and one that he was directed to use; and after suffering the same delays and evasions after as before it, he reverted to the only form of coercion that remained and prepared the Quai d'Orsay for extraordinary measures.

The state of the country and the stability of the government were delineated in a succession of pessimistic reports. "In the state of anarchy, or rather of social dissolution, prevailing in this wretched country, it is very difficult to foresee what turn conditions will take," he wrote in April. "Only one thing seems to me certain, the impossibility of remaining *in statu quo.* Everything indicates that we are approaching a new revolution. In these circumstances, it seems to me absolutely neces-

sary that we should have on the coast of Mexico a material force sufficient, whatever happens, to provide protection for our interests." He
did not refer to the bonds. For obvious reasons, the subject was too sore
to mention. He had just received a reprimand from the Quai d'Orsay
for his conduct in the incident of the Sisters of Charity, reminding him
that the French Legation in Mexico was established for the protection
of French interests and not for those of any religious community whatsoever. Charity beginning at home, however, he was lectured with the
indulgence due to a French gentleman who had allowed his chivalry
to get the better of his judgment and was scolded considerably. The
reprimand was confidential, and, to save his face, it was accompanied
by an official letter approving his behavior, which he could show, if
necessary, to cover his conduct of the Jecker affair; and at the same
time he received peremptory orders to conclude it.

Thus spurred and tamed, he presented Zarco with an ultimatum in
May. His language, remarkable alike for its frankness and moderation,
made ample amends for the insolence and bluff with which he had
threatened to break with him for the sake of the Sisterhood in February. For three months he had been hoping for the settlement of "an
important question in which the honor and interests of France are
gravely involved," he admitted. "I refer to the question of the Jecker
bonds, the only one that can raise serious difficulties between our two
countries, and prevent France from giving free rein to her friendly
intentions toward Mexico. Unfortunately, this hope has been disappointed. I cannot take it upon myself to postpone any longer the execution of the orders of the Emperor's Government. Nevertheless, before notifying you officially, I have wished to give you another proof
of the conciliatory spirit by which I myself am animated; and, accordingly, prompted by a sentiment that I trust you will appreciate, I beg
you to inform me without delay of the definite intentions of your
government." It was almost an apology, maybe an appeal, and certainly
a challenge to Zarco's charity; but the only effect was a tentative understanding, or misunderstanding, which induced Saligny to believe that
he had scored a point and allowed him to report progress to Paris.
Zarco consented, implicitly admitting the principle, to discuss the
amount to which the bank was actually entitled to be reimbursed for
the bonds actually sold, the interest paid on them, and the advances
made to the Miramon government. This concession represented an insignificant sum and a diplomatic accommodation worth some consideration, but it fell far short of the total credit for the bond issue; and as
the resistance of the government to the whole claim remained unbroken, no substantial advance had been made, and it was clear to
M. de Saligny that nothing would float the unsold bonds but a naval
demonstration. By the beginning of May there was no doubt of it:
the legitimate claims of his government had been settled to the satis-

faction of his superiors, the only hitch was the Jecker affair, and he was still a diplomat *manqué*. Intimidation had been tried unsuccessfully. The situation was, in a word, serious.

Serious was the word for it for other reasons as well. So far the French Minister had had the field to himself, but in May his British colleague, Sir Charles Lennox Wyke, arrived, and the unbroken tradition of British diplomacy in Mexico made it doubtful whether he would prove a collaborator or a competitor. With Mathew Saligny was on bad terms. In his case there was no doubt. Everything divided them—racial antipathy, religious tolerance, but above all the Jecker bonds, for the recognition of that credit threatened to wipe out the small percentage of customs revenue still available for foreign claims and to deprive the government of the resources necessary to satisfy British indemnities. Mathew was of inferior diplomatic rank, but he still doubled for Russell and Palmerston, and in the protection of preferred claims he had the advantage of having recognized the Liberal government, for which he had developed a pronounced partiality ever since its success, one month before Saligny. His conditions were accepted without question—arrears on the debt service, indemnity for the plunder of the *conducta* by Degollado and of the British Legation by Miramon, although the validity of the last was as questionable as the Jecker bonds, and awkward questions were being asked about it in Paris.

Ocampo, before he left office, had caught an echo of them from his friend in the Legation there, who tipped him off to some trade secrets. "You are not sharp enough to explain *why* that money was kept on deposit in Mexico and in the British Chancery, while *conductas* were leaving for Veracruz and when the remittance of currency to London was advantageous to the rightful owners, our pesos being quoted at that time at a premium as high as ninepence. I will tell you. Mr. Mathew made them sweat and worked them in his own way, when Mexico was so short of currency and loans were so high and speculation so fruitful with individuals and with the Apostolic faction. Familiar as he was with that faction, Mr. Mathew gave them a chance to lay hands on the deposit. This is how the business of indemnization is done, like that of speculation, and if no honor is derived from it, undoubtedly a very high rate of profit is received. I know also that he gave Señor Degollado to understand that he could seize the *conducta,* provided, of course, that he respected English property." Such imputations naturally could not be proved, but they gained currency from many known precedents in the diplomatic game, where nothing was above question but one thing: the business of indemnization was legitimate in English hands, and whether those of Mathew were clean or not could not be judged, since, unlike Saligny, he was not obliged to show them.

English favor offered the government a certain security in dealing with the French Minister. "The touchstone is England," wrote the same friend to Ocampo, "because of her intimate relations with the United States, and because, if she wishes, France will not attack us. In American affairs the reverse of what happens in Europe occurs: over there English influence will predominate, contrary to what takes place in Europe, where Napoleon III is not willing to yield an inch." English favor, however, was contingent upon the financial responsibility of the Mexican Government, and when the new British Minister arrived in Mexico at the beginning of May, the solvency of the government was a matter of urgent doubt, affecting the interests of both the creditor Powers.

3

THE end of the war had by no means relieved the chronic penury in which it was fought and against which the government was called to contend as soon as it was established in the capital. The millions of the *conducta* had carried the last stage of the war to victory, but Gonzalez Ortega was penniless when he won the battle of Calpulalpam, and the burden was laid down barely in time to avert a financial collapse. The days of expedients were over, and the first and most pressing problem of peace was a fundamental financial reorganization indispensable to the consolidation of success. Saligny himself realized it when he advised the Jecker creditors to give the government time to settle itself. So did the press and the public, but in the first flush of triumph attention was distracted from the gravity of the situation by the celebration of victory, the preferred claims of self-congratulation, the pursuit of the guilty, and, above all, by the confidence that, formidable as the problem was after three years of civil war and forty years of hereditary insolvency, the government had ample securities with which to meet it in 1861. The problem was gigantic, but so were the guarantees of confiscated Church property, and so was the financial genius of Lerdo de Tejada. Both these securities were incommensurable, however, and hypothetic.

Lerdo de Tejada was not in the government. He had left it to nurse his health and his prospects as a candidate in the coming presidential elections, which were slated for June and which were a live issue in January. In February he died. The campaign continued posthumously in the apotheosis with which the press lamented his loss. His reputation flared up, towering, immense, incomparable, and with overwhelming unanimity papers of every shade of opinion echoed the void he had left behind him. "The giant of Reform," "the most vigorous and practical mind on which the revolution could count," "the personification of progressive initiative," "the author of the Reform Laws," "the only man who could understand and formulate the idea of our revolution" —a litany of devout voices vying with one another acclaimed, in a chorus of mourning, the memory of a man whose reputation was secure, because it had never been tested. The credit of Lerdo rested on the nationalization of Church property, and great as the value of that measure was in destroying the economic strength of the enemy, its merit as a constructive contribution to national progress lay less in its conception, which was common to many minds, than in its social application and practical administration; and he died just in time to save a reputation which remained mythical.

A gloomy foreboding filled the columns of the obituaries. "In hours of solemn intimacy," wrote one of his friends, "I heard from his lips profound ideas for the work of regeneration. I heard also some of his hopes and his fears for the future of the country. With regret I must say that the latter outweighed the former, for he saw what was happening to the Reform and to the invaluable opportunity definitely to settle the peace of the Republic. He saw that the abundant capital of the clergy would be consumed without benefit to the many and without profit even in producing revenue for the nation and amortizing its enormous debt. He saw that without establishing an adequate system of finance society could not rest on a solid foundation nor peace be the fruit of so much blood shed and so many sacrifices made. What Lerdo foresaw has come to pass, what he conceived and studied for the hour of construction has not been done, because he was deprived of the participation which was his due on the day of triumph; and what the country expected, what the great party of Lerdo imagined when he would come to power, whether by electoral suffrage or the choice of the President, has been lost for ever. . . ." But the opportunity to make political capital of his passing was not lost. "What shall we do now? What direction shall we take? Who is the man to guide us?" the indictment continued. Lerdo was in the grave, and so was the government that had dropped him. "As for the man who will replace Lerdo in the great conceptions which he held for the good of his country, since we have neither the wish nor the ability to indicate him, let events discover him, let them unearth and reveal what we need, for thinking men cannot admit the theory of indispensable men. An inexorable law sends mankind the men whose names it reveres."

The burden was shouldered by Prieto. Returning to the post that he had vacated in Veracruz in favor of the expert, he faced a cruel comparison. An expert alone could penetrate and disentangle, let alone solve, the problems that had accumulated for two generations in the Treasury. Prieto had served two terms in that den of confusion and was familiar with its routine: the perennial deficits could be juggled, the legacy of the civil war could be managed, the makeshifts, the mortgages, the detritus of dead bonds and spurious conversions, the litter of forced loans and chronic default, the long wreckage of a struggle that had drained every resource and reduced both sides to highway robbery, could be repaired while the hope of an issue lay ahead. But what could neither be disguised nor redeemed was the monstrous delusion that led him into the maze and through the toils of the labyrinth to his final confusion. The saving measure to which he looked for relief from ruinous expedients was itself an expedient and the most ruinous of all. The fabulous wealth of the Church was a fable, a mirage luring him on and eluding his reach; the enormous resources of expropriation were an arid waste, guarded by glittering grit. Before he could reach them, he had first to clear away a rank tangle of conflicting claims arising out of past purchases made under Lerdo's original law of disamortization in 1856, their cancellation by the Clerical government, and subsequent adjudications under the final decree of 1859 —an overgrowth so thick and stubborn that his entire tenure of office was spent in coping with it—and then . . . then . . . He went no further, for as he burrowed he unearthed an appalling discovery.

The springs of fresh wealth had shrunk, dried up, disappeared—no one knew how or where. The causes were as elusive as the flight was certain. The wealth of the Church had always been legendary and incommensurable, and it had steadily waned as prospectors approached it. It was a public mystery when Mora valued it at 180 millions in 1838, and ever since the eye of the first reformer menaced it, the mystery had thickened and the millions thinned. In 1858, at the start of the civil war, it was roughly estimated at 120 millions; at the close of the war, it was completely inestimable, concealed by confusion and revealing only an incalculable reduction. Part of it had been dissipated to pay for the war, first by the Clerical and then by the Constitutional government; part of it had been buried by the financial subterfuges of agents of the clergy; part of it had been plundered and consumed by the Liberal forces; part of it had been converted by speculators into paper, which, subject to litigation and continually discounted as it changed hands, depreciated steadily. The whole had perhaps been overrated; but the sum of the parts was a tremendous deception, and none of these reasons accounted for a reduction of fifty to sixty per cent in the resources on which the government counted to establish itself soundly. The fact remained that, with untold wealth at its command, the State was compelled to borrow at the rate of four dollars for one to meet its immediate needs, to resort to the same shifts as during the war, and to dispose of valuable properties piecemeal for a pittance or in batches for a song to cover its running expenses. The realization of its assets resembled a proceedings in bankruptcy rather than the liquidation of national wealth.

Politically, the deterioration was even more disastrous. Depreciation of Church property was due in large measure to differences between the estimated value in normal times and in the adverse season in which nationalization was negotiated, and to the reluctance of the devout to incur excommunication in acquiring it, but principally to the operations of speculators, for the most part foreigners, who rushed in where the native feared to tread, took off the curse and cornered the market, holding their investments for a clear title and a quick turnover, and prolonging the unproductive process; and though these conditions were transient, the results were lasting. The needs of the day devoured those of the morrow. The penury of the government, the need of selling short, the prodigal cheapening of Church property, and the facilities for speculation combined to sterilize the social reform which a redistribution of national wealth was intended to serve; and what actually occurred was a transfer of title from one propertied and unproductive class to another, without relieving the masses or invigorating the national economy, while the government functioned as a broker, squandering its security for a fugitive fee. If the clergy had laid a curse on the sacrilegious hands that violated their treasure—as they had—the result was calculated to satisfy them. And the curse fell not on a financial wizard like Lerdo, who might have exorcised it, but on an amateur who succumbed to it. Prieto floundered manfully for four months, losing ground, losing credit, losing hope, and when he was finally convinced that the great lever of the civil war was a broken wrench, and that the sacrifices, the agonies, the massacres, the concessions, the betrayals it cost had been wasted, he lost heart and announced the imminence of national bankruptcy.

From so crushing a sentence common sense recoiled, refusing to believe and seeking every explanation to evade it, but betraying alarm by its very defenses. The press took a less serious, because a more personal, view of the slump. Prieto was attacked for spreading panic fears, which were counterrevolutionary since they undermined public confidence, and antipatriotic since they affected foreign credit, and which were therefore unfounded. "It is a lie that the country is perishing of inanition," wrote Manuel Zamacona, the new editor of the *Siglo*. "The country is not so much poor as impoverished; the sources of public wealth are not exhausted but choked; as soon as the hand of power

applies itself to releasing them, they will begin to flow immediately.
. . ." The Ministry was at fault—an easy mark—and imputations were
raised, if not of corruption, of incompetence—familiar and reassuring
features of Mexican officialdom. The probity of the Minister was unquestioned, but he was taken to task on every other score. He was
honest, too honest; he was hazed for the innocence with which as a
novice he exposed the veteran vices of his department, and forced to
run the gantlet of the most fearful scourging and the most terrified
tongue-lashing. He was berated for abusing public trust as a poet and
letting his imagination run away with him as a minister. Manuel
Zamacona attacked the secrecy with which he conducted the mysteries
of his department and scoffed at the "Trappist silence" broken only
by the ritual wail of "Brethren, we must all die!" that rose from it.
And when Prieto broke his silence and produced his accounts, the
party whip fell on them and plastered the front pages with triumphant
and itemized evidence of extravagance and mismanagement.

As a poet, Prieto was, by his own admission, a loose, careless, and
incorrect writer, and as a public bookkeeper he was convicted of the
same faults. Preferred claims and obsolete debts settled unsystemati-
cally; back bills for rebellion in 1856 when the government could not
meet its running costs in 1861; senescent senatorial salaries honored at
random; lavish indemnities for minor injuries while war pensions were
unpaid; a cool million a month for the army; exorbitant printers' bills;
press subsidies that the government had sworn to abolish; fat commissions for the denunciation of Church property; thirty-four thousand
pesos for the location of treasure not even concealed; twenty thousand
Mexican dollars for "the precious revelation that the Cathedral contained tapers and reliquaries subsequently sold for a song"; hundreds
of thousands for "various creditors" and unspecified sundries—etcetera
and etcetera to the crack of doom, detail consuming the core, a literary
vice fatally indulged in finance, wrecking the writer and leaving his
critics aghast. Such a picture of prodigality and disorder, incoherence
and favoritism, revealed, if not outright irregularity, a lack of planning
and system that would have been scandalous had it not been customary. But the times were not normal, and though Prieto defended himself in a prolonged controversy with pleas as sound as they were irrelevant—bad debts, Jecker bonds, congenital chaos—he was obliged
to resign. Clearing his integrity by admitting his incompetence, he
escaped with nothing to his name but a reputation shopworn and
damaged, and retired from public service as badly bruised as Ocampo
had been by the McLane treaty or Degollado by trading with the
enemy. The revolution consumed its own with relentless rapacity and
was hungry still for fresh victims; for the specter of national bankruptcy raised by each of its chosen defenders in turn was not laid by
plucking the poet.

The dismissal of Prieto minimized the danger, but not for long. His sucessor was Mata, who risked his name for a few informal weeks in the most treacherous and important post in the government. The antithesis of Prieto—"prosaic as a textbook, positive as an equation, logical as a syllogism," someone said of him—and certainly not prone to nervous panic or imaginative exaggerations, and no less honest, Mata fared no better. And as suspicion spread that conditions, and not man, were the culprit, the alarm revived and the warnings of Prieto were seriously heeded. What more could Lerdo himself have done? Lerdo had done it; he had died. Prieto did more. Before abandoning the maddening struggle, he left his critics four methods of dealing with it— sensible methods of loosening the growing incubus and taming the popular unrest, which, passing from one channel to another, now revived revolutionary bitterness and turned the latent terror against the Treasury.

The prescriptions were all based on reduction of four national liabilities: reduction of the foreign debt service, of dividends on the internal debt, of the army, and of the states to Federal authority. Of these the first offered the easiest relief because it was the heaviest burden on the budget, and the most difficult problem because of the pressure that secured it, and hence it was the one on which despair instinctively fastened. The foreign debt service absorbed almost the entire revenue of the customs, which was mortgaged in its totality in the ports of the Pacific, while at Veracruz the scale had risen from forty-eight per cent in 1856 to eighty-five per cent in 1861, and the remaining fifteen per cent was the subject of competing claims, among them the Jecker bonds. The pressure was throttling, and the critics of Prieto were the first to embrace the most desperate of his proposals. Zamacona led off with a long and eloquent article in the *Siglo,* feeling out native and foreign opinion. "The public Treasury," he wrote, borrowing the language of the poet, "has become something like the labyrinth of antiquity, guarded by a monster; the monster is the foreign debt that has closed every avenue leading to the land of reconstruction. The Republic was born like those children who bring into the world an organic ailment, the development of which makes it impossible for them to live. The debt that we began to contract in the days when we were born to political life has grown into a parasitical excrescence that chokes us, drains us, and destroys all regularity in the administrative functions of the government. Not a single dollar coming from the maritime customs reaches the general Treasury. It could be said with complete truth, as the Minister of Finance has just explained, that the coffers of the nation are in those vessels that come periodically to collect virtually the total product of our customs, assigned to cover our diplomatic engagements. Why should we suppose our foreign creditors incapable of conceding us a truce indispensable to life and health? We are not afraid that a false scrupulousness on the part of our government, or an inexorable severity on the part of the friendly Powers, will prevent the realization of this idea, which would be the salvation not only of our Republic, but also of all those who have any claim against it." And to make quite clear that it was no sentimental appeal, he remarked casually, "What will they gain by being inexorable and by killing, so to speak, the goose that lays the golden eggs?"

The idea prospered, and before long it figured in political forecasts and was propagated by rumors breathing as freely as the public they fed. Officially it was ignored, and the government gave it no countenance: for Zamacona was not yet a minister, and though the press was a ruling, it was an irresponsible, power. The nemesis that prompted Prieto to compete with Lerdo had produced a dangerous nostrum, as popular as it was prohibited, and as tempting as it was provocative. Zarco was too badly embarrassed by his negotiations with the French Minister to feel him out any further. The broaching of the Jecker bonds had already produced plain symptoms of public gagging to which M. de Saligny remained deaf; and the French Legation naturally ignored those of a general convulsion.

M. de Saligny, however, was the least risk. The British Legation was the gravest. The English debt being the largest, and English influence the heavy weight in determining the reaction of foreign opinion, it was there that the question was explored. In that quarter the possibility of a compromise was considered. The parable of Zamacona and the gospel of Mathew agreed up to a point; the necessity of some degree of accommodation was recognized by Mathew, and he prepared his government for it. "The bondholders might save their capital by submitting to a temporary suspension of interest," he advised London, "and the establishment of a more equitable tariff, which the government are pledged to me to urge upon Congress, may lay down a better basis of revenue." But he qualified his advice. "Mexico," he added, "whatever her distress, should at least commence at home, and the holders of the immense internal debt should be the first to suffer for the ruin their own folly has caused or abetted. I much fear that the Republic has not yet produced men of sufficient energy and honor to adopt this course, unsustained by some foreign interposition. The effort will always be made to make the foreigner the chief sufferer from the undoubtedly bankrupt state of the country." The appeal to his charity satisfied by that compromise, he laid the problem of public mendicancy in more responsible hands. It was his last report and he was relieved of further responsibility by the arrival of the new British Minister.

In London Sir Charles Lennox Wyke was an expert on Latin American affairs, having served in Honduras and other spheres of British influence in Central America. He had lost his health there, and it was during a prolonged convalescence in Europe that he was appointed, at the same time as Saligny, to serve in the proposed mediation of the Powers in Mexico. Of that scheme all that remained was the understanding that the two Ministers should collaborate, and though the situation had changed when Wyke arrived there a year after his appointment, it had changed so much for the worse that it provoked their spontaneous co-operation. With the practiced eye of an expert, Wyke took in the situation at a glance, and three weeks later he wrote a despatch, containing his first and final impressions of Mexico, which reflected the views of Mathew and Saligny alike. From Mathew he borrowed his worst fears of financial collapse, and from Saligny his most sinister prognostics of social dissolution, and the blend was an ominous diagnosis of a country in the last stages of decay, for which he recommended the same prescription as Saligny. In the meanwhile the trial balloon launched by Zamacona rose, wafted from hand to hand, and drifted buoyantly toward the higher spheres of a government beset by internal troubles.

4

THE government was in the last stages of the election campaign and drifting rapidly toward its dissolution at the polls without any visible means of support. One by one its props fell away. The agitation of the financial question profoundly undermined public confidence and cast a pall over the cabinet, and the President himself was taken to task for his provoking serenity. "The President is a rock, nothing moves him, nothing crushes him, he hears nothing, and hence he is good for nothing"—the tone was typical of the restlessly radical wing of the press, where grievances were being accumulated against the day of election. "Once the President stops signing pardons, supporting the employees of the reaction, holding family talks with his ministers, and misguiding his government to the best of his ability, no further reason remains for his being President of the Republic. Ah! how sad to see a whole people groaning under the burden of a Supreme Magistrate, whose sole title to power today is the one he derived from his seat on the Supreme Court! We would gladly give a thousand presidents of the Supreme Court for one man who represented the Revolution!"

The search went on blindly. It was a measure of the panic by which

the public was stampeded by the announcement of national bankruptcy that popular feeling turned against the entire cabinet, although
the cabinet had been packed with trusted names—Zarco, Mata, Ramirez, Ortega—guarantees, every one of them, of revolutionary energy.
They all suffered from the same misfortune. And in that group there
was one who could not bear unpopularity. Gonzalez Ortega was a candidate for the Presidency. The death of Lerdo had removed his one
serious competitor, for though Juarez was standing for re-election, he
was hardly reckoned by Ortega as a rival or even a handicap. Like
Lerdo, Ortega had developed the habit of running the affairs of his department independently and of ignoring the President, politely or im-
politely; once, on being asked whether he had secured approval for an
order, he was heard to reply, "I have ordered his hundred pesos a day
to be sent him, and that is all that interests him."

Idolized by the army, revered by the revolutionary clubs, profoundly respected by the press and the public, the hero of the civil war
now found himself involved in the rising unpopularity that spread
through every branch of the government and that barely stopped short
of the War Office; and his heel was touched. The time had clearly
come for a test of his political strength. He demanded the dismissal of
two of his colleagues, Zarco and Ramirez, because of their popular dis-
repute, and when Juarez refused to sustain him, resigned himself. His
exit was noisy, and a long shadow fell across the front pages of the papers, haunted by the dread of a relapse into the traditional disorders of
the past. But the threat was cast by a shadow: the mutiny was purely
ministerial, and with a single exception the press rallied to the President. That exception was a paper that demanded that the cabinet be
ousted by force, and it merely multiplied the protests of the rest, which
closed their ranks to deplore the judgment of a hero who could
cheapen the glory of Jesus Gonzalez Ortega by catering "to a few
shouts from a group of boys," which he mistook for public opinion.
Jesus hastened to agree in an open letter, professing his respect for
legality and the sanctity of the civil authority, and Gonzalez Ortega
deplored the hasty conclusions of the press and the baseless fear of
which he was a victim. His was no vulgar ambition: he prided himself on his principles, he was a civilian at heart, he was sound. The denial was accepted with relief, and the heel was planted firmly once
more on the pedestal to which the press hastened to restore him.

Though the alarm subsided as quickly as it arose, it was sharp while
it lasted. "We see in this new vicissitude a new reason for foreigners
to say 'Mexicans are incorrigible,' a new blow to public confidence, and
hence to commerce and every useful enterprise," Zamacona com-
mented—a warning well timed, since M. de Saligny was systematically
unsettling foreign credit with predictions of the approach of a new revolution. The air was cleared by the crisis, and in the relief that followed

there was a general appreciation of what the revolution had actually gained. Henceforth some things were impossible; the unholy spirit of militarism had been mastered. "The incidents that have occupied the capital for the last three days are perhaps the last manifestation that the military will make in Mexican politics," Zamacona ventured to predict, and he paid homage to the President, who, he declared, "in this affair, as in all the crises through which the revolution passed in its militant phase, has shown the most firm and enlightened faith in the vocation of the civil power and its ability to dominate the policy of the country in the future, despite all the obstacles which the military arm might raise."

The real significance of the incident lay in the reading of public opinion, and the substantial advance that it registered in the rising level and stability of the revolution was ample cause for congratulation. The fact that on the eve of a presidential election, the long-awaited test of the relative popularity of the civil and military powers produced nothing more serious than a ministerial crisis, settled by general agreement in favor of the former, was recognized, even by foreigners familiar with the customs of the country, as a guarantee for the future. The future, to be sure, was foreshortened and focused by the coming elections, but the personal prestige of the candidates was subordinated to the cardinal principles with which they were identified in the public mind. If Lerdo was hallowed as the financial genius of the Reform, and Ortega as its military savior, Juarez was respected as the incarnation of its social stamina—the least visible and most vital of the sinews on which its survival depended—and the recognition of his preeminence was a proof of political maturity that augured well even for an unlimited future.

The cult of heroes, however, was an essential part of any revolution and a stubborn survival of the civil war. Besides the dictation of the successful soldier, Juarez had also to master the appeal of the fallen hero of the war—a far more dangerous rival for popular favor. When Ortega resigned from the War Office, the post which he vacated was offered to Degollado, but as the tender was made confidentially, he refused it. What he wanted was not reconciliation, but a trial and public acquittal or condemnation, and as the postponement of that test had worn his patience raw, he was driven finally to do justice to himself. Attacked in the course of the presidential campaign by a supporter of Juarez, and harassed by what he considered the political exploitation of his case, he wheeled on the pack at his heels and turned on the President himself as a party to his persecution. "How is it possible," he exclaimed in a protest that was carried uncut by the press, "that His Excellency the President can remain a cold spectator of so many insults to one who was his most loyal supporter; who saved him from being forgotten and disowned in the interior; who refused to follow him to safety within the walls of Ulua, although he held no military command; and who never once shielded himself behind shutters during the six days that Veracruz was bombarded? What! Does disgrace deserve no respect? misfortune no consideration? and helplessness no protection?" All the gall which he had swallowed without complaint welled up at last in disgust of a martyrdom of which he was weary. "Well or ill, I have served the national cause and proved, even in my errors, my right intentions and my zeal to be of service to the cause of my country," he declared. "I expect no gratitude, gentlemen, or public appreciation of my services, for I knew when I assumed command of the Constitutional army that in all lands and at all times services to one's country have encountered only envious souls and thankless hearts. The greater the merit, the greater the ingratitude: such is the weakness of humanity. But I believe that I have the right to expect that the verdict of my judges be awaited, that I be allowed to live in peace, that I be forgotten, and that the grace be granted me that Diogenes begged—not to be deprived of the sun."

The biting reproach cast an ugly reflection on the President. Degollado called him coward, he accused him of ingratitude, he taxed him with callous indifference, he shamed him for feeling no duty of generosity, decency, or ordinary humanity and fair dealing—no motive was too mean, no slur too small, to belittle and blacken him. Public sympathy was with Degollado, and he knew it: popular judgment had settled his case out of court; only official sanction was withheld—why? He hinted at the reason in a plaintive aside. "If by any chance my moans find an echo in some generous breast, let him pity me in secret, but never dare to let his voice of sympathy be heard: no, let him not dare, for the men of fortune, strength, and power are against me," he sighed, dropping his defense in a tone to which the public was highly susceptible in the campaign literature of the day. The reproach barely stopped short of arraignment and was all the more crushing for being arrested: no words could have implied more plainly that the President was unwilling to risk a reversal of his verdict on the eve of elections.

The inference was conveyed by the complaint and confirmed by the attack; between the lines of both the public read the familiar charge of machine politics; and the charge, fraught with the full weight and fatal popularity of pain, called the whole justice of Juarez into question. While the Degollado affair remained unsettled, the question it raised could not be begged, and it was never more trying than at that moment. The real question was not why his case had not been brought into court, but why he was to be tried at all. If revolutionary justice required his dismissal, and military discipline his court-martial in a time of stress, what purpose was served, or what motive, when the emergency was over and the war won, in prosecuting a man who was guilty at most of misjudgment, whose error remained abortive, and whose lapse was outweighed by his services? Expediency was justified by its timing; what was necessary yesterday was excessive today; all justice was relative, revolutionary justice was dictated by circumstances, and the circumstances having changed, human justice demanded a higher equity; and it was that justice that was now demanded of Juarez. He had made an example of Degollado—but for what crime? The issue was uncertain, the offense controversial, and the elementary right of self-defense could not be deferred indefinitely without reflecting on his judge. The charge was reversed. Why was Degollado still disgraced? For his own weakness or for that of his case? Was that his real crime? Was he an example of the vindictiveness of the war toward its own champions and the bitterness which it bred among its best sons? Such were the searching questions raised by the delays of the law, and Degollado himself had no doubt of the answer. Persecuted on the presumption of guilt and prosecuted only by the suspension of trial, hounded, without protection but his own pathos, and surfeited with selflessness, he felt himself intolerably wronged and was, in fact, irreconcilable; and when the offer to reinstate him in office was made *sub rosa,* he spurned private satisfaction and held out relentlessly for his public rehabilitation. Although he studiously avoided politics, his case became a political issue, and in one state he was nominated for the Presidency and unanimously elected on a protest vote. His sole title to power was his talent for misfortune, and had he carried more than one state the condition of the country would indeed have been desperate.

For the resuscitation of Degollado was dangerous politically precisely because it produced a sentimental reaction that belittled the President morally. The reasons for the delay of the trial, as Juarez informed the press, were those of legal routine—the transfer of the archives from Veracruz, the assembling of documents, the preparation of the case—but the explanation was unfortunate because it was pedestrian, and the fact that he was satisfied with it produced a painful impression, provoking those who accepted it as a pretext and distressing those who believed it. The worst of it was that it was true. The administration of justice was clogged—the confusion and inefficiency that paralyzed that branch of government defied the most strenuous efforts to reform it and forced Ramirez to resign—but the case of Degollado was not one of ordinary routine. To be slow in circumstances so fatal to the accused was to warrant the belief that it was not the way, but the will, that was wanting to clear him, and the meanest motives were attributed to the President by his detractors. He was accused of aiding and abetting the abuse of a fallen hero, of burying a reputation that menaced his own, and of sealing a case to save an election. The effect of letting the case rest was to convert it into a political trial, and the imputations to which it gave rise were the penalty of its perfunctory conduct. If the failure of Juarez to realize what was expected of him revealed his limitations as a politician, his indifference to such considerations guaranteed his integrity as a magistrate, however, and that was all that mattered to Juarez himself. His justice was impersonal, unaffected by veering moods or changing conditions. If conditions changed, so did persons. Witness Degollado—an unfortunate example of that fact. Would he have ruined himself if men were the same under all circumstances? Was he the man now that he was then? Would the saint have defended himself as the sinner did? He did too much justice to himself not to make the angels weep and the judicious grieve. He weakened his own case by luxuriating in his woes; and the worst of it was that he could not see that he harmed no one but himself by nursing his grievances, that he cheapened his glory by gushing against disgrace, that he cheated compassion by self-pity, that he dishonored by chastening himself like a *meretrix publica,* and that he was turning the fallen hero of the civil war into its heroine. In this phase he was not a serious embarrassment to the President. Men had to be at their best to challenge him. With the same firmness with which he resisted the dictation of Ortega, he ignored the agitation in favor of Degollado, trusting in both cases to the common sense of his public to prove the maturity of their judgment and to hold puerile appeals of hero-worship in place and sentimental impulses in political check.

It was a great deal to expect of any public on the eve of an election. In the course of the campaign the recent past was revived, the civil war was recapitulated, and Juarez himself was faced with heroic comparisons, while the public was torn between conflicting loyalties of principles and persons. Against Ortega he was supported as the personification of the civil power, but it was the principle that triumphed far more than the man, and the prompt submission of Ortega restored the prestige of the soldier with fresh might. Here the rival claims of incorruptible principle and personal glamour appeared to be satisfied in a single man; the rare combination had perhaps been found at last—perhaps, for the proof depended on the process of elimination and the elections were the laboratory—but he might be the blend, and he enjoyed two great advantages over his competitor. Ortega at his best was the hero of a hypothesis and Juarez was a habit. The familiar portrait of the President, everyone knew it, it was a stereotype, unaffected by changing conditions. It neither faded nor gained with familiarity. It was typed for all time, without the subtle modulations of life; it was set once and for all by the war, without graduation or degree by the end of his term in power.

So his war record, reviewed by a paper that followed him from Veracruz to attend the test in the capital, was weighed once more, and the well-known score of his merits and shortcomings rehearsed, before the public went to the polls. "Señor Juarez has much claim to our sympathy," the scorekeeper conceded. "The abnegation of this man in suf-

fering, the faith with which he displayed his image of authority everywhere, the good intentions that inspired him, and other virtues that
unfortunately are purely personal, had won our favor. This man, nevertheless, did not and does not meet the requirements of the revolution,
and we may say that his elevation to the Presidency would be the ruin
not merely of the democratic party but of the nation. Señor Juarez, so
replete with domestic virtues, is unfortunately very deficient in political understanding and can be accepted only as the representative of society, not its ruler. As a ruler, his actions are unfortunately not open to
doubt: his tortuous management, his slight tact, and his obstinacy in
sustaining the contrary of what the people want, are very strong reasons for preventing his ascent to the Presidency. Alien to all the events
that occurred during the struggle with the Reaction, he performed
everywhere, but especially in Veracruz, the role of a mere partisan, re-
ceiving good news and bad together with his companions, without doing a thing to secure their success or to repair their defeat. The Liberal
troops, losing or winning battles in the interior, maintained themselves
practically unaided; inspired by their own enthusiasm and nourished
by their own exertions, they saw in the Juarez government a mere
principle of legality, not an active, intelligent, and protecting government. The name of Juarez was a banner for the revolution, not a man."

But disqualification added one deed to the undone for his final undoing: "He succeeded merely in producing the McLane treaty without
deriving from it the desired resources, and incurring, on the contrary,
the ridicule heaped on us by the Reaction for that negotiation. Don
Benito Juarez, in sum, exhibits merely something good of which he is
not the author, and much evil which owes its origin to his conduct.
Such a man not only does not merit the place of first magistrate, but
should occupy, on the contrary, the bench of the accused to be tried and
punished as he deserves. . . . Señor Ortega," the scorekeeper concluded,
"the democratic party, which chooses you today and proposes you for
the Presidency, trusts that it will not be disappointed, and that you
will not become, like Juarez, the butcher of your own people." The
curse of Comonfort had not worked itself out yet, and Ortega gained
by it. "You are young and full of noble and generous ambitions." To
be Ortega was good; but better yet to be young. To be young amid so
many hoary charges of ineptitude, which had hardened with time into
the common cant of political controversy, was an inestimable advantage. Age could not stale the confirmed habit of those settled complaints, Juarez was still guilty, arch-guilty, of being Juarez, and as he
did nothing even to secure his election, his conviction was confidently
predicted by the good bettors. The best of Ortega, however, was still
his ambition, and the worst of Juarez that everyone knew who he was.
The issue was reduced to simple terms in a cartoon representing Ar-
chimedes, on the one hand, declaring, "Give me a point of leverage

and I will move the world," and Juarez, on the other, proclaiming, with his hands behind his back, "Give me emergency powers and I will do *nothing!*"

Nevertheless, the onus of nonentity had been borne so long by the President that it weighed very little against the unknown, and by dint of repetition the persistent charge of negation had become itself an ineffectual negative. Something more positive appeared to be needed to annihilate a nobody who would not down, and as he continued to defy the laws of political gravity when the campaign drew to a close, something was done: Congress assembled, and a motion was made to impeach the President for treason. The negotiation of the American treaty was hung on his neck, and in a heated debate his friends came to his rescue. They were not many. Fortune and misfortune made friends easily, but no mean courage was needed, and a rare devotion, to champion mediocrity under a capital charge. That uncommon kind of heroism, however, was displayed by Zarco, who rose to his defense and turned the attack to account by shedding light on much that had remained dark in the vexed controversy.

Zarco had left the government and returned to his trade and was free to talk. Although he had not been one of the official family in 1859, he joined it in spirit and belonged to it by the best of all rights, being a militant civilian himself, and he recalled the conditions that had beset them all in 1859 when, as he said, Liberals had been less plentiful than they were now and the country had lain prostrate, overpowered by the Reaction within and blocked by the diplomatic league without. American recognition had been regarded at that time as a hope and an advantage, "the Liberal party expecting that the moral ascendancy of the neighboring Republic, its mercantile interest, and even its physical support might aid the national cause and hasten the triumph of right principles. Though this aspiration was general among the most patriotic and enlightened Liberals, there was one among them who did not share it, who openly refused to call foreign troops to our aid, whether they were of the regular army of the United States or volunteers who, on touching Mexican soil, would renounce their nationality and receive, at the close of the campaign, public lands on which to settle in recompense for their services to their adopted country. The man who thought this expedient contrary to the national dignity, the man who foresaw dangers to its independence in this extreme resource, who did not despair of the Mexican people, believing that alone and without foreign aid they were certain to reconquer their liberties, was the President of the Republic, and thanks to his stubborn and tenacious resistance then, the idea failed. . . . In like manner he combated every idea of loans if, in contracting them, there were any stipulations that involved large international agreements. . . . Señor Juarez earned from many of his friends then the epithets 'stubborn' and 'pertinacious,' and they were later repeated when with the same firmness he refused to accept conciliation with the reactionaries and the mediation of foreign Powers in the settlement of our internal questions. . . . We have said that the President was almost alone in rejecting ideas that were then held by many Liberals, and in saying this we give every man his due. Many military commanders declared that it was indispensable to engage foreign volunteers; some wanted officers as well as troops. Señor Lerdo de Tejada and Governor Zamora shared these ideas, which, we frankly admit, were ours as well, under those trying circumstances. In vain instances were made to the President, in vain the most studied precautions were proposed, so as not to compromise the independence or the dignity of the Republic, in vain the idea was combined with other projects, intertwining it with the need of colonization, or of realizing religious liberty, or of maintaining the nucleus of an armed force after the triumph for the pacification of the country. Señor Juarez rejected all these ideas; he differed with many even of his close friends; in his correspondence he always opposed the project, and, persevering in the struggle, events have justified him; and it is due to him that the Republic has overcome its oppressors without other aid than its own resources."

This testimony went far to clear the personal responsibility of the President, but it fell short of the mark. By analogy much could be argued; by inference, it was absurd to suppose that the man who was so careful not to compromise the independence of his country was so simple-minded as not to see the treasonable lien in the treaty, or, seeing, so faint-hearted as to submit to it and so foolish as to put his head into the noose. But the defense, adroit yet evasive, left the core of impeachment intact—the derelict danger, the deadly evidence of the treaty itself, the haunting treaty, the nightmare of yesterday, the trial of today, which returned to plague its inventors with all the fury of political persecution and which contained too much meat for the vultures to satisfy them with negative pleas of wrongs undone and extenuating circumstances—and on that score Zarco touched very lightly, admitting its vulnerability by begging the question with feeble apologies. "The text of the treaty, whatever may have been its tenor, is no ground for indicting the President of Mexico," he protested, "since it is well known that the right of introducing amendments and modifications exists until ratification is granted"; and "although great concessions were made to the United States," he pleaded, "not all the advantages which they sought were offered, as is proved by the fact that the convention was not approved by the American Senate." And attacking the author of the indictment and carrying the controversy into impalpable regions where no pursuit was possible, "How does Señor Aguirre know," he challenged, "how can the jury know, what were the intentions of Señor Juarez touching the McLane treaty, what modifications he would have proposed if the negotiation had been renewed, to what articles he would have refused his ratification? This simple question destroys all the charges and hopes so ardently voiced by some organs of the press that this incident would suffice to prevent the present holder of the Executive from ascending to the Constitutional Presidency of the Republic." Obviously it did nothing of the sort; but Zarco could do no more. Not having been one of the official family at Veracruz, his testimony was secondhand, and he left the brunt of defense to those who were in a position to know the whole truth, and above all to the man who, as the closest friend and partner of the President, had most interest in protecting his good name. "We are sure that Señor Don Melchor Ocampo," he concluded, "will not let this occurrence pass unnoticed, and that with the frankness that characterizes him he will clarify all the facts."

Congress gave the President a vote of confidence, but the discussion of the treaty remained on the order of the day. The presence of Ocampo was urgently needed to clear him completely—and Ocampo did not answer the call.

5

ON THE same day the *Siglo* carried a small item stating that "a reactionary band led by a certain Cajiga, acting under orders of Marquez, entered the *hacienda* of Pomoca and seized the person of Don Melchor Ocampo. It appears that this gentleman has already been delivered to Marquez, who will probably demand a high ransom for him or will try to murder one of the men most distinguished in the country for his probity and patriotism." The item was printed under the caption "Reactionary Feats," and mentioned several other cases of the same kind in the vicinity of the capital. Since the close of the civil war Marquez and Zuloaga had taken to the mountains, where they mustered several thousand men who eluded pursuit by the local garrisons and kept up appearances by sporadic hostilities in the back country. Leading the lives of outlaws, foraging far and wide, raiding lonely farms, dashing into Cuernavaca to round up horses, emboldened by the absence of police in the outlying valleys and steered by tips from their partisans in the capital, they resorted to the abduction of prominent persons to nourish the remains of their faction and to keep their phantom cause afoot. The repetition of these feats, multiplying with impunity, had already provoked criticism of the government, and it was primarily to meet a danger that had been underestimated and neglected too long that Congress gave the President a vote of confidence, together with arbitrary powers, to enable him to act energetically—without suspending, however, discussion of the treaty. That was accomplished by the capture of Ocampo. The news reached the capital, by a grim coincidence, at the very moment when Juarez needed the helping hand of his mate, and in the ensuing excitement he was saved by the strong arm of Marquez. Every other discussion was drowned in the clamor of alarm that rose from the press and that rekindled the furies of public vengeance of the first days of triumph. "To restore security and save the captured persons there is no measure that is not warranted and that public opinion will not applaud," the *Siglo* declared. "On the frontier, people snatch their women and children from the Apaches and Comanches and war on them like wild beasts. The soldiers of religion have a more odious character than the savages themselves. The circumstances seem to us to warrant the authorities in using actual reprisals and notifying Marquez that, unless his captives are released, the leading men of the Conservative party here will be shot, and that if he exacts ransom it will be paid by the notables of the same faction. We are sworn friends of legality, but not to the extent of seeing society succumb helplessly to bandits."

Acting in that spirit, the government attempted to save the life of Ocampo by taking hostages; as soon as his capture was reported, orders were issued for the apprehension of the mother of Marquez and the wife of Zuloaga. The former escaped, like mother like son; the latter was released for lack of evidence, but being more valuable as a contact than a hostage, she was induced to write a note to her husband interceding for Ocampo. The good offices of M. de Saligny were secured for the same purpose, and the letter was forwarded with his òfficial advice and under diplomatic seal.

Twenty-four hours later, it was too late. At seven in the morning Juarez was informed by Prieto that a *mozo* had gone to the enemy camp and had returned with a report that orders had already been given for Ocampo to be shot. Ransom would have been forthcoming, had it been wanted. For the past fortnight Juarez had been moving every lever to raise money, begging Congress for a million and begrudged a fraction, begging authority to suspend the foreign debt service and denied a hearing, begging private capital for a voluntary loan to avert a forced levy and delay a bleeding; nothing had been done; but for Ocampo blood money would have been found immediately. It was not ransom that was wanted, however, but vengeance: he had signed his own death warrant with the American treaty. Half an hour later Prieto returned with a letter that left no doubt that their old com-

rade had paid the price. The letter, written by Marquez to a correspondent in the capital, lamented the death of Ocampo and washed his
hands of it.

The day that had begun thus darkly developed into a storm, and
Juarez recorded its significant phases in his diary, as they affected him
personally. What comes to mind first in extreme danger? The fundamental in a man, and he was fully conscious of it. "Considering the
powerful sensation that this lamentable calamity will produce in the
people," he wrote, "I gave orders to double the guards at the prisons
and recommended the utmost vigilance to the Governor of the District,
the military commander, Don Leandro Valle, and the Minister of
War"—precautions that were taken none too soon, for the first thought
of the people was also for reprisals. "In a little while the news spread
through the city, and people of all classes came to us demanding that
the political prisoners be executed on the spot and even insisting that,
if the government did not, they and the people would do justice. I did
everything in my power to dissuade these persons from committing the
slightest offense, since as the legal ruler of society I would do everything possible to have the criminals punished according to law, but
would never tolerate violence against accused persons who were under
the protection of the law and the authorities. That they must bear in
mind that those who sacrificed my loyal friend, Señor Ocampo, were
murderers, and that I was the ruler of an enlightened society. Señores
Don Leandro Valle and Don Aureliano Rivera witnessed this act."
The entry had a testamentary ring, the solemnity of a sworn will duly
witnessed and vouched, the conscientiousness of a creed, and the solitude and self-consciousness of imminent peril. He put himself on record; what was fundamental came uppermost—the sacred trust of society, civilization, law—and the whole man lay there in the legacy of
legality about to be overborne.

The precaution was warranted. The prisons were surrounded by
maddened crowds demanding the surrender of the political prisoners,
and above all of the arch-scapegoat Isidoro Diaz, whose trial had been
pending for five months and whose fate would have been settled on the
spot but for Leandro Valle, who rode through the throngs and bore
witness with an arm and a voice raised wherever they were needed to
the pledge of the President. Authority was delegated to this young officer, who had defended him well on other occasions, at Guadalajara, at
Santa Ana Acatlan when he was attacked by Landa, at the Convent of
the Sisters of Charity when the law was assailed by M. de Saligny, and
who saved the day for him once more on the morning of June 4. It was
not necessary for Juarez himself to descend into the streets, as once he
had done in Oaxaca, to quell a mutiny with nothing but a stick in his
hand and his hand behind his back. Valle was young, intrepid, and
popular; he succeeded in checking the mobs if not in taming them,

and while he held the popular fury at bay, Juarez continued to commit its pressure to paper and to register the salient facts that struck him on that sinister day. The day was only half over, and the popular ferment, unspent, found an outlet in another channel. "The effervescence increased with the assembling of Congress, which decreed various measures, one of them being to empower the government to raise resources by whatever means it saw fit. Señor Degollado appeared before Congress, seeking permission to join the campaign, to which Congress consented on condition that the trial to which he is subject continue." But the bald words of the diary were unequal to what followed.

The dramatic irruption of Degollado was the culminating event of the day, provoking a scene to which the professional pen of the press alone could do justice, and to which it could hardly bear witness, being a mere plume in the wind. In Congress the mob spirit also prevailed. Before the session opened, the lobbies echoed with another riot, anarchic in the streets, antiparliamentary in the Palace. "A triumvirate, a Convention, a reign of terror, and a thousand other such ideas were discussed as political inspirations appropriate to the occasion," the congressional record noted. "The public showed that it shared to the utmost the universal indignation, and although it voiced it at times in a manner not very consonant with the dignity of the Assembly, the rules, which have spoken with much less reason on other occasions, remained mute in the hands of the chairman." The death notice, the authentic thing written by Marquez, the mocking apology which he flipped in their faces, was produced and flung, thick with blood, to a house full of law-baiters, and bedlam broke loose. Up to the last man in the press gallery booing, groaning, gasping, the whole house "broke into a roar of rage as the letter was read in which the monster who makes a profession of predatory killing sheds crocodile tears for his victim and in the name of humanity recommends an end to the savage and barbarous character of the war."

Down from the roof and up from the floor a dense clamor battled back and forth, finally cut short by the Minister of War, who dinned into the ears of the penned audience a reminder that precious time was passing and that, if funds were voted, within twenty-four hours eight thousand men would round up the gangs in the hills. At this point the chair interrupted and read a note from Degollado, begging a few minutes' hearing. In that heavily charged atmosphere the effect was electrical: the debate halted, and what went before was as nothing to the sensation he created merely by sending in his card. Even the pages of the congressional record breathed, and breathed deep, in their tense transcript: "Señor Degollado appears in the hall. The assembly rises to its feet, the galleries burst into prolonged applause and clamorous cheers. Silence being restored, Señor Degollado takes the floor and says that he has come to ask two kinds of justice: one against the perpetrators of the dastardly murder that has just stricken the Liberal party, the other for himself, so that he be convicted or acquitted in the trial instituted against him, and allowed to fight the Reaction not as an officer, but as a simple soldier. He swears by the shade of Ocampo that he will never rise to power, and that his one wish is to go to war, not to drag defenseless citizens from their homes and murder them, but to fight the assassins hand to hand; and he wonders that the city is quiet and is not roused by an impulse of rage and execration against the monsters who have sacrificed one of the most illustrious citizens of the Republic. He leaves the hall amid the din of the public that tries to hold him back."

The ovation continued in Congress, one member moving that the Assembly constitute itself a Grand Jury forthwith and declare that Citizen Santos Degollado had never forfeited the confidence of the nation, another challenging the House to decide, once and for all, whether his fate was to be oblivion or glory, a third moving heaven and earth to cry aye, and the redundant galleries rising and re-echoing him and calling the roll themselves in the thickening congestion of mounting enthusiasm. When someone objected to overruling the trial, they shouted him down with cries of *"mocho"* and "reactionary," while down below roar after roar rose, claiming parliamentary sanctuary for Degollado, acclaiming him, booming him, exonerating him, dilapidating the law courts, wrecking the prison of the unwritten law, demolishing the penitentiary of the popular will; and there were no protests when one orator denounced his persecution by the Palace as hack politics and republican backsliding to the Bourbon policy of *divide and rule*. Thereupon Degollado returned to the hall. He did not mean to surprise the Assembly, he said, but merely to rehabilitate himself in order to bear arms, and he proposed that his acquittal be not declared, but only his permission to serve. This gallantry completed his triumph, and though the vote was taken on the terms he proposed and carried by acclamation, there was no doubt in that dense jury that his trial had been definitely killed.

Effervescence—seething in the streets, fermenting in the Assembly— the word with which Juarez labeled both outbursts of the popular temper was significant of his own. Effervescence, an explosion of volatile feeling that threatened the fundamentals he was sworn to defend. The demonstration in Congress he noted in his diary as a statement of fact, like an item of bookkeeping, but it was none the less eloquent and appropriate. A score had been settled, an account closed. A council of war was immediately called, and Degollado attended it. As they sat there side by side, their positions were strangely reversed: both under the shadow of trial, but one already absolved by popular verdict and the other still threatened with impeachment, they plunged into the discussion of military plans and tacitly buried the past, brought together by the galvanizing force of the corpse of Ocampo.

But the day of reckoning was not yet over, and that afternoon an incident occurred that Juarez included among his major ordeals because it provoked his temper and betrayed the strain under which he was laboring. The diplomatic corps called on him in a body to intercede for the political prisoners and begged him to suspend the summary execution that they had learned was scheduled for that night. This was too much even for the schooled temper of Juarez. The appeal was not only uncalled for, but offensive in form, the dean declaring that they had decided to make a concerted plea "for the good and honor of the government itself, as they did not wish to see it on the same level as Zuloaga and Marquez, who were bandits." His reply was sharp, and committed to his diary, where he digested it wrathfully. "They were informed with the proper energy"—and when he was stung he had energy to spare—"that the Mexican Government, understanding its duty and dignity, had never thought of proceeding, nor would permit others to act, in a barbarous manner against persons under the shelter and protection of the law and the authorities; that I greatly regretted that they had formed so poor an opinion of the Republic, judging it capable of so base and degrading a deed, and that they had accepted as true a rumor spread by the rabble; and I desired them to withdraw an idea so offensive to the first authority of the country." Whereupon his monitors apologized profusely and withdrew. The diplomats were the last to learn who Juarez was, being a credulous rabble, but they recognized their mistake, and the day ended in a complete vindication of civilization and legality. Then, and then only, was he free to think of Ocampo, and he sent for his body.

In the crowding events and swift succession of crises produced by his fate, Ocampo himself had been all but buried; but in the next few days reports of his passion and death began to drift in, and the tragedy was slowly reconstructed. Living in the seclusion of his estate, busy with his books, his plants, his poor, and his frugal occupations, he had steadily ignored the warnings that reached him more than once that marauding bands were roaming the valley and that he was not as completely forgotten as he supposed. Nevertheless, he was troubled one evening, while the household was at supper, by a sound of scraping on the walls and ordered the women into the cellar while he went out to search the grounds; and though he discovered nothing tangible, he caught the echo of hooves and voices vanishing in the dark. An hour later a neighbor called with news that a reactionary band was heading his way and urged him to flee. "What have I to fear?" he had the simplicity to reply. "I have never harmed anyone." The following morning he refused

to accompany his daughters to the neighboring town of Maravatio for
the feast of Corpus Christi, and he took leave of them without a fonder
farewell than usual. When they were gone, however, his forebodings
returned. His housekeeper was worried by the appearance of a stranger
who put up with them for a few hours and whom she suspected of being a scout, his horse being branded on the rump with the "R" of religion, and she persuaded her master to leave. He ordered his horse to
be saddled, but the man accounted for his mount with a plausible story,
and Ocampo sent his own back to the stable, doubly disturbed because
he had doubted and because he was not reassured. The next morning
it was noticed that he was more than usually melancholy, idle, and silent. Since he had retired from public life, he had indulged his philosophical habits of mind to the full: one was a ready resignation to misfortune, and another a melancholy that verged on misanthropy; but to
the latter he had not yet succumbed, and he found comfort in the
other. He sat down to the midday meal without appetite, and when his
overseer sighted the raiders he went to the window and watched their
approach through the shutters, and he was still there when he was captured. He offered the leader the hospitality of his table—a last gesture
of dignity, which produced no impression. He was placed on a hack
with half a saddle, no reins, and a halter for a bridle, and the party set
off at a brisk pace.

At the first halt, a few miles from the *hacienda,* he was hailed by
some neighbors on their way to visit him, and he borrowed a pair of
chaps from one of them. With his customary consideration he turned
their attention into a local jest. "No one will believe that I am from
Michoacan, my boy," he said, "for you know very well that the padres
wear chaps when they give the Viaticum." The hint went no further,
and though his neighbors caught it, they could do nothing. Friends
he had all along the way, and all equally helpless. In Maravatio, where
every other man was his acquaintance, he spent the night in the inn,
under guard, and the best that his friends there could do was to send
an appeal to Marquez the next morning—after he was gone. Five
months after the close of the civil war there were no police in the
region, and the inhabitants took cover when the party appeared and
remained at a respectful distance until it moved on. For two days he
rode through a land he knew and loved as a naturalist—a land of vast
unpeopled spaces, of virgin wildernesses and lawless solitudes, where
Marquez was merely a primitive survival and Zuloaga a zoological
specimen—and on the third he was brought into their den. Here he
was held for another day while they disputed his last one. Marquez
proposed to shoot him immediately, but Zuloaga insisted on legal
formalities; the primitive insisted that Ocampo was already convicted
by the American treaty, but the specimen, who still styled himself
President of Mexico, insisted that sentence be passed only after a pre-

liminary trial; and their differences were still unsettled when the troop moved on to the village of Tepeji del Rio the next morning.

Here Ocampo was lodged in the inn, and informed that his journey had ended. He drew up a will, which closed with the words, "I die believing that I have done as much for the service of my country as in my conscience I believed to be good." Even then, and there, he found friends. A Liberal *guerrillero* having been captured that morning and summarily sentenced by Marquez, the local notables interceded for his life and won a reprieve; emboldened by their success, they appealed for Ocampo as well, but they were denied, although they were led by a priest who honored the religion branded on the rump of a horse. The priest was denied the favor of redeeming it even by the victim, who refused the last rites and waived all further formalities. "I am well with God, Father," Ocampo said, "and God is well with me." At two in the afternoon he was ridden out into the open country, and at the appointed place he dismounted and performed the customary rites of such occasions himself, distributing his remaining belongings to his last friends, the firing squad. The relics were few and poor, but the captain drew his borrowed chaps, and he found one last *peso* for a little bugler whom he had overlooked, and no one had been neglected when he took his place and the muzzles were raised level with his silence. There was a discharge, and as the convulsions that were Ocampo lashed the dust, another was fired to silence their indignities. Then the immediate heirs ran a rope under the armpits and hastened to drag the weight of a human life of which they were eager to be rid to a tree, where they hoisted it on a dead limb and left it, by order of Marquez. Through the long summer afternoon the peasants on their way home from market watched it gravitating unably toward the ground, unable to reach and forbidden to touch it; for the limb was withered and not the fruit.

The first to feel its weight was Zuloaga. When the *guerrillero* had been brought in that morning, Zuloaga had agreed to shoot him, and he was working over some papers found on the captive, confident that his orders to hold Ocampo for trial had been obeyed, when an orderly entered and reported that the prisoner had been shot. "What prisoner?" asked Marquez. "Why—Señor Ocampo," the man stammered. Furious that his authority had been flouted, the ex-President sprang to his feet and gave orders that the responsible officer should be court-martialed; but these orders also were disregarded, Marquez insisting that it was all a mistake, and though Zuloaga realized that he had been tricked, he was forced to swallow it to preserve his authority. How much of a mistake they both realized when they received the letters of intercession from Señora Zuloaga and M. de Saligny. Marquez lost no time in repairing it, writing by return courier the letter of exculpation that raised such a storm in the capital; but Zuloaga at

least realized that it was irreparable. It was the bitterest day of his
life, he said, and his life had known many. He was incapable of killing
a chicken, as one of his officers said, but he could not prove it. By then
the specimen and the primitive were too busy washing their hands to
notice what became of Ocampo. The body was cut down by the villagers and brought in after nightfall, and by daybreak anyone could
claim it, Marquez having decamped with his President at his heels.

Four days later the remains were interred in the capital with national
honors. The flags flew at half-mast, the government donned mourning
for nine days, and the weight that was Melchor Ocampo was distributed in the hearts of the thousands who crowded the cemetery; and
there it was transubstantiated into a seething and restless afterlife far
more potent than the life he had shed. The fury of the first day, subsiding in the tumult that relieved it, revived at the funeral and was
kindled afresh by the obituaries and fanned into flame by the details,
the conjectures, the confirmations of the manner in which he died.
"Señor Ocampo, who placed his personal dignity above everything,
must have suffered much," it was surmised, "from the humiliations
to which his assassins subjected him. Perhaps his characteristic pride
triumphed at the end and he returned insult for insult and humiliation for humiliation. This would account for the precipitation with
which he was killed." The theory was confirmed by powder burns on
the face, showing that he had been shot at close range, and pious pens
wrote an avenging amen across it and vowed to retaliate in kind.
But, above all, it was the tree—a tree, as someone said, twisted and
tricked into a cross—and the load hanging from it and yearning in
vain for the ground, that haunted the public mind: that last gratuitous
indignity could not be borne or buried. The burning columns of the
press towered over it night and day, Congress placed a price on the
heads of the outlaws, the government proscribed them, but every day
their reappearance was reported at some new point, and provocation
and impunity goaded the most active agitators in the capital to incite
the countryside to a general man hunt. The murder of Ocampo reopened all the unsettled scores of the civil war, the nightmare returned,
the terror revived, and the letter of Marquez, deploring its latest victim, recalled so clearly his like evasion of the massacre of Tacubaya
that both atrocities were fastened on him by the weight of mass evidence; his mate was forgotten, and the hue and cry of the hurrying
man hunt singled out as the one unforgivable felon of the civil war
the little man whose instincts ran on four legs and who still reared
himself on two.

The inextinguishable invocation of vengeance testified to the veneration in which Ocampo was held far more than to the survival of his
spirit among those who partook of his passion and death; but the

memory of a man who had lived and died without malice was honored by mercy as well. At the height of the agitation one paper had the temerity to mention the treaty that bore his name, but it was instantly silenced, and Congress, though it did not formally dismiss the controversy, buried it as finally as the trial of Degollado. There the remains of Ocampo rested; the curse was lifted; and the vexed treaty which had been meat for vultures a week before became for all time food for bookworms.

That Ocampo was captured within close range of the capital and encountered no rescue during the four days of his abduction was a striking demonstration of the powerlessness of the government beyond the limits of the city. No effort was spared to repair it, but the measures hastily taken on the morrow of the crime were themselves a humiliating admission of weakness. Every available resource had to be mustered to hunt down a fugitive band of guerrillas, regular troops mobilized, a full-scale campaign planned, and money found to place the government once more on a war-footing; and as the indemnity due to the British Legation had drained the Treasury, the President authorized a forced loan to launch the expedition. These were the humble tributes which he paid to his friend. At the funeral he was silent, leaving eloquence to the orators, who were legion; his homage took the form of bleeding the public of fifty thousand *pesos* to avenge him. It was a week before the expedition could start—an intolerable delay in the feverish pace of public feeling—and without waiting for the main body under Ortega, Degollado dashed ahead with a flying column.

Five days later, while he was being dunned by the Minister of War for another forced loan, Juarez was notified that he had been elected President of the Republic. He noted the fact in his journal as part of the day's work, among miscellaneous memoranda, jotting down the figures with which Congress had cleared his election—five votes—without further comment. That he left to others. Though he had carried the country by an absolute majority, the Opposition attempted to challenge the verdict and to throw the election into Congress, but the maneuver raised an issue—hotly discussed at the time—of how far parliamentary bodies with their cliques, their coalitions, and their intrigues represent the popular will; and Congress ratified the choice of the people, although by so narrow a margin that the question remained unsettled. The result, nevertheless, was a vindication of the elected and the electors alike, and it was all the more remarkable because, as Zarco observed, the President had not lifted a finger to secure a single vote or to defeat the electoral schemes directed against him, and had given the press unlimited liberty, suppressed its subventions, and sued none of his slanderers in court.

So spontaneous a victory was an unprecedented triumph for the democratic process in Mexico, but it was celebrated with a sobriety that led many to believe that the people were disappointed and discouraged—as they were, but not by the sound issue of the electoral urns. The absence of festivities, which also excited comment, was circumstantial evidence of a deeper depression; the public had come of age, a sobering process in itself, and under circumstances of extraordinary gloom. "In the present state of public affairs, a self-respecting people cannot indulge in demonstrations of joy before the bloody shade of Ocampo, cannot celebrate festivities when it knows that society is in danger and that great efforts must be made to save it," Zarco reminded the diehards who compared the drab advent of Juarez with the illuminations and eulogies lavished on Santa Anna, Zuloaga, and Miramon. "Señor Juarez has done well to favor no farces on his assumption of the first magistracy of the country, to make no gifts, no donations, no pledges with the public money; and those who supported his candidacy have shown him a sign of respect in not repeating the flattery and adulation with which other governments have been inaugurated." More unprecedented yet, he had cut his salary. The scrutiny was a trophy that confirmed the qualities of the man—decency, public spirit, and a complete absence of pose—and he met the expectations of his public by continuing to work quietly and steadily, with the electoral campaign out of the way, on the only campaign that mattered, under the pall that hung over the capital. The consensus of opinion was that the country had made a safe choice; and a tremendous premium was placed upon safety in June 1861.

The election returns diverted attention for a few days from the pursuit of Marquez, and the papers were still dilating on its significance when there appeared, amid the large meditations spread formally over the front pages, another of those small items that caught the eye, and the breath, of the reader, like a blood spot. Buried on the back pages, and couched in the cautious and considerate phrases due to the susceptibilities of the public, it reported the disappearance of Degollado. A raw rumor one day, it was a full-grown fact the next: his division had fallen into an ambush, he had been deserted and killed. His body was missing, and so for a few days was the comment of the press. Coming so close on the death of Ocampo, this fresh casualty caused a shock no less profound, but different in effect; the response was slower, dulled by the first blow, stunned by the second, and deadened by a numbing sense of fatality. His fate was felt to be the consummation of a career vowed to disaster, and was accepted with mute relief that a life so incurable had been arrested at last. Misfortune, mortification, disgrace, desertion, death—nothing remained for the complete fulfillment of his destiny but its transfiguration; and that morbid duty was devoutly performed. The rehabilitation hastily begun before his death was amply completed after it, and the response, when it came, rose with the cumulative force of common compunction, discharging a debt long overdue.

The obituaries were both an apology and an apotheosis. "Señor Don Santos Degollado, the immaculate patriot, the purest and noblest incarnation of the ideas of democracy and reform, has ceased to exist"— Zarco led the responses of the press in halting words attuned to the muffled pulse of prostration and dismay. "Merely to know that Degollado no longer exists is to realize that another calamity impends on our country. The soldier of the people, the most distinguished champion of progressive ideas, has ceased to exist. . . ." The desperate repetition dragged on flatly, unable to rise above the crushing fact, rehearsing it over and over in a hypnotic daze, and shifting it to a future free to cherish his death as it deserved. "The name of Degollado will be pronounced by generations to come with veneration and tenderness, as we pronounce those of Hidalgo and Morelos"—and then compunction quickened, and while the hushed tone of the pantheon relayed his apotheosis to a remote posterity peopled with juster men, the dry reiteration of the litany labored to raise the weight of leaden neglect with which his memory was still laden today. "Though fortune was frequently adverse to him on the fields of battle, his spirit was of the antique temper; he never lost hope in the cause of justice and liberty, and his consistency is all the more admirable and heroic because he fought not only against adversity, but also, we are forced to admit, against envy and calumny. But the truth is that without Degollado the leaders who were more fortunate would never have appeared, and but for the defeat of Tacubaya we would never have known the victory of Calpulalpam." The homage was heavy with humiliation and honored the hero whose mortifications it rehearsed by valuing them as he did. The capture of the *conducta* was recalled as a hallowing stigma. "More could not be done by the man who was probity itself than to plead guilty and sacrifice everything for his country. No one has carried patriotism and abnegation so far."

Echoing Degollado to the letter, the mourner made the supreme atonement and offered him the absolute satisfaction of accepting him at his own unqualified estimate. If flaws there were, they were decently veiled and mutely glossed over: there was no frailty in the flesh, no infatuation with misfortune, no fallacy in martyrdom, no pose in self-pity; whatever might mar the transparent truth was effaced by the clean breath of death. His transgressions were forgotten and his errors exonerated in his own spirit, and the devout zeal of the disciple unfleshed the master and made full amends for his worldly mortification. The cloud of his dealings with Mathew was cleared by the dark, for there are no clouds in the dark; and what shone forth in the shadows was his last gallant crusade for Ocampo. "We can still hear the accents of grief and enthusiasm with which he addressed Congress only a few days ago. As Degollado himself said then, let us not offer these victims womanish tears. His shades demand more: they demand energy, they exact justice, and nothing but justice." And on that firmly held note the meditation, moving to its own subdued music, closed. More compensation the most injured could not demand of mortality, more Degollado Degollado himself could not exact from it, and his exit was the *ne plus ultra*. The unerring pursuit of disaster by which Marquez lured him to his ultimate destination secured his transfiguration. All his old friends vied with one another in contrition. "You who trembled at the tears of a child, you who imposed on yourself the privations of a cenobite lest you squander the farthings of the poor, you who were the sanctity of the Revolution"—Prieto apostrophized him, penitent for his own apostasy. Ramirez, the iconoclast, proclaimed him his idol. Exceptions there were none; he was sanctified by common consent; the very surfeit of tribute strained to deny desertion and to forget the fatigue with misfortune which had drained sympathy dry before his death. Congress completed the consecration by discharging his trial with a posthumous decree of national gratitude. The decree was sent to the President, who published it after a noticeable delay, which left the impression of perfunctory acknowledgment of the general verdict. The immortality of Degollado, however, had long since been taken out of his hands, and he paid him the same tribute as to Ocampo, digging down into the pockets of the public for another appropriation, and with results even more melancholy.

The most shocking feature of the disaster was that Degollado had been deserted by his men; some said that one of them shot him in the back. Surrounded, outnumbered, trapped, they were dispersed because they were demoralized, and defeated because they were unpaid. The cult of glory required cash, and the multiplication of heroes regular meals. The engagement occurred in the passes of the Monte de las Cruces, where Hidalgo had flung his untrained hordes against regular troops fifty years before and had won out by sheer weight of spirit— a feat cruelly reversed by the defeat of Degollado on hallowed ground half a century later. What had been gained, what had been lost, in the interval? Another name had been added to the national pantheon: Don Santos had ascended into the empyrean with his peers. A legendary remoteness shrouded his fate, but there was nothing legendary about the rout of his followers or remote in their desertion. Signs of panic appeared in Congress when it was learned that a shipment of arms had been turned back at Veracruz for failure to pay; a delegation waited on the President, who informed them that there were arms enough in the city, but no funds with which to purchase them. Nevertheless, by dint of scraping and extortion, two thousand rifles were procured for the national guard. A new avenger volunteered, and five days after the death of Degollado, Leandro Valle took the same road at the head of eight hundred men.

But the pace of disaster was swifter than the speed with which it was repaired. The following day the back pages began bleeding again, and twenty-four hours later Valle was defeated and dead. The action occurred almost on the same ground, in the treacherous passes of the Monte de las Cruces, but this time the disaster was not due to improvidence or pinched bellies or poor generalship or the obscure curse that dogged the hero of defeat; on the contrary, there were abundant reports of a hard-fought battle and the ability with which Valle made a stand against superior numbers; and he was not deserted by his men. The droves of dead were there to prove it. They were too numerous and too nameless to be mourned in the public prints or mustered into the national pantheon, which was a privileged place with no room for the many and less and less space for the few, and already overcrowded; but for Valle in an especial manner the press raised its black banner, because he comprehended them all in their common pit. The name of Leandro Valle was not, like those of Ocampo and Degollado, one to conjure with; yet it cast a deeper spell on the public. He had the supreme appeal of youth, which supplied its own apotheosis. Cut off in his prime, when the current was flowing full in his veins, he met death with the zest of the green and the vigor of the veteran. When he was told that he was to be shot, he turned his moment to account and, choosing his tree, fell scoffing at his assassins in the style attributed to Ocampo; and by way of retort, they hung him on the trunk where he belonged.

The trunk was severed, and the body of which he had made a banner was left hanging there at half-mast, where the trail of the wilderness crossed the highroad to Mexico; and at half-mast the colors hung in the capital, waiting for the nation at large, and no other avenger, to answer the taunt. Zarco dipped his pen to write a rousing call to the reddening colors. "To kill such a man, and to treat him as a traitor, and a traitor to religion!" he raged, recalling the vigor with which only a few days before Valle had prevented the mobbing of the political prisoners. "Who speaks of religion? The beasts, the tigers of Tacubaya! And the ministers of religion accept such apostles apparently, for their lips hold gall enough to defend their property and their privileges, but they have uttered not one word to repudiate such support or to rebuke abduction, murder, and arson! A bishop cannot be silent when a cleric seeks permission of the civil authorities to legitimize his children, but the entire clergy is mute in the face of these crimes and has no censures for those who raise the cross as the standard of murder and crime or for the priests who fight in the reactionary gangs! But censures they had, and tremendous ones, for

the first insurgents who proclaimed our independence from Spain!
The Inquisition, the bishops, the chapters, thundered against the patriots and insisted that there were no privileges for them. These are
facts to which history is a witness." Witnesses were not wanting
either then or now to the timeless and untamed treason of the Church
to Christ and its tacit consent to any atrocity that served the Faith
and fouled its trust; and the blasphemous silence with which the
clergy sanctioned the latest crusade in their favor compelled the popular tribune to wield the scourge on behalf of a cowed people. Never
had the Monte de las Cruces been so close to the heart of Mexico since
Hidalgo stood there, scanning the promised land, and turned back;
the death of the youngest flung the whole nation back to its beginning
and telescoped its history in the generation nailed one by one to the
tree. "And this party of assassins proposed to form a government and
to dominate the people!" Zarco cried. "Marquez has released all those
who witnessed the murder of Valle to spread terror and has charged
them to tell us in Mexico that this is nothing, that we have no notion
as yet of his savagery. This beast promises to shoot, hang, murder,
all the notables of the Liberal party, to kill all who have acquired
nationalized property, and to put into shackles the insignificant who
merely profess democratic beliefs and set them to work rebuilding the
dens of the convents! Here is his political and religious program!"

The cup overflowed. More than Ocampo, more than Degollado, the
loss of Valle stirred the depths; it reached down into the womb of
unborn generations and smothered their existence, and the blight of
the future and the waste of the past made the popular temper implacable. The name of Valle conjured up the call of the blood, and
the nakedness of the seed, as no other could. His murder was more
fanatical than that of Ocampo, his fatality more formidable than that
of Degollado, and his tree more forbidding and more far-reaching
than theirs. He was all that was never to be, born but for barren death,
and now, under the shadow of what was seen to be a systematic campaign of intimidation, terror, naked terror, began to stir in the very
vitals of a society stalked and ruled by it, and stifled by its inability
to retaliate. "The extermination of the bandits, the action of justice,
the salvation of order and liberty"—the exhortations with which Zarco
concluded the call were feeble, were tame, with repetition. It was
clear that the strength of the enemy had been underestimated and that
Marquez was supported by more than audacity.

On the very day after the kill the suburbs of the capital were raided
by a flying detachment of the rebels, and they were beaten off not
half an hour from the center of the city. The alarm was enough to
recall Gonzalez Ortega from the field and to halt the pursuit: he was
advised not to risk a clash with the main body. But where was the
main body? Within the walls or without? The recurring provocations,

the power that waxed with impunity, the acceleration of pace, the studied terror, and the taunting threats of worse to follow, proclaimed unseen support, prospects, accomplices, and the search for them started. The public, profoundly unnerved, was prodded by a press sleeplessly ringing the knell and the tocsin, dinning day in and day out the warning that no one was safe, that henceforth every man was marked, repeating that there were persons in the capital who openly threatened the Liberal party as a whole with the fate of the elect, re-echoing others who derided the debility of the government and compared the justice of Marquez, who needed only a pistol, a rope, and a tree, with the trammels of the courts strangled in writs and chicaneries, and harking back to the fact that six months after the capture of the capital the ministers of Miramon were still unpunished and glorying in the legal guarantees they enjoyed and the accommodations so freely provided by the government.

If the smell of massacre was not in the air, it was in the papers, and Valle was not there to check it. His body was brought in unobtrusively on a gun carriage, with others collected on the mountain, and would have passed unnoticed but for an accident. His mother happened to pass the hearse, and, on learning whose it was, she flung herself on the coffin, forced open the lid, and embraced the remains, oblivious to the crowd that collected and the sensation she caused. The contents of the casket, exposed by chance, were deliberately drawn forth and cherished by the press. Preserved from putrefaction by the draining of the veins, the relics were still immune to the seasoning of time, and the tortures of extinction intact. One eye was closed, the other open, and the body was riddled by seventeen bullet holes, like pores through which the vision of his ordeal transpired. The arms, grotesquely twisted by suspension, had stiffened into the posture of a foetus reaching for life, and the whole shriveled creature resembled something between the embryo and the mummy of a man. The lid was lifted on the image of an abortive generation and closed without comment. Morbid reflections were lost in the onrush of violent resolutions.

So ended the month of June. Three such casualties in succession would have shaken any regime, and under the onrush of rising panic the government was, if not foundering, visibly cracking. A cabinet could not be formed, the coveted posts went begging, public service was provisional, and Juarez was goaded to govern by decree and to meet the emergency with the drastic measures necessary to retain national confidence. Zarco, as his stoutest champion, headed the demand, insisting that legality could be preserved only by arbitrary methods and civilization only by exceptional sanctions, and underwriting the prescription with a program—martial law, permanent councils of war, reprisals, instantaneous justice, mobilization of every resource, and the raising of money by any means sanctioned by Congress, which had already given him unlimited license. "The task is not long nor arduous; it is a matter of seven million men defending themselves against two thousand assassins," he insisted. "A week of severity will save the situation."

And three weeks later the President met the demand for extreme measures. Roused by the sting of a pygmy, the nation heaved like a giant against its bonds, which were unbreakable because they were foreign bonds. The indispensable condition of energy was control of the national resources; a beginning had been made by suspending payment on the internal debt, but the crushing burden from which there was no release was the foreign debt, and under stress of the crisis the proposal to dump it revived. The idea launched by Zamacona two months before appeared in Congress in the first days of July and was adopted in secret session and passed on to the President. In that atmosphere of brewing panic the buoyance of his trial balloon carried Zamacona to office. Called to the Foreign Ministry to convoy the measure he had so fearlessly sponsored in his sanctum, he shrank from the risks and responsibilities of its passage, however, and it required all the persuasion, the insistence, and the authority of the President to induce him to sign it. But the pilot silenced his misgivings. The risks were common and the responsibilities collective: the heroic remedy originated in a general recognition of its necessity. Passing from mind to mind, begging for adoption, diffused in the public, discussed in the press, debated in Congress, shunned and postponed, developing with the drift to disaster, maturing in the deadly month of June, and coming at last, sanctioned by the dead, into the hands of the President to be applied as a measure of public safety, the mandate was unanimous. Precipitated by an immediate crisis, but prescribed by a permanent infirmity and premeditated as an organic cure, the moratorium was converted, like the Reform Laws, from a passing expedient into an act of incalculable consequence. On July 17 Juarez issued a decree suspending payment on the foreign debt service. It was a second and more dangerous declaration of national independence, and it was made without consulting the creditor powers. A week later the French Minister severed, and the British Minister suspended, relations with Mexico.

6

DEBT suspension placed Mexico beyond the pale of civilized nations. The sentence it provoked was as formidable as the excommunication incurred by the Reform Laws. A canon had been broken as basic to the creed of modern civilization as the ecclesiastical covenant had been to the feudal culture of the past, and henceforth the forces of the world to which Mexico aspired by its progress and those of the society to which it still belonged by its backwardness were leagued against the government guilty of defying them both. Before those forces began to move, however, there was a brief period when their agents were free to guide their direction and to mold the destinies of the country at their discretion; and during that period persons were of capital importance.

Neither the French nor the British Minister was caught unprepared for the shock. The shape of things to come had cast a long shadow ahead, and its deepening density had developed into an inky cloud in their despatches. M. de Saligny, in particular, had primed his government and prepared it for drastic measures of its own by a series of tendentious reports, depicting conditions in Mexico as the ferment of an advanced stage of "social decomposition" that would eventually require intervention. In April, when the only ferment was normal agitation of an electoral campaign, he called for French fleets to patrol the coasts in anticipation of another revolution. In May, when nothing abnormal developed, he fell back on the crime wave and the preference of the assassins for foreigners. In June, when the crime wave carried off Ocampo, and all foreign claims but the British were ignored, he called for another injunction "to support the justice of our claims by force, if necessary." By the first week of July the approaches of panic and financial paralyzation were so close that he could not collect even the legitimate claims acknowledged a few months before, the Jecker business was stalled, the conduct of the government was unconscionable, and he was more than ever convinced, he wrote, "that force alone can compel this government to honor its pledges to ours." A fortnight later the crash came. For month after month he had sent up distress signals and wrought himself to the pitch of outrage that civilized people require before they can conscientiously resort to violence, and when the crisis was reached the groundwork was well laid. With unerring accuracy M. de Saligny had anticipated the collapse, and he acted with unhesitating confidence in breaking relations: he was covered. That he waited a week was due to the lag of his colleague, for the support of the British Minister was essential to his purpose, and their interests were allied but not identical.

His purpose was not clear until it was accomplished. He came to Mexico, he said later, *pour casser des vitres*. His official mission, however, was not to smash windows; that was the consequence of his failure. The systematic incitements he sent to Paris were dictated by the interests he represented and the combinations he served. His mission was important only because of the commissions it carried, his interests were many and various, he was adept at combinations of all kinds, his mind ran naturally to mergers and pools, and he was teeming with ideas when he left Paris. Investment in the Louisiana Tehuantepec Company was a scheme that had much to recommend it on more than one account; he proposed it to the Foreign Office as a feasible means of turning American enterprise to account in a field attractive to French interests by professional alliance with a powerful competitor; but it was a useful connection for other reasons as well. He counted on American as well as British and French support to force recognition of the Jecker bonds, because of the facilities which they offered for cheating the customs; cut rates opened an easy diplomatic channel for the affair, and the pool a pressure which would favor his negotiation. The hopes he held out to Elsesser were based on the prospect of bringing an international financial offensive to bear on the Mexican Government; and the promises he made to his clerical clients to do great things for Mexico were inspired by the same calculations.

All his combinations had one feature in common—an opportunity to exploit the difficulties of the Liberals. Nevertheless, before leaving Paris, he had listened to a friend who attempted to influence him in their favor, and he left France with a mind more or less open—open, that is, to the main chance. A diplomat on the make, M. de Saligny did not allow his partialities to prejudice his prospects or his sympathies to interfere with his success. On his way through Washington he assured the acting head of the Mexican Legation there that the Emperor had no *prévention* against his government, though the McLane treaty led him to think the opposite party the more patriotic; on his arrival in Veracruz he was agreeably surprised to find the Liberals amenable to his advances; and it was not until he met with insurmountable difficulties in Mexico that he began to indulge his itch for window smashing. All his initiatives had come to nothing—the Tehuantepec business was war-logged, the Jecker business was stalled, the protection of his clerical clients was no business of France—but every calamity has its compensations. M. de Saligny was never at a loss for ideas, the difficulties of the Mexican Government were the salvation of his own, and he exploited them relentlessly. Scenting bigger game, he seized the opportunity to turn them to account for his country, his career, and his clerical clients, and set to work to pave the way for a piece of really big business by a series of provocative reports on the "social dissolution" of the country to which he was condemned, the government to which he was accredited, and the party against which he was prejudiced by political bias, personal spleen, and professional flair. The disappointed agent degenerated rapidly into a sociologist, and the nervous alarmist into an *agent provocateur* sedulously instigating aggression against a government that he had wrecked in his reports long before it committed the transgression that guaranteed international sanctions. The debt suspension provided him with a legitimate opportunity to force French intervention and to serve all his combinations at once by a joint offensive of international capital; but he was still one man against Mexico, a person pitted against a people, and until he was sure of carrying his government with him, it was essential to secure the co-operation of the British Minister and to pool their interests.

This merger was not so easy. A French diplomatist has observed that the functions of his profession have broadened with the development of democracy. "The importance of persuading a Prince or his ministers has diminished, that of understanding a nation has increased. . . . The representative of a self-governing nation has been under a more direct obligation to study and interpret the social conditions of the country and has been called upon to assume a greater responsibility in advising his government and shaping its relations with a sovereign people than the minister of an irresponsible ruler." The dictum might serve as a compass pointing to the cardinal quarters and the prevailing forces by which Mexico was controlled in the middle of the nineteenth century. If Saligny belonged to the older school, Wyke represented the newer—negatively, but none the less accurately for that reason. Arriving in Mexico on the eve of a crisis which required some understanding of local conditions for its correct appreciation, he formed his judgment in three weeks and began to forward a series of reports as prejudicial as those of Saligny, not from a deliberate purpose to color or distort, but from a complacent inability or unwillingness to comprehend. He saw the same things, in the same way, for different reasons; but the bias of obtuseness was as mischievous as that of premeditation. His attitude also was determined by the nature of his mission; he came to Mexico to collect bad debts, and his mind had been pre-shrunk for the purpose in London. The Foreign Secretary had been sharply criticized in Parliament and the press for neglecting British interests in Mexico and spurred to protect investments and enforce claims in what was, commercially, an important

outpost of the Empire, before the profits of dispossession of the clergy
were dissipated. These complaints were more than the buzz of speculators; they had the volume, the persistence, and the hum of an
aroused commercial community; and it was in response to this pressure
that Wyke was recalled from sick leave on the Continent, where he
had spent the better part of a year since his appointment, nursing a
liver complaint. The long delay in taking up his duties had given rise
to interpellations in Parliament, and though, unlike Saligny, his career
was not at stake, he had no less reason to be zealous and to dispel any
doubts that he devoted more thought to his liver than to the organic
troubles of the Empire. The British debt cramped his mental activity,
and to the diagnosis of the organic troubles of Mexico he brought the
peremptory judgment of a bailiff, the diplomacy of a commercial
traveler, and the impatience of a vigorous invalid.

Under such conditions he could hardly be expected to lose time in
studying the conditions of the country, but his interpretation was
cursory even under the narrowest construction of his duty. Nothing
revealed the mentality of Sir Charles Lennox Wyke better than the
contrast between his first report and the last of his predecessor. Mathew
had learned to appreciate the difficulties of the government and to
estimate correctly its chances of overcoming them. His observations
also were governed by the British debt, but they were not subordinated
to it. "The hope of Mexico lies in the maintenance of peace," he
repeated as his parting injunction. "A wise basis of civil and religious
liberty has been laid down, and peace only is needed for the development of Constitutional principles and for the gradual enlightenment
of the country. But seeing as I do so many native and foreign elements
at work to disturb the existing state of things, I cannot but entertain
a conviction that unless the present government or principles of government are in some way upheld by England or the United States—by
a protecting alliance or the declaration that no revolutionary movement would be permitted in any of the seaports on either ocean—
further deplorable convulsions will afflict this unfortunate country, to
the heavy injury of British interests and commerce, and to the disgrace
of humanity." The heaviest liability under which the country labored
was the moral prejudice created against it by the late regime and the
difficulty of recognizing abroad the progress that had actually been
made, for "however faulty and weak the present government may be,
they who witnessed the murders, the acts of atrocity and plunder,
almost of daily occurrence, under the government of General Miramon
and his counselors, Señor Diaz and General Marquez, cannot but
appreciate the existence of law and justice. Foreigners especially, who
suffered so heavily under that arbitrary rule, and by the hatred and
intolerance toward them that is a dogma of the Church party in
Mexico, cannot but make a broad distinction between the past and

the present. President Juarez, though deficient in the energy necessary for the present crisis, is an upright and well-intentioned man, excellent in all the private relations of life, but the mere fact of his being an Indian exposes him to the hostility and sneers of the dregs of Spanish society, and of those of mixed blood, who ludicrously arrogate to themselves the higher social positions in Mexico."

The social benefits resulting from the dissolution of the old order were a material gain for British interests, and their best security. If his judgment was governed by any other consideration, it was by suspicion of Saligny, whose conclusions he contradicted point by point. The threat to peace lay not in the lingering lawlessness, which he recognized as the subsiding ferment of civil war, nor in the recrudescence of the Reaction, but in the very issue that affected the British Government. "The most imminent peril to Mexico, and one that will equally press on any future, as on the present, government," he insisted, "is the deplorable state of its finances. . . . The Mexican Government has been accused, and not without reason, of having frittered away the Church property recently nationalized; but it must be remembered that while forced contributions, plunder, and immense supplies from the Church and its supporters enabled General Zuloaga and General Miramon to sustain the civil war for three years, the Constitutional government abstained from such acts and have the sole robbery of the *conducta* at Lagos, toward the close of the civil war, to answer for. Their reserves, during this lengthened period, were drawn from advances by individuals, on bond for larger sums, payable at the close of the war, and from actual sale of a great part of this property at twenty-five per cent, or even fifteen per cent of its supposed value. . . . From the foregoing details Your Lordship will at once understand the precarious condition of Mexico, and that without some foreign interposition the dismemberment of the Republic and a national bankruptcy appear all but inevitable."

Over the political map drawn by Mathew, with its careful qualifications, Wyke passed the sponge three weeks later. "It will be very difficult, if not impossible, to give Your Lordship a correct idea of the present state of affairs in this unfortunate country," he began afresh, "so utterly incomprehensible is the conduct of the government that at present presides over its destinies. Animated by a blind hatred toward the Church party, the present government have only thought of destroying and dissipating the immense property belonging to the clergy without, however, at the same time taking advantage of the wealth thus placed at their disposal to liquidate the many obligations that at present weigh them down and cripple their resources. The Church property has generally been supposed to be worth between sixty and eighty million Spanish dollars, the whole of which appears to have been frittered away without the government having anything to show for it. A considerable amount was, doubtless, spent in repaying advances at exorbitant rates of interest made to the Liberal party as they were fighting their way to power; but still enough ought to have remained after satisfying their creditors to have left them very well off and in better position as to their pecuniary resources than any previous government." Disgusted by such incomprehensible mismanagement, he gave the government guilty of it short shrift. "The Church party, although beaten, are not yet subdued and several of their chiefs are within six leagues of the capital at the head of forces varying from four thousand to six thousand men. . . . Señor Comonfort, ex-President of the Republic, has arrived at Monterrey in Nuevo Leon, where it is said the Governor has made a pronunciamento in his favor, which will very likely be joined in by the neighboring states, and probably aided by a party in this capital, who are thoroughly disgusted with the weak and tyrannical government of Señor Juarez. . . . Those well acquainted with the country watch this movement with anxiety and say that unless promptly checked it will lead to the downfall of the present government and renew all the horrors of the civil war. In the meanwhile, Congress, instead of enabling the government to put down the frightful disorders that reign throughout the length and breadth of the land, is occupied in disputing about vain theories of so-called government on ultraliberal principles, while the respectable part of the population is delivered defenseless to the attacks of robbers and assassins, who swarm on the highroads and in the streets of the capital. . . . This state of things renders one all but powerless to obtain redress from a government that is solely occupied in maintaining its existence from day to day, and therefore unwilling to attend to other people's misfortunes before their own"—a peculiarity of human nature which completed his disgust. "Patriotism, in the common acceptance of the term, appears to be unknown; no one man of any note is to be found in the ranks of either party. Contending factions struggle for the possession of power only to gratify their cupidity or their revenge; and in the meantime the country sinks lower and lower, while its population becomes brutalized and degraded to an extent frightful to contemplate. Such is the actual state of affairs in Mexico, and Your Lordship will perceive, therefore, that there is little chance of justice or redress from such people, except by the employment of force to exact that which persuasion and menaces have hitherto failed to obtain."

The conclusion was irrefutable. Poverty was a perpetual threat to civilization, and poverty so incurable defied it, and within three weeks Wyke had worked himself to a pitch of outrage at which his views tallied completely with those of Saligny. Between the smug consternation of the one and the calculated pessimism of the other nothing but the main chance was needed to bring about their merger.

After consulting the senior officer of the British squadron, Sir Charles came to the conclusion that only two courses were open to him: not to mention Mathew's, nor to waver between forbearance and foreign interposition, but to choose between withdrawing the Legation and adopting the plan of Captain Aldham; and he preferred the flag officer's. "Captain Aldham, who during the last three years has gained a very clear insight into the Mexican character and the manner of evading their engagements so peculiar to their officials, is of opinion that the time for lenience is past, and that if we mean to protect the lives and properties of British subjects, coercive measures must be employed. He thinks that a blockade is not advisable on account of the large force that would be required for that purpose on so extensive a line of coast, to say nothing of the commercial difficulties to which it would give rise, besides the fact that by so blockading we should be actually robbing ourselves of the percentage of duties levied at Veracruz and Tampico. This plan, then, presenting so many objections, Captain Aldham is of opinion that the next best thing to be done is to take possession of the customs houses of Veracruz, Tampico, and Matamoros on the Atlantic, and of either Acapulco, Mazatlan, or San Blas on the Pacific; to lower the duties on all goods landed at those places; and to pay ourselves by the percentage to which we are entitled but which we now never obtain, owing to the rascality of the Mexican authorities." Whatever objections might be raised to the unilateral action of the British might be safely discounted. "The French have only a small debt of 190,000 dollars to recover, which is being chiefly paid off by twenty-five per cent of the import duties levied at Veracruz on cargoes brought in French ships. The Spanish claim eight per cent on all import duties on some claim of theirs, which is in suspense and therefore the interest thereon is not paid." Both creditors would undoubtedly welcome a control of the customs guaranteeing their efficient administration, and so would the debtors themselves. "From the moment that we show our determination no longer to suffer British subjects to be robbed and murdered with impunity, we shall be respected, and every rational Mexican will approve of a measure, which they themselves are the first to say is necessary, in order to put a stop to the excesses daily and hourly committed under a government as corrupt as it is powerless to maintain order or cause its own laws to be executed."

Provided that any government survived such assistance, and that any rational Mexican could be found among so many national ones, this conclusion was also irrefutable; but patriotism being merely another "ism" in Mexico, such considerations were irrelevant. What was worth some consideration was the point made by Mathew that peace was indispensable to the recovery of the country and the British debt alike. Sir Charles, however, had not yet thought so far. After six weeks in the country his mind was too jaundiced to work either fast or clearly, and, baffled by financial collapse and his inability to deal with it, he saw no further than the punishment of incompetence. Ignoring the risk that coercion might defeat his purpose and by wrecking the government and renewing the civil war prevent the protection of British interests, he recommended the course best calculated to secure that result, and his advice reached Lord John Russell at the same time that the government suspended the debt service.

Wyke was fully prepared for the crisis, therefore, and had done as much to anticipate it as Saligny; yet when it came, his conduct varied inversely to its gravity and differed in a small but significant degree from that of his colleague: where Saligny promptly severed diplomatic relations, Wyke merely suspended them. The difference, slight as it was, corresponded to a fundamental distinction in the aims and interests of the two Ministers: Saligny, pursuing a course of studied provocation for political purposes, required a rupture for their promotion and employed the negligible French debt as a mere lever; while Wyke, exclusively concerned with the economic interests of his flag, had too great a stake to protect to be uncompromising. Caution came late, but it came with the crisis and his recognition of the consequences, and either because of a professional preference for half-measures or a belated compunction, prompted by ignorance of the intentions of his government, he left ajar the door which Saligny slammed. Of this opening Zamacona took advantage to negotiate. The impulsive, confused, and choleric temper of the previous few weeks subsided on both sides; the discussions, acrid at first, strained, defensive, evasive, restored contact and gradually approached an understanding; and Wyke, working with an antagonist eager to propitiate him, proceeded to seek a solution less drastic than the one he had recommended to London. The damage, however, was already done: the problem had passed out of his hands. For a moment, for a brief fateful moment, it had been his to mold and formulate; but the decision taken in London produced complications and set forces in motion which could no longer be controlled.

Mexico had always suffered from the personalities of foreign diplomats, and in the critical summer of 1861 those of Wyke and Saligny loomed large. Together, though from different and even antagonistic motives, they shaped its destiny. The political bias of the one and the economic prejudice of the other were equally misleading; but in any assessment of their joint responsibility the British Minister was undoubtedly entitled to the lion's share, since he represented the preponderant Power.

7

BUT it was abroad that the brood of the nightmare littered. After July 17 the destiny of Mexico was shaped in Europe. Word of the debt suspension was received in London late in August, and though another two months passed before action was taken, the policy adopted by the British Government was determined by the first reports of Wyke and based on the premises he supplied—a derelict country, a government insecure, incompetent, and corrupt, and the necessity of applying disciplinary measures and foreclosing on a mortgage menaced by national bankruptcy in Mexico. His plan was adopted in all its essentials and broadened to meet the objections to it which he ignored or minimized. Russell and Palmerston formulated the problem with more foresight, and molded it even more myopically, at a distance. English interests in Mexico being purely commercial, their primary object was to isolate economic sanctions and prevent them from breeding political complications. Obviously this was impossible. Financial intervention was, *ipso facto,* political intervention: occupation of the seaports and control of the customs were calculated to throttle the government, and what was to follow its collapse? That question could be ignored only by the blind or the British, but they were old hands at evasion, and they met the question by blinking it. The Prime Minister was an expert at taking the first step and avoiding the last, his Foreign Secretary was an accomplished subordinate, and they covered their responsibility and declared their indifference to the consequences by a formula pledging the British Government to non-intervention in the internal affairs of Mexico. But the difficulties did not end there; the formula was sufficient for domestic, but not for foreign, consumption. The collection of the British debt, absorbing the bulk of Mexican revenues, could not be decently executed without consulting the other creditors, and to avoid the appearance of unilateral action it was necessary to collaborate with them. Decency raised the devil, as it always did, in England. As the interests of France and Spain were primarily political, and both were suspected of velleities of intervention, the next step was to extend the formula to include them and to commit their governments to the same pledge of neutrality. This was less simple. Time was required to adjust the English position to that of the other parties and to guarantee the freedom of action of the British Government by limiting theirs. Two months were spent in settling these safeguards, and in the meanwhile the center of political gravity shifted to France, and the primary object became confused with subordinate aims that seconded it there. English initiative was not, and could not be, neutral, since national interests were settled by national characteristics. In England, where the national character was predominantly male, the Mexican question was settled with virile simplicity; but across the Channel it was complicated by an infusion of feminine influence, and in that phase of its development women and women's motives and women's men played an important part in fostering the brood of the nightmare.

In France the effect of the debt suspension was purely political, and there the announcement precipitated a combination far more complex, the elements of which had long lain in solution, waiting to be fused and materialized. Of those elements the most visible and the least forceful, but the one that acted as a catalytic agent on the others, was the ferment of a group of Mexican refugees in Paris. The classic capital of political exiles had become the headquarters of a dozen Mexican reactionaries, dreaming of a restoration of their regime and scheming unsuccessfully to promote it. Feeble in themselves, their potential strength lay in the forces with which they were connected and those with which they had long been seeking to establish contact—the Church and the Court, the Bank and the Throne—influences of the past and the present, whose shifting frontiers met in Paris. There the refugees found protective coloring: clerical, monarchical, speculative, simian, they were nothing in themselves, and not until those forces began to stir did they find patrons; but for a brief period in France as well, persons played a decisive part in manipulating the destinies of Mexico.

Of those futile few the most important were a trio of disappointed intriguers whose names figure in the initial combinations: Gutierrez Estrada, Hidalgo, Almonte. The first was the notorious expatriate who had been expelled from Mexico twenty years before for preaching the gospel of monarchy there, and who had spent his life parading it around Europe. Possessed of a respectable fortune and married to an Austrian countess, he had obtained an entree to most of the courts of the Continent and solicited pretenders from Austria to Spain without success, since he was commonly considered a visionary and a crank. For that reason, perhaps, one court had remained closed to him, and to penetrate the Tuileries he was forced to seek an assistant; and in the person of a prepossessing young diplomat by the name of Hidalgo, who shared his obsession, he found him. The bearer of that illustrious name distinguished it from that of the liberator of his country by con-

spiring to undo the work of his namesake. The son of an officer who
had served Iturbide, he inherited the political faith of the ephemeral
emperor and was able to give it the contemporary cachet, which made
him so valuable to Gutierrez Estrada. For Pepe Hidalgo—he was known
by his familiar diminutive in the highest circles—was a salon diplomat
and an accomplished worldling, ingratiating, pliable, presentable, whose
social gifts and connections won him access to spheres that were closed
to his fanatical friend, and the assistant soon outgrew the master. If
Gutierrez Estrada was the sire of the scheme for foreign intervention,
Hidalgo was its spark, and Almonte the drudge. Almonte figured in it
by virtue of his rank as Minister of the Miramon government in Paris,
for though his functions were extinct, he retained their prestige and
traded on his position; but he never rose above the role of a diplomatic
dummy. His antecedents were glorious: he was the son of Morelos.
He was a bastard, and his name was a nickname that recalled his casual
birth in the mountains. He began life as a Liberal, but as he learned to
know the world better he turned his coat and immortalized his name
by attaching it to the treaty that secured the favor of Spain for the ultramontane government in Mexico. The Mon-Almonte Convention was
a deed of mutual adoption. His character was colorless. Such was the
singular trio of patriots—the namesake of the first liberator of Mexico,
the son of the second, and the professional expatriate—for whom the
hour had now struck to convert their phantom existence into political
life.

Timeservers all, they would have continued to stagnate in their insignificance, however, had it not been for Hidalgo. For in one respect
at least he could compare with his homonym. His was the hand that
sowed the seed and that reaped the harvest in 1861. How he did so was
also a historic story. Five years before, when the revolution of Ayutla
had triumphed in Mexico, he lost his berth in the Legation at Madrid,
but he met with better luck when he crossed the French frontier on
his way to Paris. At Bayonne he bowed to a lady whom he had known
years ago as a girl in her mother's salon in Madrid, and who had since
become the Empress of the French. She recognized him, and this
chance meeting altered the whole course of his career. Old acquaintance was not forgotten; she picked him up and invited him to Biarritz,
and there, in long outings together on the water, he entertained her
with idle reveries about Mexico and caught her fancy with a topic that
made them compatriots, for he was still a Spaniard at heart and she
had not ceased to be one by marrying the Emperor of the French.

Eugénie de Montijo had lost many illusions with her maiden name.
Unhappy in her domestic life, she longed to play a political role in
France and had already asserted herself on the Roman question—a
satisfaction that the Emperor owed her for his marital infidelities—
and the engaging young lady's man touched a responsive chord, and

touched it at the right time. The tribulations of the Mexican Church gave her a fresh lift in life, as he acquainted her with them, and he caught her attention. When she tired of the Church, he changed the subject to a Mexican monarchy, and her sympathy for him grew with her interest in Mexico. She had never heard of any other Hidalgo, and she read the history of his country through his eyes and in them. She allowed him to court her politically. In due time she introduced him to her husband, whom he attended in turn, following him from Biarritz to Paris, Fontainebleau, Saint-Cloud, Chantilly, or wherever the calendar led his seasonal promenades. Hidalgo became a member of the Imperial entourage, on the verge of the Imperial ménage, and found repeated occasions to open his heart to the Emperor. The Mexican question was a topic of remote interest, however, to the husband. The tribulations of the Church left him cold—he had his hands full with them in Rome; the idea of a Mexican monarchy caught his fancy, but without capturing it seriously. He toyed with the notion as a prophylactic to American expansion, which was his pet aversion, but both his aversions and his ambitions were indolent, and though it appealed to his prejudice against an imperialism in democratic dress, it moved his imagination only, not his ambition. His attention was engaged elsewhere. The risks of so distant an adventure, the dearth of suitable candidates, and pressing problems at home made the scheme seem chimerical even to Louis Napoleon, who was something of a dreamer himself.

Hidalgo won a hearing, but nothing more, but a hearing was enough for him. He attached himself to his host in much the same way as Madame Gordon did. When she was asked whether she loved the Emperor she smiled and replied, *"Je l'aime politiquement. A vrai dire, il me fait l'effet d'une femme."* Her mot was cited by a learned physiologist as the clue to the Emperor's character. According to this authority, his temperament was "lymphatico-nervous." "The nerves and the lymph are mingled in him, as often happens in the women of our European West; which explains a well-known mot by Madame Gordon." Perhaps. She was merely a woman; but the authority built a whole theory on her hint. "Where the nerves dominate, the intelligence is facile, comprehensive, fertile in projects, and the imagination inclined to pleasure. If the lymph is uppermost, the mind is slow, the senses obtuse, and, as someone has said, they have to be peeled to be tickled. Suppose these elements united:,from their fusion comes a new character, which partakes of both principles and modifies one by the other. Then a man is at once intelligent and dense, bold and calculating, modest and ostentatious, voluptuous and cold, mystic and skeptical, curious and indifferent, mobile and tenacious, indiscreet and secretive, credulous and scoffing, affable and haughty, hesitant and verbose, boastful and careless"—in a word, mutable as a woman and contradictory as a man. "Add to this idea a position, a rank, an elevation . . .

and you have the explanation of his whole reign." The explanation was
more mysterious than Napoleon, but it was all that Hidalgo, or Madame Gordon, or the world, had to go on. He was a subject for guess
work. Many people were mystified and fascinated by the inconsistencies
of his character without contesting his sex. A man with no woman in
him would not be a man anyway, but a male; and there was nothing
the matter with his manhood. Nor was there any mystery about him
more than the normal elusiveness of the great. In his position he kept
people guessing, as he was obliged to do by his rank and an elevation
that placed him on guard against the world, and Madame Gordon,
and Hidalgo. So it was with the Mexican question. His heart was not
in it yet; but he was mutable and married to the Empress Eugénie,
and that was enough for Hidalgo.

The whole international situation had to change, however, before
the second Hidalgo could make any headway. His ideas were premature in 1857 and ahead of their time in 1858; but the outbreak of the
civil war in Mexico boosted them, and by the beginning of 1859 they
were dangerous enough to catch the attention and excite the alarm of
a member of the Legation in Paris, of Liberal sympathies. Andres
Oseguerra, the friend, informer, and confident of Ocampo, railed bitterly at the *"cicisbeo de la Montijo"* and his fatal knack of catering to
"feminine sensuality that shrinks from the crack of a whip and swoons,
while the scent of blood and butchery thrills it. . . . Why should not
our noble *énervées* give themselves the luxury of emotions," he scoffed,
"when there are peoples to pulverize under the wheels of their phaetons
for their pleasure?" But he overrated the languid interest of the Empress and the influence of her minion. Gutierrez Estrada, gaining admission to the Tuileries with the help of Hidalgo, annoyed Napoleon
and shocked the Empress herself by his fanatical clericalism, his antiquated brand of monarchism, and his anachronistic social ideas; and
after defending them at great length he was not invited to do so again.
He was *de trop* at the Tuileries.

Almonte, in turn, tried to gain a foothold for himself in the inner
circle, and much more cleverly. He composed a pamphlet in favor of
intervention, which he entrusted to Hidalgo to polish and present at
the palace. But this bid attracted no attention there, and no notice anywhere, save from Andrés Oseguerra, who noted with satisfaction that
Almonte had completely mistaken his man when he trusted his work
to Hidalgo and thought "to throw the stone and hide the hand." "I
must tell you," he wrote to Mexico, "that by the hand of the Empress
the Emperor has received a letter from Hidalgo asking for intervention; it preceded the pamphlet; and hence in the pamphlet there is the
I, so much to the taste of the sons of Loyola, with phrases and paren-
theses of apparent modesty and humility, but the *I* that says, nevertheless, look at me, *I* am the author. Almonte thinks that he has been very

clever; he thinks that he is a person for Hidalgo, when he is merely a *thing*." Hidalgo was not the man to play second to Almonte, and Almonte came no closer to the Tuileries than he could see from the *impériale* of a public omnibus. The contact man guarded his chosen preserves jealously against poachers; but he himself penetrated no farther than the outskirts of his peculiar domain. Hovering on the verge of the domestic ménage, and familiar with the political household, he was called Pepe here and Pepe there and answered the beck and call of both and the purposes of neither, being without power himself.

So the years of civil war slipped away. In 1859 Napoleon was engaged in the Italian campaign. In 1860 the proposed mediation of France and England in Mexico revived hopes of intervention, but only to disappoint them again, and Hidalgo began to lose heart, as he confessed in an account of his disappointments which he wrote later, for like most of the Creole aristocrats he had less character than conviction and was readily discouraged by adversity. During the years of drought, however, he preserved his position at Court and was allowed to play with ideas that were still unloaded, and the prize of persistence was his in the end.

In the summer of 1861 Hidalgo was at Biarritz again when he was privately informed of the financial crash in Mexico, and he had the honor of being the first to announce it to the Empress and to direct the attention of the Emperor to its possibilities. The scene was preserved by his pen. Dinner was over, the Emperor had retired to his study, the Empress was busy with nothing better than her embroidery, and the friend of the household handed her the letter, which he had just received, containing advance information of the debt suspension. She rose, passed into the study, returned, and invited him to follow her. "Tell the Emperor what you have just told me," she said. The Emperor rose, lit a cigarette, and listened. It was an audience. "Your Majesty, I had long lost hope of seeing those ideas realized of which I had the honor to speak to Your Majesty four years ago, but England, together with Spain, is now irritated by the policy of Juarez, and they will both order warships to our ports. Thus, Your Majesty, we have what we need—English intervention. France will not be acting alone, which was what Your Majesty always wished to avoid. Spain has long been prepared. General Conchal told me not long ago that he had left six thousand men at Havana, ready to land at Veracruz, but that the cabinet at Madrid prefers to act together with France and, if possible, with England as well. French, English, and Spanish squadrons might be despatched to Veracruz and land those six thousand Spaniards. In view of the three combined flags, Mexico would recognize the full strength and superiority of the alliance, and the overwhelming majority of the nation could rely on the support of the intervening powers, destroy the demagogues, and proclaim a monarchy, which is the only salvation of the country. The United States are in the throes of war: they will not move. Besides, they would never oppose the three united powers."

Napoleon was caught off his guard, as he had received no information from the Foreign Office, but the idea was presented with a combined caution and boldness that appealed to him, and he gave it serious consideration. "I have not yet received M. de Thouvenel's despatches," he replied. "If England and Spain act, and the interests of France demand it, I shall join them, but I shall send warships only, no landing troops, and if the country declares that it wishes to organize with the support of the European Powers, I shall lend a hand. Besides, as you say, the state of affairs in the United States is very favorable."

This was sufficient commitment for Hidalgo, and with rare presence of mind he proceeded to go the British one better and to provide for the succession, which they left to chance. "Sire," he continued, "whatever may be the results, we shall have France alone to thank for it. Will Your Majesty permit me to ask whether you have a candidate in view? The Mexicans would accept him from Your Majesty as their own choice." The Emperor turned, lit another cigarette, and answered, "I have none." Before venturing to take the lead, Hidalgo glanced at the Empress. "We cannot think of a Spanish prince," he remarked. "Señor Mon has always assured me that there is no possible choice there." — "It is true," she agreed. "There is no possible choice there, and it is unfortunate, for if there were, he would be the most suitable." The search for an alternative began with two or three German princes, whom the Imperial couple mentioned but discarded because of their religion or the insignificance of their states. Then Hidalgo guided their thoughts toward an Austrian archduke. "But which archduke?" The leading question was put by the Empress and answered by Hidalgo. "I believe the Archduke Reiner was mentioned." — "Yes," said she, "the Archduke Maximilian would not be willing." — "Oh, no, he would not be willing," Hidalgo agreed. — "No, he would not accept," Napoleon concurred. Silence ensued. Then the Empress, tapping her bosom with her fan, exclaimed, "Well, something tells me that he will accept." — "We can but try," said Hidalgo promptly, "and I might write to Gutierrez Estrada to go to Vienna and sound His Imperial Highness." The Emperor assented, and Hidalgo hurried away with permission to use the Imperial telegraph.

It was the crowning moment of his career, and he could hardly be blamed if the *I* of the author dominated his account of it. Neither Almonte nor Gutierrez Estrada could vie with him; not being in Biarritz, they were nowhere. He, and he alone, had won a hearing for his cause—and what more had the other Hidalgo done? Pepe Hidalgo was more fortunate, for he arrived at the right time, and catching the historic moment on the wing, made the most of it. For a fleeting moment he dominated his hosts: the Imperial couple were merely the audience, and he was the impresario pulling crowns from his pocket and princes out of his sleeve. Then the initiative passed from his hand; but that moment was enough to turn the world. Powerless himself, he succeeded nevertheless in anticipating Palmerston, and by playing his cards well and slipping his king into the pack, he trumped the British hand. The morrow proved his accomplishment. Once the winning combination had been played, nothing could stop it, and he benefited by British improvidence, for whatever is left to chance is someone's opportunity, and as sure as anything in this world to be picked up by Pepe. The world was his head, he set it spinning, and his moment made the ephemeral immortal. Hardly believing himself that it was true, he flew to the telegraph office and flashed the name of Maximilian over the wires to Gutierrez Estrada.

Maximilian of Austria . . . Maximilian of Austria. That was a name to conjure with. For anyone who knew the world it was a find. For Hidalgo it was an open sesame. No name in the *Almanach de Gotha* conjured up more pregnant possibilities. Both for political and personal reasons it was a powerful precipitate, as the reaction to it in Biarritz proved. The reaction was as positive as the expression of it was negative, and the unanimity with which the three anglers recoiled from it, the moment it was mentioned, was significant of its fascination for each of them. There were good reasons, in fact, why the Emperor, the Empress, and Hidalgo exclaimed with one voice that Maximilian would not be willing.

Five years before, about the same time that Hidalgo happened in history by his chance meeting with the Empress of the French, the paths of Napoleon and Maximilian crossed for the first time. The younger brother of the Emperor Franz Josef of Austria paid a visit to Paris in 1856, on his first outing from Vienna. The impression that the Napoleons made on him then was described by the young prince in a candid report to his brother, which characterized the writer as well as his hosts. The Emperor of the French, he wrote, "displayed at our first meeting, and during the whole evening, an insuperable embarrassment, which hardly produced a favorable effect upon me. His short unimposing figure, his exterior wholly lacking in nobility"—"vulgar" was the word that first occurred to him, but he crossed it out—"his shuffling gait, his ugly hands, the sly inquiring glance of his lusterless eyes, all these things made up an ensemble that was not calculated to correct my first unfavorable impression. I found the Empress, whom I visited immediately afterward, in a state of great lassitude and weakness; she took uncommon pains to be agreeable, but was at the same time extremely embarrassed. . . . She is quite thoroughbred, but essentially lacking in the august quality of an Empress, and the impression produced on me by her appearance was dimmed by memories of Imperial Vienna." As for the other Bonapartes, they were all very Corsican: old King Jerome reminded him of a senile Italian dentist, and Prince Plon-Plon of a shabby Italian basso; the Princess Matilde was unpleasantly common in appearance. At a state dinner at Saint-Cloud, the Court confirmed his estimate of the master. "The Emperor's incredible lack of ease was particularly obvious; it occurred to me that he still felt uncomfortable in the presence of a prince of more ancient lineage than his own; when he overcomes this constraint, he displays great candor, and the more closely I come to know him the more founded does his confidence in me seem to be. In general, there seems to be a most commendable intention of giving a proper setting to the Court, but the machinery does not work very smoothly as yet, and in spite of the unconstrained manner they try to affect, the parvenu etiquette comes through. . . . I need hardly assure Your Majesty that I take great pains to be agreeable and to let no signs of the unpleasant impressions that strike me here and there appear."

On closer acquaintance the Archduke modified his opinion of his host, albeit with becoming reserve. "Napoleon is one of those men whose personality has nothing winning about it at first sight," he added, "but ends by producing a favorable impression by his great calm and noble simplicity of character. The reckless way in which he speaks in the presence of servants is most remarkable; he often lets fall the most incredible statements in their presence; this seems to me typical of the parvenu, utterly lacking in that *esprit de corps* that makes one careful not to expose oneself in the presence of inferiors." Gradually, however, he warmed to him. "The pleasantest time is at *déjeuner,* when the Emperor can be very attractive in his frankness and amiability. He speaks well and with animation and the effect is heightened by a certain flash in the eyes. On these occasions great candor prevails, in which I join with due moderation." His final impression was almost favorable, and on the eve of his departure he condescended to flatter Napoleon—just to show him how it was done. "Napoleon I had genius," the young Hapsburg remarked. "Napoleon III has cleverness. Genius moves the world, but cleverness rules it." The compliment was a little left-handed, perhaps, but Napoleon accepted it and was extraordinarily friendly and betrayed a certain emotion on parting with his guest— they were like old friends, he said. Once they touched on politics— but only once—and lightly. Maximilian, who was just learning to walk politically, put a candid question to the clever antagonist of his house. "May I assure the Emperor my brother that Your Majesty will proceed in perfect harmony with him in the Italian question, as in all others?" The answer was satisfactory, and the Archduke left Paris highly pleased with himself.

The impression that Maximilian made on Napoleon was unfading. Five years had passed since their meeting, but his first thought, when Hidalgo proposed that name, was that naturally the Archduke would be unwilling to accept a throne from his hand; for however carefully the young prince had concealed his superiority, he was a Hapsburg, and Napoleon would not have been a Bonaparte had he not suffered from condescension. For a long and unforgettable fortnight in 1856 he and his consort had been daily undressed by the appraising eye of their guest, and in 1861 they were still self-conscious at the sound of his name. The Imperial Adam shrank, and his blood turned blue with the chill which the bare mention of it recalled, but the vanity of the Imperial Eve overcame the pride of her partner. The vanity of the female was less modest and more enterprising than that of the male, and an unerring intuition told her that the Hapsburg could be conquered. She tempted, and he consented, and Hidalgo triumphed. None of them suspected that Maximilian might be a Bonaparte too. That discovery remained to be made by a scholarly sleuth, who deduced it from a letter left by L'Aiglon, suggesting that his captivity in Vienna had been consoled by the Archduchess Sophia and that she had borne him two sons, one of whom was the reigning Emperor of Austria and the other his lesser brother; but the proof was as doubtful as it was suggestive, and it was still locked in the secret compartment of an old desk in Vienna. So far as the Napoleons knew, Maximilian was pure Hapsburg. The only family secret of which they were conscious was the family failing of their inferiority in the eyes of the hereditary enemy of their house, and that was an open secret. Had Napoleon been deterred by such considerations, however, he would have been unworthy of his name and would have merited the mot of Madame Gordon on whom he produced the effect of a woman.

There were far better reasons for courting Maximilian politically. The opportunity to patronize the hereditary enemy of his house might be a personal satisfaction, but it was dignified by greater considerations. Many things had changed in Europe since 1856, and the Archduke was a valuable pawn, and the offer of a throne, however remote, a diplomatic gesture liable to relieve tension with Austria over the Italian question, which since the intervention of Napoleon in Lombardy had become so acute as to threaten a general war. Vienna, Venice, Victor Emmanuel—combinations of all kinds were conjured up by the name of Maximilian, and the dream of a Mexican monarchy began to materialize in the mastermind at Biarritz as a febrifuge for old Europe. Nothing was risked by indulging it but a snub, of which Hidalgo would bear the brunt; and vanity, discreetly varnished with politics, involved all three in an adventure which lacked neither the pettiest nor the largest motives for the ruin of Mexico.

The time, the place, and the man had been found by Hidalgo, and out of that tentative conversation a larger and more entangling alliance developed. His mercurial mission ended when he wired Gutierrez Estrada to hold himself ready to leave for Vienna. The old man, who in the course of peddling a Mexican throne for twenty years had kept his head only by riding his hobby, now cleared the ground with one bound. He hurried to the Austrian Embassy, and in the absence of the Ambassador—it was the dead season—submitted the proposal to a secretary, who transmitted it *pro forma* to Vienna. Two months before, he had laid it before the Ambassador, on his own responsibility, and Prince Metternich had humored him to the extent of forwarding it to his Chancellor, whose verdict was what might have been expected: Rechberg declared the idea absurd and unworthy of serious consideration. The telegram from Biarritz, however, turned the steadiest heads. Supported by the tacit sanction of Napoleon, the notion that the Chancellor had described as absurd two months before now commanded serious attention, and he took the train for Miramar to consult Maximilian—a step that conveyed the implicit sanction of the Kaiser. Maximilian had been sounded before and had turned down the idea, but he was accessible to it now on two conditions suggested by his brother and accepted as essential safeguards by himself: that he be assured of the consent of the Mexican people and of the formal support of the great Powers. There was no further need for Gutierrez Estrada to go to Vienna: Vienna came to him. His was the faith that moved mountains, and the conditions imposed were mere hitches. The consent of the Mexican people was not a serious hindrance. The Archduke was famous for his liberal principles. They had won him some popularity in Austria and Italy, and the disfavor of his brother, who was not averse, therefore, to an adventure in America which promised to relieve him of a family problem. The consent of the governed was a concession to the idiosyncracies of the Archduke, covered by the guarantee of the great Powers upon which his guardian insisted as a matter of political dignity and natural affection. This guarantee, however, raised a formal difficulty.

For, in the meanwhile, another factor had come into play—the independence and routine of the French Foreign Office. The first report of the debt suspension in Mexico reached Paris on the same day that the Emperor left for Biarritz, and the first steps to deal with it were taken during his holiday by the Bay of Biscay. M. de Thouvenal, who was also on vacation, came into Paris occasionally to give it perfunctory attention without suspecting the importance it was assuming in the villa by the Bay of Biscay, for Napoleon did not deem it necessary to inform him of an idea that was still nebulous, embryonic, and contingent upon the consent of Maximilian. Following the usual practice in foreign affairs, M. de Thouvenel consulted the British Ambassador and acceded to the British plan for joint intervention. An ultimatum requiring repeal of the moratorium, and the appointment of English and French Commissioners to collect their credits at the customs, was to be presented by both Powers, backed by their fleets; but intervention was to be purely financial and limited, as London insisted, to political neutrality. To this formula M. de Thouvenel made no objection, nor did Napoleon when it was referred to him, since his participation was contingent upon English co-operation, and it was not until the overtures made in his name to Vienna produced a response that the consequences became embarrassing.

In the meanwhile, following another normal precedent, M. de Thouvenel proposed that Spain be included in the expedition. This step was warranted by several considerations. Spain was an acknowledged creditor, with a strong garrison in Cuba waiting to be landed at Veracruz, and a more or less willing protégé of Napoleon. The suggestion was coldly received in London, however, for those very reasons. The aims of Madrid were likely to lead to political complications, which the British Government wished to avoid, and to the resuscitation of a regime in Mexico that was unpopular in England. And had it not been for the growth of the monarchical intrigue, Spain might have been ignored.

But Spain was not to be ignored. There the crisis in Mexico produced an effect that was political only in the narrowest sense of the term, affecting international affairs merely because it excited local politics. National interests were not involved, but national characteristics were. Spain in the middle of the nineteenth century was ruled by the psychology of a decadent nation struggling to recover the position of a major Power in the family of modern nations, and considerations of prestige and national pride, prompted by nostalgic sentiment far more than by material interest, dominated all its governments alike. The government of Marshal O'Donnell then in power was peculiarly susceptible to the question of face, for Marshal O'Donnell had conducted the conquest of Morocco in 1859 and given a fillip to the revival of national sentiment by that enterprise. He had also refused to make an issue of the expulsion of the Spanish Minister to Mexico at the beginning of the year and had discredited him in the Cortes, to the scandal of the Opposition, which, led by Pacheco himself, attacked the government for neglecting the national dignity with a vigor that shook it. The parliamentary feud was at its height in May and had barely subsided when the crisis in Mexico arose, but as it arose in the dead season O'Donnell had time to anticipate its domestic repercussions before the Cortes reconvened.

No sooner was it known that two of the great Powers were consulting than his Foreign Minister took steps to forestall the unfortunate impression at home and abroad of the omission of the third. He telegraphed to his Ambassador in Paris to ascertain the intentions of the French Government and stated his own, which were to act independently, energetically, and without delay. Calderon Collantes compressed into that message the dilemma of a people equally sensitive to neglect of its right to rank as a great Power and condescension toward its claims, and of a government conscious that it could not act without England and France, and he teamed the two horns in a warning that Spain could neither be left out nor left behind. A gesture of independence and a bid for support, the message was so understood by M. de Thouvenel, who invited the Spanish Government to consult and collaborate. As the protection of Spain formed part of the Napoleonic policy in Europe, this step was as automatic as consultation with England, and he did not expect it to be contested in London. Thus encouraged, Calderon Collantes took the lead in two other directions. Without consulting London or Paris, he sent orders to Cuba to occupy Veracruz and Tampico, and, without approaching the English Government, he suggested to the French that the scope of the conversations in Paris be broadened and that the three Powers should combine not merely to exact satisfaction for injuries, but to establish "a regular and stable order in Mexico." Thouvenel replied, after consulting Napoleon, that their views coincided.

Thus the situation stood at the end of September. In the first week of October, when Maximilian accepted the crown conditionally, the principal condition could not be met: a formal offer by the great Powers was, on the face of it, impossible. His candidacy, of which rumors were circulating, excited jealousy in Madrid, where the Bourbons had preferred claims to the hypothetic throne of Mexico; the projected monarchy ran counter to the policy of Palmerston; and Napoleon had been committed to contradictory pledges—to the British definition of intervention on the one hand, and the Spanish version on the other. This involved situation had developed partly, no doubt, because of the slack season, which allowed Thouvenal to shape the preliminaries of French policy in the absence of the Emperor from Paris; but the negligence of the master was no seasonal indolence; it was the habitual state of mind of a dictator who had not received the power of decision from nature and who readily abandoned it to his subordinates. That mongrel psyche of his was to blame. It was during one of those slack periods that he drifted toward the idea that entangled him at Biarritz: impelled by the importunities of Hidalgo and the Empress, he was hurried into a step for which he was unprepared and which carried him further than he contemplated—until he caught up with himself. The prompt if provisional acceptance of Maximilian made it as impossible to withdraw as to square the offer with the conflicting views of

Spain and England, and before the confusion became embarrassing he dispelled it. Thouvenel was instructed to consult the British Ambassador in Paris on the advisability of establishing a stable government in Mexico, and the French Ambassador in London was directed to approach the Foreign Secretary with the same proposal.

Russell welcomed the prospect of a stable government in Mexico, but insisted that it should be brought about by the Mexican people themselves; and at the same time he took a step to break the combined weight of France and Spain and to bring them both under control. On the old and tried principle that the best way of foiling an opponent was to become his ally, and a combination of opponents by joining their company and spoiling it, he consented to include Spain in the expedition, and proposed to keep the combined hands of Paris and Madrid off Mexico by binding them to the English formula of intervention in a written engagement subscribing to its principles. This maneuver compelled Napoleon to declare himself. Duplicity was abhorrent to him—he had no gift for it—and he met the difficulty with candor. In a personal letter to the French Ambassador in London, who was directed to read it to Lord Russell, he set forth his first thoughts and his second and explained his conception of the joint enterprise, not in the ambiguous formulas of professional diplomacy, but in his own direct, forthright, and first-personal style. He spoke English, in short.

What had been a mania with the Mexican monarchists and an idle reverie with Napoleon had developed so rapidly that he was obliged to assemble his ideas hastily to justify it; they were still vague and unformed, but he advanced them boldly. He began by dwelling on the advantage of establishing a stable government in Mexico to check the encroachments of the United States and to open a commercial field equally profitable to the three partners, particularly at a time when Mexican cotton would go far to supply the shortage caused by the American civil war. These considerations had long struck him, he said —but they were addressed to Liverpool rather than to Lord Russell. When Mexicans had appealed to him in the past to rescue their country from anarchy, he had had no pretext to intervene and had been unwilling to risk a rupture with the United States; that hazard was now removed. The outrages of the Mexican Government gave England and France legitimate grounds to act, and though the tripartite pact limited their action to the redress of grievances, he wished to look further and "not to bind his hands benevolently and prevent a solution that would be to the interest of all concerned." And now came the cotton for Lord Russell. Mexicans had assured him that the mere appearance of a naval force would cause the proclamation of a monarchy; they had asked him to name his candidate; he had none, he wished to have none, but the Archduke Maximilian seemed to offer the desired guarantees, and the Mexicans had sounded the cabinet in Vienna and were inclined to believe that the Prince would accept the crown, provided he were formerly invited by the Mexican people and assured of the support of the Powers. He did not press the point; he merely notified Lord Russell. Lastly, there was cotton for himself as well. He would be wanting in sincerity, he concluded, if he pledged himself not to support, at least morally, a political change, which he desired not from selfish motives or unjust antipathies, but from a consciousness that he was working in the interests of civilization as a whole. The final consideration was as sincere as the others and the most compelling of all for Napoleon; a high-minded and unconscionable dreamer, ambitious for humanity and fatal to it, he was incapable of deceiving others without first deceiving himself, and material considerations were always secondary to those large, general, congenial, and cloudy views in which his mind was at home.

Of this notice Lord Russell took no cognizance, since he had no official knowledge of it. He had no desire to embarrass Napoleon, and he did the decent thing. He continued to press for the conclusion of the pact on his own terms, carefully excluding those ulterior aims of which he was privately apprised and which he discouraged by a diplomatic deafness that made them inadmissible. Time was pressing, too; the season for operations on the fever-ridden coast of Mexico was short, and two months had been spent in harnessing the creditors, underwriting the expedition, and adjusting their interests. Under the combined pressure of British consistency, Spanish impatience, and Austrian condescension, Napoleon consented to join the undertaking on terms that converted his false situation into a formal agreement. The London Convention, signed on October 31, represented the triumph of British policy. It provided for consultation among the three Powers in the organization of an expedition to occupy the ports and military points of Mexico; it bound them not to seek any acquisition of territory or private advantage, nor to exercise in the internal affairs of Mexico any influence liable to impair the right of the Mexican people freely to choose and constitute their own form of government; and to complete its international character and guarantee its rectitude, the Government of the United States was to be invited to join it. Nothing apparently could be more explicit; but as a working agreement it rested on the assumption by one party that it meant what it said, and by the others that it was open to interpretation and compatible with mental reservations; so that full intervention was merely a matter, after all, of mutual confidence.

8

TO COMBAT the designs of their creditors during the two critical months when these engagements were forming, the Mexican Government commanded the diplomatic service of one man. The foreign service was the first to suffer from the need of drastic economy and was reduced to indispensables: the Legation in Washington was maintained, and a single minister was appointed to cover Europe in an omnibus character.

Don Juan Antonio de la Fuente, on whom the choice fell, was neither poor in spirit nor an untested Christopher. A fellow traveler who had had joined the government and supported it before, in bad weather, and been seasoned by adversity, he had sat in the Veracruz cabinet, where he fought the McLane treaty alone and signed the decree of religious liberty, and had built up a Spartan political record, which schooled him for the task of representing his country abroad at a time when the principal qualification of a Mexican diplomat was a capacity to suffer without complaint. He had also built up a certain rigidity of character, which was the professional defect of his qualities. Although he was appointed at the beginning of that stringent year, his departure was delayed by the difficulty of raising his traveling expenses, which he supplied himself, and when he arrived in Paris in April he encountered another delay in presenting his credentials, deliberately prolonged by the Quai d'Orsay on the pretext that Almonte had not yet been formally recalled; and after contesting it for four months he won his first diplomatic victory by forcing his reception at Saint-Cloud on August 10. Depressed by the unpopularity of his party and his poverty, he was prepared for the worst. He dreaded, he confessed, "a cold reception, at the very least, if not a harsh and bitter one, but, on the contrary, the Emperor displayed the most exquisite benevolence." Gratefully surprised, he was not dazzled, however, by the amenities of the occasion and accepted them with mental reservations. "I cannot describe the flattering reception accorded me by the Emperor as decidedly favorable to our interests," he reported, "until I see that the claims of M. de Saligny are less exacting and bellicose in the extremely serious negotiation of the Jecker bonds and the new French Convention."

His reception at the Foreign Office ten days before had put him on his guard, and his account of it was uncanceled by the benevolence of the Emperor. "The threats of M. de Saligny," he had written then, "the immoderate expressions employed by M. de Thouvenel; his statement that he approved all that M. de Saligny had done; demands so strong, so unseasonable, and so inconsiderate as those conveyed to the Constitutional government, while every consideration is lavished on the lifeless remains still lingering here of the Reaction, in which I include Almonte, who maintains his good relations with the Emperor, and Miramon, who was invited with his wife to the festivities at Court; the efforts of the bondholders in London to induce the English Government to assume a tone of hostility toward us and their success in many respects; the claim to intervene in the collection of our Federal revenues to take up the dividends of the English debt; the desires of which the correspondent of the London *Times* has made himself the echo, proposing the political intervention of England in our country, also suggested by the *Frankfurter Zeitung;* and above all the union of England and France, admitted by M. de Thouvenel and Lord Russell, and designed to crush the legitimate government of the Republic, which has done them no wrong, while they maintain with the Miramon government, which has offended them, relations of friendship or at least of tolerance . . . all this leads me to conclude that there is some grave design against the Republic on the part of France and England, or that the governments of those two nations may readily carry their demands so far as profoundly to injure the sovereignty of Mexico and make the constitution of the Liberal government impossible."

The telltale catalogue was discouraging, and it was with these signs of a campaign to mobilize public opinion for a coming *coup* in mind that he went to Saint-Cloud and listened with misgiving to the Emperor expressing his sympathy for a country ravaged by civil war and menaced by American invasion, his desire to preserve its independence, and his regret that "so beautiful a country should be so unfortunate." He caught the Emperor in a holiday mood, just before leaving for the seashore, and what he really heard was the hush before Biarritz.

His misgivings were fully confirmed three weeks later, when the first reports of the debt suspension reached Paris. Recognizing the coincidence of the crisis with a premeditated plan of aggression which had developed before it and which would have materialized without that provocation, he realized better than anyone the full fatality of the crash and the futility of opposing the forces that conspired to produce it; but he made a conscientious attempt to avert the consequences. He wrote to Thouvenel, requesting him to waive the rule that limited audiences to one day a week and to grant him an immediate interview, so that he might communicate with his government by the mail boat leaving the next morning. Three days later he was received, and the interview lasted only a few minutes. Thouvenel, who had consulted the

GONZALES ORTEGA

DOBLADO

ZAMACONA

British Ambassador before answering De la Fuente's note, refused to listen to any explanations and, abandoning himself to the utmost excitement, said, "We have fully approved the conduct of M. de Saligny. We have given orders, in agreement with England, for a fleet composed of warships of both nations to exact satisfaction of the Mexican Government, and your government will learn through our Minister and our Admiral what the demands of France are." Then, irritated by his own temper, Thouvenel spoke for Thouvenel. "Personally," he added, "I have nothing against you, and I wish that events permitted me to use more friendly expressions." The Mexican relieved his embarrassment by putting an end to the interview himself and retired with a stiff expostulation. After that there was nothing to do but to suspend relations, and he did so on the same day in a note that needed no answer. He had been recognized for exactly four weeks, and his mission was confined to forcing one door and being shown out by another.

By the same mail that notified him of the debt suspension, De la Fuente received a note from Juarez, directing him to explain the situation to Napoleon in person and to Queen Victoria, and enclosing a draft for five thousand pesos to secure a hearing for the Mexican side of the question in the press. After his experience at the Quai d'Orsay, De la Fuente decided that it would be useless to proceed to London, "since it is practically certain that this step would win us another rebuff such as we have received here. I am further moved to this opinion," he explained, "by the information, sufficiently to be expected by now, that it is in England that the infamous intrigue of European intervention in the politics and government of our country had its origin and is most in vogue." Official doors being closed to him, he could no longer act upon governments or against them except by appealing to public opinion; and that arbiter was also inaccessible. Public opinion meant, if it meant anything, parliamentary opinion—and the parliaments of both countries were in recess—or the press. In France the press was muzzled and not venal enough to be influenced by five thousand pesos. In England the government organs were booming intervention, and the Minister sent some clippings to Mexico with a caveat. "It is quite clear that our British creditors would willingly see us delivered over to any nation in the world, and subjected to the most despotic government that men can imagine, provided the Convention of the English debt in Mexico and the law covering the debt contracted in London were completely observed; and everyone knows that the influence and interests of those creditors make themselves felt only too well in the regions of power." All the channels to public opinion being choked, he chose the only course left to him and remained in Paris in the hope, as he put it, "of penetrating the capital idea of France and England in relation to Mexico." Paris was the listening post of Europe, and if he could not be heard there himself, he could at least overhear the hum of the machinery; and to that post he clung, stranded.

The machinery creaked, creaked loudly enough to give him some hope. "We may be able to profit by the small and doubtful respite granted us by the mutual antipathies of France, England, and Spain," he wrote as the alliance was being forged. But he was too close to the machine to mistake a hitch for a halt in its momentum. If the mutual antipathies of France, England, and Spain had been purely political, there might have been some hope that the combination would break, but they were harnessed to the preponderant Power, whose economic strength and interests gave it the lead and the control of the whole enterprise, and whose initiative determined its nature. The driving power of the capital idea that united those incompatible Allies lay precisely in the competition of capitalist forces from which there could be only a brief respite, but no ultimate escape, for a colonial country. Friction was its fundamental note, and the proof that the machine was functioning; and he dwelt on that note incessantly, urging his government to draw back while there was yet time and to repeal the decree of July 17 at all costs.

His warning was anticipated. The emergency that provoked the moratorium subsided as rapidly as it arose. Early in August Gonzalez Ortega met the forces of Marquez and dispersed them, and though the result was not decisive, the relief was sufficient to allow the government to reconsider the expedient of debt suspension and to take steps to avert the coalition forming abroad: progress in one direction allowed of retreat in another. By forcing the government to such shifts and provoking the crisis, however, Marquez had scored a formidable triumph, which his rout could not efface. The victory of Gonzalez Ortega dispelled the mere wraiths of the nightmare, and it fell to Zamacona to disperse its brood and appease the irritated Powers.

With one of them he found it impossible to treat. M. de Saligny was irreconcilable. Shortly before the moratorium was announced, the government had approached the creditors of the French Convention with an offer of pledges and promissory notes secured by Church property, which they were inclined to accept; but on consulting their Minister, they were advised to refuse any settlement. If there was any doubt that he was acting as an *agent provocateur* before July 17, it was dispelled by his conduct after it.

The return of Ortega to the capital was celebrated by cheering crowds parading through the main streets, and several days later the diplomatic corps called upon Zamacona to protest against an attempt made on the life of the French Minister in the course of the demonstration. Surprised that he had not heard of it before, and that it had not been reported to the police, he ordered an immediate investigation.

The testimony was unanimous that the behavior of the crowds passing the French Legation was orderly; no one had heard the cries of "Death to France!" of which the diplomatic corps complained, or noticed any demonstrations of hostility toward the Minister. There had been some shouts of "Death to Reaction!" which no one supposed to be directed against him, and some singing of the "Marseillaise," which no one construed as an offense to his flag. To the attempt on his life there was no witness but himself. According to his account, he was standing in the courtyard of his house, at dusk, when he heard a report and noticed that a column near which he was standing had been nicked by a bullet. The police studied the story and the premises; the trajectory of the shot that no one had heard was traced to a point that no one could see; and the story missed its mark as completely as the bullet that M. de Saligny produced to prove it. The investigation was dropped at that point, but it brought out some facts to which the press gave publicity. The French Legation was known to harbor a reactionary general wanted by the police and to be a notorious center of conspiracy from which communication with the enemy was carried on with diplomatic immunity. Wisely, no doubt, M. de Saligny was silent, but in his report to Paris he capitalized the attempt on his life, representing it as the culmination of an inspired system of terror to which the French residents of the capital could testify, many of them having brought him letters left in their homes by night, threatening them with fire and death. "Our nationals have not let themselves be intimidated by these maneuvers, which everyone attributes to subordinate agents of the government," he added. Witnesses to this charge were also wanting; but he was never at a loss for ideas, nor embarrassed by contradiction. Far from representing the French colony, which was predominantly Liberal in its sympathies, he was denounced even by its conservative members as a menace to their interests, and the leading bankers and merchants proposed to draw up a representation against his interference and warmongering—testimony which Zamacona hastened to forward to Paris in the fond belief that his Minister there could still be heard and oblivious to the fact that the correction of calumny, under the best of conditions, always comes too late.

Against M. de Saligny there was no defense, and the means which Zamacona adopted to disarm him were the most deadly: he ignored him. The French Minister could not be ignored with impunity; he had already been ignored too long for the good of the country; and he was now isolated by the negotiations that Zamacona was conducting with the British Minister. Incensed by the desertion of his colleague, M. de Saligny retired into the Legation, nursing his spleen against the day of reckoning and relieving it in inflammatory reports to Havana. The protection of Spanish nationals, which he owed to Pacheco, provided him with the nearest means of offsetting English influence, and in his correspondence with the Captain-General of Cuba he harped on the pride of Spain, which had also been ignored too long, and discharged the congested venom he generated into the hospitable mind of Marshal Serrano.

With the British Minister, Zamacona fared better. Wyke was not irreconcilable, he was merely irritated, and though he acted in concert with Saligny up to the rupture with the government, after it the fundamental differences in their interests led to a divergence in their conduct. Wyke was without ulterior aims and not without scruples; and Zamacona, attributing their agreement to the dominant influence of Saligny, set to work to break it on the assumption that Wyke had "innocently seconded" the designs of his colleague and could be weaned away. So, at least, he chose to believe, and not out of charity, for on the slight distinction between a dupe and an accomplice he built his hopes and his diplomacy. The first steps were the most difficult. Wyke was less shocked by the fact of default than by the manner in which he had learned of it, like everyone else, by opening the morning papers, a feature of the case on which he laid great stress in his note of protest. For this lapse Zamacona made ample amends. On the ground of form he was an accomplished apologist, and he lavished all the amenity of which he was a master on his opponent, but with no effect at first except to irritate him further, for Sir Charles had a liver, a legitimate motive to indulge it, and a limited command of language, and he was exasperated by the glib tongues of Mexico that could talk themselves out of anything. It was all that Zamacona could do to induce him to listen; but listen he did rather than to reply indefinitely to Zamacona's insufferable politeness. Wyke had served in the army, had never married, and was inclined to be abusive in his own language, but a foreign tongue was a bit, and from the moment that he was reduced to mere irritation, progress was possible.

Progress was slow, however, for at the outset Wyke insisted on repeal of the decree as the preliminary, instead of the object, of discussion. Discussion was established, nevertheless, by an exchange of communications arguing the ethics at stake. Here the Englishman was at home; the opportunity to moralize was irresistible, and he rose to the bait and was hooked and drawn into a controversy which raged furiously for four weeks. The Mexican took a hard lashing, but he would not let go. Confident of the rectitude of his wrongs, Sir Charles laid down the law with a finality which left nothing to add to it but incessant repetition, and repetition was heaped on the head of his antagonist with indefatigable vigor and crushing weight. "Congress has thought fit to make a free gift of other people's property to the government of the Republic," Wyke ruled. — "Sir Charles Wyke will now allow the Undersigned the liberty of stating," Zamacona demurred, "that the application of the term 'free gift' to what is merely the act of ratifying certain obligations and specifying the mode of fulfilling them amounts to a misnomer." — It amounted to many millions of pesos, Wyke retorted. Whereupon Zamacona condescended to simpler language and, unwinding himself elaborately, went on: "The nation has paid its creditors with the blood of its citizens. . . . It would be sad, indeed, if history were to be obliged to record that this country, after the most trying vicissitudes, came to be governed by men who, without any supernatural ability and inspired solely by their experience and their patriotism, have not shrunk from one final effort—an effort such as never yet has been made—to establish in Mexico the rule of reason and morality, and that this effort was wrecked on the prejudices and skepticism of the most enlightened nation in the world." — "That which is wrong can never come right," came the retort, "for it is a well-known axiom that spoliation as a source of revenue soon exhausts itself." And by way of illustration Sir Charles grounded Zamacona in fundamentals: "A starving man may justify, in his own eyes, the fact of stealing a loaf, on the ground that imperious necessity compelled him thereto, but such an argument cannot, in a moral point of view, justify his violation of the law, which remains as positive, apart from all sentimentality, as if the crime had not had an excuse. If he was actually starving, he should have first asked the baker to assuage his hunger, but doing so of his own free will, without permission, is acting exactly as the Mexican Government has done toward its creditors on this occasion." But he was Old Bailey talking to a schoolboy. "His Excellency has employed a simile, the ineptitude of which is strikingly apparent," Zamacona objected, rehearsing his arguments once more in as homely language as he could manage. But Wyke held his ground against all the circumlocutions in which he was involved and kept the incorrigible casuist at a distance, and the bout continued in a futile discussion of the priority of property over human rights, without practical result other than to maintain the contact, which Zamacona was determined not to relinquish.

Apart from the arguments involved, the honors of the debate undoubtedly went to the Mexican, who maintained the altercation within diplomatic limits and in a tone of indomitable urbanity, which exhausted his adversary; and he had another asset on his side. He conducted the dispute with an eye on posterity—a witness of which Wyke was unaware—and with unflagging confidence continued to add to the record against a day of judgment when, as he reminded Wyke in a pointed aside, "this correspondence will come to light." The warning went unheeded, however; winded but unweakening, Wyke continued to insist on unconditional surrender, and as Zamacona had nothing to offer but appeals and persuasion, no advance would have been made by either side had not help come from another quarter. The deadlock was broken by the American Minister.

A cataclysm had improved the relations of Mexico and the United States. As one nation emerged from its inner convulsions, the other slipped into civil war, and their neighborly relations were so radically altered as to be almost reversed. For the first time in history a Mexican Government found itself courted. The Lincoln administration exercised conspicuous care in the choice of a new Minister to Mexico, and the selection could not have been more considerate. Thomas Corwin was notorious on both sides of the border, like Lincoln himself, as an outspoken champion of Mexico during the American war, and the significance of his appointment was immediately recognized by the Confederate press. "The man who more than any other can attract the sympathies of Mexico" was the warning spread in New Orleans. "He will have great influence in the efforts that are being made to prevent us from being recognized as a nation; and we believe that his appointment has no other purpose. Mr. Corwin has all the talent necessary to occupy a place in the cabinet or to discharge a first-class mission in Europe." The *Mobile Advertiser* took up the cry. "We think that our government should consider seriously how to neutralize the maneuver which the Lincoln administration is putting into play in Mexico. Lincoln has sent to that Republic a man of high capacity, whose presence in Mexico, for various reasons, will be very detrimental to the interests of the South. The Southern States are the ones that principally desired and sustained the war against Mexico. The Mexicans know it and will do everything in their power to avenge themselves on the partisans of our President, Jefferson Davis. They know also that the North was opposed to the war and took none but a very small part in the shedding of Mexican blood."

The appointment of Corwin, like the election of Lincoln, presaged a new deal in American diplomacy. With the rise to power of the Republican party and with control of the Federal government by the Northern and Western states, a pioneer era opened in the relations of the two countries; the sectional split revealed the roots of the past, and it was generally recognized on both sides of the border that the long, wretched history of American imperialism represented sectional rather than national interests and was due to the almost unbroken domination of the American Government by Southern statesmen. Honest Tom Corwin, as he was called in Ohio, did much to honor his name in Mexico. He was the only recruit to the diplomatic corps who presented his credentials unconditionally, and by his accurate and unbiased reports on conditions in Mexico he performed a service to both countries and succeeded in creating mutual confidence and sympathy and effacing many of the bitter memories of the past. His mission prospered; and when an agent of the Confederacy appeared on the scene, all doors were closed to him.

Arriving in Mexico at the same time as Sir Charles Wyke, and making the trip to the capital with him, he continued to act as his traveling companion after the debt suspension; and he put his insight at Wyke's service. In the critical weeks that followed Corwin took steps to exorcise the catastrophe that everyone foresaw by a solution so simple that no one had thought of it: he advised Seward to underwrite the Mexican foreign debt and guarantee the interest on it for five years. With all his sympathy, however, he was as little of a sentimentalist as Wyke himself, and he befriended Mexico in Washington with Hoosier honesty and shrewdness. He was a diplomatic servant, subdued to the element he worked in, and as Seward was an apostle of Manifest Destiny, Corwin adapted his idea to the traditional views of the State Department. "England and France," he pointed out, "are now in possession of the best of the West Indian Islands (for I consider it certain that San Domingo is certain to fall into the hands of Spain before our rebellion is quelled), and Mexico, a colony of England, with the British power on the north of our possessions, would leave on the map of this continent a very insignificant part of the United States, especially should the present unnatural rebellion end in the severance from us of eight or nine, or all, of the slave states. Mexico, I am persuaded, would be willing to pledge all her public lands and mineral rights in Lower California, Chihuahua, Sonora, and Sinaloa, as well as her national faith, for the payment of this guarantee. This would probably end in the cession of sovereignty to us. It would be certain to end thus if the money were not promptly repaid as agreed upon. By such an arrangement two consequences would follow: first, all hope of extending the dominion of a separate Southern republic in this quarter or in Central America would be extinguished; and second, any further attempt in all times to come to establish European Powers in this continent would cease to occupy the minds of either England or Continental Europe. . . . The United States are the only safe guardians of the independence and true civilization of this continent; it is their mission, and they should fulfill it."

The proposal differed from previous liens of the same nature by the sympathy that whetted it. But for the double emergency on both sides of the border and the inability of Mexico and the other republics of South America to defend themselves, he said, "I should not desire either to intermeddle in their concerns or to add any of their territory to ours, except, perhaps, Lower California, which may become indispensable to our Pacific possessions. . . . I cannot find in this Republic any men of any party better qualified, in my judgment, for the task than those in power; if they cannot save her, then I am quite sure that she is to be the prey of some foreign Power, and they, I fear, cannot without *our* aid. I say *our* aid, because she will look in vain for help elsewhere." The aid thus offered was valuable precisely because it was not disinterested. Seward agreed, and Corwin was authorized to open negotiations with the Mexican Government. No more was needed to bring the British Minister to terms, and Wyke began to bargain with Zamacona.

The deadlock was broken. Under the stimulus of American mediation and American competition the British negotiation developed. The American deal, on the other hand, made no progress. No government, and least of all one so recently scorched by the McLane treaty, could be induced, however desperate its extremities, to accept the mortgage proposed by Corwin, but as an equivalent Zamacona proposed a fifty per cent reduction on tariffs for a period of five to ten years. Corwin declined to recommend this offer for fear of antagonizing England and France, and because it offered no real advantage; the most-favored-nation treatment being guaranteed to both those Powers by treaty, he pointed out that their Ministers would undoubtedly demand the same favor. And so it proved. Rejected by Corwin, the idea was adopted by Wyke, to whom it was of more value than to his American colleague, British trade suffering severely from the high Mexican tariffs, and its volume being more than double the American, which was the lowest in the market. Besides eliminating any risk of an American loan, the idea he borrowed from Corwin had other advantages to recommend it: under the high protective tariffs a lucrative contraband trade, which defrauded the government of half its revenues and of which the English held the monopoly, had grown up; and as the British Minister was nothing if not honest, he recognized the necessity of cleaning his own house and was willing, for the sake of a solid moral and material gain, to reconcile ethics and business by a tariff reduction. On that spar his negotiation with Zamacona was brought to a successful conclusion. After three months of hard work, he was satisfied by a concession that made the claims of the bondholders a relatively insignificant matter. "I explained," he reported to Lord Russell, "that so long as Mexico by reducing her tariff really benefited trade, we had no right to insist upon her effectually crippling herself for the sake of being able to square the balance sheet of the bondholders, or fix the exact ticket to be placed on each separate piece of shirting that came into the country."

But an explanation was also due to Lord Russell for the remarkable conversion by which his agent now spoke the language of Zamacona; for such was the result of a trade favor. Association with Corwin had cured Wyke of the diplomacy of a commercial traveler, and borrowing another idea from his American friend, he reflected his sympathetic attitude toward Mexico; sentiment was also a commercial asset. On November 21 a convention covering the most difficult points in dispute and allowing of the resumption of normal diplomatic relations was ready for signature. The *status quo ante* of the 17th of July was restored, plus the tariff amendment, and the rights of the bondholders were insured by a stipulation for the appointment of British inspectors to control the collection of the Mexican customs.

But there were several other factors with which Wyke failed to reckon. One of them was the French Legation. M. de Saligny had followed the progress of the negotiation for three months with growing agitation, and its conclusion provided him with a final argument to embroil Spain with Mexico, for all the others that he found failed to move Marshal Serrano. "But Spain is threatened abroad by other dangers and causes for anxiety," he wrote to the Captain-General of Cuba on November 23. "The English Legation, true to the *frank and loyal policy* which you already know, has concluded, or rather completely closed, an agreement which has aroused public opinion on all sides and which cannot, to my mind, be approved in London. The French Legation is further than ever from any accommodation, however, and aside from the question to which the orders I have received from the Imperial Government refer, and which they refuse to admit here, new incidents have arisen even more serious than those that occurred in the month of August, and they render impossible my stay in this capital, where not only does the press daily and scandalously attack France and her representative, but my life is publicly threatened by the Chief of Police, a consummate criminal, a former highwayman notorious for the many crimes he has committed, and a man who has spent many years of his life in the jails of Chapala and Mexico City. I am preparing, therefore, to leave with the whole Legation, and I hope to see you in Mexico, convinced as I am that you will come in command of the expedition. In Robles' letter you will see the intrigues of England laid bare. The sudden about-face, performed with as much duplicity as stupidity by Wyke (a nigger diplomat), is explained by the reply of my colleague to someone who expressed astonishment at the strange attitude assumed by the British Legation: 'What shall I say? We feel an invincible repugnance against entering into any common action with Spain, no matter what the question may be, and especially when behind Spain we see France.'"

The negotiation of the Wyke–Zamacona convention, which threatened to settle British complaints and to eliminate the necessity of punitive measures, roused M. de Saligny from his state of captive spleen and stung him into furious activity; but his efforts to precipitate intervention from the nearest available quarter were not necessary. The negotiation came to nothing. The stipulation providing for British control of the customs was the last hitch, but an insurmountable one, and for purely sentimental reasons. "The difficulty of getting the President to see the question in its proper point of view," was the apology offered by Zamacona for his failure to overcome it; but Congress was equally stubborn and threw out the convention on that condition, although as an earnest of good will it repealed the decree of July 17 at the same time. But the major concession, which Wyke had demanded four months before, no longer satisfied him; like Saligny, he was bent on bigger business, and he had scented Saligny's running counter to his own. The Mexican objections were more than he could bear, his patience was exhausted, and he called for the passage of the convention or his passports. His ultimatum was accepted; Congress refused to pocket the national pride, and Zamacona resigned.

Great was the satisfaction of M. de Saligny. "Here is more news," he wrote to Serrano the next day. "The famous agreement in which Wyke shamelessly sacrificed all the principles heretofore invoked by England in agreement with France produced a serious revolt yesterday, and I have just learned that at a late hour last night Congress rejected it. Wyke is furious and is preparing to leave. Now more than ever I can say, *nigger diplomacy.*" The failure of the treaty by no means relieved his anxiety, however, and twenty-four hours later he was rattling confidential incitements to Havana at the same breathless pace. "In the enclosed clipping you will find new proof of the duplicity and stupidity of the British Minister, and curious revelations as to a project of alliance between Mexico, England, and the United States against France and Spain. . . . I send you the *Trait d'Union* and two extracts from the *Siglo,* in which you will find curious details about the convention that was rejected the day before yesterday. Every article of this strange document reveals the shrewdness and insincerity of the Mexican Government, no less than the incredible naïveté of perfidious Albion. . . . There is talk of submitting the Wyke treaty to Congress again; I should be greatly surprised if the second attempt fared better than the first. The number of votes against it, seventy to twenty-nine in favor, seems to me to indicate a secret understanding with Doblado to overthrow Juarez. I should not be surprised if he and his ministers had to flee within the next fortnight. . . . I insist that, if you are to act, there is no time to be lost."

But his fears were unfounded. Though the defeat of the treaty did not reconcile him to his British colleague, it restored their collaboration. Wyke was now committed to an uncompromising position. The peremptory judgment of a bailiff which he brought to Mexico was fully justified when he closed the Legation, and he could indulge the impatience of a vigorous invalid with a clear conscience. He had exhausted the possibilities of conciliation. The effort had not been wholly wasted, however, and before leaving the capital he felt it his duty to

pay two deserved tributes to his collaborators. "I have only now to express to Your Lordship," he wrote to Russell, "my high sense of Mr.
Corwin's conduct through the whole business. He has stood by me in
the most honorable manner and, on learning of the rejection of my
convention by Congress, refused in the most positive manner to advance the government one dollar of the proposed American loan. Nor
can I pass over in silence the service of Señor de Zamacona, the Minister of Foreign Affairs; he at all events has been sincere in trying to
second my late endeavors, and his resignation of office proves that there
is an exception to every rule, even as regards Mexico."

His late endeavors had been doomed beforehand, in any event, by
Russell and by himself. The possibility of a peaceful settlement had
been eliminated by Lord Russell as soon as he learned of the negotiations that Wyke was conducting: the proposed terms satisfied the separate requirements of Great Britain, he admitted, but they provided no
security that they would be observed any better than previous stipulations and agreements. The conviction so assiduously instilled into his
mind that the bankruptcy of Mexico was due to the irresponsibility and
dishonesty of its government, that folly was coupled with bad faith
and incompetence with corruption, had taken root too firmly for correction and could no longer be retracted after the signature of the
London Convention, which had no other writ or ostensible reason for
its execution. The late endeavors of Wyke as a peacemaker, indeed,
caused his government some embarrassment. When the solution conceived by Corwin was communicated to London, Russell was hard put
to refuse the American guarantee and to produce a plausible reason for
rejecting the security which it provided, but he was not to be bought
off by a trade rival, and the reason he needed was supplied by the
American Government itself. The price of the loan destroyed its political value, as the American Minister in London reminded Seward.
"You will permit me," Adams wrote, "to make a single remark upon
the importance of appearing to divest the United States of any personal
or selfish interest in the action it may think proper to adopt. The view
customarily taken in Europe is that their Government is disposed to
resist all foreign intervention in Mexico, not upon any principle, but
simply because it is expecting, in due course of time, to absorb the
whole country for its own benefit. Hence any proposal like that which
I had the honor to receive, based on the mortgage of portions of Mexican territory as security for engagements entered into by the United
States, naturally become the ground for an outcry that this is but the
preliminary to any entry for inevitable foreclosure. And then follows
the argument that if this process is legitimate in one case, why not
equally in all?" But it was Lord Russell who made the most cruel
comment on the plan for American mediation when, as a counterpro-

posal, he blandly invited the United States to join the Allied expedition. The invitation was declined, and Seward allowed his plan to lapse. With it vanished the one substantial hope of averting intervention.

9

WHATEVER hope remained was visionary, though not for that reason negligible. The action of foreign opinion—that factor might be expected to make its influence felt in time, but it was of small value as yet, since it was still dormant and uninformed. Inaccessible in August, it had begun to stir, however, in November. The awakening appeared first, where it counted most, in England. Plans for the expedition had been prepared during the parliamentary recess, without consulting the country, and the publication of the London Convention at the end of October confronted the public with an engagement which commanded attention and required explanation. The alliance contracted by the cabinet—or a fraction of it, for not all the members had been consulted—and the rumored ambitions of the foreign partners to the enterprise, raised questions as to its ultimate purpose and original responsibility, which the ministerial press anticipated and met with explanations so inconsistent as to thicken the confusion and quicken the suspicion of those who studied its erratic behavior.

One of the first and most alert of these was the London correspondent of the *New York Tribune,* who came to the rescue of Mexico with an activity that ferreted out the whole affair and a clamor that raised a general alarm, and as his name was Karl Marx he commandeered Mr. Greeley's paper to good purpose. To raise a general alarm by way of the transatlantic press was a circuitous route, but in the tense relations between the war-torn New World and the war-ripe Old Continent his warnings had a wide resonance and were addressed to a quarter vitally concerned with the moves of the British Government and the combinations of the European Powers, because of their bearing on the war of secession in the States. A foreigner in England himself, an international exile, and a citizen of the world, Marx was in a better position than the stranded spokesman in Paris to act as a Christopher for Mexico. "The contemplated intervention in Mexico by England,

France, and Spain," he wrote in the first week of November, "is, in my opinion, one of the most monstrous enterprises ever chronicled in international history. It is a contrivance of the true Palmerstonian make, astounding the uninitiated by an insanity of purpose and imbecility in the means employed, which appear quite incompatible with the known capacity of the old schemer." He said no more than De la Fuente thought; but he spoke and thought more formidably, because he knew whereof he spoke. Reviewing the evident motives of the Allies—the value to Napoleon of a foreign diversion, the ambition of Spain to recover colonial dominion and foreign prestige—and collating them with the professed purpose of the English Government, he came to a conclusion confirmed by the English press itself. "It is, therefore, certain, and has even been expressly admitted by the *Times,* that the joint intervention in its present form is of English—i.e. of Palmerstonian—make. Spain was cowed into adherence by the pressure of France; and France was brought around by concessions made to her in the field of foreign policy." The motives of England were cloudy, but one thing was clear. "There are no people in England who desire an intervention in Mexico, except the Mexican bondholders, who, however, had never to boast the least sway over the public mind. Hence the difficulty of breaking the Palmerstonian scheme to the public. The next best thing was to bewilder the British elephant by contradictory statements proceeding from the same laboratory, compounded of the same materials, but varying in the doses administered to the animal." As an example he cited the first feelers put out by the *Times* and the *Morning Post,* both of them ministerial organs, the latter maintaining that there would be no territorial war, but that, as it would be impossible to deal with Mexico as an organized and established government, the principal ports would be temporarily occupied and their customs revenues sequestered, while the former hoped that "the mere presence of a combined squadron in the Gulf, and the seizure of certain ports, will urge the Mexican Government to new exertions in keeping the peace." Intimidation as a constructive trick was not original with the English, but they reduced it to absurdity. "If then, according to the *Post,* the expedition was to start because there is no government in Mexico, it was, according to the *Times,* only intended to encourage and support the *existing* Mexican Government. To be sure! The oddest means ever hit upon for the consolidation of a government consists in the seizure of its territory and the sequestration of its revenues!" With the conclusion of the tripartite pact these contradictions deepened and multiplied to such a degree that they could no longer be sustained. "The *Times,* which ever since its first announcement on September 27, seemed to have forgotten the very existence of Mexico, now again steps forward. Anyone ignorant of its connection with Palmerston and the original introduction in its columns of his scheme, would be induced to consider today's leader in the *Times* as the most cutting and merciless satire on the whole adventure. It begins by saying that 'the expedition is a very remarkable one' (later it says a curious one). 'Three States are combining to coerce a fourth into good behavior, *not so much by way of war as by authoritative intervention in behalf of order.'* Authoritative interference in behalf of order! This is literally Holy Alliance slang and sounds very remarkable indeed on the part of England, glorying in the nonintervention principle!" So little had times changed in 1861 that the text would have been as true half a century earlier or at any time later.

Out of the mouth of the Thunderer, Marx plucked the teeth of his indictment. "In the progress of its article," he continued, "the *Times* veers around and explains: 'We shall, no doubt, succeed in obtaining at least a recognition of our pecuniary claims; in fact, a single British frigate could have obtained that amount of satisfaction at any moment. We may trust, too, that the more scandalous of the outrages committed will be expiated by more immediate and substantial atonement; but it is clear that, if only this much was to be brought about, we need not have resorted to such extremes as are now proposed.' The *Times,* then, confesses in so many words that the reasons originally given out for the expedition were shallow pretexts. What, then, is its real aim and purpose? . . . *An authoritative interference in behalf of order.* England, France, and Spain, planning a new Holy Alliance, and having formed themselves into an armed Areopagus for the restoration of order all over the world." Was it necessary to labor the point or possible to finish the sentence with a period? " 'Mexico,' says the *Times,* 'must be rescued from anarchy and put in the way of self-government and peace. A strong and stable government must be established' there by the invaders, and that government is to be extracted from 'some Mexican party.' Now, does anyone imagine that Palmerston and his mouthpiece, the *Times,* really consider the joint intervention as a means to the professed end, viz., the extinction of anarchy and the establishment in Mexico of a strong and stable government? So far from cherishing any such chimerical creed . . . Palmerston and the *Times,* then, are fully aware that there 'exists a government in Mexico'; that the Liberal party, 'ostensibly favored by England, is now in power'; that 'the ecclesiastical rule has been overthrown'; that Spanish intervention was the last forlorn hope of the priests and bandits; and finally, that Mexican anarchy was dying away. They know, then, that joint intervention, with no other avowed end than the rescue of Mexico from anarchy, will produce just the opposite effect, weaken the Constitutional government, strengthen the priestly party by a supply of French and Spanish bayonets, rekindle the embers of civil war, and, instead of extinguishing, *restore* anarchy to its full bloom. The inference the *Times* draws from those premises is really remarkable and curious. 'Although,' it says, 'these considerations may lead us to look with some anxiety to the results of the expedition, they do not militate against *the expediency of the expedition itself.*' It does, consequently, not militate against the expediency of the expedition itself, that the expedition militates against the only ostensible purpose. It does not militate against the means that it baffles its own avowed end. The greatest 'curiosity' pointed out by the *Times,* I have, however, still kept *in petto.* 'If,' it says, 'President Lincoln should accept the invitation, which is provided for by the Convention, to participate in the approaching operations, *the character of the work would become more curious still.*' "

And that point Marx felt it necessary to underline. "It would, indeed, be the greatest curiosity of all if the United States, living in amity with Mexico, should associate with the European order-mongers and, by participating in their acts, sanction the interference of a European armed Areopagus with the internal affairs of American States. The first scheme of such a transplantation of the Holy Alliance to the other side of the Atlantic was, at the time of the Restoration, drawn up for the French and Spanish Bourbons by Chateaubriand. The attempt was baffled by an English Minister, Mr. Canning, and an American President, Mr. Monroe. The present convulsion in the United States appeared to Palmerston an opportune moment for taking up the old project in a modified form. Since the United States for the present must allow no foreign complication to interfere with their war for the Union, all they can do is to *protest.* Their best well-wishers in Europe hope that they will protest, and thus, before the eyes of the world, firmly repudiate any complicity in one of the most nefarious schemes."

A protest at that moment might have produced a sharp, and even an arresting, effect on foreign opinion, but in the strained relations between England and the United States it was impossible. Toward the end of the month the *Trent* affair brought the two countries to the verge of hostilities, and when the tension relaxed the correspondent of the *Tribune* returned to the attack with bated breath. The conduct of Palmerston throughout the crisis was highly revealing: bold to the brink of disaster, he retreated at the last moment. And recognizing Palmerston's fondness for "a spirited policy," Marx reduced his recklessness to a professional play for popularity. The frivolity of the motive aggravated the offense, and if Palmerston proposed to apply the same tactics to Mexico, the danger was even greater for Washington. "Many weeks ago he urged Bonaparte to propose a joint armed intervention in the 'internecine struggle,' supported that project in a cabinet council, and failed in carrying it only because of the resistance of his colleagues. He and Bonaparte then resorted to the Mexican intervention as a *pis aller.* That operation served two purposes, by provoking just resentment on the part of the Americans, and by simultaneously furnishing a pretext for the despatch of a squadron ready, as the *Morning Post* has it, 'to perform whatever duty the hostile conduct of the government of Washington may require us to perform in the waters of the North Atlantic.' . . . I may add that the *Nord* of December 3—a Russian paper and consequently initiated into Palmerston's plans—insinuated that the expedition was from the first set on foot, not for its ostensible purpose, but for a war against the United States." That conjecture at least paid Palmerston the compliment of supposing that he had not taken the first step without calculating the last.

Of all the interpretations to which the London Convention was open, that of Marx was the most logical. It was based on conjecture, but the conjecture was shrewd because it was scientific. His analysis was the result of intuition, experience, and *a priori* knowledge of the traditional workings of British policy, which anticipated the palpable proof; and the evidence already confirmed all his deductions. The erratic behavior of the ministerial press was an admission of ulterior aims. The bad news that it was trying so uneasily to break to the British public might be that intervention in Mexico was merely the preliminary for eventual intervention in the American civil war. To that policy the British public was solidly opposed, but its attitude toward Mexican intervention remained to be determined, and by December the expedition was already on the way. A better brake was the impossibility of conquering Mexico, also admitted by an English Government organ, which Marx cited. "If it is desired," wrote the *Economist,* "to thrust upon her a British prince with an English army, then the fiercest wrath of the United States is excited. France's jealousy would make such a conquest impossible, and a motion to this effect would be rejected almost unanimously by an English parliament the moment it was submitted to it. England, for her part, cannot entrust the government of Mexico to France. Of Spain there can be no question whatever." For purely practical reasons, it was not easy to foist a Holy Alliance upon England or smuggle it into Mexico in 1861. But reason had nothing to do with the Mexican question; and the most sensible people in the world became the most erratic when it was necessary to rationalize their interests. If Marx erred, it was in being too logical about the British people; the inconsistencies of their statesmen and their inveterate habit of muddling through the contradictions they created were the greatest danger for Mexico at that moment.

The abortive plans, the secret and still-born aims, and even the conjectural motives of historical events are as material to the record as the facts themselves, and in the inception of a scheme fraught with so much confusion and consequence there was ample matter for the his-

torical critic; and as an historical critic Marx was in a better position
to serve Mexico than as a correspondent for the *New York Tribune*.
To the practiced eye of the revolutionary the full scope and importance
of the enterprise was immediately apparent. Whether it was a deliberate reprise of the Holy Alliance or the casual international foreclosure which it purported to be, it was equally reactionary; consciously
or unconsciously, the outcome was the same; but the ambiguity was
characteristically English. The confederacy of England, France, and
Spain was a politically unnatural alliance of the leading liberal nation
of the age with two partners, one of which definitely represented the
past and the other an indefinite compromise with it, and the issue was
monstrous because the leading liberal was also the leading capitalist
power, and the contradiction of economic and political interest produced one of the typical miscarriages of nineteenth-century civilization. The plight of Mexico, emerging from its long struggle for
modern civilization only to be overwhelmed by it, was no chance
paradox, nor was the course of England in capturing a country both
backward and progressive for that civilization fortuitous; the one and
the other obeyed the polar attractions of the same axis. And as it was
on the revolutions of that axis that the mind of Marx turned, Mexico
had a peculiar claim to his scientific interest.

The space which he occupied in the *New York Tribune* was hardly
the place to ventilate his professional views, and after the protest which
he lodged there in the first white heat of indignation, he gave to the
violation of Mexico only the passing and topical attention of a journalist. In his correspondence with Engels he glanced at it occasionally, but
as casually as in his letters to America, and Engels ignored it altogether. On Mexico Engels had pronounced himself once and for all
after the American war, and his judgment then was wholly scientific
and unsentimental. "We have witnessed with due satisfaction the defeat of Mexico by the United States," he wrote in a scholarly review
in 1849. "This also represents an advance. For when a country hitherto
involved in its own affairs, perpetually torn by civil wars, and without
any issue for its development, a country whose best prospect would
have been industrial submission to England, when this country is
forcibly pushed into historic progress, we have no alternative but to
consider it a step forward. In the interest of its own development, it
was right that Mexico should fall under the tutelage of the United
States. The evolution of the whole American continent will lose
nothing if the latter, taking possession of California, faces the Pacific."
It was absurd, he maintained, "to place a sentimental value on narrow
national prejudices when the existence and free development of great
nations" was at stake. Forsyth employed the same argument a few
years later. What mattered to the revolutionary was not nationalism,
but "facts of world-historical importance" in social development, and

he approved the annexation of Mexican territory because "the energetic Yankees" were more capable than "the lazy Mexicans" of developing their resources and of opening the Pacific to civilization.

An equally harsh view of Mexican character was held by Marx at
that period. Comparing the conqueror and the conquered in a summary of the soldiership displayed in the American war, he wrote: "We
find in the Yankees the sentiments of independence and individual
valor in an even greater degree perhaps than in the Anglo-Saxon. The
Spanish are degenerate beings. But a degenerate Spaniard, that is the
ideal! All the vices of the Spaniard, grandiloquence, bragging, quix-
otism, appear in them raised to the n-th power, without the solidity
of the Spaniard. The guerrilla war in Mexico is a parody of the
Spanish, and even the regular troops that flee the field seem to be infinitely surpassed. One must recognize, on the other hand, that the
Spanish have never produced a genius the like of Santa Anna!" The
summary judgment formed in the days of Santa Anna were subject
to revision, however, in the days of Juarez. Since then another breed
of Homo mexicanus had developed, and a new generation had pushed
their country into historic progress by a social revolution which entitled its protagonists to the respect and support of the leaders of
world revolution, and their achievements could be measured by the
degree to which they won their championship.

Little as they could do to influence public opinion, Marx and Engels
were in a position to serve Mexican progress by the recognition they
granted it. The kind of polar power generated by their minds was a
fluid intellectual electricity none the less potent for being isolated from
the current of events: diffused in the atmosphere of the age, and ac-
cumulating energy in polemics and criticism, it flashed forth on occasion with positive and dynamic effect. Such an occasion was the American civil war, to which they rallied public opinion in the English
working class, the support of the Second International abroad, and the
partisanship of progressive forces wherever their radius of agitation
could reach. In the case of Mexico, however, there was only heat lightning. The achievements of the Mexican Liberals were recognized by
Marx in the same measure as he noticed every other progressive movement of his time; but no more. The revolution in Mexico, deriving its
ideals from the eighteenth century, was a colonial aftermath of the past,
a forced growth and a relative advance in a remote province of nineteenth-century civilization. The aspect in which it could claim his attention as a genuine revolution, and a significant part of the forward
movement of the world, lay in the transformation of the property relations of society, and the expropriation of Church property was a
partial reform which transferred public wealth from one section of
the middle class to another, under private title, without affecting the

control of production or the exploitation of the masses. As a part of the class struggle, the conflict was confined to the middle class: the proletariat was nonexistent as a conscious or potential political force in a feudal and backward country. It had begun to develop, on the contrary, in the powerful industrial nation to the north, and the passionate interest of Marx and Engels was wholly engrossed by the civil war in the United States, where the destruction of Southern feudalism, the preservation of the Union, and the progress of bourgeois democracy were vital pre-conditions to the growth and progress of the working class; and they agitated its significance strenuously. The fate of Mexico, intertwined though it was with that of its neighbor, fell into second place and was considered only in connection with, and in the intervals of, the decisive stages of the conflict in the States. The sacrifice of the weaker was an outrage, but a side issue, for Marx; his mind was exercised by it, but his heart was not in it.

Finally, the revolution in Mexico suffered from the inactivity in the revolutionary movement in Europe since 1848 and the conviction of Marx that the ascendant curve of capitalism had a long and prosperous course to complete before it could be challenged. "The difficult problem for us is the following," he wrote in a survey of the situation at this period. "On the Continent the revolution reveals, inevitably, an immediately socialistic character. Will it not be crushed in this little corner, given that, in a vastly more extended territory, the movement of bourgeois society still advances in an ascendant line?" If the Continent was a little corner, Mexico was a mere tangent on the chart of social change. The nature of the struggle there, the competition of the American civil war, the lingering influence of former indifference, the scanty information available abroad, the overwhelming odds—everything combined to make the fate of De la Fuente's country a subject of remote and intermittent interest to the seers and surveyors of world revolution.

The isolation of Mexico in the last months of 1861 was bitterly felt by its two representatives abroad. A ghost of a diplomat in France, De la Fuente crossed to London, led by a sense of neglected duty rather than by any hope of being heard, and called on the American Minister—"rather for the purpose of gaining than imparting information," Adams remarked—and through the good offices of Adams was received by Lord Russell, who, caught in the mechanism of an enterprise which nothing but the most rigid consistency could palm off on an awakening public, naturally had nothing to say to him. The interview was a duplicate of the one with Thouvenel, differing only in the frigid indifference with which the English Foreign Minister heard him out before showing him the door. Accustomed by now to that familiar routine, the mortified Mexican returned to Paris, where he invented duties for himself and continued to serve his government with desperate advice.

The expedition had started, and with public opinion beginning to stir, but too feebly to question the venture, the sole hope which he saw of defeating it lay in the expedition itself: in the nature of its composition, the haste of its preparation, the ill-welded divergences, the lines of cleavage which might lead to its disintegration if they were skillfully exploited. Signs of such flaws were not wanting, and he speculated on them. Imprudence in London, uncertainty in Madrid, equivocation in Paris: the common state of mind in the three capitals was one of instability, while the concerted measures taken were materializing with the swiftness of complete confidence. Mastery of the situation clearly belonged to the partner capable of consistency and decision, and it was the confidence of one of them that caused the first crack in the common front. In September, when Calderon Collantes had made his bid to join the expedition, he had sent orders to Cuba to mobilize the garrison, and in December a sharp jolt was caused in London and Paris by a report that a large Spanish force had left for Veracruz without awaiting the arrival of the Allied fleets. Explanations were demanded of Madrid, and though the original orders were promptly canceled, the explanations of Calderon Collantes were accepted by Thouvenel and Russell with conspicuous reserve and mistrust. From the flurry De la Fuente snatched an inspiration. The reaction of the French and English Governments, he pointed out, was vigorous, guarded, and ambiguous. Prompt to check the surreptitious initiative of Spain, they were by no means averse, nevertheless, to profit by the Spanish advance: if it succeeded, they would collect the common spoils; if it failed, they would disavow it as a flagrant breach of treaty. An English paper, in fact, had gone so far as to say that if the Mexicans gave the Spanish a lesson, they would emphasize the absurdity of the recent Spanish conquest of Morocco—"the strange origin and repeated theme of the much-touted restoration of Spain."

"Either I am deceived in what seems to me as true," De la Fuente continued, "or the triumph of our army over the Spanish is certain to be very favorably received in Europe, and the opinion of it formed there will powerfully influence the counsels of the Allied governments; we shall be able to treat with them without difficulty and without great collisions; our name and credit, prostrate at present, will rise, and we shall offer a solemn refutation to those who accuse us of being able to fight only against ourselves. . . . At the point which matters have reached, I think the Spanish invasion, isolated from the Allied forces, is the best thing that can happen to us." It was a case

in which a skirmish might save a war, and he urged his government
to provoke Spain to take the aggressive and to focus the fighting
spirit of the country on the hereditary enemy.

The despatches of De la Fuente passed through Washington, where
they were opened, read, and digested by his solitary colleague in the
foreign service. The Legation in Washington was in charge of Matías
Romero, a junior member of the band of reformers, young enough
to add daring and initiative to the zeal with which he defended his
country abroad. To the task of winning support from the one people
that were inclined to befriend his own he applied himself strenuously;
he had to contend with the prevailing apathy or hostility of the American press and an appalling ignorance in public opinion, which cul-
minated in Congress, but he left no stone unturned to present the case
of Mexico on its own merits and in its bearing on the United States
alike. He went once to the President. Early in that fateful year for
both countries, he approached Lincoln while he was still the President-
elect, and made a trip to Springfield to meet him on his home ground
The memorable defense of Mexico that Lincoln had made in the
Illinois Legislature in 1848 was well worth a pilgrimage to the wilderness in 1861, and Romero, born in Oaxaca and a close friend of Juarez,
perceived the importance of establishing personal contact with a man
whose origin, whose rise, and whose faith offered so many points of
analogy with his own President and so many opportunities for a sympathetic understanding between them.

The interview in Springfield was encouraging. Romero was rewarded with pledges of honest friendship for Mexico, which impressed
him as something more than official platitudes, for they were uttered,
he noted, "in an explicit and even vehement manner," and were
confirmed by the turn the conversation took. Lincoln questioned him
particularly on the condition of the Mexican peons, revealing what
Romero described, a little sensitively, as "the exaggerated ideas held
here of the situation of the Indians who work on the *haciendas*. It
is said that they are more abominably treated than the Negroes on
the Southern plantations, and it is believed that the abuses which are
unfortunately committed in some parts are general throughout the
Republic and are sanctioned by law"—an impression he hastened to
dispel. "I explained to him in detail how such abuses have been committed, and he showed much satisfaction on learning that such practices were contrary to the laws of the Republic, and that as soon as
there was a solidly established government, it would try to correct
them. Mr. Lincoln," he went on, "does not seem to be well informed
on Mexican affairs, and since the way in which he sees our situation
will be the basis of his policy, my first concern was to inform him of

the cause of our upheavals, which have become proverbial here and which are regarded by many as incurable, and to show him that they have already been radically cured."

Romero was sanguine, or he would not have gone to Springfield. The liaison with Lincoln was a bond of character, and above all of a class character, which offered a new guarantee for the future of both countries, and Romero was satisfied that "his administration will be guided by the good sentiments which he expressed, since he is a simple and honorable man, and his words bear the stamp of sincerity and not of those pompous and hollow phrases employed by persons trained in the school of false policy, which is accustomed to offer much and perform nothing." The promise of the first interview remained a promise, however, and the contact was no sooner made than lost. In Washington the war-logged President was inaccessible, and his inexperience in foreign affairs left a free hand to his Secretary of State. So far as Romero was concerned, Seward was the President of the United States.

Seward mystified the Mexican from the first day they met, and after studying him for a year Romero still found him "impenetrable." "I find it hard to believe," he wrote, "that a man of his perspicacity and experience should really be ignorant of our internal and external questions; but from the manner in which he speaks and in which he has worked so far, one must infer either that he does not know them in fact, or that he affects to be ignorant of them." He took Seward's antecedents as a politician into account. "Mr. Seward, either because he conducted a systematic opposition to the government of Mr. Buchanan, which favored the Constitutional cause in Mexico, or acting in good faith, was the mainstay of our Reaction in the United States Senate and the most severe and bitter critic of the policy toward Mexico pursued by Mr. Buchanan. Since then he has undoubtedly had to accept facts independent of his will, but which seemingly have in nowise served to enlighten his judgment."

Of the great change in American policy toward Mexico presaged by the triumph of the Republican party there was little evidence in the attitude either of Seward himself or of the Republican press. In an article in the *New York Times* of December 1860, headed "Shall We Have Mexico?" that organ of the incoming Secretary of State had given a fresh twist to the policy of his predecessors and declared frankly that "we are happy to know in view of threatened dissolution of the Union and the consequent disruption of commercial enterprises and other affairs, that prominent members of the Republican party are already beginning to consider the annexation or acquisition of Mexico as a sure means of immediately indemnifying the North for the partial loss of Southern trade and frustrating the projects of propagandizing slavery which constitute a great incentive to disunion."

The policy advocated by the *Times* was developed at great length and with complete candor. "Although we profoundly deplore the disorganization of the Confederation as it now exists, it is a consolation to know that so sad an event will remove the last obstacle to the consummation of the obvious policy of the American Republic. The slavery question will no longer be an impediment, and the people of Mexico can receive from our hands the guarantees of a stable government without incurring the risk of being ruined by slavery. The Mexicans, ignorant and degraded though they are, entertain a healthy prejudice against an institution that would reduce them to the level of slaves. . . . A protectorate, followed by free trade and the right of colonization, would be the beginning. But it is evident that the effect of this intimate contact with the free people of the North would have as its result the *Americanization* of Mexico in its ideas of government and civil liberty; so that after a few years of pupilage the Mexican States would be incorporated into the Union under the same conditions as the original ones. The South would thus be surrounded by states and territories in which the idea of civil liberty, in its broad application, would be the bond of union. . . . This, then, is the policy which ought to have the ardent support of every man in the North, and particularly of those who are engaged in manufacture and commerce. It opens an unlimited field for enterprise and cannot fail to compensate whatever temporary loss we may suffer by the dissolution of the South. If that dreaded event should come to pass, it would undoubtedly harm the commerce and traffic of the North; but we have already shown that, in the Union or out of it, the South cannot do without the manufactures, the ships, the seamen, the tools, and the capital of the North; and when we consider the facilities and attractions which the separation of the South would give the North for the acquisition of Mexico, we can console ourselves with the reflection that, although disunion may be censurable from the point of view of patriotism and national honor, it will not prejudice essentially and permanently the commercial and industrial prosperity of the North."

Although the *Times* of New York was not, like the *Times* of London, an acknowledged ministerial mouthpiece, Seward had identified himself among the prominent leaders of the party as an extravagant disciple of Manifest Destiny, and in a campaign speech in which he gave wings to his historical imagination, he had advocated the inclusion of Canada as well as Mexico in the American Union. The disruption of the Union and his accession to office had undoubtedly sobered him, but, as Romero remarked, independently of his will. And in dealing with the Secretary of State the Mexican was baffled by an insuperable reserve.

That reserve deepened with the approach of intervention. The paralyzing effect of the civil war on American foreign policy and the

necessity of neutrality imposed on the Department were recognized
by Romero, but there was, he felt, a margin between caution and
callousness and a decent difference, which he expected the Lincoln
administration to observe. Any other Secretary of State would have
been bound to be noncommittal, but the manipulation of prudence by
Seward betrayed the hand of the politician in the glove of the statesman. The aid which he proffered, and the support which he reserved,
both obeyed his inveterate habits of mind. The lien on Mexican territory in return for a loan to avert intervention was a proposal as unfortunate in its effects on the creditor Powers as on the debtor nation:
it reminded the world that American policy was manufactured in the
interest of Springfield, Massachusetts, rather than of Springfield, Illinois, and guaranteed the aggression and legitimized the competition of
the European Powers in Mexico. If ever there was a time when it
would have been politic to be disinterested and statesmanlike to be
generous, it was at that moment, when the security of Mexico was a
safeguard for the United States and an antiseptic to the league of
three governments eager to favor the South and exploit the disintegration of the American Union. And even in the negative aid which
Seward extended to Mexico there was a deliberation which discouraged
Romero. The invitation extended by the Allies to the United States to
join the tripartite intervention was a transparent diplomatic gesture,
which no one, and least of all the framers of it, expected the American Government to accept. Nevertheless, when Romero called on
him, Seward declined to commit himself immediately as to the reply
he would make. "The coldness and reserve of Mr. Seward," he wrote,
"have finally confirmed me in the impression that I had already
formed, that if, while Mr. Seward is in the State Department, the
United States take part in our difficulties, it is only to derive from
them what profit they can at our cost, and not because they have the
slightest desire to aid us sincerely to maintain our nationality and our
liberties."

The reticence of the old Republican on this occasion was a gratuitous offense which inspired Romero with a desperate idea. "After
leaving the State Department, I set myself to thinking of the impenetrable designs of Mr. Seward," he continued, "and I should not be
surprised if this government approved the plans of the European
Powers and joined them, if it found any advantage to be derived
from such a step. Reflecting on this subject, it occurred to me that if
we cannot prevent intervention, it would be better for us were the
United States to take part in it, since in that case, besides increasing
the reasons for dissension among the interventors, we should be sure
that the Liberal cause would have at least as many votes as the reactionary, for it would not be hard for the United States, with so able an
agent as Mr. Corwin, to decide England, which otherwise would be

vacillating, wholly in favor of the Constitutional cause. I shall reflect maturely on this matter, and if the result of my reflections is worth the trouble, I shall impart them to Mr. Seward."

Feliciter audax! Meditation convinced him that the most reckless course was the most secure, and as inspiration required speed and there was no time to consult his government, he laid the idea before Seward on his own responsibility and was rewarded with serious consideration. "Apparently impressed by my observations, Mr. Seward said that the matter was sufficiently serious and required time for reflection. Afterward he added in a lively tone, 'It is very hard to have to declare war on a good friend in order to help in saving it'; to which I replied that circumstances and complications made such anomalies necessary, adding that our wish to see the United States appear as our enemy was a proof of the confidence we felt in them." He was not facetious. Paradoxical, extravagant, and supremely precarious as the maneuver was, it was inspired by a boldness of spirit commensurable with the situation, and it succeeded at least in entertaining the seasoned politician for an hour and leading him to declare himself. A few days later Seward definitely rejected the invitation of the Allies, as he had always intended to do, and quite independently, of course, of the exertions of Romero.

Tantalized, mystified, and fascinated by a mentality which he could not master, the Mexican was at his wit's end when he snatched a fresh inspiration from the despatches of his colleague in Paris. The desperate idea of De la Fuente that the best thing that could happen to Mexico was a Spanish invasion was an expedient even more intrepid than his own, and he adopted it and submitted it to Seward for approval, together with evidence he had collected to prove that the anti-American spirit of Spain made such an eventuality a matter of common concern to them both. Although Romero was ostracized by the diplomatic corps in Washington, he had been pursued with attentions by one of its members, and it was from the Spanish Minister that he had obtained his arguments. In a confidential conversation Señor Tessara had pointed out to him, as a friend and racial brother, that the only escape for Mexico lay in submitting to the demands of the Allies; that nothing was further from the mind of Madrid than a reconquest of Mexico, the natural field for Spanish expansion lying in Portugal and Morocco; that, in case of war, Washington would doubtless decide in favor of the European Powers; and that the forces that they would accumulate in the Gulf would be directed not against Mexico, but against the United States. With these disclosures and passages from the reports of his colleague referring to the ambition of Spain to place a Bourbon on the throne of Mexico, Romero attempted to alarm Seward and to ascertain his attitude in the event of a clash with the Spanish contingents at Veracruz. Seward listened "with an incredulous smile" and replied that, for the moment, he could do nothing.

Suspicion of Spain was Seward's weak point. Only a few months before he had attempted and failed to challenge the reoccupation of Santo Domingo by Spanish forces, and that reverse compelled him to depreciate dangers with which he could not cope and to minimize with wary skepticism the alarms with which the Mexican so solicitously fed him. It was a trying moment for them both, for each saw through the other without the possibility of further delusion. "The statement of Mr. Seward that 'the United States have nothing to do with a war between two independent nations' and that 'they cannot impose republican institutions on the people of Mexico,' made under these circumstances and when the memory of events in Santo Domingo is still fresh, are highly significant," Romero informed his government, "and must make us lose all hope, I believe, in this government. No one saw with more pleasure than I the arrival in power of the Republican party in this country, since its antecedents led one to believe that it was animated by really fraternal feelings toward Mexico; no one conceived greater hopes than I of the good results which such an event would produce for my country; and no one has been more bitterly disappointed than I am by the manner in which I see this government proceeding toward my country. . . . All these considerations confirm me in the belief that I have always held," he concluded, "that we must expect nothing from this country in our hour of trial, and that we must rely only on our own elements and internal resources." And he urged his government to engage Spain alone. When the recommendations of Romero and De la Fuente reached Mexico, however, the course of events there had already relegated them to the limbo of lost motion.

IO

A SOLID front against Mexico being the one certain prospect, and self-help the only resource on which the country could rely, the necessity of building a solid front of defense was generally realized there as the hour of trial approached. Concurrently with the diplomatic negotiations, some preparations for military mobilization were made and some precautions taken for the political consolidation of the revolution; but these measures were tentative, because the object of intervention was obscure and beclouded by confused and conflicting reports from abroad. Its primary and ostensible purpose engrossed public attention; rumors of political complications and the attempts made to graft monarchist schemes on financial foreclosure were bruited by the press but discounted by it with sober public spirit. There was a general disposition to minimize alarms and prevent a return of the panic terror which had unsettled the government throughout that trying year. The negotiations with the British Minister inspired a false sense of security, and not until they broke down at the end of November, and the conclusion of the London Convention was confirmed a fortnight later, did the public at large awake to the gravity and the imminence of the danger. Then the convergence of foreign and domestic forces leagued against the nation, the party, and the man that represented it, imposed on all the saving obligation of union; but the fusion was not accomplished automatically.

The nation was identified with a party, and nothing less than foreign intervention could have soldered the schism of the civil war. The remains of the Clerical faction had succeeded in unsettling the country and provoking the crisis, and one of the first steps that the government took to meet it was to issue the general amnesty that the ferment of popular feeling had forbade it to decree at the beginning of the year. The measure was mortifying in the circumstances in which it appeared, and the amnesty was far more liable to embolden than to reconcile the unsubdued remnants of the reactionary party. But a greater guarantee was provided, and a better contribution to closing the breach, by the steps that the Mexican monarchists in Paris took to reopen it. Realizing the responsibility they had assumed in promising Napoleon that an overwhelming majority of the nation would rise on the appearance of the Allied flag, and none too sure of their premises, they took the precaution of appointing an agent to pave the way and guarantee the spontaneous proclamation of a monarchy. Having long lost contact with their country, it was not among their own number that they looked for a missionary. Their choice fell on Father Miranda, who was well qualified to act as their delegate, having a high reputation in Mexico as an agitator. He accepted the commission and moved from New York, where he was wasting in exile, to Havana, where he carried on an active correspondence with his following across the Gulf.

The reports which he received were discouraging. His correspondents were unanimous in painting the party as prostrate and inert, disorganized and demoralized, willing to be saved but unable to lift a finger in self-defense, and confused and alarmed by the prospect of foreign intervention. No one knew what it meant. Some believed that the object was to restore Miramon—"an idea that is intolerable to them"; others supposed it to be instigated by "the few German and English speculators, together with some French socialists, who benefited most from the property of the Church by odious combinations which we all know"—everyone had another inside story to tell. No one knew where intervention would lead, and all looked to Father Miranda for light, guidance, and leadership. For, more than the service of an interpreter, the presence of a reliable leader was indispensable to make proselytes and revive the spirit of a party that was morally cowed and materially crushed. Marquez and Zuloaga had fallen out among themselves and lost every opportunity as it arose; Miramon, after proclaiming in Paris that there was no such thing as a monarchist party in Mexico, was waiting in New York to draw his sword in defense of his native land. Marquez himself warned Miranda that any appearance of coercion would lose them the country and that, unless absolute freedom in the choice of a government were guaranteed beforehand, the remnants of the party would rally to the Liberals as the lesser evil. They were Mexicans after all.

Miranda labored to correct these errors by mail, but correspondence was not enough to dissipate them. There was but one man in Mexico with the moral authority to dispel all doubts, and he was in Havana. He, and he alone, could carry conviction. The confidence which he inspired, as his brother in New York assured his patrons in Paris, was unique: the soldiers would obey blindly whatever word they heard from his own lips, but in his absence they distrusted everyone else. "The first question will always be: Where is the Doctor? If this is what we are told, why is the Doctor not with us? And short of the death of the Doctor, no reply to these questions will satisfy these people. In short, amid so much misery, imbecility, disloyalty, and cowardice as we have seen, the Doctor is the only one who inspires them with unlimited trust. With him everything will be easy; without him all will be difficult." Father Miranda determined to answer the call, but as he was also wanted in Mexico by the police, he decided to remain in Havana until the arrival of the Allied fleets. There was a price on his head in Mexico, and his head was indispensable where it was; but it was also indispensable for an agitator to be on the spot, and as he lacked the first qualification of an advance agent, his influence was indifferent. Instead of preceding the expedition, he followed it; and in the meanwhile his partisans remained passive and patriotic, the boldest hesitating to betray the land of his birth, the most timid clinging to it with tenacious inertia, and the party accepted the amnesty of the government with pathological submission. The unsettled conflict of patriotism and party spirit neutralized the reaction.

If the shadow of intervention was enough to fuse, or confuse, the national feud, not until the expedition actually materialized did the internal dissension of the Liberal party disappear. Success was a severe test of its discipline: the solidarity developed under stress relaxed as soon as the pressure of necessity was removed, and during the first six months of the year the personal rivalries of its leaders and the factional loyalties of their followers were wrought to such a pitch by the presidential campaign that at the close of it Zarco raised a warning against what was fast becoming an incurable and congenial condition. "Shall we always need the needle of danger to make us unite?" he wrote when the catastrophes of the month of June once again closed the ranks. The recrudescence of the Reaction, the difficulties of consolidating the revolution, and the menace of foreign complications combined to revive the agitation of the party and the demand for revolutionary leadership. Death had thinned the ranks of the original protagonists, and of the survivors only two figures of tested capacity and national stature stood out—Juarez and Ortega—as the shadow of intervention took shape. The forging of national unity was the supreme test of the party that was identified with the nation, and of the man who represented them both.

The presidential election had not settled the questions that it raised. In spite of the large plurality with which the country—the quiet, inarticulate country as distinct from the political clubs and partisan press that produced the surface agitation of the capital—had declared for Juarez, the verdict was not accepted without question by the defeated candidate or his followers, who drew a pointed distinction between the choice of the people and the popular choice and counteracted the effect of the election by undermining confidence in its result. Their first move was to secure the succession. Congress appointed Gonzalez Ortega President of the Supreme Court. The elevation of a soldier to the bench and of a defeated presidential candidate to a position that carried with it the Constitutional title to the Presidency in case of emergency was a step the ulterior purpose of which was emphasized by its irregularity, election to the Presidency of the Supreme Court being vested not in Congress, but in the people; but it met with no open opposition. "Señor Juarez has put all his power into play to prevent my appointment," Ortega wrote to his wife, "because he is tottering in the presidential chair and is afraid of falling with my ascent to the Supreme Court. I have offered him no opposition and I despise the meanness of the government, which is discredited to the last degree."

Ortega turned himself inside out in telling the inside story of his appointment, and between man and wife that was proper; but he could not keep it to himself. The appointment was made when he was leaving for the campaign against Marquez, and on his return in August, flushed with victory, his credit was higher than ever; and on assuming his seat in the Supreme Court, he made an address remarkable for its faulty political tact. Readily admitting his lack of professional training for the bench, he repudiated the suspicions to which it might give rise and declared that, if his position there were ever to prove an impediment to the President of the Republic, he would resign. "To foresee such an antagonism is to recognize that it already exists," was the comment of one paper. His followers, however, had no tact at all. Early in September the Opposition in Congress presented a petition to the President of the Republic, signed by fifty-one deputies, requesting him to resign.

The petition was, in effect, a pronunciamento in legal form, a parliamentary mutiny that reversed the verdict of the electorate, and it was made at a time of growing emergency, which heightened its gravity. The method was not less subversive because the lever employed was moral pressure. The petition was designed to discredit the President in public opinion and—more dangerously yet—in his own. His tested capacity was contested by the same charges of inefficiency and inertia that had served to combat his election, and they were pressed home with deadly effect by the approach of an international invasion, which demanded vigorous and undisputed leadership. "The present President of the Republic, to whom we address ourselves," the petition read, "cannot save the situation, and his retirement from the high position that he holds is a necessity as imperative for the salvation of the country as his presence there was important in the first days of the revolution. Throughout it and in the days of trial, he spent the noblest thing he possessed, his prestige and moral power, which he has vainly sought to recover by means of various ministerial combinations that have merely sacrificed other such reputations and sterilized noble and fertile minds. The revolution needs them, Citizen President; it must save the name of Juarez from passing to posterity with the stigma that history will stamp on it if he appears as the man who smothered the seeds of a great revolution."

The Opposition was an amalgam of contradictory elements, dominated on the one hand by the Moderates, the timeserving liberals who had weathered the civil war without suffering it, and on the other by the impatient, battle-worn, radical youth. The latter were the serious dissidents, and they found an eloquent spokesman in Ignacio Altamirano, who had denounced the sloth of the President during the civil war and who returned to the attack as the most ruthless leader of the parliamentary Opposition. "This is a vote of censure," he concluded a scathing review of the work of the ministries, "and not only of the cabinet, but of the President of the Republic, because amid so much confusion he has stood firm, but with the deaf, dumb, immovable firmness given to the god whom the ancients named *Terminus*. This is not what the nation wants; it wants a locomotive, not a milestone. Señor Juarez, whose private virtues I am the first to respect, feels and loves democratic ideas, but I believe that he does not understand them, and I doubt it because he fails to display that vigorous, continuous, energetic action which circumstances such as those through which we are passing demand. . . . What is needed is a new name in power.

The President will render the greatest service to his country by retiring, since he is an obstacle to democracy. . . . To want to remain in a position only to prove a great and continual disappointment in it, is to be willful and to lose the country, carrying the legal principle to the point of sophistry."

Among the radical youth a doctrine was developing, which opposed the free creative spirit of revolution to the deadening legality in which it had set: this was the serious sense of a complaint which paraphrased in ideological terms the personal insurrection against a President whose creed, whose character, whose career, and whose conduct were bound by the book. "The letter of the law kills!" was the text on which one speaker after another rang the changes in Congress; and despite its partisan distortion, it was a genuine cry of distress, incident to any revolution threatened with arrest and defeat from within and without. It was irrelevant and irrational, a maddened revolt against insoluble problems, a confusion of men and things, and a blind search for a personal panacea, prompted by gathering panic, and the rebels called for an autocrat because they felt themselves balked by a bureaucrat.

Public opinion rose to the challenge. The attack failed. In reply to the petition of the Fifty-One, fifty-two deputies drew up a counter-statement in support of the President; but the bare margin was a serious symptom of his insecurity. The response of the press was a solid rally to the principle of legality; but personal defense was subordinate to the principle he represented, and though he was warmly defended, the point of the attack was conceded by some of his most zealous apologists. "Citizen Benito Juarez is not fitted to govern. This has been said for a long time, and we agree. Citizen Benito Juarez is a man of sincerity and firm principles, democratic, staunch in his decisions, honorable, of exquisite sensibility, and he loves his country only too well"—but his qualities were negative. By acceding to the Fifty-One, however, "anarchy would be the fruit of a step as false as it is ill considered," and "the weakness of Citizen Juarez at this moment would be an unpardonable crime." The treachery of the attack lay precisely in its appeal ad hominem. "Perhaps the most skillfully contrived part of the document is the appeal to the patriotic sentiments of the Citizen President; but in so presenting the question there is no generosity, no justice, and no political advantage. To expect a man, however strong he may be, to realize that he is the obstacle to the happiness of a whole people for whom he has so often exposed his life, as Señor Juarez has done, is to bewilder and blind him, to expect him to renounce all freedom of choice in the supreme decision imposed on him." He was "the perfect type of what the Constitution requires in the person of the Executive: not men of strenuous initiative, apt for great struggles, but administrators of laws, ready, as Señor Juarez has always been, to receive the inspirations of the Chamber, from which he has drawn his ministers ever since he was installed." His complete identification with his office raised the fundamental question of how far revolutionary progress was compatible with the democratic process: a system was put to the test in his person, and the fusion of the man and the function was a political fact, an organic growth, which made it impossible to separate the one from the other. Gradually emerging from the heated controversy in the capital, where it was obscured by the polemics of Congress and the press, the issue was clearly visible at a distance, and it was a writer in the provincial press who stated it in the simplest and most sensible terms.

"Citizen Juarez is the model man to execute the laws. Give him those laws, and if he does not execute them, then represent against him, but do not wound the delicacy of the virtuous citizen without reason. A profound sensation had been excited in everyone's mind by a phenomenon hitherto unknown in the long catalogue of our aberrations: the petition of the Fifty-One." And submitting it to analysis point by point, "supposing," he said, "that the resignation were made and accepted, and that Citizen Ortega as President of the Supreme Court assumed control of the Supreme Government; supposing, also, that this citizen surpassed Citizen Juarez in civil and moral virtues; that he had more abnegation, more energy, more political science, more prestige with the diplomatic corps, more circumspection—would all these guarantees be of any use to the country during the interregnum? Unquestionably not; for he would be enclosed in a circle of the same persons and the same difficulties as those that have foiled the great qualities of Citizen Juarez. . . . It would offend common sense to suppose that Señor Juarez is not aware of all the evils that afflict the country, and it would be the greatest injustice to think that he does not wish to remedy them. If he does not, it is because neither he nor any man alive can do so in his circumstances. It would be extremely interesting to have a diary of what happens about him, of all that he says and that is said to him; the world would then know the truth and do him justice. The time will come when his greatest glory will consist in what he has neglected to do, and in having done what no one now wants him to do. More energy of character and more civic courage are needed, unquestionably, to keep to the legal course than to use extraordinary powers and to defy and scuttle the laws, which is what is meant by *political tact*. That *political tact* has been shown by Santa Anna, Comonfort, and all the governments of the Republic, and it has brought us to our present pass. The greatness of Juarez obviously lies in his lack of *political tact*." And the last word on the whole controversy was pronounced by the same distant and unbefogged observer: "Señor Juarez is forced to be the expiatory goat on whom are visited all our sins without number, sins of which he is entirely innocent, and the only one innocent."

Prepared for protests, the Fifty-One carried their case directly to the states in a letter to the governors, inviting their support, but the states refused to stir; with three or four exceptions, the governors declared their determination to deny recognition to any power that did not derive from the legal order; and nowhere was this position maintained more firmly than in the native state of Ortega. Throughout the controversy a studied attempt was made to dissociate Ortega himself from it. A public-spirited conspiracy to exonerate the national hero was maintained by silent agreement between his friends and opponents. The latter, indeed, were his best apologists; when they mentioned his name, it was to applaud his probity and to point out how little he would gain by compromising it. "His time will come," as one of them said, "but never by cabinet intrigues. We are certain that he has had no part in whatever has been done on his behalf, which he appreciates, but does not accept." Not all his opponents, however, displayed the same glaring sense of tact. "What heroism! What greatness of soul not to have been a traitor!" one plain speaker interjected. "We are thrilled by such virtue, such abnegation, such fidelity! But do the fifty-one petitioning deputies know why the victorious soldier gave way to the depository of the supreme powers of the nation? Do they know whether this was a spontaneous act of his will or an unavoidable necessity? . . . If for the first time in the history of our country the victorious soldier respected the law and did not place himself in the supreme power, it is because education has taught us that winning a battle is not title enough to govern." Ortega himself maintained an exemplary silence, and the other principal to the affair met it with equal propriety.

The President rejected the petition of the Fifty-One on constitutional grounds and ignored their attacks as a routine incident of political life. It was not even mentioned in the diary, which was supposed to contain so many revelations of intimate truth, as he best knew it. Whether the omission was a sensitive or a sensible one, indicating the degree of importance which he attached to a public discussion of his merits, he gave no sign at the time that he felt the attack. For a man, however, whose acknowledged merits included "an exquisite sensibility," the experience could not but be a severe ordeal. His capacities challenged, his limitations explored, the springs of his being searched out, he was spared no humiliation to undo him, but he was inured to it by habit and heredity.

The psychological vivisection to which he was subjected was fundamentally a blood test. During the election campaign some attempts had been made to drum up race prejudice and to identify his deficiencies with those of an inferior, fatalistic, and apathetic people. These imputations had been indignantly repelled by the press; race prejudice was taboo in Mexico, an alien abuse, and foul blows were promptly challenged. In refuting them a College of Indians published a tribute testifying to the pride, the vanity even, which they felt, that "for the first time since our emancipation from Spain the majority of the inhabitants of Mexico, composed of its real natives, sees that its destinies will be governed by one of their blood brothers, that Mexico will be represented in the eyes of other States as it is, for Juarez is its very incarnation, for Juarez represents its virtues by his modesty, its craving for progress by the progressive laws he has issued, its love for the land by his pre-eminent patriotism." His own people, at least, knew who he was, and to all the other motives, public and private, for retaining his position was added the obligation of redeeming their reputation and vindicating their faith in him. But he was braced by a far greater responsibility. For the President of Mexico his race could not be his people; he was the personification of the nation as a whole and forbidden to fail it by a battle only half won. The damage to his self-confidence, which was the most treacherous effect of the maneuver of the Fifty-One, was blunted by striking the bedrock of a secular trust. Time was for him, but the times were against him, and it was fifty to one that he would fail, for the attack was no routine incident of political life. It was the climax of the terror lurking in the year of the comet. With all due allowance for what was factitious in such agitation, it was demoralizing because it was made at a time when the nation, the party, and the man needed all the self-confidence they could muster to meet a great emergency. The perfunctory support which he received was not sufficient to dispel self-doubt; he alone could do that, and he was the one against fifty who turned the wavering balance. He was baited into being supremely himself, and there was nothing Indian in the way in which he met the test, unless it was the muteness with which he muffled, and the indifference with which he dismissed, the attack. When the crisis was over, the world knew nothing of what it had cost him, but it knew that the inner dissension of the party had been mastered by the man who represented the nation where it mattered most vitally—within himself.

As the agitation subsided, Zarco hastened to depreciate its importance and to congratulate the party on its discipline. "This calm, after so much effort to excite agitation, this publicity and the clash of the most divergent opinions, and the dignity with which the President has acted, and even the polemics carried on by the Opposition, seem to us auspicious symptoms and a clear demonstration that democratic institutions and republican customs are taking root in Mexico." The legality in which the revolution had set had allowed its sinews to knit and braced it against the day of reckoning. When the day came, and intervention materialized, the President and the party were, to all outward appearances, at one. The demonstration of the Fifty-One had produced a sober and unanimous recognition that Juarez was an institution and, as such, inviolable. Whatever the revolution had or had not accomplished, it had achieved the fusion, or confusion, of the parts in the whole, and the result was the best proof of the leadership of the President. His scrupulous selflessness, the collective conscience that consistently governed his conduct, the complete identification with his position, which made him invisible in it and which made a democracy work, were a focal force that compelled his collaborators and competitors alike to conform to a criterion that none could ignore, on pain of losing caste and forfeiting all that, as revolutionaries, they had lived and fought for. The religious inspiration of revolution was safe; and its value was felt when moral power was the only power upon which the nation, faced with an invasion that threatened to sweep away all its other gains, could count.

An English journalist commissioned by the parliamentary Opposition to Palmerston to visit Mexico and report on actual conditions there, arrived in the capital just in time to witness the dissolving scenes of 1861. His first impressions were formed from a seat in the gallery at the closing session of Congress on December 15, when Veracruz was already invaded and emergency powers were conferred upon the President. The setting was a far cry from the House of Parliament: "There was no ornament or gilding, the painting and glazing were of the most ordinary and trumpery description, and the galleries were filled with all kinds of riffraff, both men and women, but there was no interruption or sound except from the members themselves, who made noise enough for all." The performance, nevertheless, was impressive. "At about three the President, Juarez, entered amid an astonishing din of cannon and trumpets. He is a dark, small man, quiet and self-possessed. He is affectionately known in Mexico as the little Indian. Juarez is a very respectable, well-meaning man, and of fair talents . . . and he deserves very great credit for his firmness and tenacity in maintaining the struggle and the cause of legitimacy. . . . All sorts of intrigues and combinations have been formed against him, both in Congress and out of it, thwarting and opposing in order to compel him to resign, but he has stood firm, and they have not yet dared to resort to force, and will not. He has scarcely had fair play in England. On taking his seat, he bowed gracefully on all sides and immediately made the following address in a clear and remarkably pleasant voice. . . ." The address expressed the President's hope that a reasonable settlement might yet be made with the Powers, and the determination of the nation, if that hope were defeated, to defend its revolution and its independence. It was not a speech but a statement, and it received the undivided tribute due to a statement of fact which was at the same time a profession of faith.

When the cheering subsided, the President of Congress replied. Stressing the responsibility placed on the President by the grant of full powers, which made him legally a dictator—"the greatest proof of confidence ever given to the depository of the executive power"—he reminded Juarez that "upon the Executive it now depends (and upon no other) to save the Republic or to plunge it into the abyss," and that when Congress again convened it would exact "an accounting of the power which it delivers into his hands today with such perfect trust." Thereupon the President rose and retired as quietly as he had come in, amid the respectful silence of a House that recognized the stature of the man whom the nation needed in its own hour of humiliation, and who had been hammered into being its man of destiny. That mute tribute was more eloquent than the ovation he had received a year before in the theater at Veracruz or the one that Gonzalez Ortega had given him in the capital.

In the streets the English scout was struck by the martial enthusiasm of the crowds accompanying the volunteers leaving for the front, conscripts whose enthusiasm and confidence, fired by the cry that the Spaniards were in Veracruz, was for once completely unforced. More impressive, perhaps, as a proof of the personal confidence of the President, was the fact that he chose this moment to buy himself a house in the capital of his country.